David
Susskind

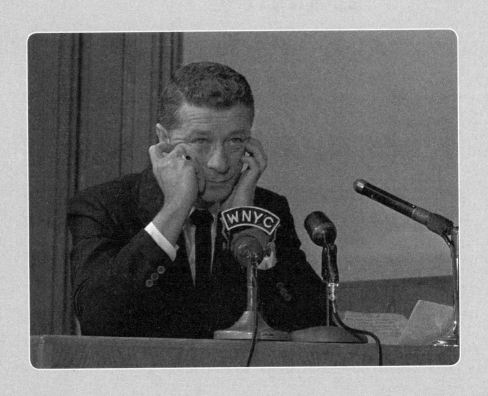

David Susskind

A Televised Life

Stephen Battaglio

ST. MARTIN'S PRESS ❧ NEW YORK

DAVID SUSSKIND: A TELEVISED LIFE. Copyright © 2010 by Stephen Battaglio. All rights reserved. Printed in the United States of America. For information, address St. Martin's Press, 175 Fifth Avenue, New York, N.Y. 10010.

www.stmartins.com

Library of Congress Cataloging-in-Publication Data

Frontispiece courtesy of Associated Press

Battaglio, Stephen.
   David Susskind : a televised life / Stephen Battaglio.—1st ed.
       p. cm.
   ISBN 978-0-312-38286-5
   1. Susskind, David, 1920–1987.   2. Television producers and directors—United States—
Biography.   3. Television personalities—United States—Biography.   4. Motion picture producers
and directors—United States— Biography.   5. Theatrical producers and directors—United States—
Biography.   I. Title.
   PN1992.4.S86B37 2010
   791.4502'32092—dc22
   [B]   2010022067

FIRST EDITION: October 2010

10   9   8   7   6   5   4   3   2   1

To my wife, Candice

David
Susskind

Prologue

O n the evening of October 10, 1982, *The David Susskind Show* celebrated the start of its twenty-fifth season on television. The program opened with its light orchestral theme, "Gateway to the
West," played over a compilation of host David Susskind's introductions from
over the years. His sonorous, formal "Good evening" greeting never wavered,
even as the black-and-white videotape of the program's early days turned to
color and his hair changed from flecks of gray to wooly white. "Right before
your eyes you see a man age—you see the whole death process coming," Susskind told viewers after watching his televised life flash by. It was not Susskind's nature to look back and reflect. As a producer, he was addicted to the
adrenaline rush that came from making a deal to put together a TV show or a
film. He was always consumed by the desire to move on to the next project.
He insisted he had nothing to do with his anniversary program, which had
been planned by his wife, Joyce, and Jean Kennedy, the longtime producer of
The David Susskind Show.

As always, Susskind was dressed immaculately for his taping at the WNEW
studio on the east side of Manhattan. He wore a crisp slate-colored designer
suit, an elegant pink shirt, and a silk tie to match. Perched on a swivel chair on
the show's set, his shoulders slightly hunched, he looked a bit older than his
sixty-one years and well beyond his days as the tightly wound, noisemaking,
angry young man who railed against the timidity of the TV industry of the
1950s and 1960s. "I could see him visibly shaking," said Jim Shasky, who was
in the WNEW control room directing the show. "His hands were shaking.
He wasn't well." But he became energized as he recounted taking on Nikita

Khrushchev, facing off with furious feminists, and unleashing Mel Brooks's hilarious revelations on being a Jewish son. His hands popped at the air with the rapidity of a featherweight boxer as he spoke excitedly. Susskind's role in exposing a wide range of ideas, trends, and personalities to viewers at a time when their media choices were minuscule was indelible, and he knew it. *The David Susskind Show* rarely made any money over its long run, and by 1982 Susskind was covering the losses out of his own pocket. It was still worth every dollar for him to have a TV platform.

Joyce Susskind joined her husband for the anniversary program. Ten years younger than Susskind, she still had the high cheekbones and soft feminine look that made her one of Canada's biggest TV stars since the 1950s, as Joyce Davidson. Several times during the hour, she gently took Susskind's arm to steer him into a commercial break or another clip of a past show highlight. There would not be many more tender moments between them. In the following year, a tumultuous one in many ways for Susskind, the glamorous New York couple's marriage ended.

The second half of the commemorative broadcast featured guests considered longtime friends of *The David Susskind Show*. The lineup included Truman Capote, who made his first TV appearance on Susskind's show, at the time called *Open End*. The writer had been the Susskinds' neighbor at the UN Plaza apartment complex along the East River when it was a magnet for glitterati residents in the 1960s. He had spent hours in the Susskinds' living room having drinks and gossiping with Joyce, who became a close pal. Gloria Rabinowitz, an associate producer for the show at the time, remembered how Susskind would corner Capote in the elevator and inveigle him into coming on whenever he needed a lively segment.

Capote was joined by Norman Mailer, who over the years had sparred on the program with the likes of William F. Buckley Jr. and was once banned by station management in the 1960s because of his volatile reputation at the time. Rounding out the group was Anthony Quinn, a Susskind favorite since the early 1960s, when they made the film *Requiem for a Heavyweight* together, and actress Maureen Stapleton, who had recently won an Academy Award for her work in the film *Reds*. It was the kind of hodgepodge panel that was typical in the early years of Susskind's show, a modern-day salon where accomplished actors, writers, and journalists could get together for unguarded, freewheeling conversation.

Shortly before the taping began, Susskind's associate producer, Dan Berkowitz, had gone to the station's makeup room where he typically had guests sign release forms. "The door was closed, which it never was," he recalled. "And I had to get the releases from everybody. I sort of knock-knocked, opened the door, and there was Truman Capote, sobbing into Maureen Stapleton's ample bosom. We were basically saying, 'We're ready to go.' And I just looked at them. And she just looked at me and mouthed the words 'Give us a minute.'"

Capote's health had been in a major decline. He looked dissipated and out of it. Yet he still managed to be impishly funny on Susskind's program that night, especially when recounting his pronouncement that rich people were different because "they eat little tiny vegetables." Norman Mailer told the story of how he was convinced he would be the alpha guest on a literary panel Susskind put together with him, Capote, and a frightened and shy Dorothy Parker that aired on January 18, 1959. That night, Susskind had become impatient with Mailer's provocations that "all politicians are whores" and started looking at his watch. "All right," Mailer said to himself, "David isn't satisfied. I'm going to sit back and see what kind of show he has." Mailer stopped talking. "It was the greatest mistake of my life," he said. When the topic of *On the Road* author Jack Kerouac was raised before the panel, Capote disposed of the beat writer in five words: "That's not writing, it's typing." The power of the put-down spoken by Capote in his bizarre, nasal voice reverberated among New Yorkers who watched, much to the massively egotistical Mailer's dismay. Mailer admitted that the response to Capote made him feel "like an actor who thought he was the star and suddenly the next day they said, 'That featured player is fantastic.'"

Many such moments of Susskind's earliest talk shows existed in memory only. In the 1950s and 1960s, TV stations considered videotape too expensive to use only once and then store. The reels were regularly degaussed and then used again. Susskind's evenings with such luminaries as James Baldwin, Lionel Trilling, Alan Jay Lerner, Roald Dahl, Jackie Robinson, Thurgood Marshall, Isaac Stern, Preston Sturges, Bertrand Russell, Adlai Stevenson, Claire Booth Luce, Bette Davis, and dozens more were gone forever. Quinn remembered one of those occasions in 1961 when he appeared with Tennessee Williams on a panel described in the TV listings as "Interesting People with Strong Opinions." The playwright had "too much tea," he said, and passed out on the actor's lap.

Dan Berkowitz had started working on *The David Susskind Show* in the late 1970s, when the program often alternated between serious discussions with powerful and influential figures in politics and business and people who traveled along the fringes of society. On his first day on the job, Berkowitz called whorehouses to find johns willing to come on and talk about why they paid for sex. His next task required him to wrangle an appearance by Jody Powell, President Jimmy Carter's press secretary. Berkowitz believed he had seen everything during his six years with the program, but he always remained fascinated by how Susskind and Jean Kennedy could pull together a disparate group of important big names and have them talking candidly on television as themselves. "One of his great gifts is that people like that *loved* coming on the show," Berkowitz explained. "Because they knew that they could talk about anything. Secondly, that the conversation would be kind of intelligent. Where else would you get to sit down with Truman Capote, Norman Mailer, and Anthony Quinn and David Susskind and just say, 'Hey, let's talk about stuff'? Maybe if you went to a dinner party in one of their houses."

For Susskind, the weekly session in front of the camera was the only constant in his tireless and turbulent career as a New York mogul responsible for thousands of hours of television, much of it outstanding, some of it groundbreaking. More than once, that career appeared to be on the brink of oblivion. There were often maelstroms of conflict surrounding his impossibly prodigious output. He publicly blasted the TV networks and Hollywood hierarchies that didn't always support his risk-taking attempts at innovation. His angst over achieving perfection on screen and balancing artistic ambitions with financial solvency was palpable. His compulsive philandering made marriage and family life precarious. David Susskind's life was worthy of a show of its own.

1

David Susskind was dressed in his navy lieutenant's uniform when, in the winter of 1947, he showed up at the Manhattan headquarters of the talent agency Century Artists. He stood at a compact five feet seven inches tall. He once described his face as resembling "a bankrupt Dana Andrews," the film actor who played the alienated World War II veteran in *The Best Years of Our Lives*. Susskind had a large head, with thick, wavy brown hair on top. His complexion was smooth, and his skin milky white, as if it had never been exposed to sunlight.

Susskind had become a familiar figure in waiting areas of the East Fifty-seventh Street office. He had made several appointments for job interviews with Dick Dorso, the dapper president of the company that represented such stars as Judy Holliday, Ethel Merman, and the Andrews Sisters at a time when radio was still the primary source for home entertainment, although not for much longer. Susskind finally made it through Dorso's door when another partner at the firm, Al Levy, had noticed how the young man kept showing up. Levy told Dorso that anyone with that much perseverance deserved a look.

Once he had an audience, Susskind launched into the details of his education at Harvard, his record of service during World War II, and his stints as a publicity agent for two movie studios. As Susskind summed up his story, he leaned that large head across Dorso's desk and fixed his intense blue eyes on him. His voice took on urgency as he said, "Now at this point, I should be able to stand up and say to you that I can bring clients here—Bing Crosby, Bob Hope, and Greta Garbo. I can't. I don't have a client. All I have is myself. But I think it's *awfully* good."

Dorso had seen and heard many agency job aspirants, but never anyone with the intensity Susskind had on that day. "He made the best pitch I've ever had made to me," Dorso recalled. "Most people come in and say, 'I love show business and I want to be in it, and if you have anything here that I can do, I would love to do it.' Those are the pitches that you get. And his was totally different. He said it so forcefully, so clearly, and so imaginatively." Dorso hired Susskind as a junior agent for $85 a week. As he would prove over his career, David Susskind was a brilliant salesman and never better than when he was selling himself.

David Howard Susskind was born in New York City on December 19, 1920. Before he was one year old, his family moved to Brookline, Massachusetts, just outside of Boston. By the end of the nineteenth century, Brookline was calling itself the richest town in America. When Susskind grew up there during the 1920s and 1930s, the children of Jewish and Irish families of different income levels attended the community's highly regarded public schools together, mostly in harmony. Susskind, who was Jewish, claimed he never experienced anti-Semitism during those years. "It was almost a place of fantasy," he once said. Susskind spent most of his youth living in one of the redbrick attached buildings on Claflin Road, in a modest tree-lined neighborhood. His father, Benjamin, the son of Russian immigrants, spent most of his adult life working as a sales agent for the Metropolitan Life Insurance Company. While he was intelligent and had an appreciation for high culture, Ben Susskind spent his days "cold-canvassing," as they called it in the insurance business. He went door to door in Boston neighborhoods to sell policies and take in premiums of 35 cents for $1,000 worth of coverage. "I had a sense that he was working far below what he thought he might be doing," said Norman Lear, a first cousin of David Susskind. "Ben was a quiet man. He was meek." Lear remembered the Susskinds living a reasonably comfortable middle-class existence in Brookline. But in the years after the Depression hit, in 1929, there were some lean times. David always carried the memory of the family car being repossessed by creditors, his son, Andrew, said.

Susskind described Saturday afternoon as a "sacred" time in the family household, when his father listened to the Metropolitan Opera broadcasts over the radio. Sundays were devoted to attending lectures at Old South Church and Ford Hall in Boston. When he was thirteen years old, David began to join his father, reluctantly at first. But it soon became their Sunday ritual. Susskind recalled hearing the political theorist Harold Laski, Supreme

Court Justice Felix Frankfurter, and the economist John Maynard Keynes on some of those occasions. He was in the audience when Orson Welles and the Mercury Players came through town with a production of *Julius Caesar*. David soon developed an appetite for culture and the exchange of ideas.

Susskind once described his mother, the former Frances Lear, or Fanny as she was often called, as "the antithesis of Father." Norman Lear, the son of Frances's brother, said the description was accurate. "Fanny was clearly the dominant figure," he said. "But she would be the dominant figure if she had a hundred people in the house. She was a firebrand of a woman. A ballbuster on wheels." Also of Russian descent, Frances Susskind's family settled in and around New Haven, Connecticut, in the late nineteenth century. Her generation of Lears was a collection of rogues and rascals. When Norman Lear was ten years old, his father, Jack, began a three-year jail sentence after being involved in a get-rich-quick scheme. Lear said he often described his father as "having a screw in his head which, if I could have turned it a sixteenth of an inch one way or another he would have known right from wrong." Another of Frances Lear's brothers, Eli, was a radio sports announcer who took on a second career as a holdup man. The newspapers nicknamed him "the Nylon Bandit" after he was arrested in 1946 for the armed robbery of a store that sold women's undergarments. Frances may also have gotten in trouble with the law for floating bad checks, Norman Lear recalled. When the Lears got together for weddings or holiday gatherings, the occasions always ended unpleasantly. "My friend Herb Gardner spoke of his family living at the end of their nerves and the tops of their lungs," Lear said. "I've always credited him, but I've always said that of my family."

As different as their personalities may have been, Ben and Frances Susskind both recognized the intellectual capabilities of their eldest son. "He was precocious and exceedingly bright," said Norman Lear. "They treated him as an adult. His mother gave him the car keys when he was fourteen." Susskind said automobile privileges were a reward for good grades. But he developed a true affinity for English literature at an early age, having had to learn Shakespeare soliloquies in the seventh grade at Michael Driscoll Elementary School in Brookline.

Susskind took pride in winning a William H. Lincoln medal for his English studies at Brookline High School. Many years later, his second daughter, Diana, would wear the medal on a charm bracelet. In his junior year, he became news editor of the student newspaper *The Sagamore*. His first byline was an editorial that praised the student marshals' efforts at policing the school. It ran adjacent to a humor column written by Murray Susskind, who was twenty months younger than David and spent much of his life in the shadow of his high-achieving brother. A doctor who performed cataract surgery on Frances Susskind in the 1960s said she once introduced Murray to him as "my other son." Susskind also had a sister, Dorothy, who was eight years younger.

When Susskind graduated from Brookline High with honors in 1938, he listed his ambitions in the school's yearbook as "college, fame and fortune." He received financial aid as he went on to study at the University of Wisconsin. There he met Phyllis Briskin, a bright, dark-haired coed who was not afraid to speak her mind. She came from a financially well-off Bronx, New York, family. Her father had been a drummer boy in tsarist Russia before coming to the United States, where he found success in the theater concessions business. Susskind and Briskin married in August 1939. "She was very beautiful when she was young and had a mouth on her like a sailor," Andrew Susskind said of his mother. "That was a pretty compelling combination in those days."

Ben Susskind was said to be opposed to his son marrying at the age of eighteen. Norman Lear, two years younger than David, said he envied his cousin. "I remember being so jealous because he was married and having sex every night," he said.

In the fall of 1940, Susskind and his bride moved to Boston. He transferred to Harvard University's Department of Government and began to consider a career in teaching. "I guess what I was seeking was a captive audience," he would say. Phyllis Susskind attended nearby Simmons College. For his honors thesis, Susskind wrote a lengthy analysis of organized labor's attitudes toward the events leading to World War II. Other papers he wrote on philosophy and literature reflected a genuine intellectual curiosity. Off campus, Susskind was likely getting another kind of education. He worked as a candy vendor at the Old Howard Theater, a famed burlesque house in Boston's Scollay Square. Between performances by such renowned striptease artists as the astoundingly curvaceous Sherry Britton and the snake-handling Zorita, Susskind hawked chocolate bars that promised an arousing picture card insert under the wrapper. "I would hold up a card and say, 'In each and every Hershey bar, there is a card so revealing that we can't describe it to you,'" he recalled. Over time, Harvard and the Old Howard reflected the full spectrum of Susskind's interests and instincts.

After his graduation from Harvard in 1942, Susskind worked briefly as a junior economist for the War Labor Board until his commission in the navy came through. His four years of service during World War II started out with the dreary assignment of selling insurance to sailors in New York, quite possibly a dismal reminder of his father's toiling. He finished with a full year at sea as a communications officer on the attack transport *Mellette,* where he witnessed some of the most brutal action at Iwo Jima. "It seemed that all the wounded in the world must be here," he recounted after one of the teams of the Twenty-fourth Marines landed on the island. "Men with shattered limbs, arms and bodies lay everywhere."

In the spring of 1946, Susskind returned to civilian life and settled into a New York apartment with Phyllis and their first child, Pamela. Their second daughter, Diana, was born in September. The routine of the navy—even the time spent on the *Millette*—was an "excruciatingly stultifying experience," Susskind said. It made him believe he was ill suited for the quiet life of a teacher, so he sought a more exciting career path in show business. He applied for a position at Warner Bros. publicity office. The job entailed planting newspaper column items about the studio's stars. Susskind once recalled how his learned persona put off the head publicist who did the hiring.

"You can't do this kind of work unless you're born to it," the publicist told him.

With his innate confidence, Susskind said, "I can do anything."

The publicist asked: "Can you change the way you talk with the big words?"

Susskind got the job, but soon left for a better one in the publicity department at Universal International Pictures, where his responsibilities included going on promotional tours with movie stars. Before long he determined he could never be happy with the publicity man's position in the show business food chain. During a trip with Yvonne DeCarlo in a small Texas town, he watched with envy as the actress's agent swooped into town and just as quickly got back on a plane to Hollywood after securing her approval of another film project. "I hated it," Susskind told journalist Tom Morgan years later. "I was always the least important member of an actress's entourage. Her manager was important, her agent was important, her lover was important. I wasn't. So I started looking for a job as an agent because what you had to say then was important."

After Susskind made his entry into the agency business by winning over Dorso at Century Artists in 1947, he immediately demonstrated that he was built for the job. For the persuasive Susskind, hearing the word "no" was the beginning of a negotiation. He was described as a Sherman tank that could not go in reverse. Dorso learned as much when a call came in that year from a West Coast agent, asking for help in resurrecting the career of his client Lucille Ball. "We represented the top agency in California, Berg-Allenberg," Dorso recalled. "They represented Clark Gable and Judy Garland, and hundreds of other people. And we represented them in New York. So Phil Berg called me one day and he said, 'Lucille Ball is coming to New York. She is dead in pictures. We can't give her away. I'm taking advantage of you by asking you to represent her in New York, because there's nothing you can do, either. But she's a client, and you represent our clients, so I'm asking you to do it.' That was the gist of the conversation. And Lucille Ball came into New York. And so I called David into the office, and I said, 'What can we do with Lucille Ball? What can we do?' So we thought, and we talked about it at great length. And we finally had the idea—and I don't know whether it was his or mine—of having her go out and play summer stock. We found a play for her that had been successful on Broadway, called *Dream Girl*. No one would buy her. So David and I decided to invest the money ourselves. We thought that the play would work. He went out and forced—I don't know how he did it— the summer stock people to buy her in the play. He worked like a Trojan. He got the rights to the play. Made her do it when she was doubtful that she could do it. That's the wild kind of energy that he would invest in a project. The play opened in Princeton and she was a smash. The show was a huge hit and it went for forty weeks and it ended up in Los Angeles where she got her radio show. And she became one of the biggest stars in the country again. It was a direct result of *Dream Girl* and David sticking with it and finally getting it done."

While working at NBC during the late 1940s and early 1950s, network executive Michael Dann said he dreaded having to turn down a pitch from Susskind. "When David went into a meeting he looked you in the eye, and if you turned him down, he could make it so personal you can't imagine," he said. "He would explode at you. He was the toughest agent I had to deal with in my life."

Within his first year on the job, Susskind was overseeing the New York office of Century Artists while the firm's partners were spending more time in Hollywood in an attempt to do more business in the movies. But a personal rift among them brought one, Al Levy, back east. Levy was a lawyer from Tucson, Arizona, where his family had a successful department store. He had been a personal manager for Frank Sinatra in the 1940s and produced the singer's radio show. He also discovered Doris Day in 1946 when she was a band singer and was instrumental in guiding her early career. "Al worked very well in the organization," said Dorso. "But an unfortunate thing happened. He was in love with Doris Day, and she fell in love with Marty Melcher. And it really split the agency." Melcher, the third partner in the agency, had been married to Patty Andrews of the Andrews Sisters, another Century Artist client. "They told Al that they wanted him out and that Doris was going to be managed solely by Marty Melcher," according to screenwriter Larry Cohen, a protégé of Levy. Melcher divorced Andrews and became Doris Day's third husband.

After Levy joined Susskind back in New York, the two sensed that radio's days as a major purveyor of big-name stars were numbered. By late 1948, the Federal Communications Commission had issued one hundred licenses for television stations throughout the United States. Even when carrying only a few hours of programming a day, the new medium caused a major upheaval in the way Americans were spending their leisure time. The cities with TV saw a major decline in movie attendance. Jukebox receipts dropped. Library book circulation started to slide. Within three years, the national audience ratings for radio's biggest star—Bob Hope—were down by nearly 50 percent.

As the stars of radio moved to television, they were most likely to be represented by the same established agents. But television was generating a new crop of writers, directors, and producers. Levy and Susskind decided to focus their efforts on representing them. The two men were well suited as partners. The avuncular Levy had family money and experience. He chain-smoked cigars and when he spoke sounded a bit like James Cagney in the gangster movie *Public Enemy*. Susskind, seven years younger, pulsated with tenacity and drive. They soon began to pursue clients. But even as they gathered new business for their venture, they were still pocketing the agent fees on Century's New York clients. Word eventually got back to Dorso and Melcher. On Christmas Eve in 1948, Susskind and Levy found that their keys no longer worked in the doors of Century Artists.

OFFICIALLY SEVERED from the company, Levy and Susskind formally christened their new firm Talent Associates Ltd. (Susskind, a budding Anglophile, suggested adding the Ltd. affectation.) The two men set up headquarters in a townhouse on East Fiftieth Street between Park and Lexington avenues. Every day they rode up a tiny rickety elevator to a floor on which they shared a switchboard operator with a theatrical producer. Within four months, Susskind and Levy landed their first client, the Philco Corporation, a major radio and appliance manufacturer that had moved into making TV sets. Talent Associates negotiated the deals for writers and directors who worked on an hour-long live dramatic show that Philco sponsored on NBC. At the time, advertisers controlled TV programming, buying the entire time period from the network and then supplying the show. Philco's total cost for doing a one-hour program in 1948 was about $25,000 a week, a small marketing investment, since television set sales were on their way to exponential growth. But the producers struggled with the challenge that faced much of the nascent television business, finding enough material to constantly feed the pipeline of a weekly live show. Videotape was not yet in use. Kinescopes—filmed off a TV monitor for playback—were generally of too poor quality for broadcast. The major movie studios were not yet in the TV production business. While movie companies were early investors in the technology of television, they were still wary of embracing the new competitor for their audiences. They held back on making their vast libraries of films available for broadcast. Hollywood studios also had the money to maintain their hold on the best and most popular stage plays for adaptations. As a result, a show such as *The Philco Television Playhouse* had to settle for material the movies had rejected. Susskind and Levy signed the Book-of-the-Month Club as a client, in the hope of getting the Philco show access to new novels the company featured. But Fred Coe, director and producer of *Television Playhouse,* urged Susskind and Levy to allow him to develop a new generation of young writers who would create original stories and scripts for television. Coe was a Mississippi native who had studied directing at Yale Drama School, a breeding ground for many of television's early producers. He landed a job as a studio manager for NBC during the mid-1940s when its New York station was broadcasting to only the few thousand homes that had television. After overseeing a number of early live-drama presentations for NBC, Coe was put in charge of *The Philco Television Playhouse,* which aired live on Sunday nights out of Studio 8G of the RCA Building in New York's Rockefeller Center.

Coe was famous for his temper tantrums. The constant pressure of mounting a new live production every week likely contributed to a drinking problem.

But he was a father figure—Coe and his writers affectionately called each other "Pappy"—able to nurture talent and create an atmosphere that was the closest thing to a bohemia of the electronic age. Writers such as Paddy Chayefsky, Horton Foote, Robert Alan Aurthur, and J. P. Miller, all prolific in movies, television, or theater during the decades that followed, received their earliest exposure on *Television Playhouse.* For Philco, they created powerful, emotionally charged human dramas in intimate settings that could be conveyed within the technical limitations of a cramped soundstage. Television sets were still luxury items for most Americans in the late 1940s and early 1950s, and those who could afford them were upscale and fairly well educated. There was little concern about scripts being too smart or sophisticated for viewers. Coe gave his writers an unbeatable combination of creative freedom and repeat business.

Writer-producer Robert Alan Aurthur encapsulated the era with this story. He was in Fred Coe's office when Paddy Chayefsky came in to pitch what became *Marty,* one of the most memorable live dramatic plays of the era when it aired in 1953. "Paddy came in and said, 'I want to write a love story about a fat butcher in the Bronx,'" Aurthur said. "And Fred said, 'Go and write it.'" What Coe got was a poignant, relatable portrayal of a lonely single man in his thirties who breaks away from the overbearing commitments of family and the pressure of friends to find his own life through a romantic relationship. "Nobody knew what they were doing, so there was nobody to say no," was how Sidney Lumet, one of several great film directors whose career started in early television, once described the atmosphere.

Susskind was an effective buffer between the show's creative types and Philco's ad agency. He also learned about dealing with writers and developing material by watching how Coe shepherded his staff at story conferences. Eventually, executives at the Music Corporation of America took notice of how *The Philco Television Playhouse* was prospering under the new management of Talent Associates. In 1949, MCA called Susskind and offered him a position as an agent in its New York office. It was a heady opportunity for a twenty-eight-year-old, and with Levy's blessing he pursued it.

MCA was big-time show business. At the time it represented such major stars as Dean Martin, Jerry Lewis, Jack Benny, Cary Grant, and Marlon Brando. The agency's New York office on Madison Avenue and Fifty-seventh Street had a stately, elegant, English look, with dark wood furniture and lithographs of racehorses on the walls. Susskind adhered to the dress code established by agency bosses Jules Stein and Lew Wasserman. Dark suit. White shirt. Blue or gray tie. Writer Walter Bernstein described their look as "eager undertakers." While Susskind was successful at selling projects with MCA clients, he chafed at what he believed was a stifling corporate culture that had little use for individuality and executives he described as Orwellian. "I was known as the egghead, the troublemaker—the iconoclast," he once said. "But I was making a lot of money."

One of Susskind's discoveries as an MCA agent came right off his family tree. In 1950, Susskind was on a West Coast trip where he saw comedian Danny Thomas at Ciro's, a Los Angeles nightclub. Thomas had killed the crowd with his six-minute routine. After the performance, Susskind asked the comedian who prepared the material. Thomas told him it was Norman Lear and his partner Ed Simmons.

Lear was living with his own young family in a one-room bungalow in Los Angeles at the time. He was selling baby pictures during the day and developing comedic routines with Simmons at night. A few years had passed since he had last heard from his cousin David. After seeing the Danny Thomas show, Susskind called Lear and told him to get to New York as soon as he could. MCA was putting together another season of *Ford Star Revue,* a comedy variety show fronted by Jack Haley, the actor who played the Tin Woodsman in *The Wizard of Oz.* Susskind wanted to make Lear and Simmons part of the package as writers for the show.

"Listen," he told Lear. "I'm going to New York tonight. Send a couple of samples of your work over to the hotel so I can show them to Haley."

"What samples?" said Lear, who revealed that he and Simmons had no material other than the one Thomas routine. They had never even seen a television script and certainly did not know how to write one.

"Listen," Susskind said. "You guys write?"

"Yeah."

"You think you write funny?"

"Yeah."

"You write a couple of funny things, send it over to the hotel, and I'll give someone $30 to make it look like a television script."

A few days later, Lear and Simmons were in New York working on the Haley program. The show lasted less than three months. But Susskind landed the pair their next job as writers for *The Colgate Comedy Hour,* a wildly popular NBC show that launched the successful nightclub comic team of Dean Martin and Jerry Lewis into major TV and film stardom. Lear was on his way to steady success as a comedy writer for TV, and ultimately he became the most successful producer of TV sitcoms in history, starting with *All in the Family* on CBS.

For Susskind, *The Colgate Comedy Hour* ended up as a potent lesson in ruthlessness. Once the show was a huge hit, MCA bosses instructed Susskind to ask NBC for an increase in talent fees for Martin and Lewis. In return, the duo would agree to do additional episodes. But Susskind knew that Martin and Lewis already had firm commitments for movies and club dates. There was no way they could extend their TV run. Susskind was told to go to Colgate's ad agency, which owned the show, and make the deal anyway. When Susskind suggested there might be some aggrieved parties once the extra shows didn't materialize, the stance of his MCA management was that he should not worry about it. When you have the talent or the property that someone wants, people will always do business with you, no matter what happened earlier. Susskind may have acted appalled at the time, but it turned out to be a career-defining experience that clearly helped him become a steely deal-maker himself.

ONCE ASKED by the editors of his high school yearbook to list his "suppressed desires," Susskind's response was, "None. I have no suppressed desires." This was especially true when it came to women. Susskind's actions on that front cost him his job at MCA. According to the public story he gave for parting company with the agency around the end of 1951, management was unhappy with his personal style. He said they complained he wasn't considered cutthroat enough. But it became widely known among Susskind's associates that he was fired because he had a sexual relationship with the wife of an important revenue-generating client for the agency.

Several months before the dismissal, Susskind received tragic news from Brookline: his father, Benjamin, had committed suicide. On the morning of June 30, 1951, David's sister, Dorothy, found their father in the bathroom of the family home on Manton Terrace. The coroner listed the cause of death as "asphyxiation by hanging while mentally depressed." Andrew Susskind said he learned years later that his grandfather had tried to kill himself several times and had been in and out of mental hospitals in the years preceding his suicide. Few of David Susskind's friends or coworkers knew the cause of his father's death. As a child, Andrew had been told that Ben Susskind died of cancer.

For years, Susskind never spoke of his father's suicide or the impact it had on him. Lear pointed out that the gate to his cousin's emotional state was rarely open to anyone. "Introspection was not a part of his lexicon," Lear once said. "He never cared to dig into himself and he certainly wouldn't let you dig there."

After being dismissed from MCA, David Susskind put in a call to Al Levy, who invited him to come back to Talent Associates.

By the spring of 1952, David Susskind was back at Talent Associates as an executive vice president earning $27,000 a year. The firm had prospered as it negotiated deals for the writers, producers, and directors for a number of shows, including *Mr. Peepers,* a popular live half-hour comedy that starred Wally Cox as a mild-mannered high school teacher, and *Television Playhouse.* Sponsored on alternate Sunday nights by Philco and Goodyear Rubber Company, *Television Playhouse* was among the top ten shows in the ratings. But there was another way to gauge its success. "They counted all the television sets that were sold Monday," was how writer Paddy Chayefsky once described it to Susskind.

Several years of operating under the grueling pace of live production took its toll on Fred Coe, who supervised the making of both *Television Playhouse* and *Mr. Peepers* every week. In 1953, he decided to take the summer off. As Coe's representative, Susskind had to inform the executives at the Hutchins Agency, which handled Philco's advertising, that the producer would be gone for more than a month. Susskind was told to come up with a replacement. Susskind had never produced a show on his own, but he had certainly seen Coe handle the job enough times. He offered to do it himself.

After learning Susskind would take over, Coe blithely took his leave as planned. He gave his loyal stable of writers the summer off as well. For Coe, the decision was the television equivalent of New York Yankees first baseman Wally Pipp sitting down for a day and giving a chance to Lou Gehrig—who would go on to play the next 2,130 consecutive games. The summer break launched Susskind as an indefatigable show-maker, while Coe's importance in the TV industry began a slow fade.

Susskind had only a few weeks to mount his first production, and his start was not auspicious. His first *Playhouse* entry aired on August 2, 1953. It was a hastily written script based on the real-life story of an imprisoned murderer proven innocent due to the diligence of a New York newspaper reporter. The story needed to convey the passage of years, which was too difficult to execute inside an hour of live TV. By the end of the harsh review that appeared in *Variety,* the critic was pining for the return of Coe.

Even before the misfire aired, Susskind had begun to search for material that was more in line with the kind of intense, personal stories that won plaudits for *Television Playhouse* from critics and audiences (and required few sets or costume changes). He started working the phones, contacting every literary agent he knew. One of them, Priscilla Morgan, presented Susskind with some sample scripts from Tad Mosel, an airline ticket clerk who had just started to break into television writing. Susskind asked Mosel to expand one of the samples into an hour show. Within ten days, Mosel delivered *Ernie Barger Is 50.* The story centered on how a middle-aged midwestern business man is forced to come to terms with the sorry relationships he has with his neglected wife and self-absorbed son. Mosel's unflinching look at family dynamics was tautly written and well played, with Ed Begley Sr. in the lead. The show turned the *Variety* critic around on Susskind. "*Playhouse* is far from a one-man operation despite the deserved kudos for Coe," the paper wrote. Mosel delivered a second well-received play called *Other People's Houses,* starring Eileen Heckart and Rod Steiger as anguished family members who decide to put their elderly father in a retirement home. Susskind also discovered a play by dramatist N. Richard Nash called *The Rainmaker,* the Depression-era tale of an old maid who falls in love with a charismatic charlatan who claims he can bring rain to her drought-stricken town. After it aired on *Television Playhouse,* *The Rainmaker* was adapted for the Broadway stage and later made into a movie with Katharine Hepburn and Burt Lancaster. Inside of two months, Susskind had established himself as a television producer with a good sense for quality material.

The notion of an agent stepping in for one of his clients was unorthodox and led people in New York television circles to gossip that Susskind had somehow undermined Coe by taking over for him. There is no evidence of that being the case. Before his return in September, Coe sent Susskind a gentlemanly telegram congratulating him on the fill-in work. Coe left *Television Playhouse* a year later, in 1954, largely because he no longer wanted to deal with the pressure from the sponsors. They wanted him to lighten up the downbeat nature of the material turned out by his writers, who had been nicknamed "the Agony Boys" by the press. As one ad executive complained to *Time* magazine, "One week there'd be a story about a blind old lady in Texas, and the next week a story about a blind young lady in Texas." Once television proved to be a powerfully effective medium for selling consumer goods, serious and often somber dramatic anthology shows became less appealing to advertisers. The intimate kitchen-sink stories about ordinary people grappling with the often bleak state of their existence was not the platform they wanted to lure prosperous 1950s America into buying Philco's self-defrosting refrigerators or Goodyear tires made to travel along the country's expanding interstate highway system. As the medium became a powerful tool in driving consumerism, advertisers who bought the time demanded that producers appeal to the widest possible audience. "In the early days the television sets were very expensive and only the well-to-do could afford them," said Ed Vane, an executive for NBC and ABC during the medium's early years. "When the cost of a set dropped dramatically in the course of the 1950s and into the 1960s, more and more people were able to obtain television sets and watch. But that meant that the socioeconomic level of the set owners began to drop too. So the dramatic appetite of the audience changed. Rod Serling's *Patterns* (an intense, unsettling look at survival in the corporate executive suite that aired on the CBS anthology show *Studio One*) would not appeal to Joe Sixpack. Westerns would be more his style."

But just before *Television Playhouse* ended in 1955, Susskind produced a new play that broke ground in a way that no other had during the program's run. *A Man Is Ten Feet Tall* was an urban tale by Robert Alan Aurthur. It centered on the friendship between Tommy Tyler, a gregarious and charming black stevedore (played by Sidney Poitier) who befriends a shy addition to the dock's crew named Axel North (Don Murray). North turns out to be an army deserter, but Tyler remains devoted to him. He also defends Axel from a belligerent, bullying crew chief named Charlie Malik (played by Martin Balsam), which results in a confrontation that has tragic consequences. A representative for Philco contacted Susskind to ask if it was true that the story had an interracial storyline. Susskind said the man "almost had a heart attack" when he confirmed it. "This was the first and certainly major instance wherein a Negro was unqualifiedly integrated into a teleplay," *Variety* noted in its review. Having the story play out without making race an issue was what made the show radical. Tommy is not only Axel's friend but also his supervisor, something viewers had never seen on television or in the movies. Most of the angry calls that flooded the switchboards at NBC the night the show aired were from viewers who thought Hilda Simms, the actress who played Poitier's wife was white (she was a fair-skinned black actress). Some of Philco's dealers in the South were incensed by the program and ended their franchise agreements with the company.

It was not until the civil rights movement rattled the nation's consciousness in the 1960s that black actors would show up on network television with any regularity. But *A Man Is Ten Feet Tall* was compelling enough to become one of the elite original teleplays of the era that was made into a theatrical film, joining *Marty* and *Patterns.* Less than two weeks after the show aired, MGM agreed to finance a film version by Susskind and Aurthur that was ultimately called *Edge of the City,* with Poitier reprising his role as Tommy. It was the first time he was billed as a costar in a feature film. John Cassavetes played Axel and Jack Warden was cast as the malicious Malik. The film was even bolder in its portrayal of blacks and whites working, socializing, and living side by side. When Poitier and Warden faced off, using baling hooks as weapons and surrounded by crates and chain-link fences, director Martin Ritt turned the fight scene into an unnerving urban ballet. Susskind secured the train yards on the west side of Manhattan as a location for the film, allowing Ritt to give the story all the visual authenticity he needed. Aurthur believed MGM backed the project to see if a low-budget film (estimated at $520,000) could succeed without playing in the segregated South, where it would not be booked in 1957. The film performed modestly at the box office—Susskind maintained that MGM overplayed the violence in the movie in its advertising and instead should have marketed *Edge of the City* as an art film in smaller theaters. Nevertheless it stands as a cinematic landmark for the social strides it made.

AFTER PROVING HIMSELF ON Philco, Susskind was able to develop a couple of shows of his own. His first series, a half-hour drama called *Justice,* was a left-wing version of *Dragnet.* It starred Gary Merrill as a court-appointed attorney who handles indigent defendants in criminal and civil cases. Susskind paid an honorarium to the Legal Aid Society so that he could say the shows were taken from the organization's files, but Roger Hirson, a writer on the series, said most of the stories were entirely fictional. The following year Susskind launched a second half-hour anthology show, *Appointment with Adventure,* which did stories based on historical events. The two shows put Susskind in the thick of one the most repressive political acts to occur in twentieth-century America. The fearmongering over communism propagated by Senator Joseph McCarthy and the House Un-American Activities Committee (HUAC) in Congress during the late 1940s and 1950s manifested itself in economic sanctions in a number of professions. The blacklisting of professionals in the TV business based on current, previous, suggested, or even imagined political affiliations was a powerful way to get the message of redbaiters in front of every citizen. Throughout the 1950s and even into the early 1960s, the casting of television shows was essentially held captive by several organizations that threatened boycotts of sponsors if their determination of who was politically acceptable was not followed. One boycott was led by a Syracuse grocer named Laurence Johnson, who threatened to banish products from the shelves of his store if a company sponsored a show that featured "Stalin's little creatures." He had all of four stores. Three former FBI agents had formed an organization called American Business Consultants and published a weekly newsletter called *Counterattack* devoted to exposing communism. A self-described security consultant named Vince Hartnett founded AWARE and provided an ongoing list of performers deemed undesirable because of perceived or alleged political leanings in a publication called *Red Channels.* Fanned by the HUAC hearings and flag-waving newspaper columnists, the groups were able to control the talent used by terrified sponsors and ad agencies. The heinous practice ruined careers. Philip Loeb, a costar on the enormously popular CBS comedy *The Goldbergs,* took his own life after he was forced off the show by sponsor General Foods when it was faced with the threat of a boycott.

The slightest provocation of government institutions could lead to suspicions of communist leanings. In August 1954, Susskind invited FBI director J. Edgar Hoover to appear on a *Television Playhouse* episode that dealt with the increasing crime rate in the United States. Hoover declined the invitation and then ordered the bureau to investigate Susskind, even though he had no history of political activity up to that time. The report said a confidential informant "advised that David Susskind was a member of the Communist Political Association." The name cited on a 1937 petition turned out to be a different David Susskind. Susskind was fortunate: he was not blacklisted, unlike some artists who were, simply because they shared the name of a suspected communist sympathizer.

As a producer, Susskind had to choose between dealing with the blacklist or simply getting out of the television business. When Susskind sold *Appointment with Adventure* and *Justice* to Young & Rubicam, the ad agency that represented the shows' sponsors, it was with the condition that every name of all personnel involved be submitted for "political clearance." No one could be hired until the ad agency had checked the name. When a name was rejected, no explanation could be given to the agents who sent clients for jobs on the shows. Food company Borden, the sponsor of *Justice,* was so fearful of reciprocity from the blacklisting groups that Susskind was limited to a list of 150 performers designated by Johnson and AWARE as patriotic and good Americans.

Susskind said he pressured Young & Rubicam executive David Levy into expanding the list, reasoning that being restricted to the approved names was hurting the quality of the programs. "Human beings are suffering loss of employment without any charges, without even knowing they can't be hired, and I am being embarrassed constantly with the agents and the lawyers of the actors and the writers and the directors by saying, 'I am sorry we cannot hire you on the fact of political rejection,'" he told him. "I know a great number of the people you rejected. I know them socially and professionally and there is no question about their political reliability or their good citizenship or their loyalty in this country, and on all these grounds I beg you to let me confront these people with whatever you have on them and let them answer and you will find that they will be all right and you will have a much better show."

When subjected to the "whitelist" of whom he could use for *Justice,* Susskind inundated Levy with additional names of actors, writers, and directors he wanted to use, thinking the more names he could get cleared, the fewer would be blacklisted over the long term. He submitted a dozen names for every one he actually needed. When Levy protested, the executive revealed that the blacklist was essentially blackmail. The private groups that informed ad agencies whether an artist was politically acceptable were charging anywhere from $5 to $25 per name submitted. "You are breaking us," David Levy told Susskind. The ad agency and Borden had paid nearly $17,000 to Vince Hartnett for information on the names submitted for *Justice.*

Even child actors had to be cleared. Susskind once recounted how he submitted the name of an eight-year-old girl for a role on *Appointment with Adventure*. It was rejected. The ad agency told Susskind the decision was based on the alleged political leanings of the child's father. Susskind's exasperation over the issue was apparent in a letter he sent to Levy after Lorillard, the maker of Kent cigarettes, dropped its sponsorship of the show. "May I close with the fervent hope that you will do everything possible to improve your product," he wrote.

Hirson believes Susskind had some success in widening the number of performers used on *Justice*. As weeks went by during the show's run, he would be surprised by the arrival of many performers who showed up in the Rockefeller Center studio after not being seen anywhere for years because they had been prevented from getting work.

JUSTICE AND *APPOINTMENT with Adventure* each lasted about a year. Around the same period as those shows, Susskind had also taken over the production of an anthology drama called *Armstrong Circle Theatre*. Sponsored by the linoleum maker Armstrong, based in Lancaster, Pennsylvania, it was a workmanlike show, even though Paul Newman, James Dean, and other major stars passed through it in the early stages of their careers as New York actors. While much of the material performed was not as distinguished as *Television Playhouse* or *Studio One*, Susskind made sure that the sponsor received full value for its money. In December 1954, Kim Stanley was cast in a *Circle Theatre* play called *H Is for Hurricane*. She played a woman with a sick child who is trapped in a New York apartment without heat, electricity, or telephone service during a severe storm. Stanley was fine during the run-through but fell ill hours before the broadcast was set to air. The doctor who was called to the studio strongly recommended that she sit out the dress rehearsal so she could rest and be ready for the live show. Stanley went on the air that night and "did amazing things to the script," according to Mary Cummings, the ad agency executive who oversaw the show for Armstrong. Whether it was her illness or creative license (Stanley was a legendary Method actor), the live broadcast was running two minutes over by the first commercial break. Susskind rushed from the booth where he watched the show with the sponsor and into the control room. He worked with director Dan Petrie to delete scenes that had no dialogue, the credits, and a blurb that plugged the following week's play so that the viewers would see the end of *H Is for Hurricane*. But what made them heroes to the ad agency was getting all of Armstrong's commercials for vinyl flooring and other products in by the end of the hour show.

Even with such efforts, *Armstrong Circle Theatre* looked as if it was going the way of *Justice* and *Appointment with Adventure*—until Susskind reinvented the program as television's first contemporary docudrama, dramatizing true-life stories and recent news events. He started out with the story of Charles Steen, a geologist who discovered a high-grade uranium deposit in Utah in 1952, presenting it with the flashy title "I Found $60,000,000." Jackie Coogan played the geologist, but viewers met the real Steen in a brief film clip at the conclusion of the show, a gimmick that became the signature of the series. "The protagonist, or his mother or his psychiatrist or his high school teacher or someone went on camera in an interview dispensing uplift and hope, and the idea became a big success," wrote Robert Foreman, an executive with the ad agency Batton, Barton, Durstine & Osborn who worked with Susskind on many of his shows. The Armstrong people loved the new format and remained committed to *Circle Theatre* for another eight years as it sold many a roll of linoleum.

Susskind attempted to distinguish the *Circle Theatre* shows from other types of dramas by calling them "actuals" in the press. The term did not really take hold. "Here's my problem," he said to screenwriter Jerry Coopersmith. "How can we let the audience know that they are watching dramatizations of real events? If we make an announcement at the beginning of the show, the viewer who tunes in a little late won't hear it, and a newspaper ad will be read by comparatively few. Think about that."

Coopersmith suggested having a news anchor as a narrator introduce the principal scenes in the show. Susskind hired John Cameron Swayze, the voice of NBC's *Camel News Caravan,* for the job; in later years he used Douglas Edwards when *Armstrong Circle Theatre* ran on CBS. The ethics of using a newsreader performing as himself in a role on a scripted TV program with actors was not an issue in the days before network television news had any real journalistic heft (once it did, Edwards was forced by CBS News to leave the show).

The writers for *Circle Theatre* had to be reporters too, as Susskind made sure the show was diligent in its fact gathering. Coopersmith agreed to spend six days aboard the *Nautilus* to research an episode about the first atomic submarine (on condition that Susskind pay for a $1 million insurance policy for the writer's wife and children, which he did). While the scripted shows were played out live in the studio, newsreel footage was blended in to give the stories more authority. The *Nautilus* episode called for moving images of the sub plowing through the sea. A public relations officer for the U.S. Navy was contacted and happily agreed to supply it. "Minutes later a yeoman arrived with a can of 35-millimeter footage, which we threaded onto a projector," Coopersmith said. "We stared at the screen with puzzlement. Where was the submarine? It was not on this film. All we saw were endless shots of machinery that none of us understood." A call then came from the panic-stricken navy officer, who asked if anyone had seen the film.

"Yeah, a few of us," said Bob Costello, a producer on *Circle Theatre,* told him. "What the hell is it?"

"For God's sake, don't show it to anyone else. We sent you the wrong footage. What you've got there are top-secret shots of the atomic engine!"

"I've often thought that story should be included in a compilation called 'Great Tales of Naval Intelligence,'" Coopersmith said.

Creating audience-grabbing sagas based on fact did not make the sponsor any less sensitive about the content. Well into the show's run, screenwriter Dale Wasserman was sent to Israel to research his *Circle Theatre* episode called *Engineer of Death,* which depicted the Mossad's hunt for Nazi war criminal Adolf Eichmann. The first script that was sent to Armstrong's ad agency came back with the words "too Jewish" written across the top page, according to Barbara Schultz, a story editor on the series. Wasserman recalled how Susskind fought for the show. "It was the first exposure of Eichmann—who he was, what he was guilty of, why the Israelis so desperately wanted to get their hands on him," he said. "What I learned and initially wrote, with David's sanction, alarmed the network and the agency involved, and modifications were forced upon us. David largely fought the battle in my behalf and the story did largely come through."

BY THE TIME Susskind built up his reputation as a prolific and reliable producer of live television in New York, the city's reign as the industry's creative Mecca appeared to be dimming. By the mid-1950s, Lucille Ball became the biggest TV star in the nation, and her situation comedy *I Love Lucy* forever altered the television production business model. The half-hour show was made with three 35-millimeter cameras shooting simultaneously on a proscenium stage in Hollywood in front of an audience. The technique embraced by her husband, costar, and business partner Desi Arnaz and cinematographer Karl Freund captured the energy of a live performance. But by being on film, the "three-camera comedy," as it was called, could be edited, perfected, and, most important, shown repeatedly after its initial airing on the network. The rerun became the financial foundation of the television business. A hit program could play for years, be enjoyed by future generations of viewers, and generate hundreds of millions of dollars along the way. Ball and Arnaz became millionaires from *I Love Lucy* (which they owned at the insistence of CBS, which did not want to take the financial risk). By January 1957, the couple was producing 222 hours of television a year out of their Hollywood studio Desilu Productions, including hit series such as *Our Miss Brooks* and *December Bride.* By that time they had turned down a $12 million offer to sell their company. Ten years later Paramount purchased it for $40 million.

Another sea change was set in motion in 1954, when Leonard Goldenson, the owner of the American Broadcasting Company, agreed to invest in Disneyland, Walt Disney's first theme park, located in Anaheim, California. In return, ABC received the weekly series *Disneyland* and Disney became the first significant Hollywood movie studio to provide a filmed program made especially for television. Soon other movie studios geared up their operations to produce shows as the number of homes with TV sets grew and the economics of the business expanded. Live television's obsolescence was sealed on April 15, 1956, when, at a broadcasters convention in Chicago, the Ampex Corporation unveiled the first videotape recorder for commercial use. Within days, CBS and NBC purchased several of the machines and started putting them to work.

The perpetual activity at Talent Associates could not offset the competition from TV production on the West Coast. The company's profits were under pressure. Susskind wanted to get into the even riskier business of producing Broadway shows as well. Susskind and Levy considered giving up on being an independent outfit and sought to make an arrangement with NBC, in which Talent Associates would be an in-house supplier of programming to the network.

They never made a deal, but NBC remained committed to live production in New York. CBS had become the ratings leader, thanks to *I Love Lucy* and other filmed weekly series. Shows with regular characters formed a habitual bond with viewers (and more predictable ratings). NBC's innovative chairman Sylvester "Pat" Weaver believed he could counter the trend by bringing lavish production values to live TV, giving viewers big events, or "spectaculars," as he dubbed them. They were produced in color, to help NBC parent RCA sell recently introduced color sets. Jerome Robbins recreated the Broadway production of *Peter Pan* with Mary Martin. It would become a favorite of young audiences, as it was taped and repeated over the years. Humphrey Bogart, Lauren Bacall, and Henry Fonda appeared in a staging of *The Petrified Forest*. Other big-name actors such as Lee J. Cobb, Fredric March, and Joseph Cotten were showing up on the small screen.

NBC's approach did not close the ratings gap as much as it garnered plaudits from the press. That was enough for CBS to respond with colossal productions of its own (and to insist on using its own terminology, calling them "extravaganzas"). In 1956, CBS made a deal with E. I. du Pont de Nemours to sponsor a splashy monthly series that could rival NBC. Talent Associates was invited to be one of the producers, pending approval by DuPont.

After a few months of planning, Susskind and Al Levy made the trip to Wilmington, Delaware, to make a presentation to the company that promised consumers "Better Things for Better Living Through Chemistry." Susskind's executive assistant, Michael Abbott, made the trip as well. They did not bring along flip cards or easels or fancy brochures. It made Abbott curious as to what exactly they were going to present. "We're on the train to Wilmington— David, myself, and Al Levy—and I'm sitting and reading a newspaper and they're playing cards. And I'm saying, 'David, what kind of show are we going to do? I mean, what do you have in mind?' And they're playing cards. We get to Wilmington and we're met with a chauffeur and a limousine. We're taken to DuPont headquarters, the most gorgeous paneled room with crystal chandeliers. And it's the DuPont board of directors. Pretty impressive. We were introduced. I sit there. Al Levy sits there. David gets up and for twenty minutes he spellbinds them. He says, 'It's going to be the greatest shows of all time, the great classics of all time, with the greatest Hollywood stars, John Wayne and this one and that one, and naming the greatest stars of Broadway and Hollywood actors and the greatest directors, and they were thrilled. 'Cary Grant, Jimmy Stewart, Clark Gable, whoever, we're going to get all of them. And we're doing *The Prince and the Pauper,* which is about two kids and it's a swashbuckling guy that Errol Flynn played in the movie.' The DuPont board thought, 'Oh great, he's going to get Errol Flynn to do it.' Al Levy and I are looking at each other, saying, 'We didn't know that.' Anyway, we did the series and we got a lot of money for it."

When the first production meeting was held at Talent Associates for *The DuPont Show of the Month,* Abbott was surprised when he met Leslie Slote, the writer who was hired to adapt *The Prince and the Pauper.* "I never heard of him," Abbott said. Why, he thought, would Susskind hire an unknown to handle such a high-profile project?

Slote turned out to be a writer for *The Chief,* a newspaper for civil service workers. He was a friend of—and a front for—the actual writer of the script, Walter Bernstein, whose name had shown up in *Red Channels.* Susskind could do only so much to get blacklisted actors onto his shows. But he was aggressive in employing writers who were willing to allow their work to be presented under someone else's name.

Bernstein was an example of a blacklisted artist who came of age during the 1930s and found himself aligned with the views of the Communist Party because he believed it was a force for good. The son of a New York City schoolteacher, Bernstein found capitalism had caused wars, unemployment, the Depression, and fascism and thought there had to be an alternative. He had admired how the sports columnists from the party newspaper *The Daily Worker* were the first to promote the idea of black baseball players getting tryouts in the then all-white major leagues. He had heard citizens' arrests were being made in the Soviet Union of people who made anti-Semitic remarks. "There was no other government that was doing that," he said. When Bernstein served in the U.S. Army during World War II and fought alongside Yugoslav and Italian partisans, "the communists were the most courageous people, but it was all around fighting fascism."

After writing for *Yank* and *The New Yorker,* Bernstein tried his hand at screenwriting. He wrote Hollywood screenplays and eventually sold a script to *Television Playhouse,* an adaptation of F. Scott Fitzgerald's *Rich Boy,* which starred Grace Kelly. He was blacklisted in 1950 after he refused to cooperate with HUAC. When his name turned up in *Red Channels,* there were as many as eight political affiliations for Bernstein that were cited as unacceptable. He had written for two Communist Party publications, he had joined organizations that supported the antifascist Republican side in the Spanish civil war and another that demanded rights for black World War II veterans. "All of them were true," Bernstein wrote in his autobiography. "I would have felt insulted if I had not been included." He started writing TV scripts under other names, but not every producer wanted to take a chance on using him, including Fred Coe, who previously hired him for *Rich Boy.* "We had a very good relationship," he said. "And when I was blacklisted, I came to see him for work. And I had a front at that time. He wouldn't do it. Too scared. I assume that was the reason, because he was very sympathetic."

Bernstein did get regular work from Charlie Russell, who produced the series *You Are There* for CBS. But once the show was moved to Hollywood, Russell was fired. Clearly the use of fronts was an open secret, as Susskind sought Bernstein out once he became available. He started giving work to Bernstein along with two other blacklisted writers in his circle, Abe Polonsky and Arnie Manoff. Manoff, who had been named as a communist before HUAC, was the husband of actress Lee Grant, who lost all of her TV and film work as well when her name showed up in *Red Channels.* Bernstein said Susskind was putting himself at risk, just as Russell had, by hiring them. "David was sticking his neck out," Bernstein said. "He really was. He didn't have to."

Over time Susskind developed an admirable reputation for using blacklisted artists. After Joseph Papp lost his job as a CBS stage manager when he refused to testify before HUAC, Susskind instructed his staff to hire him to work on the technical crews for his productions. Martin Ritt's promising career as an actor had come to a halt when he was listed in *Red Channels.* It was Susskind, at the urging of Robert Alan Aurthur, who put him behind the camera to direct *Edge of the City.* Ritt's circumstances enabled Susskind to get his services at a deep discount of $10,000. But it got him off the blacklist and launched his career as a director. "David was the first one I know to really fight the blacklist," said Loring Mandel, who began his long career as a television writer during the era. "He was a patriotic man. And he believed in the Constitution and there were things that were going on he felt were wrong."

Marc Merson, a casting director during the 1950s, said the practice of blacklisting actors faded when it became apparent that groups such as AWARE never came through on threats to boycott advertisers. "As that threat began to recede, independent producers like Susskind and other people who didn't believe in this would hire a Lee Grant," he said. "And so that made it easier for the next one, and the next one. It was a process of chipping away." But the remnants of the fearful era lasted for years.

Bernstein appreciated Susskind's courage and wanted a friendship with him, but it seemed impossible. He recalled how the writers' meetings with Susskind, conducted after business hours and away from the Talent Associates offices, often became contentious. "I would be glad to see him and it would last about thirty seconds," Bernstein said. "I wanted to kill him. I really did like him. I sensed a kind of good-heartedness about him that he had, that he was out to destroy. It was like he deliberately set out to antagonize me when I would see him. He would say something. He would do something. And not to be too psychological about it, but it was as though he couldn't deal with the fact that I liked him, really. I almost felt that there was a need—just speaking for me, particularly—to alienate me. And that in some way, it was concealing something opposite that he didn't want to have to deal with—some kind of intimacy, some kind of affection, some kind of warmth. That in some way, that probably emasculated him, in his own mind. Now, this is cheap pop psychology, but I always felt that. I felt like shaking him and saying, "David, you don't have to do this. Don't do this. Come on. Stop it. Let's be friends. I like you, and I appreciate what you've done.' But he had to kill it, in some way. He'd make some crack about a girl. Or if he knew I was seeing somebody he would say something to get your back up and push you away. He was afraid of the intimacy. And this was his way of making sure he wasn't going to get it."

CHRISTOPHER PLUMMER—not Errol Flynn—starred in Susskind's production of *The Prince and the Pauper,* which aired on October 28, 1957. The show was exactly the type of sumptuous production DuPont and CBS were looking for, utilizing nineteen sets and a hundred performers. The critic for *Time* said Dan Petrie directed the show with "the fluidity of a movie" and that the production "abounded in virtues that spell 'long run' in Hollywood." The other DuPont shows that followed, including *The Count of Monte Cristo, Wuthering Heights, The Prisoner of Zenda, The Bridge of San Luis Rey,* and *The Browning Version,* elevated Susskind to the status of supreme showman. Kraft Foods, Kaiser Aluminum, and other sponsors hired Talent Associates to produce their live-drama shows and specials. Paul Bogart, who was a director on many Talent Associates shows, said Susskind was a force to be reckoned with when he arrived on a set to observe a rehearsal. "People would respond to his mere presence," Bogart said. "The fact that he was there used to elevate them a little bit. And their performances would move up. The men too, not just the women. Everybody would get a little electric because David was there. He would have a big pad of paper and a pencil and he'd walk around following them and would be looking at them with great eagerness. He'd get up real close, and a little too close while they're acting. And if he didn't like what they did, he'd write. But if he liked it you could see it written all over him. He was not a man to conceal what he felt. You could see it in his face all the time. I did enjoy what he did for the work. The best that a producer can give to a performance is presence. He electrified them."

After fighting the battles over the angst-ridden material that TV writers served up earlier in the decade, Susskind found that producing shows based on classic literature was an easy sell to sponsors and respectable enough for highbrow critics to praise. It was also cheaper. Many of the properties chosen for DuPont and other sponsors were in the public domain and did not require rights fees. His cost for the material was the hiring of a writer to adapt a work. Often his associate producers, Jacqueline Babbin and Audrey Gellen, did it in-house.

Susskind's goal was to be recognized as a showman in television the way Cecil B. DeMille had been in the movies. Soon his name on a production became a beacon for viewers searching for quality. He promoted the belief that Hollywood could not offer the energy and excitement he created in New York, where he used stage-trained actors who performed live. Susskind was a lover of London theater and frequently visited the city to see plays and find actors to import for his shows. Talent Associates gave the first American TV exposure to such performers as Richard Burton, Sir John Gielgud, Richard Harris, and Laurence Olivier. "British actors, actresses, directors, and so on are so talented, so agreeable to work with," Susskind once said. "If it is possible to like actors at all, one must like British ones." British stage actors who were steeped in the classics were more suitable for the literature-based material he produced for TV. "Most of the American actors were more naturalistic by then because that's how plays had been written in the last decade," said British actress Rosemary Harris, who worked in a number of Susskind's shows. "England was far behind. They were still doing artsy-fartsy things."

Robert Foreman was astounded at what Susskind was willing to try on live television (although by the late 1950s many shows contained videotaped scenes). "He collapsed the bridge in *The Bridge of San Luis Rey* and plunged the cast into a mat below," Foreman wrote. "For the hurricane in *Swiss Family Robinson* he used gallons of real water and a score of wind machines . . . the swordplay in *The Prisoner of Zenda* was so real it was positively frightening—especially to the actors." Susskind sought perfection in every production and asked for scenes to be rewritten or music to be rescored hours before airtime.

He even replaced lead actors on short notice, a highly risky endeavor, as a 90-minute special required three to four weeks of rehearsal.

Susskind had originally wanted Rosemary Harris to costar with Richard Burton in an adaptation of Emily Brontë's Gothic romance *Wuthering Heights* on *The DuPont Show of the Month.* She had played Desdemona in a production of *Othello* with Burton at the Old Vic in England and worked well with him. But Harris was booked to star in a *Hallmark Hall of Fame* special, *Dial M for Murder,* scheduled two weeks before the DuPont show was set to air on May 9, 1958. She could not fathom working on two major productions so closely in succession. "*Dial M for Murder* was incredibly difficult," she said. "The cameras were like big lumbering elephants with the cables as thick as your thigh. To have four of those in one small room and have them try not to record each other—it was like unraveling knitting." Harris recommended another actress to play the role of Cathy Earnshaw. Susskind was grateful at first. But at some point he became unhappy with the choice and he let Harris know it. The aggrieved producer telephoned an exhausted Harris shortly after she finished the Hallmark show and demanded that she step in to take over. "I remember the call waking me up," she recalled. "He said, 'You started the fire and you better get your ass over here and put it out.' I said, 'David, aren't you going on the air in four days?' He said, 'Yep.'"

Harris relented and took the job. "It was a challenge," she said. "But it was a lovely script and I'm a quick study, I have to admit." Harris confessed that she kept a piece of paper with her lines on it under a pillow in the final scene where she plays a dying Cathy. "I think I had my lines written on scenery all over the set," she recalled.

But actors were loath to turn down any Susskind show at the time. "It was very prestigious to be in one of David's productions," Harris said. "We were thrilled to be part of the pond that he put his hook into. We jumped at the bait. He spent money and the shows always looked wonderful. When we did *A Tale of Two Cities* for *The DuPont Show of the Month* it seemed like a hundred actors were storming the Bastille."

Whenever a new standard was set in television specials, Susskind would try to raise his own game. On March 30, 1957, a then-record audience of 100 million viewers watched Julie Andrews in *Cinderella,* a musical rendering of the fairy tale with an original score by Richard Rodgers and Oscar Hammerstein. Later that year, Susskind enlisted composer Alec Wilder to write an original score for the Italian fable *Pinocchio* for a special sponsored by Rexall, a drugstore franchiser. Wilder had written the pop standard "While We're Young" and was a favorite songwriter of Frank Sinatra. Hanya Holm, the German modern-dance innovator who staged numbers for the Broadway hits *Kiss Me Kate* and *My Fair Lady*, was brought in for the choreography. The script by Yasha Frank, originally written for the Federal Theatre Project in the 1930s, was entirely in verse.

Mickey Rooney gave a first-rate performance as the wooden boy who comes to life. The score was memorable, the dances were intricate, and the set had a hallucinatory look. While *Pinocchio* wasn't as successful as *Cinderella,* the production was distinctive and different for television but did not give short shrift to the sponsor's commercials. Stubby Kaye, the Broadway star who played the Town Crier in *Pinocchio,* actually sang the segue into the first Rexall message while in character and even held up the company's Sunday newspaper circular. After a scene in the show went to black, the lights came up on a druggist standing in front of shelves filled with products on sale "for only one cent more at your Rexall store." Foreman claimed that one of the displays for the commercials was built inside the whale set that swallowed Pinocchio and Gepetto.

As Susskind brought bigger spectacles to television, he still could not stop the industry's exodus to the West. Even *Studio One,* considered the finest of the live New York–based dramatic anthology shows, made the move to Los Angeles, where it would have better access to what CBS executives called "box office names." Susskind became a gadfly on the issue of preserving New York as a production center, heading a committee of industry types who lobbied for the creation of a centralized production facility in the city. He always talked on the record to the press about his disdain for Hollywood, calling it "a world of lotus blossoms, swimming pools, smog and indifference." He insisted that television would be ruined once it became part of the movie studios' assembly line. "Live television enlisted the kind of man who, using a strained analogy, was doing custom-tailored work," Susskind often said. "Film television is buying your clothes off the rack; it comes down by the yard. Every two and a half days another one is made. It is edited, processed, shipped east or projected from California. The live function, the live technique had about it the elements of a crusade. We thought we were shooting for the Academy

Award or the Pulitzer Prize every time, or we hoped we were. And we suffered most immediate comparison to the theater because the theater was next door."

Susskind had become the king of live television in New York, and he was intent on keeping his throne. He even resorted to remaking some of Hollywood's best-known films for television through a crafty deal he and Levy made with MGM.

As Susskind told it to his son, Andrew, it was a morning in the spring of 1958 when Levy mentioned an announcement in the Hollywood trade papers that preproduction had begun on MGM's $12.5 million widescreen extravaganza of *Ben-Hur*. Susskind acknowledged that he had seen the ads.

"What can you tell me about *Ben-Hur*?" his partner asked.

"Well, you know, Al, it's a biblical story with a chariot race."

"And who owns it?"

"Nobody owns it."

"Well, let's call up *Variety*."

Susskind asked why.

"We're going to take out an ad," Levy says. "It's going to say that David Susskind and Al Levy have announced the commencement of preproduction for their live television version of *Ben-Hur*."

Taken aback, Susskind wondered out loud if Levy had lost his mind.

"Just do it," Levy said.

Soon afterward, the ad appeared in *Variety*. It was a fraction of the size of the spread MGM bought. Television reporters were told about Talent Associates' *Ben-Hur* plans as well.

"What do we do next?" Susskind asked.

"We wait for the phone to ring," Levy said.

As absurd as the concept of attempting to stage *Ben-Hur* in a New York television studio was, Jerry Wald, a top Hollywood movie producer at the time, said he was appalled at what he called an act of "thievery" by Talent Associates and the damage it would do to MGM's planned epic. Wald threatened that the movie industry could strike back at advertisers who sponsored *Ben-Hur* or any other property TV producers attempted to poach. "Let them name the product and we'll spend millions to give it a quick death," he told the *Los Angeles Times*.

Levy's prediction was correct. After the outrage brewed for a few days a call did come in to Talent Associates from a business affairs executive at MGM. He requested that Susskind and Levy come by his New York office.

At the meeting Susskind and Levy were told that the studio was investing millions in its *Ben-Hur* production: building sets, training horses, designing period costumes. He asked just what exactly Talent Associates was doing.

"We think it's a great story," said Levy. "Live television has never seen anything like it."

For good reason. Mounting such a spectacle would be next to impossible on live TV. But as Levy and Susskind laid out their vision with straight faces, the MGM executive was getting the picture.

"How much do you want?" he said.

"We don't want any money," said Levy.

Levy reached into his pocket with a list of MGM movie titles that included *Meet Me in St. Louis, The Philadelphia Story, Ninotchka,* and *Mrs. Miniver.* In return for dropping Talent Associates' "plans" to do *Ben-Hur* for TV, Levy and Susskind wanted the television rights to at least a dozen MGM properties.

"You got 'em," the MGM exec said.

Once the deal was made, Susskind informed the press that Talent Associates was scrapping its *Ben-Hur* TV show. He said MGM had too much riding on its production and he could not with a clear conscience pursue a project that could be damaging to the studio. As old MGM movies kept being remade as television specials by Talent Associates in the years that followed, reporters rightfully became suspicious of Susskind's claim that he was acting out of altruism.

The MGM deal helped make Talent Associates the biggest independent supplier of network television specials in the 1958–1959 TV season, with revenue of $12 million that season. There were nights when Susskind productions aired opposite one another on different networks. By the summer of 1958, Talent Associates had outgrown its East Fiftieth Street town house and moved into larger quarters on the seventh floor of a high-rise building at 444 Madison Avenue. Susskind's office overlooked St. Patrick's Cathedral.

David and Phyllis Susskind had moved up in style as well. A few years after Andrew was born in 1954, the family moved to 1125 Fifth Avenue, into a large $20,000 seventh-floor cooperative apartment overlooking Central Park. The apartment was described in the *New York Post* as having a "a kind of Hollywood elegance in the dining and living rooms." A family room had a wall completely filled with books, while another had photographs and memorabilia from Susskind's career. A staff of three handled the cooking and housekeeping.

David Susskind loved his children. He used their names, alone or in combination, for different production entities he set up for certain projects (Paman,

Pamandia, Andrew Productions). But in the years he was building Talent Associates and mounting several productions per week, he acknowledged that work was a priority. When a journalist once mentioned to Susskind that Phyllis complained about his absences from home, he said, "I tell her this is not a job—it's a way of life. It's my whole existence."

AS LUCRATIVE AS they were, many of the TV adaptations of the old MGM titles did not enhance Susskind's creative reputation. He maintained that he wanted to do original material but had no choice, as advertisers did not want to take the risks. DuPont executives complained mercilessly when he produced a depressing rural family drama by Horton Foote called *The Night of the Storm.*

In many cases it was difficult for Talent Associates to improve on the original movies. Roger Hirson remembered when he was assigned to write a television adaptation of *Ninotchka,* the beloved Ernst Lubitsch comedy that starred Greta Garbo as a Soviet envoy sent to Paris to retrieve three errant comrades and the jewels they were supposed to recover.

"David had optioned *the* Billy Wilder script," Hirson said. "So I took the script, and about ten or twelve days later I turned in my draft of the script. In those days, you got $10,000 for it, whatever it was. And I did that. I hadn't changed one word. I chopped it up into television segments and turned it in."

Susskind was not happy when he saw Hirson's work.

"What the hell did I give you $10,000 for?" he said.

"I think you gave me $10,000 because you knew that I knew enough not to touch the script," Hirson shot back.

Nevertheless, Dick Dorso said it was hard to comprehend the level of Susskind's remarkable output of programs during the late 1950s. "People would ask me, 'How did that picture get made?'" he said. "And I'd say, 'Because two people wanted it to get made. They just had to get it made.' That was David all day long. Every week. It was impossible. As somebody once said, it's very difficult to make a bad picture. It's impossible to make a good one. He was doing it every week. Now, some weren't perfect, but he certainly made a lot of distinguished pictures. It took enormous psychic energy to do it."

Susskind's greatest achievement of the era was in the fall of 1959 with *The Moon and Sixpence,* a brilliant production based on W. Somerset Maugham's novel about a forty-year-old English stockbroker, Charles Strickland, who abruptly leaves his wife and heads first to Paris, then to Tahiti, to become a painter. The program was the first American television performance by Sir Laurence Olivier. Susskind offered varying accounts of how the deal came together, but it clearly came down to money. Susskind met with Olivier in London during the summer of 1958 and offered him $100,000 to star in the program—double the previous high of $50,000 that NBC had paid to Bogart for *The Petrified Forest*. It was ten times the going rate for what name American stars received for a lead role in a dramatic special. For a British actor who saw much of his income eaten away by his homeland's high tax rate, it was too rich an offer to pass up. Susskind made the deal with Olivier without having a commitment from a sponsor or a network for the program. The stipulations from Olivier were script approval and production dates that accommodated his schedule.

Olivier was happy with writer S. Lee Pogostin's adaptation of Maugham's novel, loosely based on the life of Paul Gauguin, whose paintings were recreated for the show's sets. Taping dates were set at NBC's Brooklyn studios for the last week of December 1958. In early January 1959, Olivier was booked to go to Hollywood for the filming of *Spartacus.* But in the months leading up to the taping, ad agency executives and potential sponsors were not nearly as impressed as Susskind with the idea of Olivier on television. He was unable to sell the show to a single sponsor. Even having one of the world's greatest actors committed was not enough to overcome qualms about the grim nature of Maugham's tale of a callous man who, in the most basic terms, abandons his family to pursue his desire for artistic expression and ultimately dies a leper.

Susskind met resistance on every aspect of the play. "I was told artists are kooks and not very commercial, make him something besides an artist," he said. "I was told that the man better stay home with his family because audiences don't like fellows who leave their wife and families. I was told 'You can't have him die. We can't go off the air with a dead man. How are we going to put our last commercial in there? And if he's going to die, for God's sake let it not be leprosy. That's an ugly way to go. Let him have cancer or a heart attack.'"

As the taping day approached, Susskind had to decide whether to make the program without a commitment from a network or a sponsor—a practice that was simply unheard of in the television industry—or delay the project and risk losing Olivier. He pressed ahead. With the hard deadline for the actor's departure, it meant twelve- to sixteen-hour days of taping on three days between Christmas and New Year's at the end of 1958. Olivier was generally easy to work with, but time pressure closed in on the production when it came to do the final scene. It called for the burning of Strickland's Tahitian home filled with his paintings. In order to permeate the set with smoke, the producers learned they would need a permit from the New York City fire marshal. Even a short delay would have been disastrous, so production manager Renée Valente got around the need for a permit by inviting officers in the fire department to the studio for a quick meet-and-greet with the famous actor.

Robert Mulligan, by that time the best of the television drama directors, brought out splendid performances from a cast that included Dame Judith Anderson and Jean Marsh, with Hume Cronyn as the hack Dutch painter who befriends Strickland and is then cuckolded by him. Cronyn's real-life spouse, Jessica Tandy, portrayed the Dutch painter's wife with heartbreaking brilliance.

It was several more months before Susskind got NBC to commit to airing the show on October 30, 1959. Susskind never found a major advertiser to do a full sponsorship of *The Moon and Sixpence* (French automaker Renault purchased a tiny *TV Guide* ad touting its local sponsorship in New York). The reviews for *Sixpence* exhausted TV critics' supply of superlatives. *The New York Times'* Jack Gould called Olivier's portrayal "a work of towering accomplishment" and designated the program as the finest in Susskind's career. "It rated uppercase hosannas as TV artistry at its very best," raved *Variety*. *Sixpence* won Susskind his first Peabody Award, the honor given by the University of Georgia for excellence in broadcasting. Olivier won an Emmy for his performance and Mulligan was honored for his direction. But the advertising community's attitude toward sponsoring challenging dramatic works did not change. That attitude was best summed up in a conversation Susskind had with one ad executive, who told him, "I want happy shows for happy people with happy problems." Susskind asked him for an example, and "he said, 'No, that's your job. If I could do that, I wouldn't have to hire you.'"

3

From 1947 to 1957, the number of television stations had grown from 22 to 467; programming had grown from two hours a night to more than sixteen hours a day. "There was a lot of blank space," said Richard D. Heffner, one of the unlikely people called upon to help fill the void. A historian, Heffner authored *A Documentary History of the United States,* a paperback collection of critical American documents, speeches, and articles from the Declaration of Independence through the Marshall Plan and the start of the cold war. When the book first became a success, "I began to realize that you can teach anything on a large scale," Heffner said. "You can expand the classroom with paperback books and popular media. I began to think about further expansion, which meant radio and television." He eventually became the point man for FCC commissioner Newton Minow's effort to get an educational television station launched in New York during the early 1960s.

Before the idea of educational TV gained any traction, stations needed programs that served the community, which the government demanded in return for free use of the airwaves. In 1953, Heffner was the public affairs director for WRCA, the NBC-owned station in New York. Heffner created shows about what he knew best. "I did *Man of the Year,*" he recalled. "I'd pick a year. 1776. Who would be the man of the year? Thomas Jefferson. I'd give a lecture next to projected images on the screen. They used to put the commissioner of agriculture for New Jersey on every week because in those days when you filled out your station license renewal form, you had to indicate what agricultural programs you put on. Even on WRCA in the midst of Manhattan you had to have an agricultural program. There were needs and I was a cheap way of filling them."

When Heffner was asked by WRCA management to create a weekly public affairs discussion show, he came up with *The Open Mind,* one of TV's first roundtable discussion programs. It premiered in May 1956 and was still airing on public television stations with Heffner as host as recently as 2010. *The Open Mind* was scholarly in its approach to contemporary issues, as Heffner often used fellow academics and educators as guest experts. The opening titles showed a metal sculpture of a stylized male profile with an open space cut out of the skull. It inspired the logo that has been used for years by the Public Broadcasting System.

In October 1957, Heffner wanted to tackle the subject of television criticism, which was still evolving, along with the medium itself. He booked Marya Mannes, a thoughtful journalist who worked at a magazine called *The Reporter,* and top screenwriter Rod Serling, responsible for several of television's best live plays, including *Requiem for a Heavyweight.* Looking for an industry spokesman, Heffner asked Ted Cott, a television executive at the DuMont network station WABD to appear. "I don't do that," he told Heffner. "But my cousin, David Susskind—you've got to get him. He's well known as a producer. But he's not been on the air."

Heffner added Susskind to the panel. It was splendid timing. The week of the show, Susskind had just done his elaborate production of *Pinocchio* for NBC. It drew raves from many critics across the country, with the exception of Jack Gould of *The New York Times.* "In those days you'd do the review after the show and than you'd reprise it frequently on Sunday," said Heffner. "*The Times* reprises Gould's pan that morning and David comes into the studio to do this live program, shaking with rage."

Susskind knew better than to unload on the highly influential Gould. He praised *The Times* critic but branded TV criticism in general as the work of second-class journalistic citizens who didn't have the analytic skills necessary for the job. "I think actually it is too flippant, too cursory, too gossipy and not constructive enough, not important enough to create a body of critical judgment toward one of the most important mediums of our time," he said with his typical loquaciousness.

"He was brilliant," Heffner recalled. "Mannes and Serling were nothing compared to him. He loves himself. He had such a great time." (Despite his comments, Susskind respected the power of TV critics and enhanced it considerably in 1957 when he became the first producer to make his taped shows available to be screened in advance for reviews. Until that time, TV shows were assessed the day after they aired and were of no help from a promotional standpoint.)

But Susskind's passionate performance made for a lively half-hour of television, and that was not lost on Cott. An innovative broadcast executive (whose notable achievement outside of television was the deflowering of a young Barbara Walters), Cott had already developed the hottest talk program on television. In 1956, Mike Wallace was toiling as a journeyman radio announcer and television host out of Chicago. He even toyed with becoming an actor, taking a role in a Broadway show that lasted for several months. When Cott was at WABD, he let Wallace and his producer, Ted Yates, try a new spin on the talk format with a show called *Night Beat.* Up until *Night Beat,* interviews with celebrities on television were breezy and insubstantial. Even esteemed CBS newsman Edward R. Murrow did not charge very hard at subjects on his series *Person to Person.* Wallace and Yates wanted to ask questions with substance that would make the guest squirm a bit. *Night Beat* was a confrontational confessional that introduced drama and tension to the format. White cigarette smoke wafted over the black background of the set, designed to have the guests looking as if they were floating in limbo. The camera focused tightly on the tense face of the interview subject after Wallace launched a question delivered in the accusatory style that later became his signature on the CBS News magazine *60 Minutes.* ("Isn't it true that an uncommon hatred of women—so typical of homosexuals—has been responsible for the dress absurdities of recent years?" This query, posed to a male fashion designer, was the usual tone of *Night Beat.*) Wallace and Yates had the look of the show down, but they did not perfect the format until Bill Lange, a retired radio booth announcer, showed up one day at their office at WABD. In the idle hours he spent in studios waiting to read station identifications over the years, Lange had filled the time by clipping newspapers. "He had a garage full of newspaper clippings from year one by subject and person—I mean anything," said Marlene Sanders, who booked guests on *Night Beat* years before she became one of the first women to work as a network news correspondent. "So we made a deal with him. I called him every week, I'd give him names of the guests, and the folder would arrive with stuff about them." Wallace often floored guests when he pulled out a wild statement or quote that had been made years before that they probably hoped was long forgotten. Viewers loved it.

"It was so hot," said Sanders. "We never came in first in the ratings but always a strong third behind Jack Paar and the late movie. But we were always talked about. In the beginning, Ted Yates would suggest whom I would go after, and I was relentless on the phone. But in the meantime we were overwhelmed with people trying to get on. Either they were scared to go on and I had to talk them into it or I had to push them off. Because everybody knew this was how they would become famous in New York. I used to come in and the phones would ring all day."

Night Beat made Wallace a hot commodity. After the show was on the air for just a few months, he was offered a $100,000 long-term network contract from ABC. Soon after he left in 1957, DuMont folded and WABD was sold. Cott moved on to WNTA, another New York station that had been taken over by entrepreneurs Ely Landau and Oliver A. Unger. A former TV ad salesman, Landau, along with his partner Unger, made an advantageous purchase of the 20th Century–Fox film library when the studio ran into financial difficulty in the 1950s. They packaged the movies under their own company's name, National Telefilm Associates, and became a major supplier of programming for independent television stations desperate for product in the 1950s.

After heading up the group that purchased the station for $4.5 million, Landau envisioned turning WNTA into an outlet that served New York's intelligentsia. The highbrow intentions of television's so-called Golden Age were largely abandoned after TV sets became common in homes and advertisers demanded programs with more mass appeal. Landau's WNTA, unveiled on Channel 13 in the spring of 1958, was the first attempt by a commercial TV outlet to attempt to serve a niche audience: culture vultures who could not be bothered with the shoot-'em-up westerns and detective shows being served up by the networks at the time.

After succeeding with *Night Beat,* Cott believed he needed a new controversial talk show to get people talking about the station. Susskind's spirited performances on Heffner's *Open Mind* and on Barry Gray's radio show on WMCA, where he was often a guest, demonstrated the kind of fearlessness that might make for a provocative host. "David Susskind was glib," recalled Edythe Landau, who ran the station with her husband. "He had a silver tongue." Cott and the Landaus approached Susskind with the idea of hosting his own weekly program on WNTA. Susskind was flattered, and he certainly loved to talk. But he was sensitive about being attacked for not coming up with original ideas. If he was going to do a talk show, it needed to be distinctive. Cott came up with an appealing hook. If Susskind's guests were engaging, the show could go as long as they wanted. If the discussion was dull, Susskind had the option to wind it up as soon as he liked. He could say good night, and the station could run a film or sign off. To emphasize the format, Cott suggested calling the program *Open End,* practically appropriating the name of Heffner's show. (Heffner never did anything about it besides telling people "I'd rather have an *Open Mind* than an *Open End.*")

Susskind agreed to give it a try, much to the dismay of his staff at Talent Associates. It was already a challenge to keep Susskind focused on the many TV, film, and stage projects that were constantly in the works at the company. The commitment of hosting a weekly television show was not going to help. "Everyone in the office was hoping that it would be a big flop," said Michael Abbott. "They didn't want David to do this."

When they got a look at the first show, on October 14, 1958, Susskind's employees believed their wish was going to come true. For the premiere episode of *Open End,* Cott had Susskind go on location at the opening-night party for the Broadway show *The World of Suzie Wong.* Susskind was set to interview Broadway producer David Merrick and members of the cast at a Chinese restaurant on Mott Street in lower Manhattan's Chinatown. As part of the public relations spectacle staged to promote the opening, France Nuyen, the beautiful young French actress of Vietnamese descent who played Suzie Wong, was transported from the Broadhurst Theatre to the party by a rickshaw. She was pulled along by Buddy Hackett, the rotund comedian who had recently had two hit comedy records that mocked the accents of Chinese waiters. "He was dressed as a coolie Chinese man," Nuyen recalled. "I was told what to do."

As Susskind told it, his show opened with him introducing himself and the program outside of the restaurant while rain poured down on him. He made his way up the crowded stairway during a commercial break. Once inside he saw a table, a microphone, and a single camera, but no cast members from the show. Needing a tease to keep viewers tuned in, he promised that a telephone call would be coming in with a report on what the newspaper theater critics had to say about *Suzie Wong.* He found one of the show's stars, William Shatner, and chatted with him for ten minutes before he caught up with David Merrick and France Nuyen. The two sat nearby before Susskind took the phone call with the reviews. In a moment that presaged the kind of humiliating scene that became a staple of reality television years later, Merrick and Nuyen listened as Susskind repeated the negative notices for the show as they were conveyed to him. "There was that indescribable hush that suddenly makes champagne taste like 7-Up," Gould wrote in *The New York Times* about Susskind's debut broadcast. Gould reported that a dejected Merrick bowed his head and that Nuyen, "looking frightened and terribly alone," told Susskind she didn't want to hear the critiques. "But Mr. Susskind continued to read the last critical rites," Gould wrote. "The effect, however inadvertent, was wholly barbaric and tragic."

France Nuyen recalled the opening-night party, although she had no memory of being on *Open End* when asked about it fifty years later. She does not believe there was any way she could have comprehended what was going on around her. "I couldn't speak English in those days," she said. "I was taught to say 'yes,' and 'thank you.' I had a few sentences I translated with my French. I didn't understand anything." When put in social situations, Nuyen usually stayed close to *Suzie Wong* director Joshua Logan, who spoke French and interpreted for her. But Logan never made it up to the restaurant for Susskind's show. "All I can tell you is whoever was there was talking to a girl that did not understand a word they said," said Nuyen.

Susskind rolled his eyes and shook his head in exasperation when years later he recounted his version of his chaotic first night on the air and the negative reactions that he elicited. But Nuyen believed Susskind had to be aware that the raw emotional responses to the notices that often determined the fate of a Broadway opening would be compelling television. "As a professional, he had to have known that it was a possibility that the reviews could have been disastrous or could have been brilliant," she said. "It's possible in retrospect he realized his lack of care. At the time, he was just thinking of himself. And rightfully so. That's what show business is about."

Susskind's debut was viewed as an embarrassment the next morning at the Talent Associates offices. "When David came into the office, no one would look at him," said screenwriter Larry Cohen, who watched the night before. "As he walked down the hall, I remember, everybody's eyes were on their desks or on their papers. Nobody looked up. Nobody said hello. He just walked down the hall, and everybody thought, well, that's going to be the end of it; he's going to pull the plug on this show and just go back to producing his shows."

But the New York theater critics had little bearing on the success of *The World of Suzie Wong*. It ran for 508 performances on Broadway. Nor did the first impression of *Open End* deter David Susskind. "To his credit, he just stuck with it," said Cohen. "And the show became popular." Critics may have been unduly harsh about Susskind's first-night performance. Josh Logan even told Susskind he was pleased at the exposure his Broadway show received on the debut program. "We're happy about Suzie and the help you gave her," Logan wrote to Susskind in a note apologizing for having missed the show. He claimed he couldn't find the restaurant.

After the rainy night in Chinatown, Susskind no longer did opening-night parties. Instead, the parties came to him. For the next three years, the show aired out of WNTA's studios in the Mosque Theater on Broad Street in Newark, New Jersey. As television's most prolific producer in New York, Susskind had access to every big-name star, writer, director, and producer who worked or lived there. It did not take long for Susskind to figure out that TV airtime was an effective means to massage not only the egos of those he wanted to do business with but his own as well. *Open End* became a stature-building calling card that no other producer had. The show also became a new electronic crossroads for movers and shakers to speak their minds—at length.

The set for the early *Open End* programs looked like the backstage of a theater. A klieg light and a ladder were set off in the darkened background as guests sat at a low round table cluttered with coffee carafes, cups and saucers, flatware, and ashtrays with burning cigarettes. The informal ambiance gave the viewer the feeling of being at an intimate New York celebrity gathering. At times, the klatch continued after the show was over. One week in late 1958, Susskind assigned Larry Cohen to deliver Adolph Green and Betty Comden to *Open End* after the Broadway opening of their show *A Party*. Cohen accompanied the legendary theatrical duo over to WNTA, and they literally walked onto the *Open End* set while Susskind was in midconversation with actors Ben Gazzara, Laurence Harvey and his then wife Margaret Leighton, Patricia Neal, Robert Q. Lewis, and *Gypsy* composer Jule Styne. Susskind stood up and introduced the newcomers to the other panelists as if they had just arrived late for a bridge game.

A wide-eyed Cohen had been instructed by Susskind to take all the guests back to Manhattan for a post-show meal at a restaurant where the host would meet up with them. After the program ended, at 1:00 a.m., the elegant cadre was herded into the Cadillac limousines outside the WNTA studios. Once they were at the restaurant, Cohen began to order food and wine. As a young man from Brooklyn trying to get into show business, he believed it was the greatest night of his life. "I'm sitting at the center of the table," he said. "I'm twenty-one years old, and I'm hosting this party for all these celebrities along with Comden and Green."

But after two and a half hours of eating and carousing had passed, there was no sign of David Susskind. "The evening goes on and on and on," Cohen said. "And I have no money."

Cohen started to panic. He turned to Jule Styne and said, "I don't know what to do. David never showed up, and I haven't got any money." Styne told Cohen he had heard Susskind mention something about Rueben's, the all-night delicatessen near the Plaza Hotel. Why Susskind would head to a deli instead of a meal with his celebrated guests was a mystery.

Cohen telephoned Reuben's and sure enough, Susskind was there. "David, I'm over here with all these people, Comden and Green and everybody," Cohen told him. "Get over here. You gotta pay the check." Susskind arrived just in time for the tab.

TALKING EXTEMPORANEOUSLY for two hours or more on live TV was new for actors who were used to having lines written for them. Politically active stars such as Sidney Poitier and Harry Belafonte could authoritatively expound on the civil rights movement and the struggles facing black Americans in 1959. But it was a trickier task for performers whose reading list was predominantly TV and movie scripts. Poitier, Belafonte, Shelley Winters, and her then husband Tony Franciosa were in the middle of a three-hour session of *Open End* when the discussion turned to a recent newspaper ad placed by a right-wing group. The ad claimed the group had a letter written by Abraham Lincoln that stated blacks were an inferior race. According to Winters' recollection in her second autobiography, Susskind asked an inattentive Franciosa for his opinion about the assertion made in the ad. The actor replied that Lincoln was "the greatest president we ever had." Winters later said it was during the course of that program that she decided to divorce Franciosa.

Open End may well have been the birthplace of the TV sound bite. The show generated headlines, sometimes just on the basis of its staggering length ("Jewish, Protestant, Catholic Spokesmen in 205 Minutes of Talk on 'Open End,'" read one). But author Truman Capote provided the revelation that it was the pithy phrase that stuck with viewers afterward when during a 1959 *Open End* he panned Jack Kerouac's work with the line "That's not writing, it's typing." The moment also established Capote as a compelling TV talk show guest. To some, his many memorable TV appearances that followed in the 1960s and 1970s overshadowed his literary work. "Television killed Capote as a writer," said Larry Gelbart, who remembered watching the *Open End* that brought Capote into many people's living rooms for the first time. "Instead of sitting there and creating and waiting all that time for a reaction from people, whereas if you did it on television, they would talk about it the next day or if there was an audience they were laughing right there. So it was much easier for him to perform as a writer than it was to write as a writer."

For Gore Vidal, who wrote a lot and could talk even more, Susskind's show was an ideal forum. He appeared frequently as a liberal voice on the early free-flowing panels the show had in the late 1950s and early 1960s. "It was a way of getting a larger audience than writing could ever get, so I quite liked that," he said. "David and I got along personally quite well and politically he got it. He would lead you along and he knew where he could lead me to and it worked very nicely. There were certain things he couldn't handle. One of them was anything that happened before yesterday. So if you said, 'According to the Bill of Rights'—well, that was a long time before yesterday and his eyes would glaze over. He was not happy about being led down memory lane as it were, or into history, and I'm never happy without it. That was the only thing that frayed our appearances together."

But Susskind's ease in skimming from theater to politics to books to sex (usually more than once) in the course of a single program made *Open End* a destination for viewers who wanted the experience of being at a table at Sardi's, a cocktail party in a Park Avenue apartment, a tea at the Plaza Hotel, a stool at the Lion's Head bar in Greenwich Village, or in the thick of a smoky pressroom at a political convention. "It's to Susskind's credit that he rarely allows a subject to be brushed off," wrote one *Variety* reviewer in 1959. "In his gentle way, he needles his guests into stating their views and he good-naturedly shrugs off the digs that come his way." Susskind called the show his graduate school. Before long, he would be faced with his first major exam.

4

Upon entering through the door of Talent Associates for the first time, it was impossible not to notice how many women were working in the office. During the 1950s, David Susskind developed a reputation for hiring women for roles that went well beyond the secretaries and receptionists that populated most New York workplaces at the time. "David did not have a hesitation about moving us into a responsible job and he paid us well," Ethel Winant told an interviewer in 1996. "David always paid everyone well." Many female employees at Talent Associates went on to have significant careers in television, including Winant. She became the first woman executive hired by CBS, after working as a casting director for Susskind in the first half of the 1950s.

Women found opportunities throughout television in its early years because the business itself was still considered a gamble. There was also generally a limit as to how high they could ascend (NBC as a rule did not hire women directors). Susskind continued the practice of hiring women even after TV became big business. His motivation was by no means an early flash of feminist enlightenment. It was a by-product of his producer's instinct to get the best available talent. Getting it at a better price than what he would have to pay a man likely made him feel he was outsmarting the competition. But the women who worked at Talent Associates in the 1950s and the prefeminist 1960s truly believed that Susskind respected their abilities. "He used to kid around and say he liked to have a lot of women because he didn't have to pay them as much," said Barbara Schultz, who began a long and esteemed career as a TV story editor and producer when she started working for Susskind in the late

1950s. "That was partly true, but it was not the main thing. I think that it was easier for him to work with women in a certain way. And he worked very well with them. And he did give them a lot of responsibility."

Dick Dorso believed Susskind felt safer around women and believed they were more honest in their response to material. "He thought women aren't as competitive," Dorso recalled. "They don't argue as much. They're more helpful. They're more sympathetic. They're more sensitive to a script then men. Men read scripts with the idea of 'I wouldn't have written it that way.' Women don't read scripts that way. They read them to get emotionally involved. If they are emotionally involved in a script, the script is a success. In many cases women are better then men, and I think David, as a number of us do, felt more secure with women."

If a woman job applicant had no experience but demonstrated intelligence and potential, he would bring her into the company and give her the opportunity to learn the business. One of those women was Audrey Gellen, a Barnard graduate who had also studied writing with Vladimir Nabokov at Cornell University.

Lucy Jarvis, a Talent Associates employee before she became a prominent producer at NBC News, recalled the day Gellen applied for a secretarial job in the mid-1950s. Gellen was striking, with reddish brown hair and freckles. Her face resembled that of a young Elizabeth Taylor, but Gellen's look was more waiflike and she was often unkempt. When she showed up to inquire about the position, her white blouse was dirty and there were runs in her stockings. Her frizzy hair was a tousled mess. "It looked like she never combed it when she got up in the morning," Jarvis said.

Susskind wanted someone who could take notes while he attended meetings with network and ad agency executives. Gellen was clearly not presentable enough for such a task, but Jarvis had her take a typing test nonetheless. After more than an hour went by, Jarvis checked up on Gellen and found her hunched over the typewriter, chewing her fingernails. Jarvis picked up Gellen's typing sample, which was full of erasures.

"What is this?" she asked Gellen. "You're not a secretary."

"No," Gellen told her.

"Then why did you apply?"

Gellen had heard about Susskind from writers and directors she had met on weekends at Fire Island. She had been an avid viewer of his shows. "I think he's a genius," she told her. "I really want to work for him and the only way I could get in here was to apply for a job. When I heard he needed a secretary I applied for that."

Impressed by Gellen's passion, Jarvis took the poorly typed letters and brought her in to Susskind's office. "I told him the whole thing," she recalled. "I said, 'David, I think you have a winner here.'"

Susskind had Gellen sit down. He peppered her with questions on how she would handle challenges that might be presented to a television producer. "He started to hit her with some of the things he was worried about," Jarvis said. "And she was brilliant. He said, 'Okay, I'll give you a chance.' It took some doing to clean her up."

Gellen was teamed with script editor Jacqueline Babbin, a Smith graduate who had worked for several Broadway producers before joining Talent Associates. Together, Gellen and Babbin used their skills to adapt literary classics, ranging from *A Tale of Two Cities* to *Ethan Frome,* to fit into the ninety-minute television specials Susskind produced. The well-read Gellen showed a real sensitivity toward writers who otherwise might not have wanted to deal with the abrasive Susskind. She could charm and captivate a conference room full of men—a situation in which she often found herself as she was producing shows for Talent Associates within a few years of joining the company.

People who knew Gellen over the years described her as a brainier version of the Holly Golightly character in Truman Capote's *Breakfast at Tiffany's*. Capote's book even inspired Gellen to write her own roman à clef, *Wait Till the Sun Shines, Nellie.* "She read *Breakfast at Tiffany's* and she said, 'Oh, I could do this easily,'" noted Gellen's first husband, David Padwa. Gellen and Padwa married after having known each other for only ten days when she was at Barnard and he was at Columbia. "It was an impulsive thing to do," Padwa recalled. "Arthur Miller had just married Marilyn Monroe and we found the same judge that was up in White Plains." After Padwa graduated law school and started a career in international law, they moved to an apartment in Greenwich Village. "We had all kinds of friends down there—James Baldwin, Delmore Schwartz," Padwa recalled. "It was a bohemian scene and in those days bohemian meant something. We had a beautiful pad on the top floor of 20 East Tenth Street. We gave lots of parties and went to lots of parties. It was definitely fun times."

David Susskind personally adored Gellen. People who knew them both said they may have had a fling at some point, but the connection was far deeper. Gellen represented the kind of free spirit that Susskind could never be himself. "David was that combination of a guy who wants to make money but also wants to be an artist," Roger Hirson said. Susskind was heard to say that if he were a woman, he would want to be like Audrey Gellen. "She knew no fear," said Verity Lambert. "I think David listened to her because she was clever. She had taste and she was a fighter."

Renée Valente also learned about Talent Associates through writer friends she met on Fire Island. As a teenager growing up in the Bronx, Valente was a beauty pageant queen and winner of a citywide dance contest. A short and shapely redhead, she performed for a while in a ballroom dancing act called "Dorio and Renée." Valente toured nightclubs and USO circuits until her partner got drafted into the military, but she had no real serious aspirations to get into show business. In the mid-1950s, she attended New York University in the morning and then headed to Talent Associates in the afternoon, where she had landed a part-time job. She did some typing and walked the standard poodle that belonged to another employee, the wife of a CBS executive named Hubbell Robinson. But Susskind latched onto an almost offhand remark Valente made during a staff meeting, in which she suggested that the costumes and sets he used in his productions be put out for competitive bids from outside firms instead of automatically being rented from the networks. He gave Valente the job of handling budgets and made her a production manager. By the end of the 1950s she was earning $500 a week and never returned to college to earn her degree. Valente was fiercely loyal to Susskind. She became his enforcer inside the Talent Associates office and was the troubleshooter on the outside, dealing with union officials and production crews. "She told you where you stood in no uncertain terms," said Verity Lambert. "She was very tough."

Rose Tobias came to the United States from Poland in 1930. She and her family traveled in steerage on the USS *George Washington* so they could join her father, who had come to New York after he deserted the German army. She grew up in Harlem while her father worked as a window cleaner and her mother toiled in a factory. As they spoke Yiddish and Polish in the home, Tobias had to quickly learn English on her own. "I was a real Yankee Doodle," she said. Tobias, blond with a well-developed figure by the age of sixteen, left high school to study modern dance at the Martha Graham School. Through her classes, she met choreographer Jerome Robbins and had a brief romance with him before he left her for actor Montgomery Clift.

Once she gave up the idea of being a dancer, Tobias became a stylist for an advertising agency that served the fashion industry. She parlayed her contacts into jobs as a guest booker for television and radio shows and did publicity for several theatrical productions, even traveling around the world on tour with one. By 1956, Tobias was familiar with every working actor in New York. On the recommendation of agent Ted Ashley, she became casting director for Talent Associates after Ethel Winant left for CBS.

Rose Tobias, Jacqueline Babbin, Audrey Gellen, and Renée Valente had become the core of Susskind's operation as Talent Associates reached the peak of its success in live television specials in 1959. They posed for a double-page spread in *TV Guide* for a story with the headline "Where Women Are Welcome." The story pointed out that thirty-two out of the forty-five employees at Talent Associates were women (including Jean Kennedy, whom Susskind hired to produce *Open End*). The one who went on to have the most accomplished career was Verity Lambert. As an executive for the BBC she helped develop the science fiction classic *Dr. Who* and was one of Britain's most prolific and accomplished producers of TV drama right up until her death in 2007. At Talent Associates, Susskind always wanted her on the switchboard, as he loved the idea of having callers greeted by a British accent.

The significant jobs held by Talent Associates women were presented as a novelty in the press. "Even in this age of electronics there aren't many little girls who want to grow up to be big television production managers like Renée Valente," the *New York Herald Tribune* wrote in 1961. Maureen Hesselroth, who was hired away from *Playhouse 90* to assist in the production of Susskind's DuPont shows, was portrayed as "TV's Handy Gal" in another newspaper spread. It was a series of photos of the pert blonde demonstrating the various hand gestures she used to cue performers.

During a 1959 TV interview, Mike Wallace suggested to Susskind that he exploited the women he hired because they were so willing to put in long hours and work on weekends. "It's been said you hire them because they marry you—in a sense they marry Talent Associates," he said. Susskind winced at the metaphor but did not dispute the level of dedication from his staff. "They will work New Year's Day, Christmas and Easter," he noted.

Lambert never felt she was being taken advantage of at the time. "I felt I was working in a place I wanted to work that was making programs that were respectable and I could admire," she said. "And I was learning."

THE OPPORTUNITY FOR WOMEN to prosper at Talent Associates was undeniable. But in an era before there were laws against sexual harassment in the workplace, they at times had to deal with the incorrigible behavior of their boss (and likely other men who worked there as well). Being propositioned by Susskind was nearly a rite of passage for women at Talent Associates in those early years. Some were told as much by the others when they first arrived. The one mitigating factor in Susskind's behavior was that by all accounts there were no repercussions for rebuffing him. When it came to womanizing, Susskind was a volume operator. If a woman employee rejected his move—typically made in the back of a taxicab—he simply moved on to someone else (yet he was capable of making a successful second attempt, Lucy Jarvis pointed out). Susskind even pursued Jacqueline Babbin, although it was hardly a secret around the office that she was a lesbian. "Jacqueline claims he made some kind of pass at her and she said something about how she liked women too, and that sort of shut him up," said Barbara Schultz. "And he liked Jackie a great deal. But he was terrible. I mean David really couldn't keep his hands off people."

As Susskind emerged as a successful force in the entertainment industry, so did his reputation as a compulsive philanderer. Whether they were starlets or secretaries, Susskind pursued women with the same relentless dynamism that he put into negotiating deals or producing projects. Valente recalled how an actress who sat down in a restaurant with Susskind was asked at the outset about whether she was going to go to bed with him. If not, he was ready to move on to another appointment. "He liked every actress that worked on any of his shows and a lot of young women that worked on his shows that weren't part of the company," said Valente. Susskind once used one of his paramours, an actress named Ludi Claire, as a front for the blacklisted Walter Bernstein when he was rushed into an office to do a last-minute rewrite on *The Bridge of San Luis Rey.* "I remember looking through the door and seeing Ludi, who was there on the set and carrying on as though she were the writer," Bernstein recalled.

Many women were receptive to Susskind's advances. When TV screenwriter and playwright Roger Hirson once asked a friend why she had slept with Susskind, she replied, "I wanted to feel what it was like to have all that energy inside of me." Norman Lear said he even knew of a few wives Susskind had been with in New York. "I gave him the key to my apartment," he said.

Susskind often dined out on the story of how his affair with Faye Emerson, a sexy blond actress and TV personality of the 1950s, came to an abrupt end. Emerson's husband at the time was bandleader Skitch Henderson, then musical director at NBC. Susskind and Emerson apparently lost track of Henderson's schedule, and he arrived home to find them together. Susskind gathered his clothes and slithered out of the apartment. (Henderson, who divorced Emerson in 1961, apparently did not hold a grudge against Susskind. He showed up on a guest list for a party at Susskind's home years later when they both worked at TV station WNEW. "Show business," said Valente.)

Michael Abbott was impressed at how Susskind was able to succeed with women without possessing the physique of an Adonis. During a business trip he once shared a suite with his boss at the Beverly Hills Hotel. "I had my bedroom, he had his bedroom, there was a living room and whatever," he said. "We went to sleep. The next morning I was all dressed or I was in my pajamas and David yelled to me, 'Breakfast is being sent up.' So I went out and David came out and he was just in his little shorts. And he had milk white skin with no hair, and I said, 'David, that's the great lover? I can't believe it. Please put on a robe.' It was just too much." But Susskind radiated a presence and magnetism that transcended conventional good looks. Rose Tobias said she could always feel his energy when he was in the office. "I knew whether he was there or not," she said. "I might not have seen him. There was a certain something. I really can't verbalize it. It's like you got it or you ain't got it."

Once they got past Susskind's caddish behavior, the women at Talent Associates deeply appreciated getting the opportunities not open to them elsewhere and liked working for him. Susskind's anger over a mistake could be volcanic, but it never lasted long. His door was always open. Hesselroth said it was not his way "to snap his fingers and ask for coffee," unlike other male producers she worked for. He was not grand or self-important around the office. "David would say to me, 'You don't work for me, you work with me,' " said Anita Grossberg, a personal secretary to Susskind and Al Levy in those years. "He gave us a lot of respect. He was very loyal to his employees. He was really very good." Grossberg and her movie producer husband Jack gave their adopted son Michael the middle name of David in honor of Susskind.

"We all loved our jobs and we all loved being there," said Tobias. When she was not going through actor headshots for the next Talent Associates production, Tobias was selling secondhand clothes in the office. "We'd have 'yenta sales' on Tuesday," she said. "They were my personal clothes. I knew a lot of designers. So I used to get clothes wholesale and somehow when I brought them home they didn't look so good. I'd bring it to the office. David would yell at us, 'Why isn't there any work being done here?' We were like children really."

SUSSKIND'S WIFE PHYLLIS worked at Talent Associates sometimes. She read scripts and occasionally pitched in as a production assistant. It may have been the only way she could spend much time with her husband, who often came home near midnight and worked on his talk show on weekends. Phyllis Susskind possessed many of the personal traits of the women who worked in her husband's company. Trim, dark-haired, and attractive, she was described as extremely intelligent, independent-minded, and well read. She could get through as many as three books a week, many of them serious novels. "Books were just sent over," Andrew Susskind recalled. "She was voracious. Intellectually, she was probably as close to my father's equal as you could be. They had a serious physical connection and certainly a powerful intellectual thing." And like her husband, she had strong opinions and didn't hold back in expressing them, he added. Phyllis Susskind was active in Democratic Party politics in Manhattan. She was involved in the Lexington Democratic Club and opened storefronts for Adlai Stevenson's presidential campaigns in the 1950s. She made speeches to civic groups. Like her husband, she was an intense follower of national and world affairs. Andrew Susskind remembers his mother coming into his childhood bedroom and crying the morning she learned that Winston Churchill had died.

But as Susskind's behavior with other women became undeniably apparent, the couple's relationship deteriorated. Over time, Phyllis demonstrated her anger publicly, making caustic remarks that belittled her husband during show rehearsals or in the Talent Associates office. "I see a lot of associates but not a lot of talent," she was once heard to say. One producer who worked for Susskind had it in his contract that Phyllis could not be in the control room when he worked on a show. Michael Abbott remembers the couple getting into a heated row at Sardi's. He slid down under the table and waited until they got up and left. Abbott also recalled the day Susskind showed up at work and bitterly complained that in a fit of anger over his infidelities, Phyllis had taken a pair of scissors and cut up the suits that hung in his closet.

"There was always tension," Andrew Susskind said. "They always argued. It was not a comfortable place. I always thought what happened is that the program she bought into changed a lot. Whether she thought she was marrying someone who was going to be a teacher or whatever, what she didn't know was she was getting someone who was not just successful but in the public eye. While I don't think she minded that, I think it came with other stuff she wasn't really ready for."

"She adored him," said Valente. "He absolutely broke her heart. I thought she was going to go crazy."

5

s *Open End* was transforming David Susskind from TV producer to TV star, he grew more confident in his role as host. After a year on the air, the panels on the program no longer resembled just a table of show business ramblers at Sardi's. By the fall of 1960, Susskind had lengthy sessions with Adlai Stevenson, Hubert Humphrey, and Nelson Rockefeller. Politicians liked to talk, and not being constrained by a program end time was ideal for them. Ted Cott, who ran WNTA at the time, said the format had made *Open End* preferable to more established network public affairs programs such as NBC's *Meet the Press*.

That reasoning was likely in play when Richard Nixon, then vice president and leading candidate for the Republican Party's presidential nomination, turned down *Meet the Press* and chose to appear with Susskind on May 15, 1960. "We are not fettered or inhibited by the clock," Susskind assured his guest at the outset of the program, which *Variety* described as "an unqualified coup."

The complexity of Susskind's questions and Nixon's long-winded, multipart responses pushed *Open End* to a staggering three hours and forty-five minutes, probably making it the longest television interview ever conducted. When Nixon was whisked off in his limo from the Mosque Theatre studios and into the Newark night, it was almost 2:00 a.m. Along with exhausting every possible domestic and international issue of the time, Nixon set television history in motion near the end of the interview when he said he was open to the idea of participating in the first-ever broadcast debate of presidential candidates during the general election campaign.

Susskind attempted to leverage the appeal of potentially limitless airtime into landing more high-profile guests. He used it to try to cajole Cuba's new prime minister, Fidel Castro, to appear with him. "Since he conducts his own *Open End* with great frequency in Havana, I am sure he would find our format compatible," Susskind wrote to a Castro contact.

Castro didn't bite. But shortly thereafter, Susskind reeled in a much bigger fish. In early September 1960, he read that Soviet premier Nikita Khrushchev was on a ship headed to the United States for a monthlong visit planned around his attendance at the UN General Assembly. Susskind, who had interviewed several members of the Soviet Union's UN delegation several months earlier, immediately wrote to the Soviet embassy to request the leader's appearance on *Open End*. For weeks, Susskind heard nothing. Finally, an invitation arrived at the Talent Associates office, asking Susskind to attend an October 4 cocktail reception Khrushchev would be hosting at the Soviet consulate. Egyptian president Gamal Abdel Nasser, Yugoslavia's communist leader Josip Broz Tito, Ghana's president Kwame Nkrumah, and Castro were the honorees. "Nice crowd of people," said radio host Jerry Williams when Susskind told him about the event.

Not knowing what to expect, Susskind arrived at the consulate and joined the receiving line behind James Wadsworth, the U.S. ambassador to the United Nations. When Susskind reached the guests of honor, he greeted Castro, ignored Nasser (likely in protest over Egypt's enmity toward Israel), and went on to Nkrumah. When he reached Khrushchev's party, Mikhail Menshikov, the Soviet ambassador to the United States, leaned forward and said, "Ask the premier the question that's on your mind."

"Here? Now?" Susskind asked.

"Yes, go ahead, ask him," Menshikov replied. "He's a simple man. He'll give you a simple answer."

Susskind requested that Khrushchev appear on *Open End* that Sunday. "I'd like to very much ask you questions Americans are thinking about," he added.

"Well, it's an interesting idea," Khrushchev said through an interpreter. "Let me think about it."

Sure enough, at 9:00 a.m the following day, a call from Menshikov came into Susskind's office. "Where do you want Mr. Khrushchev to be Sunday night?" he said. "He has decided to do your program."

Viktor Sukhodrev, the legendary interpreter for several Russian leaders, including Khrushchev, believed the Soviets agreed to Susskind's offer because it was apparent that *Open End* would be the only high-profile television opportunity for the premier. The State Department had issued what Sukhodrev called "an advisory," asking the press to limit its coverage of Khrushchev to his speeches before the General Assembly.

"None of the leading talk shows of the day in America wanted to give Khrushchev a platform," said Sukhodrev. "So he was glad to grasp at the opportunity offered by David Susskind. It was explained to him by the experts that David was the host of a very popular program, rating-wise." Actually, all three American TV networks wanted Khrushchev to appear on their air. But that changed after *The New York Times* disclosed the State Department's request that the networks not give Khrushchev "extended use of this country's free communication system for the purpose of trying to subvert its policies and principles." The networks were already getting mail from organizations and individuals urging a news blackout of the Khrushchev visit. Executives clearly felt pressured to state publicly that coverage would be limited to Khrushchev's activities during the day and that he would not be invited on a studio program.

Soviet officials were also aware that with Susskind, the premier would not be dealing with an expert on foreign affairs. "He had had Nixon as a candidate," Sukhodrev said. "But at the same time, he had Gypsy Rose Lee and other strippers. You know, he was that kind of guy."

Khrushchev had sat for a lengthy American TV interview only one other time. Daniel Schorr, then Moscow bureau chief for CBS, and two other journalists, had queried the premier for an hour on *Face the Nation,* which aired on June 2, 1957. Schorr remembered being surprised when he got a call from the Soviet foreign ministry's press department after having a long-standing request for a face-to-face meeting with the premier. In the months leading up to it, tensions between the Soviet Union and the United States were heightening. After Khrushchev's efforts to de-Stalinize the Soviet Union and take the country closer to the outside world, Soviet tanks moved into Hungary in 1956 to stop the anti-Communist revolution there. It was followed by the Soviets siding with Egypt against Israel, Britain, and France in the war over the Suez Canal. "These two events marked the real beginning of the cold war with the Soviet Union," Schorr said. But in the interview, Khrushchev seemed intent on returning the Russians to Western society. "That was evident in the friendly interview he had with us," said Schorr. "There was talk on disarmament, the need for getting along with countries."

Nevertheless, distrust surrounded the proceedings. Khrushchev often came off as impulsive and unpredictable. He used those traits to his advantage when he met with Schorr, *Face the Nation* moderator Stuart Novins, and B. J. Kutler of the *New York Herald Tribune* at the Kremlin to film the program. "Just before we started he asked, 'What kind of questions are you going to ask me?'" Schorr recalled. "I said, 'Mr. Khrushchev, it's a rule with *Face the Nation* that we don't give questions in advance.' He said, 'Well, if you're going to use this as an opportunity to bait me, then perhaps I will not do it.' Then he calmed down, having achieved the effect that he wanted by just sounding threatening. Then everything went all right again. You were dealing with a guy who doesn't understand television very well, but a really intelligent guy who knew what he was doing, and especially knew how to make his point and put you on the defensive. There's no doubt that he would have lived up to that threat that he might not do it or might walk out. I won't admit I took it easy, but I will admit that it was in my mind that we don't know what this guy is going to do. In the end we did ask him the questions. I asked him a question about China, which is usually a no-no between two Communist states. But on the whole it was a cordial interview."

President Eisenhower, however, criticized the program. He accused CBS of airing it for purely commercial reasons. Schorr viewed that as an odd complaint. As significant as the interview was, it played on a Sunday afternoon news program without tremendous fanfare. Yet the president's public disapproval made CBS chairman William Paley and the network's chief executive, Frank Stanton, nervous. The country was still emerging from the fearful atmosphere of the McCarthy-era red-baiting of the 1950s. The week following the interview, CBS aired a panel that was "one hour of talking back to Khrushchev," as Schorr described it. "It had a lot of Radio Free Europe people and others," he said. "In television, people get very scared when they find a lot of people who don't approve of something. Even CBS gave an hour of criticism of Khrushchev just to show we were not taken in by this guy." .

The public reaction to the *Face the Nation* interview was mild, perhaps because it was conducted overseas and not broadcast live. In the days before satellite transmissions, overseas TV reports were done on 16-millimeter film and often hand-carried by courier to network news headquarters in New York. Schorr's program was historic, but lacked the immediacy of a live event and therefore gave Khrushchev the look of being a safe, unthreatening distance away.

Susskind wanted a live interview with Khrushchev just when relations between the United States and the Soviet Union had deteriorated further. As the premier was preparing to attend Moscow's May Day festivities in 1960, he learned that a Soviet missile had shot down a U.S. spy plane. Francis Gary Powers, the CIA pilot of the U-2 jet, parachuted onto a state-run farm and was captured by KGB agents. Khrushchev maintained that the U.S. military had launched the reconnaissance flight without President Eisenhower's knowledge. But Eisenhower later admitted he had known about it and didn't apologize for it. An enraged and embarrassed Khrushchev delivered a blistering tirade against Eisenhower at a summit of world leaders in Paris that summer. "Khrushchev was deeply, personally offended by the U-2 incident," said Sukhodrev. "Eisenhower had his invitation to visit the Soviet Union. He would have been treated royally. He was supposed to be in Moscow, have talks, and go to Lake Baikal, and things like that. And suddenly, this thing happened." As Nixon told Susskind during their marathon session, "There is never a right time to make one of these flights if you get caught."

On September 19, 1960, *Baltika,* the ship carrying Khrushchev and his party, arrived at Pier 73, a dilapidated dock on New York's East River. *Baltika* was greeted by hostile longshoremen waving placards that urged the Russian visitors to "drop dead." The boycott forced the *Baltika* crew to board a lifeboat and moor the ship to the dock themselves. In the days that followed, Khrushchev gave several agitated and lengthy speeches at the United Nations, denouncing colonialism. There were impromptu news conferences from the balcony of his residence at the Soviet embassy and a very noisy public visit with Castro at the Hotel Theresa in Harlem. Americans saw a lot of the premier in their morning newspapers and evening TV newscasts during the trip, and he did not win them over. The lasting iconic image from the trip was of a boorish Khrushchev banging his shoe on a table at the UN General Assembly to protest a charge by a delegate that the Soviet Union deprived Eastern Europe of political and civil rights.

ONCE KHRUSHCHEV AGREED to appear on *Open End,* Susskind and Cott met privately with Ambassador Menshikov and Sukhodrev at the UN Secretariat headquarters. They discussed the ground rules of the interview. Did the premier mind if David Susskind smoked during the interview? No. Would the premier like to be served coffee as most guests were on *Open End*? He preferred Borjami mineral water from what was then the Soviet Republic of Georgia. Khrushchev's entourage traveled with a supply of the brand. The exchange between the two sides continued amicably until Susskind requested that other journalists who were experts in covering the Soviet Union be allowed to join him in the questioning. Susskind was often portrayed by the press as brash and arrogant. But he was fully aware that he did not have the qualifications to take on one of the world's most powerful and forceful leaders alone. Menshikov nixed the idea of a panel. "You didn't have anybody else with you when you had Mr. Nixon on, or when you spoke with Governor Rockefeller," he pointed out.

The two sides bargained. In return for having Susskind as the sole interrogator, Menshikov withdrew a request that his questions be submitted in advance. There were no restrictions on what Susskind could ask Khrushchev. But Susskind and Cott lost on their request to use simultaneous interpretation as heard in broadcasts of the UN General Assembly sessions. They were told that Khrushchev conducted all multilingual discussions by consecutive interpretations. The question was interpreted for him into Russian. He answered in Russian. The answer was then interpreted back. The unwieldy process did not promise to be compelling television.

For security reasons, the State Department restricted Khruschev's travel during the visit and he was not permitted to go to the WNTA studios in Newark. The UN headquarters was chosen as the location for the program. Cott believed that the UN Secretariat consulted with the State Department before committing to using the site for the broadcast and therefore had to be aware that Khrushchev was doing the program. Despite the earlier advisory to limit coverage, no one from the State Department contacted Susskind, Cott, or anyone else at WNTA about interviewing Khrushchev.

In the days after Susskind confirmed Khrushchev was to be his guest on *Open End* on October 9, members of the press and the public lashed out at him. Hungarian freedom fighters shouted insults as they picketed in front of

Talent Associates headquarters at 444 Madison Avenue. The office was deluged with telephone calls, telegrams, and hate mail from people who called Susskind a "dirty red" and a "kike." Susskind claimed that threats were made against his children.

Conservative newspaper editorialists stoked the anger over the program. "Mr. Susskind (never yet famed as a red-baiter) swears he won't let the Red Hitler take over the show and make a propaganda forum out of it," fumed the New York *Daily News,* which described the short, bulky Khrushchev as "Mr. Commie Five by Five." If Susskind succeeded in getting answers to the questions on Americans' minds, that would be fine, the paper said. If not, "the affair will be a service only to Communism."

"Disgusting!" was the headline on the *New York Daily Mirror* editorial denouncing the interview. "We draw the veil," it said. "When Susskind comes on, we shall turn the television off."

When a newspaper clipping about the upcoming program landed on the desk of FBI director J. Edgar Hoover, he scrawled under it, "What do our files show on Susskind?"

SUTRO BROTHERS, a Wall Street brokerage firm that regularly sponsored *Open End,* was eager to run its commercials in the Khrushchev program. The company had wanted to run custom announcements that said, while it did not support Khrushchev's views, it wanted to uphold the principles of free speech. But senior partners of the firm started to hear objections from customers and friends. They then asked that their commercials be replaced with announcements (at no charge) that said, "We are not sponsoring this program tonight because we don't feel Prime Minister Khrushchev should be given a television audience to espouse his Communist dogma. We disclaim any relationship to tonight's program." Management at WNTA turned down the request and Sutro Bros. never sponsored *Open End* again.

The growing tension caused by the program became worrisome to Ely Landau, chairman of the board for WNTA. According to Susskind, Landau was initially excited about the Khrushchev interview coup. Landau had arranged for television stations in other cities that carried *Open End* on tape to get a live feed of the interview. He made audio of the program available to radio stations that wanted to carry it as well. Susskind claimed that Landau's support diminished once complaints came in from a bank that loaned money to

WNTA, which had been struggling. "I don't think you should go through with it," Landau was said to have told Susskind. "I think the world will cave in on us."

The protests and heated warnings only made Susskind more determined to go ahead. He studied all the key UN sessions involving the Soviet Union. He read endless transcripts of Soviet propaganda. He met with British prime minister Harold Macmillan's press attaché, who briefed him on Macmillan's conversations with Khrushchev. Max Lerner, Marguerite Higgins, and Joe Newman, all newspaper journalists who covered the Soviet Union, briefed Susskind as well. "This is a free country and this is our enemy," Susskind said he told Landau. "Whatever he says, it will be a revelation. If he lies, it's one kind of knowledge. If he answers, it's another kind of knowledge. We have no reason to be afraid."

Susskind's partner Al Levy believed there was plenty to fear, and it was all on Talent Associates' balance sheet. Alan Hirschfield, who went on to become the chairman of Columbia Pictures in the 1970s, was an investment banker at Allen & Company at the time, advising Susskind and Levy on their company's finances. Talent Associates had started to see a decline in its fortunes as the networks moved away from the kind of live television productions the company had specialized in. Troubling publicity over an interview with a despised enemy foreign leader was not going to help.

"They were having their financial issues, as they always did," said Hirschfield. "Money was coming in and David was spending it faster than Al could get it in. And I did a good deal of work with them, trying to rationalize the company and get them on a much firmer footing. They weren't looking for an investment at that time, but they just needed guidance. David was not easy to control. But because I was an investment banker and kind of an outside guy, he paid more attention to me. I remember going over those numbers almost on a daily basis and figuring out what they were making, and what they could afford to do, and what they couldn't afford to do. Al was always the conservative one, and David was the total opposite. Al just wanted to have a good, comfortable, viable, successful operation. But he wasn't willing to take the kind of risks that David was. And then, of course, David, because of *Open End*, became somewhat of a superstar. Al wasn't thrilled, in a sense, with *Open End,* in that it took David's focus away from a lot of stuff."

Interviewing Khrushchev was a whole new level of risk, one that Hirschfield and Levy didn't want Susskind to take.

"We begged him not to do it," Hirschfield said. "It was clear that David at that point felt he could control anybody. He was the master. And you know he probably could have controlled any kind of governmental figure from the United States. But we kept saying, 'You don't know what you're getting into.' Given my bent, I could not care less what the State Department thought in those days. Al was concerned about what impact it would have on sponsors; on the people he was doing business with, who were very white-shoe people: DuPont, Hallmark, Armstrong. They were vital to the company's future."

On the evening of October 9, the tension became palpable in the Susskind home on Fifth Avenue. Landau and Cott had shown up to go over questions for the program—something they had never done for any previous *Open End*. Susskind had written more than a hundred questions for Khrushchev. While Ambassador Menshikov indicated that Khrushchev was usually in bed by 10:45 p.m., Susskind was prepared if the premier felt the need to extend the dialogue into the early-morning hours. Just before Susskind was out the door to head over to the United Nations for the program, he got some advice from his son, Andrew, then six years old. "Dad, whatever you do, don't let Nikita Khrushchev declare war on your show," he said.

Susskind did not have a credential to park at the United Nations. He left his car a block away and had to walk over to the heavily guarded UN head-quarters. Across the street on the southwest corner of Forty-seventh Street and First Avenue, about a hundred sign-waving anti-Soviet demonstrators were gathered along the sidewalk. Their messages read "We got plenty of murderers on TV, we don't need Khrushchev," "Dial K for Murderer," and one that could not have made Levy and Hirschfield very happy: "Mr. Susskind Deals with Khrushchev, Can Madison Avenue Afford to Deal with Susskind?"

Susskind, Khrushchev, and Sukhodrev were seated side by side at a long table in Conference Room 3 at the United Nations, which served as a TV studio for the broadcast. Through Sukhodrev's interpreting, Susskind chatted with the premier in the moments before the live feed went out at 9:00 p.m. Susskind asked Khrushchev if he slept calmly while knowing that the destiny of mankind depended largely on him.

"I always sleep calmly," the premier replied. He then said he wanted all the questions and replies to be keyed toward an improvement in the relationship between our countries.

"I beg you to ask the kind of questions that will help improve our relations," he said.

"We have a good word, 'yes,'" said Susskind. "That's the English for *da*."

"I also would like to hear *da* from you," said Khrushchev.

Amused by the response and Khrushchev's jovial manner, Susskind observed that he found it hard to fathom how a man who has "such a sense of humor can inspire a fear of war." If the two could remain in the conference room where they were seated instead of the hall where the General Assembly had been listening to Khrushchev in recent weeks, "the world would be in complete safety."

"You are mistaken," Khrushchev told him.

Susskind opened the program with a short, earnest speech about his intentions for doing the interview ("In a free republic, it is our job, I think, never to trammel inquiry . . ."). With corked bottles of Borjami mineral water on the left and the right of him, Khrushchev impassively looked straight ahead as he awaited the questions in Russian from Sukhodrev, who sat to his left. The premier appeared to be awash in the bright television light that reflected off the shiny crown of his round, bald head (he refused to wear makeup). It conjured up the image of a man's face in the moon.

Once the interview began, Susskind's tone immediately took a confrontational tack. He became an advocate for America rather than a civilized interlocutor. He asked Khrushchev why he continued to "perpetuate the myth" that the U.S. government was warmongering and deceitful. Khrushchev ranted on about the U-2 and the RB-47, another U.S. reconnaissance plane that had been shot down over Soviet territory that June. In short order, the interview turned into a ponderous debate. Susskind demanded the premier take a stand on Eisenhower's call for a plebiscite asking Eastern European nations to vote on whether they wanted Communist rule—just as the *Daily News* editorial had demanded. He was no match for the crafty Khrushchev, who barreled along with his standard bromides about how if people truly understood communism and socialism, they would embrace them. "They were like boxers in different weight classes," said Sukhodrev. "Basically, Khrushchev was his usual blustering long-winded self and there was no way that David could stop him."

The consecutive interpreting didn't help. Both Susskind's questions and Khrushchev's answers went through Sukhodrev, causing a single exchange to go on for nearly ten minutes or longer. Khrushchev suggested bringing mattresses into the conference room in case the interview went late into the night.

Susskind grew frustrated and asked again if Khrushchev's answers could be interpreted simultaneously. Khrushchev used the request to mock the United States. "I don't know how it can be done," he said. "It seems that American technology is not up to that. You come along and we'll do it immediately." Khrushchev leaned into Susskind as he gave his answers in Russian, repeatedly jabbing and grabbing his arm while making points.

"Khrushchev was a very difficult guy," Sukhodrev said. "And he would never accept the American way—or, I'd say, the normal way—of doing an interview. That is, short question, short answer. Khrushchev would go into lengthy discourses on any subject, digressing. He could never give a short reply."

Susskind's dissatisfaction over the proceedings likely led to a verbal swipe he made at Khrushchev's pronouncement that communism is "the most noble teaching in the world." It became his signature line of the night.

"You're baying at the moon," Susskind said to the man he had deemed responsible for mankind's destiny just moments earlier.

Khrushchev became visibly agitated. He believed Susskind had crossed the line from robust debate, which the premier appeared to be enjoying, to disrespecting him. "I am old enough to be your father, and, young man, it is unworthy to speak to me like this," Khrushchev scolded.

Susskind was alarmed by the response and apologized. Looking back, Sukhodrev believed his interpretation of the word "baying" as "barking" exacerbated the exchange. "There was no absolute word in the Russian idiomatic language," he said. "In hindsight I didn't do too well. I should have softened it. Khrushchev was offended by that likening of him to a dog barking. I should have said maybe you're trying to break into an open door. That might have been a mistake on my part. What else could I say?" But he noted that Susskind had been somewhat careless himself. "It was not a statesmanlike thing to say to a head of the government of a major power."

The contretemps escalated during a commercial break when Khrushchev was handed a note by one of his advisers. It said the *Open End* broadcast was carrying public service announcements for Radio Free Europe, the CIA-funded broadcast service that beamed pro-democracy messages and programming into Eastern Europe. RFE spots typically used blunt imagery of hands grabbing onto barbed wire or broadcasters from captive nations being bound and gagged. The one that aired on *Open End* showed a Communist soldier smashing a radio set with an axe.

Edythe Landau, the wife of WNTA board chairman Ely Landau, said her husband was not aware of the decision to run RFE spots on *Open End* until he saw them on the air. "I remember sitting in the den watching this," she recalled. "I thought he was going to have a heart attack. He called the station and screamed and raved and ranted." The station ran the spot once more before it was replaced by promotional announcements for the panel discussion of journalists set to follow the interview.

But no one was angrier than Khrushchev, who immediately denounced the RFE announcements as a dirty trick while he and Susskind were off camera. "You are afraid of communism, afraid of the truth!" Khrushchev said after receiving the note. "Well, all right, let them screen it. We are not afraid. This will only make us stronger. . . . Let them do it."

"He felt he was being set up," Sukhodrev recalled. "Because he didn't see them. He couldn't argue with them. He couldn't object to them. We didn't see them. That's why he got mad. It was like the U-2 incident. In a way, he was deeply, personally, offended. And, well, during another station break, David tried to say that he had nothing to do with that."

In the days that followed the program, no one at WNTA took responsibility for running the RFE spots. It was common for stations to fill unsold commercial time with the announcements in those years, and it was certainly conceivable that their placement on *Open End* was coincidental. But in fact, it wasn't. Ted Cott later acknowledged that he signed off on the idea, fully aware that running the announcements adjacent to Khrushchev's rants was a political statement. "The intent of putting this on was to dramatize the fact that we in the United States were giving Mr. Khrushchev unlimited time to say whatever he felt, on American television, whereas they were jamming all our broadcasts in the Soviet Union—and this was the editorial point we were trying to make," he told an oral historian two months later. Over Cott's objections, Landau issued a public apology to Khrushchev the day after the broadcast.

When the program resumed, Khrushchev eventually calmed down and answered a few more questions. But with no prompting from Susskind, the premier stood up from his chair and appeared ready to leave. Susskind stood to remove the microphone cord from around Khrushchev's neck. As he reached for it, the feared Soviet leader gave Susskind a playful bear hug. (The embrace caused Susskind to stiffen up "like an unwilling virgin," he later said.) But there was also a bit of panic on Susskind's face as he realized the interview was ending without generating any real news. He kept the discussion going, pressing the premier to categorically state he would never start a war.

As Khrushchev went on about how the Russians wanted friendship and peace with the United States, he noticed he was no longer wearing his microphone and wondered out loud if viewers were hearing his remarks. "How tricky you Americans are," he said. Susskind assured Khrushchev he could be heard as they continued to talk for nearly another half hour more. Sukhodrev, eager for the night to end, removed his microphone and nervously rubbed his fingers over the top of it. It made a scrapping sound that viewers heard at home. "I felt this could go on forever," he recalled.

When the interview ended after running nearly two hours, a drained-looking Susskind joined the roundtable discussion of journalists broadcast from another UN conference room. He massaged his brow and drew deeply on a cigarette as he mostly listened to the analysis. The panel spared him any criticism of his performance, largely saving its barbs for Khrushchev's propagandizing. Afterward, Susskind went over to Talent Associates at 444 Madison Avenue. Al Levy, who had watched the proceedings on the set in the office, parodied the protestors who had shown up in front of the building in recent days by taping a sign to Susskind's door. It said "David Go Home." Susskind was not in a laughing mood. He knew the night had been a near debacle. Despondent, he sat alone and stared at his desk. Levy became concerned and called Alan Hirschfield. "You've got to call him," he said. "We can't get him to go home."

Hirschfield reached Susskind on the telephone. "David, you know, I'm not going to kid you. It was a tough night," Hirschfield told him. "But you know, you've got to look at who else could have gotten this guy to go on the air, and who else could have done this. It wasn't a total disaster."

They talked long into the night. "He must not have gone home till four or five o'clock in the morning," Hirschfield recalled. "He didn't want to face anybody. He was just almost like a broken person, because it never occurred to him that he couldn't control Khrushchev."

Critics were not kind to Susskind's effort. *Time* magazine called it a sideshow. The *New York Times* TV critic, Jack Gould, described it as an "international turkey." But they missed the historical significance of the event. Joseph Newman, who had long covered the Soviet Union for the *Herald Tribune,* rightfully noted that the evening was a modern milestone in news coverage. During the panel discussion that WNTA aired after the interview, Newman recalled the pretelevision days of covering Stalin. Even though the Moscow bureau where he worked was blocks away from the Kremlin, no one could be sure who was making policy, what the policy was, or whether Stalin was even alive. Khrushchev's appearance on live American television was a major advance that forever changed how viewers saw the world. "We've had the benefit of a man coming out of that cave in the Kremlin and standing right there in front of you," he said. "If this is the enemy, how valuable it is to know who the enemy is and how he's thinking, how he evades and exactly what he supposes to do." As a result, Newman said, the United States was in a far better position to deal with Khrushchev and the Soviet Union than it was before.

Open End also demonstrated that television would not just settle for covering the news. It was going to package it too. The Khrushchev interview aired within the same month that American voters were swayed by John F. Kennedy's performance over Richard Nixon in the first televised presidential debates. Nixon, like Khrushchev, refused to wear makeup before going in front of the cameras. In a democracy, that decision proved to be costly.

The overheated criticism of Susskind for booking Khrushchev wasn't based solely on a desire to keep the premier from being heard. Some of the backlash was clearly due to jealousy from other journalists who believed Susskind was a show business charlatan treading on their territory. He was not a trained member of their ranks, yet he was able to land an exclusive booking that generated global attention. The program was shown in Australia, Great Britain, Canada, and Russia. A transcript of the entire interview ran in the Soviet state newspaper *Pravda*. "All of us who did interviews back then envied David," said Mike Wallace years later. "We were secretly pleased when Khrushchev filibustered him. We snickered, but we remained envious nonetheless." At the time, Susskind was still a novice as a talk show host able to tackle complex issues. But as a showman, he instinctively knew how to get viewers' attention. "If you have this show out in Jersey and you get the big enemy of the United States on your air who threatens God knows what, you're doing pretty well for your show," said Schorr. "You've got to look at this as seen by a guy trying to make his way in talk television." There were apparently no hard feelings from Khrushchev over the Radio Free Europe spots. The day after the interview, a case of Borjami spring water arrived at Susskind's office at Talent Associates.

For years, Susskind chastised himself over his performance that night with Khrushchev. He frowned and shook his head when he recounted the details about how he was overcome by the pressure from the protests and criticism, and felt forced to prove he was a good American who was "not giving this monster a chance to proselytize and convert us to atheistic Communists." He said it was his biggest failure, the one professional episode of his life he wanted to rewrite. "I wish I hadn't been so nervous," he once said on his show years later. "I wish I hadn't been so defensive about America and its ideals. I wish I had done it well."

Having done it at all made him more famous than ever.

6

The United States survived the *Open End* interview with Nikita Khrushchev and so did David Susskind and Talent Associates. In April 1961, Susskind and his partner Al Levy announced they had sold 50 percent of their company to Paramount Pictures in exchange for Paramount stock valued at about $1.6 million. Paramount had fallen behind the other major Hollywood studios in television production. "David was going to change television for them and make them an important factor because they had no experience," said Michael Abbott. Another possible catalyst was Paramount's interest in buying New York TV station WNTA, the flagship outlet for *Open End* that was owned by National Telefilm Associates. Earlier in that year, Susskind fronted Paramount's $6.6 million bid for the station, and his credentials certainly would have passed muster for approval by the Federal Communications Commission. But the FCC delayed any possible deal by asking for hearings on the need to bring a noncommercial educational station into the New York and Los Angeles markets. It discouraged the commercial bidders and cleared the way for transferring the station to National Educational Television.

While Paramount may have wanted Susskind for his prowess in television, he clearly went into the deal with dreams and schemes for a greater presence in the movie business that he had entered by the end of the 1950s. The high quality that Susskind delivered in his first feature, *Edge of the City*, earned the attention of the film industry, and he was offered a job at MGM that would have put him in line to be head of production. He turned it down, he wrote, because it would have meant pushing through the kind of musicals, adventure stories, and costume pieces that "had no thematic content or consequence, pictures that didn't influence hearts and minds." Instead, Susskind had signed a production deal with Columbia Pictures. As advertisers shied away from TV programs that attempted to make any kind of social statement, Susskind was convinced film would offer him more creative freedom to do so. He argued that movies needed to give the audience something they could not get from television.

Susskind backed up those words when he made *A Raisin in the Sun* as his first film for Columbia. Based on Lorraine Hansberry's 1959 play, it was a timely story of a multigenerational black family looking to improve on the life they have known in a worn-out tenement apartment on Chicago's South Side. While they are not poor, Walter Langer is a chauffeur and his wife Ruth is a domestic who works in white people's kitchens. Walter's mother, Lena Langer, is the weary family matriarch who has spent her life cleaning other people's houses, while his younger sister, Beneatha, is a college student who wants to attend medical school and embodies the hopes, ideals, and anger of the black Americans who would come of age during the civil rights movement. Their different views of the world and each other are tested when a $10,000 insurance payment on the death of Lena's husband is paid out. Walter, willing to take risks to improve his family's situation, wants to invest in a liquor store. His mother intends to use it to buy what she thinks will be serenity in a home located in an all-white blue-collar neighborhood.

Susskind had a chance to invest in the stage version of *Raisin*. The show's Broadway producer, Philip Rose, said Susskind was concerned that a virtually all-black cast limited its commercial potential. However, once *Raisin* opened to strong reviews, on March 11, 1959—and earned back its initial investment within a few weeks—he immediately pounced on the movie rights. He got Columbia to pay $300,000 once he secured the original Broadway cast, which included Ruby Dee, Claudia McNeil, Diana Sands, Louis Gossett Jr., and Ivan Dixon. Most important, Susskind also had Sidney Poitier, who was ascending into a box office attraction after starring in *The Defiant Ones*. The two men had become friends after making *Edge of the City*. When the deal was announced, Hansberry gave her blessing to the involvement of Susskind, whose bona fides as a liberal voice were well established. "I am sure Mr. Susskind could give the play the kind of sensitive treatment it deserves," she told *Jet* magazine. Susskind in turn raised Hansberry's profile by inviting her onto *Open End* to discuss the Broadway season along with director

José Quintero and former MGM studio president turned playwright Dore Schary.

While *Raisin* was an immediate hit on the stage, putting it on the big screen for audiences across a racially divided nation at the start of the 1960s was considered a risk. Susskind pitched the movie to Columbia with his usual dose of hyperbole—he noted that six other producers were vying for the property—but he also encouraged the studio to look beyond race. The play, he said, presented "a warm frequently amusing moving story of Negro life in which, for once, the race issue is not paramount."

If Columbia executives really believed that, it was another example of Susskind's stunning salesmanship. While family and money are the driving forces in the plot of *Raisin,* the examination of the emotional toll of racial discrimination, segregation, and oppression are at the center of the piece (along with discussions about atheism, the emancipation of women, and abortion). Hansberry wanted to heighten the social aspects in her screenplay by restoring some of the scenes and dialogue that had been cut from the play and adding new ones. In the earliest scene, she has the Langers' young son asking his parents for 50 cents for an unspecified school expense. For the film, Hansberry wanted to make clear that it was to pay for special "Negro schoolbooks." Columbia executives resisted the idea of augmenting any of the racial issues out of fear they would alienate white audiences. They even pruned a mild remark by Beneatha about French and British colonialism in Africa, for fear of offending moviegoers in the European markets.

But Susskind and Rose (who was a coproducer for the film at Hansberry's request) were largely successful in battling or ignoring the dozens of changes Columbia executives Sam Briskin and Arthur Kramer suggested for the script and kept the movie faithful to the original stage work. Most of the difficulties the production faced were from external forces. One of the few scenes shot on location was the Langer family's visit to the house on which Lena has put a down payment. When the scene was shot in early July 1960, the racial hatred and fear in America examined in Hansberry's work came to life. "They found a house in the neighborhood that would be right," recalled *Raisin* director Dan Petrie's widow, Dorthea. "The woman who rented the house was thrilled to have a movie being done. She was about eight and a half months pregnant. But the neighbors were terribly upset. They were really afraid the house was going to be sold to a black family."

Even more dispiriting was when the cast headed west to Hollywood to shoot interior scenes on the Columbia Pictures lot. The actors believed racial discrimination kept them from finding desirable hotels for their stays. Even Poitier was unable to rent a decent home for himself and his family for the three-month stay. "I speak with pain," Poitier said when he told *The New York Times* about the housing problems, "because I would like not to say that these things exist."

Gossett, a New York actor who had been working steadily since he was in his teens, was stunned when faced with the situation on what was his first trip to Hollywood. "It was very, very racist," he said. "We had to stay in motels. Hollywood was full of people from the South after the war and their sons and daughters worked in the factories and they were in the police force and they brought their prejudices with them. I stayed in a motel around La Brea and Washington boulevards. We were at different places like that. We wanted to stay at a Hilton or some place near the studio." Eventually, the cast was able to get rooms in the showbiz-friendly Montecito Hotel. Instead of renting a house, Poitier put his family up in three suites in the Chateau Marmont.

On screen, *Raisin* looked very much like a television play, which had largely been the experience of director Dan Petrie up to that point. Columbia would not let Susskind use location footage of the rundown Chicago neighborhood where the Langers lived. But Petrie succeeded in capturing outstanding performances from the actors. The highest praise was for Sidney Poitier. His Walter Lee was "one of the few fully realized character portraits ever to come onto celluloid and one of the most moving," Arthur Knight wrote in the *Saturday Review*. The film won raves from critics and a special award from the Cannes Film Festival, where it was shown. Susskind was hailed for getting the film made while the issues it confronted were still fresh in the nation's consciousness. "The final thanks should go to David Susskind for daring to bring it to the screen," Knight noted.

Segregation in the United States undermined the box office success of *Raisin*. Many southern theater owners refused to book the film. In cities with segregated movie houses, black patrons most eager to see it were limited to sitting in balconies. Susskind calculated that the studio was only able to book 2,187 play dates out of a possible 14,000 for *Raisin*. The initial box office take was a modest $1 million. But by the end of the decade, *Raisin* was repeatedly shown on network television, exposing Hansberry's story to tens of millions of people and cementing its status as a classic.

Susskind's second film for Columbia was *Requiem for a Heavyweight*. The gut-wrenching story of an aging, washed-up professional boxer was one of the most memorable live television plays of 1956, with Jack Palance in the lead role when it aired on *Studio One.* For the film version, writer Rod Serling was allowed to present the story with the original ending he intended, in which Mountain Rivera, the once proud palooka who "never took a dive," humiliatingly performs as a pro wrestler in order to pay off his manager's gambling debt. Susskind and director Ralph Nelson lined up a strong name cast for the film, with Anthony Quinn as Mountain. Jackie Gleason took the role of the boxer's corrupt manager Haish while Mickey Rooney played the loyal trainer Army. Julie Harris was cast as a compassionate employment counselor who is drawn to Mountain, a small role in the TV play that was expanded into a romance for the screen version (apparently to Serling's dismay).

Stylistically, *Requiem* had a gritty texture that came from extensive location shooting around New York, including Stillman's Gym, a training mecca for pugilistic greats on Eighth Avenue. Susskind hired fight referee Arthur Mercante to be a technical adviser on the film. He recruited many of the real-life boxers who appeared as extras, helped choreograph the fight scenes, and played himself in the ring. (Susskind ended up hiring one of Mercante's boxers, a journeyman Argentinian named Alex Miteff, to be his driver for many years.) Mercante had a second job as a public relations man for Rheingold Brewery, a popular New York beer at the time. In what may be the earliest example of product placement, he made sure some of the fighters in the barroom scenes were holding bottles of the brand.

Mercante recalled that in his first meeting with Susskind, the producer asked that he find an actual heavyweight contender to use in the opening sequence of the film, when Mountain Rivera takes a brutal beating in his final bout. Mercante brought in a nineteen-year-old fighter from Kentucky who had won a gold medal at the 1960 Summer Olympics in Rome. It was Muhammad Ali, who was still known as Cassius Clay at that time.

Ali was explosive in the scene, which Nelson shot from the point of view of Rivera, his vision blurred and on the verge of being knocked out. "Here Arthur Ornitz's camerawork is so personal, going out of focus with every blow from flailing fists that he makes the viewer feel that he is taking the beating," the *Variety* critic observed. It was a stunning early glimpse of Ali, an image that everyone in the country would soon recognize when he became the most dynamic and polarizing sports figure of the decade. Off camera, Ali charmed the cast and crew so much that they passed a hat around the ringside set on

Randall's Island Arena to take up a collection to supplement the modest fee he was paid. Quinn tossed in $100 when the hat got to his trailer. Even the usually prickly Gleason was amused when the engaging fighter sat in the director's chair with the star's nickname "The Great One" stenciled on the back. Ali, already calling himself "The Greatest," reasoned that Gleason's moniker was close enough to suit him.

Ali provided some of the few light moments on the *Requiem* set, which was generally tense when the two outsized personalities of Quinn and Gleason were together. Quinn got under Gleason's ample skin when he got Susskind to side with him on a choice he made in his portrayal of Mountain Rivera. In his 1993 autobiography, Quinn recounted how he struggled over how to play the character until he heard the raspy wheezing voice of Abie Bain, a former light heavyweight who helped coordinate the fights in the film. Quinn said Bain "sounded like a man who had been kicked in the throat a thousand times." He thought it conveyed a poignant weariness he was looking for. According to Quinn, director Ralph Nelson disagreed and made a retching sound as if he wanted to vomit when he first heard Quinn use the voice. "It sounds like shit," Nelson told him. Susskind liked it and wanted to give it a try, but was willing to look at some dailies first. After a screening, Nelson said he still didn't know if it was right. "I don't know" was the wrong answer for a director to give to David Susskind. "If you don't know I'll have Tony Quinn direct the picture," Susskind replied. Quinn used the voice. Seeing Quinn get his way over the director of a film did not sit well with Gleason, who reacted by telling his costar, "Don't fuck around with me." Gleason was once so frustrated by Quinn's constant questioning on the set, he went to his dressing room, stripped naked, and threatened to come back to work unclothed unless Susskind reined in his costar.

Quinn's performance was even hailed by critics otherwise not enthralled by the movie. The actor regarded it as one of his best and admired Susskind for standing up to Nelson. "Too many producers are afraid to upset the touchy artists in their employ," Quinn wrote. But Nelson never worked with Susskind again.

Susskind again ran into interference from Columbia executives on *Requiem,* and this time he went public with his unhappiness about it. In a three-part memoir by Susskind that was published in *Show Business Illustrated,* a short-lived glossy entertainment magazine published by Hugh Hefner, he recounted how Columbia's creative chief Arthur Kramer told him *Requiem* was "a grimy, depressing, downbeat, rotten unpleasant script—and a picture we shouldn't make, it's a sure loser." According to Susskind, Kramer also suggested that the story be built around the heavyweight at the height of his success. "That's fascinating, Arthur," Susskind told him. "Except we wouldn't have *Requiem for a Heavyweight*." Susskind offered the exchanges and other unflattering comments about his relationship with Columbia even though the studio was releasing his movie later in the year and had two projects left on his deal.

Perhaps realizing that the brass at Columbia and numerous others he skewered were people he wanted to do business with again someday, Susskind sent a frantic telegram to Hefner asking that his *Show Business Illustrated* pieces be killed. But it was too late to pull them. Besides, Hefner knew it was great copy. "You can only come off as the hero, the fighter and the believer in truth and integrity, as a result of this piece," Hefner wrote to Susskind. (Susskind did scrap plans for a voluminous and even more provoking autobiography he was working on with one of the magazine's journalists.)

As much as Susskind wanted to be successful in the movies, his initial instinct was to blast the people who interfered with his vision. Members of the television industry accepted Susskind's finger-pointing, perhaps because he was one of them almost from the beginning. The movies were a far more established and exclusive club in the late 1950s and early 1960s.

"Television was a freewheeling business," said Dick Dorso. "You can create something that gets on the air and it's a hit and you're wealthy. And you have a lot of opportunities. In those days, when David was active, there were dozens of advertising agencies that bought television and the opportunities to create things were unlimited. That was not true in the picture business. In those days, there were six studios. They controlled everything. Everybody played the game. David didn't know how to play that game of being supplicant and obsequious. When Dore Schary was head of MGM, we used to play tennis together. I used to call it 'Good-Shot-Dore Tennis.' Whenever he'd hit it, any kind of a shot, we'd say, 'Good shot, Dore.' And that's what the business was in those days. They were kings, and they ruled empires. You had to honor them that way. David couldn't play that game. It wasn't in his nature."

When Susskind had his first extended stay in Hollywood during the shooting of *Raisin* at Columbia in the summer of 1960, he tweaked the industry town whenever a reporter was in earshot. "In New York there is a thrilling connection with human beings—it is a symphony, a spectrum in life," he told a *Newsweek* writer who trailed him one day. "Here I go to work each morning and wonder if we're at war or not—it would take you three days to find out." On one of several editions of *Open End* that he taped in Los Angeles, Susskind unloaded on a group of actors who had taken to writing, directing, and producing, citing Tony Curtis, Rock Hudson, and Jerry Lewis among others. "They barely qualify as actors," he said. "The idea that they are creators is nonsensical and maniacal." The comment set the stage for a feud in the press, in which Curtis threatened to assault Susskind. "I never met Mr. Susskind," the actor said. "But when I do I'm going to punch him right in the nose. Nobody has to tell me how bad an actor I am. Better men than Susskind have told me." When asked to respond, Susskind described Curtis as "a passionate amoeba."

Susskind was more comfortable in New York, and he tried to convince his partners at Paramount that he could create his own movie-making empire there in spite of the lack of facilities and the migration of talent and film crews to the West Coast. In the late spring of 1961, before he went into production on *Requiem,* Susskind embarked on an experiment that attempted to shift some of the film business away from Hollywood and onto his own turf. Many of his productions for television were as good as or better than what moviegoers were paying admission to see in theaters. Why not make them as theatrical films? With Paramount's backing, he put together a spectacular television adaptation of Graham Greene's novel *The Power and the Glory.* Television was moving away from such expensive one-shot specials. Susskind's plan was to shoot the program on videotape for airing on a network and then present it as a theatrical movie overseas. The show was to be made with a television budget and shot on a TV schedule—typically $500,000 and eight days of shooting for a two-hour play at that time. The price and the pace were unheard of for a studio movie with a big-name cast. Susskind used a process he had learned about from a CBS engineer, called electronic film production (a more advanced version of the technology was known as Electronovision, used to film a 1964 Broadway performance of *Hamlet* that starred Richard Burton). While the show was being taped, the video image was simultaneously recorded onto 35-millimeter film. Using electronic film production, Susskind could immediately play back the videotape to see what was done instead of waiting a day for film rushes, enabling the production to move faster and more efficiently.

In order to give the project the best chance of working, Susskind needed a star with box office appeal overseas. He turned to Laurence Olivier to play the role of Greene's debauched whiskey priest who seeks martyrdom as he keeps up his sacramental duties, while being pursued by anticlerical Marxist authorities in 1930s Mexico. The actor who had given Susskind his most celebrated television triumph two years earlier with *The Moon and Sixpence* was playing on Broadway in *Becket* and was in New York until early June. Olivier liked Susskind and loved the kind of money the producer paid him to be on American television even more. He reportedly earned $100,000 for the role, but a line in the show's budget listed $290,000 for "other expenses, including Olivier." The rest of the cast Susskind put together was arguably the best ever assembled for a dramatic television production up to that time, with George C. Scott, Julie Harris, Keenan Wynn, Martin Gabel, Cyril Cusack, Fritz Weaver, Roddy McDowall, Mildred Dunnock, and Patty Duke. The $7,500 earned by Scott and $5,000 for Harris were both well below their usual rates, but they wanted the chance to work with Olivier. The production was budgeted at $620,000, reportedly the most money spent on a single television program at the time. CBS paid $250,000 for the rights to air it one time, so it was realistic to believe it could turn a profit after a theatrical release. But Susskind's pursuit of perfection in less than ideal circumstances drove the actual total cost to $1.24 million.

Paramount executives were initially enthusiastic about the concept. "I am beginning to get the thrill that only comes to us once in a while," the studio's vice president, George Weltner, wrote to Susskind. "I have the feeling that this picture may pioneer a whole new successful formula which will [be] to the benefit of both great television shows and important and profitable motion picture releases."

A typical two-hour TV play used eight sets. *The Power and the Glory* had forty, built in NBC's Brooklyn studio, the same site where *The Moon and Sixpence* was taped. Art director Burr Smidt was asked by Susskind to re-create an authentic-looking Mexican village. He was the right man for the job. Smidt had studied painting in Mexico with Diego Rivera before becoming a set designer. During the 1950s, he was vice president in charge of color at NBC. The network's parent company, RCA, was manufacturing the bulk of color TV sets sold at the time. "He would call a hundred people at their homes at ten o'clock in the morning and tell them 'We're going to have five minutes of color programming tonight,'" said Renée Valente, who was married to Smidt for nearly forty years. "He would call them back and ask them how they liked it." Susskind admired Smidt and lured him back into production design with the promise of work. "David said to him, 'Why are you wasting your time at NBC? Why don't you go back to your art? If you do, I'd love to hire you to be an art director,'" Valente recalled.

Unfortunately, Smidt's brilliant eye for color was not put to use in *The Power and the Glory*. The show needed to be shot in black-and-white to contain costs. He did his best, however, importing $15,000 worth of tropical foliage, including live banana trees, and building mountains and stucco huts out of polystyrene foam. The sets were rapidly built over twelve days. The studio was filled with a hundred extras and live farm animals, including a horse and a burro. After a few weeks of rehearsal, filming and videotaping of the show was scheduled from May 30 to June 4, with little room to maneuver, as Olivier was scheduled to board the *Queen Elizabeth* for England on June 7.

Once production commenced, Olivier was relaxed and playful with the rest of the cast and crew. He often dined with them at Ratner's Delicatessen after rehearsals in Central Plaza, a space on the Lower East Side that doubled as a Dixieland jazz hall. Olivier's favorite topic of discussion was women, according to Dale Wasserman, who wrote the screenplay for the program in one week to accommodate the actor's schedule. "I had breakfast with Larry a few days in a row, at the Algonquin Hotel," recalled Wasserman. "I introduced him to a girlfriend of mine passing by our table, and he said, courteously, 'Oh, how d'you do, I'm terribly good at making babies.'" Giddy after a long day and evening of taping, Olivier once had his driver drag-race another car containing Valente, Smidt, and other Talent Associates employees while traveling back into Manhattan from the Brooklyn studios.

Barbara Carney, who worked in the Talent Associates office as a production coordinator, was also an actress. She had a small part as a prostitute who practices her trade in a jail cell where Olivier's priest is held after he is apprehended for possessing brandy. Carney and another actor had prerecorded the moans and groans of a sex act that was to be played in the background during the scene.

"We were in the studio and we were shooting that scene with Olivier and Mildred Dunnock," she recalled. "It's dark, and they're in the center of this cell, where they are talking to one another. And David says over a loudspeaker, 'Larry, while you and Millie are talking here, we will be using a recording of some sounds that will be happening in the cell while you're in there.' And Larry said, 'Well, what sounds are those?' David said, 'Don't worry about that.' And

Olivier was cute, really cute. He said, 'No, I want to hear it.' So David said okay. And they played our grunting over the loudspeaker. When it was over Olivier said, 'And who did that?' And I raised my hand and he applauded us. It was very sweet." But underneath his casual "call me Larry" style, Olivier was protective of his star status. After rehearsing his scene with Patty Duke, then a phenom child actor who played the daughter of an American couple who hide the priest from authorities, he told Wasserman that she was brilliant. He then asked the writer to cut some of her lines.

Olivier became less convivial as the tightly scheduled production wore on and shooting days lasted as long as fifteen hours. Having a finite amount of time with the star gave Susskind no margin for error, and he repeatedly asked for retakes after reviewing the video. "David was in his 'one more, let's do one more,' mode," Carney recalled. "And one day Larry finally said, 'Enough, that's it, I'm finished.' He was wearing contact lenses at that time that were not comfortable, because he had blue eyes and they wanted brown eyes for the character. His eyes were so bloodshot because he was exhausted."

The shooting went two days over schedule, putting it close to its rock-solid deadline. Olivier, who did not fly, was determined to be aboard the *QE* whether the show was complete or not. "We worked a hundred and eight hours straight through," said Valente. "Everybody was sleeping on floors."

CBS aired *The Power and the Glory* on October 30, and it garnered strong reviews, especially for the compelling performances of Olivier and the rest of the dream cast. It certainly stood out during a TV season that was awash in mediocre detective shows, westerns, and a sitcom about a family that raises three chimpanzees as children. "Olivier very nearly reaches the actor's dream state of absolute emotion, absolutely disciplined," said *Newsweek*'s critic. "Attention must be paid to this sort of excellence, on pain of having it disappear from television entirely." A poll of television editors and critics voted *The Power and the Glory* as the best program of 1961 and named Olivier as the best performer.

Susskind proposed the use of electronic film production for *All the Way Home,* the next film he made for Paramount, based on the play adapted from James Agee's novel *A Death in the Family.* Those plans probably changed after Paramount's ninety-eight-minute film version of *The Power and the Glory* made its way into European movie houses. Smidt was nominated for an Emmy for his work on the program. But what looked elaborate and rich on the mono-chromatic TV screens of 1961 came across as cardboard and cramped on the big screen. Cinema trade writers overseas noted "fuzziness" in the corner of the movie frames.

"I happened to see it in Malaga, Spain," Wasserman said. "It was poorly executed as a movie, muddy in its lighting and simply not up to the technical quality as a feature film." Paramount president Barney Balaban told Susskind in a letter that the movie was unsuccessful "due largely to the fact that prints of sufficient quality could not be made from the negative." The studio lost $500,000 on the project.

While the experiment with *The Power and the Glory* failed to turn Susskind into a movie mogul, he was clearly on to something. Three years after his project, MCA developed "world-premiere movies" for NBC, the first full-length motion pictures made especially for television. They were also released in theaters outside of the United States after their initial TV airings. MCA's Universal Studios was able to make the movies more efficiently on Hollywood back lots. The made-for-television movie, as it would be known, quickly grew into a major programming staple in the 1970s, and Susskind ended up being one of the most prolific producers of the form. But in the short term, his cinematic aspirations were put on hold.

7

Being a TV star added to the mystique David Susskind had as a TV producer. Ely Landau, the head of WNTA, wanted to tap into that power. Landau was intent on trying to find more programming that catered to a high-minded New York audience, and he needed more than smart talk shows such as *Open End*. His ambition was to stage a first-class theatrical production of a serious play on the station every week. It was a bold idea for an independent TV outlet, especially since Landau was struggling to keep his operation afloat financially. Landau believed he could make his TV plays cost-effective by taping the presentations and repeating them over consecutive nights during the same week. But he needed David Susskind to kick it off. "Ely Landau was a rough-and-tumble kind of a guy in the film business," said Marc Merson, who worked on Landau's program, called *The Play of the Week*. "He was more like the original studio moguls, on a small level, than he was an intellectual or somebody who knew about plays or culture."

Susskind agreed to help Landau get *The Play of the Week* off the ground in the late fall of 1959 in return for a stake in the show. For the first program, he convinced Dame Judith Anderson to play the lead in a production of Euripides' Greek tragedy *Medea,* a role that theater aficionados knew her for. He enlisted José Quintero to direct it. Susskind introduced several of the episodes he produced, including a pair of short plays from John Mortimer, which introduced the British writer's works to American audiences.

But the challenge, as it was in the days of *The Philco Television Playhouse,* was to find enough worthy plays that were not already claimed by the movies or Broadway. For that job, Susskind designated Bob Rafelson, a young Dartmouth graduate he had recently hired as a story analyst. His job consisted of sitting in a tiny supply closet turned office and reading all the scripts that came into the Talent Associates office that the producers didn't want to deal with. "I read everybody that I could and made notes on those who I thought were good writers, and so on and so forth," said Rafelson, who a decade later became a groundbreaking film producer with *Easy Rider.* "This put me in some considerably good stead as training way later in my life. But I was working till two o'clock in the morning. I was married. I just came out of there looking like a rodent, staying up, reading, reading, reading."

One day Rafelson was literally pulled out of his office by Susskind and brought into a conference room where Landau was seated. Susskind introduced Rafelson. "He has been associated with me for years," said Susskind, who proceeded to tick off a list of production credits that Rafelson had nothing to do with. Rafelson suddenly found himself working as the story editor for *The Play of the Week.*

The Play of the Week became an extraordinary platform for established New York actors who wanted to work on the stage again. It wasn't for money, as lead actors were paid $750 for a show. But for many it was an off-Broadway run on television. A number of formerly blacklisted performers could slowly restart their careers on *The Play of the Week* because the show did not air on a network, which would have required names to be politically cleared.

Most of the material for *The Play of the Week* consisted of adaptations of classic works in the public domain or older material that could be acquired inexpensively. But Susskind did use the show to present *Black Monday,* an original contemporary work from writer Reginald Rose that the networks would have never touched in 1961. The play depicted the first day of class for a black child entering an all-white school in a southern town (with a cast that included Ruby Dee, Ossie Davis, Ivan Dixon, James Caan, Robert Redford, and Ed Asner). Susskind bought the rights from Rose after having returned from New Orleans, where he had done an *Open End* session about the federal district judge decision that ordered the city to desegregate its schools. While *Black Monday* was simply staged and at times didactic in its tone, the production effectively depicted the hatred, tension, and violence that bubbled up throughout the South at that very moment in early 1961 when it aired.

While viewers saw many great television shows they could talk about the next day, *The Play of the Week* allowed those who missed it to tune in and catch it the following night. "People stayed home on Monday so that they could watch," said Rafelson. "The numbers were often very good, but it wasn't so much the numbers as the kind of self-congratulation that the audience could have, by saying, 'Did you see the play that José Quintero directed last night? I saw it first. And I highly recommend it to you tomorrow night, and the next night, and the next night.' It ran six nights in a row." The scheduling for the show was a model adapted years later by HBO and other cable TV networks that attracted small or niche audiences.

Launching a prestige platform such as *The Play of the Week* was second nature for Susskind. But at the start of the 1960s, that type of television was less welcome at the networks. They wanted fewer anthology dramas with new casts every week and more series with recurring characters. Nearly all the shows were filmed on the West Coast. Even third-place weakling ABC was emerging as a ratings competitor as it became a regular customer of glossy caper shows supplied by Warner Bros.' growing television unit. Affable, pretty-boy actors populated such series as *Hawaiian Eye* and *77 Sunset Strip,* aimed at attracting younger viewers in the cities where the network had its strongest TV stations. All the networks were loath to disrupt the habit of TV series viewing by preempting shows for the one-shot special programs that Talent Associates did best.

By the end of the 1950s, the cost of production and airtime had shot up, along with the number of homes TV was reaching. Many advertisers found it too expensive to sponsor and produce an entire program themselves. They instead looked to spread their sixty-second messages over a schedule of shows. The networks used the trend to exert greater control over their program lineups with the intent of maximizing ratings and getting higher rates for those commercials. Fewer shows were put on the air simply because a sponsor or an advertising agency wanted to back them: a program had to deliver a big rating too. As a result, Susskind no longer could depend on having to convince just one out of dozens of ad agencies or sponsors to agree to make a program. It really was up to one of the three networks. "If three men and their minions reject your program conceptions, you simply don't get on the air," Susskind lamented. "The fact that you could sell it to an advertiser or his agency is academic." Susskind believed the process was contributing to the deteriorating quality of TV. He began to refer to the network decision makers as "mental pygmies" in the press.

But out of the public eye, Susskind was adapting to the shift in the television balance of power that now tilted toward the network executive suite. He made a point of cozying up to James Aubrey, who rose to the presidency of

CBS after running its TV station on the West Coast. Aubrey was a Princeton-educated ad salesman who climbed to the top of the executive flow chart at CBS, thanks to keen commercial instincts that he executed with what most of his peers believed was a ruthless lack of humanity. His nickname was "the Smiling Cobra." "He could be as cold as permafrost to any star he felt was no longer useful," *Life* magazine once wrote. Aubrey was uniquely unsentimental while working in one of the most emotional of industries. Years later, when he was president of MGM, he infamously sold off the studio's memorabilia from its golden era of the 1930s, including the ruby slippers Judy Garland wore in *The Wizard of Oz*, to raise cash.

On the surface, the two men appeared to be polar opposites. Aubrey was a tall cool WASP who never apologized for putting profits over what critics perceived as quality. For Susskind, artistic credibility was as important to his ego as money, if not more. But Susskind used his charm and intelligence to win over Aubrey. According to Jack Willis, who worked on *Open End* as an associate producer, Susskind made it a point to find out when Aubrey was having his hair cut at the Warwick Hotel barbershop so that he could settle into the chair next to him. Over time, they became fast friends.

Aubrey found Susskind useful as well. When he needed a superbly produced special, Susskind could deliver. CBS once had an opportunity to land a big chunk of ad money from an advertiser, and Talent Associates turned out a handful of one-hour plays called *Family Classics*. One of them was a memorable rendering of *The Heiress* with a splendid performance by Julie Harris. But those opportunities were coming along less often. The pressure was on Talent Associates to come up with series programming, an area where it had never succeeded. The company made several filmed comedy pilots throughout the 1950s. The ones that got on the air lasted only a few weeks. Susskind liked the idea of the profits generated by hit series, but he was always more personally invested in his lavish endeavors, such as *The DuPont Show of the Month*.

Even though Talent Associates eventually set up an office at Paramount Studios in Hollywood, Susskind spent little time there. He was determined to develop a series that could be made in New York. In 1960, he sold to CBS a clever albeit flawed reality-based concept called *The Witness*—a drama that was staged like an actual government hearing or congressional investigation. The defendants were rogues from recent history such as Al Capone, Ma Barker, and John Dillinger. *The Witness* used actual attorneys to present the questions during the inquiry. "It was kind of ludicrous, the idea of bringing these famous villains before a committee," said screenwriter Larry Cohen. "I mean, Dillinger was dead. He's been killed. Everybody knew that. But there he was before a committee answering these questions. It was nonsensical."

All of the action in *The Witness* took place in a single hearing room. Shot on videotape, the set was brightly lit and looked realistic enough that CBS executives had to confer over how to prevent viewers from confusing the show with an actual news event. The network eventually ran a strange disclaimer that read: "THE WITNESS is not a trial, not a court of law, not a legislative inquiry but a simulated hearing before a simulated committee." The show lasted for half a season.

Susskind also believed he could turn Harry Truman into a TV star. He signed the former president to do a twenty-six-episode series in which he could describe in his own words the decisions that helped shape the future of the world during his six years in office. Truman seemed an unlikely candidate for such a project. When he left the White House, he returned to his wife Bess's family home in Independence, Missouri, and insisted on leading a quiet civilian life. He refused to cash in on his status as a former president and turned down easy earnings from corporate board memberships, consulting jobs, and commercial endorsements. But as the years went on, it was clear that Truman needed money. His lack of financial resources led to Congress enacting the Former Presidents Act in 1958, providing an increase in the pensions for former White House occupants and funding for office staffs. Susskind agreed to pay Truman $25,000 an episode for his services; over twenty-six episodes, he would have been one of the highest paid stars on TV.

After the deal was announced, Susskind had Truman touting the educational and historic value of the series. The former president appeared at a press conference and on *Open End*, parroting prepared lines about how unfortunate it was that TV had not been around to record the recollections of past leaders. "It is my hope that the free people of our own land and free people everywhere as well as future generations will be helped by this series to understand better the role of our nation in the world today," he dutifully said. But Susskind could not sell Truman to the networks. He was told they already had shows in the works about the Roosevelt and Eisenhower years. "We're up to our necks in presidents," ABC chief Tom Moore told Susskind. CBS believed such a concept was better handled within its own news division. But it may also have been that network executives knew Truman was still not very popular with the public and certainly not as compelling on the TV screen as the "Give 'em hell, Harry" mythology that was later built around him. Rather than embarrass Truman by telling him he was not ready for prime time, Susskind insisted he would finance the program on his own and sell it to individual TV stations. "I shall take the film under my arm and go city to city and station until I get it on the air," he told the *Chicago Tribune.*

Susskind believed he caught a break in the series business in early 1961, when CBS called to say it was going to cancel a game show called *You're in the Picture*, hosted by Jackie Gleason. One of the most renowned debacles in TV history, Gleason's show lasted one week. The humbled Great One filled the time period the following week with a personal apology to viewers. The rare quick yanking of a series created an opening for a show Susskind had pitched the year before called *Way Out*. It was a creepy anthology drama in the spirit of Rod Serling's *The Twilight Zone*. Susskind put a twist on *Way Out* by hiring Roald Dahl, whom he had met through the British writer's wife at the time, Patricia Neal. Dahl introduced the macabre stories each week, just as Serling did on his show. Instead of Serling's earnest intensity, Dahl opened each show with dark, humorous monologues that offered advice on how a woman should kill her spouse without raising suspicions.

In selling *Way Out* to CBS, Susskind learned a tough lesson in the new ways of the network TV business. In exchange for putting the show on the air, CBS demanded that Susskind hand over half ownership of the program. Even though Talent Associates developed the show, hired the writers, approved the stories, and created a unique look and atmosphere with Dahl as host, the network wanted to control the property. It became a common practice in television at the time and was often unavoidable, as series producers had only three networks to sell to. Susskind was dismayed over the deal, especially since Talent Associates was not even listed in the end credits. Had the show been a long-running hit, his financial rewards from syndication to local TV stations would have been limited. But with the networks buying fewer of his specials, he badly needed the company to have another series on the air. He took the deal, essentially becoming a producer for hire on a CBS show.

Susskind was not alone in his frustration about the greater control the networks exerted over programming and the dire effect it was having on what got on the air. After taking office in 1961, President Kennedy appointed a young Chicago attorney named Newton N. Minow as chairman of the Federal

Communications Commission. Television had grown into a billion-dollar industry by 1960 and delivered profits of 19 percent during a year when the country was in a recession. The license to broadcast was appearing more like a license to print money, and some believed there was little regard for serving the public interest. Minow rode into Washington as one of Kennedy's "new frontiersmen" who wanted broadcasters to do better on that front. He sent a chill through the industry on May 9, 1961, with an address on the issue in front of an audience of station executives at the National Association of Broadcasters in Washington, D.C.

"I invite you to sit down in front of your television set when your station goes on the air and stay there without a book, magazine, newspaper profit-and-loss sheet or rating book to distract you—and keep your eyes glued to that set until your station signs off," he said. "I can assure you that you will observe a vast wasteland."

The words "vast wasteland" became part of the American lexicon as a description of everything that was wrong with TV, largely because newspapers, threatened by the new competition, latched onto the phrase.

"It was a big surprise to me," Minow recalled. "I had a lot of help on that speech, and a good friend of mine, John Bartlow Martin, a very gifted writer, had given me a draft. What John had written was 'a vast wasteland of junk.' I crossed off 'of junk' and I never paid any attention beyond that. I never anticipated it was a term that was going to endure and I think it did endure because an awful lot of people agreed with me, and also I think many of the print journalists at the time who were anti-television, grabbed onto it. What I meant more than anything else was the word 'waste.' I felt that this extraordinary technology, the ability to send a picture and a voice into every home, was being wasted in terms of what it could contribute. That was my point, and I was focusing particularly on children, and it seemed to me that this was the greatest educational medium ever invented and we were wasting it."

What station and network executives heard was a warning to clean up their act with an implied threat that licenses would be revoked if they failed to do so. Before Minow joined the FCC, the commission had already started an inquiry into network programming practices, especially as they related to the decline of live shows and drama programs. A report called "The Quality of American Life" had been prepared for President Eisenhower during his last year in office. It stated that "the temptation to let fourth-rate material replace the better shows seems all too often to be irresistible to the advertiser." The Writers Guild of America was raising concerns as well on how attempts at serious dramatic works were no longer welcome at the networks. Minow went ahead with hearings on the issue, which were set for the courthouse in New York City's Foley Square that June. An all-star lineup of witnesses, mostly directors, writers, and producers who made their bones during the golden age of television, had been lined up to testify.

Minow recalled running into President Kennedy at a Washington party after the testimony had gotten under way. "I'm watching your hearings," he told Minow. "You've got to get a little more life in there." President Kennedy got his wish on June 21 when David Susskind took the stand. Among those who testified, Susskind had the highest profile, thanks to *Open End* (Kennedy was a viewer), and he was the only producer appearing who still had regular business dealings with the networks. For four hours, Susskind delivered the equivalent of a public session on a psychoanalyst's couch. He recounted the barriers he faced through the years in trying to bring serious drama to television, how the networks and agencies closed the door on him when he first approached them with *The Moon and Sixpence* starring Laurence Olivier, how they chastised him for attempting to present programs that were gloomy or downbeat, and their timidity in approaching any social issues in their programming. They wanted happy programs about happy people with happy problems.

Even DuPont, the company that had enjoyed the prestige of having its name attached to the elaborately staged productions of well-known literary properties, had become concerned that many of the works Susskind had chosen were too serious for a broad audience.

"Ratings began to come in and they trembled," Susskind told the commission. He trashed competitors, calling Revue Television, the filmed TV operation run by his former employer Music Corporation of America, "a Who's Who of Clap Trap. Everything from inane situation comedies to excessively violent westerns and private eyes . . . celluloid sausage that comes down the pike by the ream." As for the networks, he warned of their "unfortunate and dangerous grip on programming. It is a three-pronged grip: NBC, CBS, and ABC. It constitutes a terrible minority of decision." He complained that none of the networks would buy his series with President Truman.

TV executives had been used to hearing Susskind's rants. It was a trade-off for getting his considerable talents as a producer. But Susskind took it a step further this time, when he pulled the curtain back and revealed how CBS required him to give the network half ownership of *Way Out* in return for placing it on the schedule.

"Well, now, did they give you any reason why it had to be a CBS production?" a commissioner asked.

"They gave me a pretty good reason," said Susskind. "They said take it or leave it."

Over at CBS headquarters at 485 Madison Avenue, the network's top programming executive, Michael Dann, was listening to Susskind's testimony as it was broadcast live over radio station WNYC. He was flanked by two of his bosses, CBS chairman William Paley and CBS Inc. president Frank Stanton. Dann had cut the deal on *Way Out* and was stunned when the details, which sounded like a government antitrust case ready to happen, came through the speakers. Dann said later he asked for the stake because CBS had lost money on a previous project with Susskind. But at the moment, he thought his career was over. "I was almost in tears," Dann recalled. "I didn't know what to say."

A shaken Dann went to dinner that night with his wife at a diner near their home in Chappaqua, New York. Still reeling that Susskind chose to reveal private business dealings to the commission, he got up from the table and called him at home.

"David," Dann said. "How could you possibly have done that, said that?"

Susskind replied, "Mike, when you're underneath those lights, you've got to tell the truth.'"

8

David Susskind paid a price for his candid remarks before FCC chairman Newton Minow. "It's hard to put your finger on it," he told journalist Drew Pearson in the summer of 1961. "But I can't get people on the phone who used to be anxious to talk. The attitude seems to be 'Oh brother, it'll be a cold day in the Sahara Desert when you sell us something.'" Susskind later said that none of the three networks would buy a program from him for more than a year after the June 1961 testimony.

There were no Christmas bonuses in 1961 for Talent Associates employees except for those who worked on the biweekly *Armstrong Circle Theatre,* the only network show Talent Associates had left on the air. "He was a pariah," recalled George C. White, the founding director of the Eugene O'Neill Theater, who worked for Susskind at the time.

Susskind was also losing the stability that had been provided by his partner Al Levy. The two men had grown apart after *Open End* made Susskind a TV star. "You see David Susskind over there?" Levy once said to White. "He wants to walk down Madison Avenue and have everybody say, 'There goes David Susskind.' Me? I want to go to a delicatessen and have one waiter say to the other, 'That's the richest Jew in New York.'" Levy had a congenital stomach disorder, which had put him in ill health for years, and it was getting worse. By 1962, his condition kept him out of the office most days. He died in June of that year and Susskind gave the eulogy at the memorial service.

Unable to sell anything new to the networks, Susskind had to look for other routes to bring income into the company. He pushed ahead with his Harry Truman series, making trips to Independence, Missouri, to film the interviews himself. When he showed up at Truman's home with a film crew at 6:00 a.m. or 6:30 a.m., former First Lady Bess Truman answered the door. But she never invited him in as he waited for Harry Truman to emerge. "She'd close the door and let you stand in the vestibule, which was about 20 degrees below zero in the winter," Susskind said.

Later Susskind learned why. When he interviewed the wife of Eddie Jacobson, a Jewish haberdasher who had been in business with Truman, she told him she had never been inside the Truman house either. "What do you mean, never?" Susskind asked. "Your husband was a partner of Mr. Truman." Bluma Jacobson informed Susskind that the home belonged to Bess Truman's family, the Wallaces, who never had Jews inside. Since Bess managed the family home, neither did the Trumans.

Soon afterward Susskind handed the project over to Robert Alan Aurthur and a writer named Merle Miller. But correspondence between the representatives of Susskind and Truman indicated that both sides were looking for a way out of the deal when it was apparent a network sale was never going to happen. It took more than a year for Talent Associates to sell off the rights to the series to Screen Gems, at a loss of at least $330,000. It never got on the air. Miller used the candid interviews he did with Truman for his 1974 biography *Plain Speaking.*

The Talent Associates staff spent hours in Susskind's office spinning out other program possibilities. He managed to get one out of the new family connection of his top producer, Audrey Gellen, who had recently remarried. Her new husband was the writer Peter Maas, then a journalist for *Look* magazine. His father, Carl Maas, oversaw international cultural affairs for Standard Oil of New Jersey (which later became Exxon), where he doled out corporate dollars for artistic endeavors. Maas once paid $150,000 in commissions to sixteen American painters asked to depict the activities of the oil industry in the United States and overseas during World War II.

Audrey Gellen went to her father-in-law with a proposal for a series of shows called *Festival of Performing Arts,* in which musicians or actors would get a full hour to perform works of their choosing. Standard Oil had already sponsored *The Play of the Week* and *An Age of Kings,* a series of Shakespeare plays, both of which earned good press. *Festival* would generate similar accolades.

The concept of artistic freedom on the program was irresistible to the performers approached by Talent Associates to be on the show, mostly classical musicians and highly respected stage actors. "We went to people with the most seductive proposal you could have," said George C. White. "It was going to Paul Scofield and Joy Parker and saying, 'If you had an hour on television, what would you do? If they said, 'I'd like to do Chinese poetry or T. S. Eliot,' we said yes. If Rudolf Serkin said, 'Well, I always wanted to do the Schubert Quintet.' Okay. No one had ever said that before, and you get paid relatively a lot of money for doing one rehearsal and one performance." Susskind also personally wooed impresario Sol Hurok, who represented many of the artists he wanted for the show, by having him as a guest on *Open End*.

Festival aired in only ten markets, mostly where Standard Oil distributed its Esso brand gasoline. Critics marveled at the cultural video treasure trove presented in the first ten installments. Margaret Leighton performed the poetry and prose of Dorothy Parker. Master violinist Isaac Stern played a program of Bach and Mozart. Cellist Pablo Casals repeated the program of classical works and Catalan folks songs he had recently played for President Kennedy at the White House. The series was immaculately staged, with spare, elegant sets designed by Burr Smidt. Kirk Browning, a veteran of fine arts television broadcasts going back to the NBC Symphony Orchestra and active until his death in 2008, expertly handled the direction. The series won three Emmy Awards and was praised on the floor of Congress.

Festival and *Armstrong Circle Theatre* sustained Talent Associates while Susskind explored other projects in film, stage, TV, and beyond. One notion he had was particularly surprising to Jack Willis.

"David and I were walking down the street to go to a meeting," Willis recalled. "I don't even remember who the meeting was with, some movie star, some celebrity. And David put his arm around my shoulder and he said, 'Look, I'm thinking of running for the Senate, for Jacob Javits's seat. And I would like you to take over the company. So I want you to be in my office. When you come in, I want you to be on every phone call. I want you to be involved in every meeting.'" Willis was twenty-nine years old at the time with no experience in show business beyond his work for Susskind's talk show and a few other Talent Associates projects. But the next morning he dutifully showed up in Susskind's office and settled himself on the couch to watch and listen as his boss and new mentor worked the phones. Halfway through the second day of the setup, Susskind looked at Willis and said, "What are you doing here?" Willis got up and left and went back to working on *Open End*. Susskind mused about a Senate run in the press, but when the idea never gained any serious traction, he moved on. Willis believed Susskind was fully aware of his own impetuous behavior and made no apologies for it.

"He acted on the spur of the moment all the time," Willis said. "And he accepted that he did that, and then he changed his mind and did something else. It was whatever grabbed him that day."

One day in spring 1962, that impulse led Susskind to take a courageous stand on behalf of John Henry Faulk, a comedian from Texas who had been a popular radio and TV personality during the 1950s. In 1957, Faulk was part of the leadership of the American Federation of Radio and Television Artists and backed a union resolution to oppose blacklisting. His support led to his being made the subject of an AWARE bulletin put out by Vince Hartnett. It falsely claimed that Faulk was booked to perform for communist front groups. Shortly thereafter, he lost his show at WCBS radio and remained unemployed for years. He filed a libel suit against Hartnett and cohort Laurence Johnson, the Syracuse grocer who threatened to boycott sponsors who employed artists with alleged communist ties. When Faulk's case finally came to trial, he was looking for a TV executive to testify on how the blacklist worked. Faulk and his attorney Louis Nizer were aware that Susskind had gone on record about having to clear names for his show during the 1950s and expressed his disdain for the practice. In 1960, Susskind hired actress Jean Muir for his series *The Witness* after she had been blacklisted for nearly ten years, and proclaimed in the press that he would no longer submit names for the network to clear when casting his shows.

Faulk wrote in his book *Fear on Trial* that during a meeting at the Talent Associates office Susskind seemed almost euphoric about the prospect of appearing as a witness on his behalf. When Faulk mentioned that he was broke, Susskind had his assistant cut him a company check for $1,000. Susskind was scheduled to travel to England in May 1962 to oversee a BBC coproduction of Henrik Ibsen's *Hedda Gabler* with Ingrid Bergman as the star (a major gamble as he did not yet have a buyer for the show in the United States). But he committed himself to make a special trip back to New York for a few days if necessary to appear at Faulk's trial.

On April 27, 1962, just before his scheduled overseas departure, Susskind appeared before the New York Supreme Court and became the first person to testify on the workings of the blacklist in broadcasting. His notoriety (thanks to *Open End*) as a TV star sitting on the witness stand intensified the interest of the jury and press coverage of Faulk's situation. Susskind laid out the blacklisting process in detail—naming sponsors, ad executives, and shows for which he had to submit names of actors, writers, directors, and technicians—over five thousand in total during 1954, with a third of them rejected, he said.

"Did you even submit the names of children. . . . Could you put a child on without getting clearance?" Nizer asked.

"Even children," said Susskind, who went on to recount his efforts to clear the name of a child he wanted to cast in a show, only to have her rejected as "politically unreliable." It was great courtroom drama, and effective. Game show mogul Mark Goodson followed Susskind on the stand with another insider account of the process. At the end of the eleven-week trial, Faulk won a $3.5 million judgment—later reduced to $550,000 on appeal. He would work in the entertainment industry again, as Susskind signed him later in the year for a role in his feature film production of *All the Way Home*.

THERE WAS NO NEGATIVE response from the TV industry toward Susskind for speaking out on Faulk's behalf, but business at Talent Associates was still sluggish for much of the year. Susskind attempted to wrangle an assignment from the White House to produce a documentary film to promote the federal government's Food for Peace program in Brazil. Its aim was to use food surpluses from the United States and distribute them to developing nations. The White House supposedly wanted the film to record President Kennedy's scheduled visit to the country as well. Susskind decided to take his talk show on location to Brazil to coincide with the project.

The White House contact for Talent Associates was Robert S. Dole. Willis and others at the company remembered Dole (no relation to the U.S. Senator from Kansas) as a mysterious character who occasionally stopped by to see Susskind in the early 1960s. "He was always hustling," Willis said. "And he said he had an office in the White House. But what he had was a phone in the White House that somebody answered for him. And he came to David. I was in that meeting. And he said President Kennedy wanted to do something around Food for Peace. And the next thing I know, we were talking about doing *Open End* in Brazil. So we all went down on Varig Airlines to Rio. David, [*Open End* producer] Jean Kennedy, Bob Dole, and me. We're going down there for a week, or ten days. And Dole travels with a shopping bag, with just one suit and a couple pair of underwear. And that's it."

The Food for Peace film never got made, as Kennedy backed out of the Brazil trip. "Kennedy cancellation plus political situation plus hostility to Americans make show impossible," producer Robert Alan Aurthur wrote in a telegram to Susskind after having spent several weeks in the country and thousands of dollars in Talent Associates money preparing for the project. But Susskind went ahead with his *Open End* plans. He had lined up Brazil's socialist president João Goulart, who proved to be an elusive guest. "We went into the interior to Brasilia, to do a show with Goulart," said Willis. "He had married a young woman who had never been photographed [Maria Teresa Goulart, who was twenty-one when her husband took office in 1961]. He wouldn't allow her in public. There were stories when we were there that some young army lieutenant had been seen talking to her, and the next thing you know, they had taken him up in a helicopter over the Amazon and he had to jump without a chute. And then, Goulart wouldn't show up. So Jean and I, just on our own, went out and traveled around Brasilia for two or three days. After this nonsense of waiting for this guy, he showed up and we did the *Open End* and he brought his wife on the show. So that was a big coup."

Willis also learned during the trip that he should steer clear of any woman Susskind might be interested in. "Varig Airlines, in those days, had women they called hostesses," said Willis. "They were basically prostitutes. They would be on the plane and they would change into an evening gown. And they'd come and talk to everyone. And they'd give you a card and say, 'And if you want to go shopping, here's my card.' So coming back, the plane was only half-full. And Jean and David were sitting behind me and I was sitting in an empty row. And I began chatting up the hostess. And she came and sat down next to me for about forty minutes. And we're talking and talking, and then she had to get up to work. And the next thing I know, Jean comes and sits down next to me. And David got the hostess to sit next to him. We get off the plane. Jean and I take a cab into the city. David takes the hostess in his car. The next day he says to me, 'Don't you ever try and upstage me with a woman.' He was serious. But she really liked him."

BY THE FALL of 1962, Susskind had lost his status as the preeminent name in New York television production. Herbert Brodkin had been with the CBS show *Studio One*. After the show headed west, he remained in New York and began to develop his own series. For the 1962–1963 TV season, he had two hour-long dramas on the CBS schedule—his legal drama *The Defenders* and a new series, *The Nurses,* set in a Manhattan hospital.

Brodkin was a Brooklyn native who became interested in theater while at the University of Michigan. While serving in the U.S. Army Signal Corps during World War II, he directed more than forty training films and produced stage shows for the USO. "We used to always laugh about a film he made called *Horse Gas Mask,*" said George C. White. "It showed how to put a gas mask on a horse in case of attack." After the war Brodkin studied at the Yale Drama School and became a scenic designer on Broadway and later a producer of live TV drama. Talent Associates represented him until Susskind started producing himself. "David had once been Herb's agent," said Buzz Berger, Brodkin's longtime business partner. "Herb fired him because David was trying to get a job that Herb was offered."

Brodkin's best-known work in early TV drama was a 1957 episode of *Studio One* called "The Defender." Written by Reginald Rose, it starred Ralph Bellamy and William Shatner as a father-and-son attorney team that tries for the acquittal of a butcher shop deliveryman. Played by Steve McQueen, the unsympathetic nineteen-year-old is accused of having robbed and strangled a woman living in a fancy New York apartment. Brodkin and Rose developed the episode into a series in 1960, with E. G. Marshall and Robert Reed cast as the lawyers. The elder Lawrence Preston, played by Marshall, analytically pursued the letter of the law while Reed's Kenneth Preston was more impulsive and emotional. Between the two of them every angle of a case was presented, sometimes without real resolution. The Prestons even lost on occasion.

CBS put *The Defenders* into production as a series in 1960, but it was not scheduled until the networks became nervous about FCC commissioner Newton Minow's pronouncements about the sad state of programming. Fearful that Minow would impose significant regulation on programming content, all of the networks scrambled to find something other than the westerns and detective shows that had been saturating the airwaves in recent years. Some existing programs were even reedited to tamp down on screen violence, another one of Minow's concerns. CBS founder and chairman William Paley forced *The Defenders* onto the 1961–1962 schedule so he could cite an example of an intelligent dramatic series on the network during another hearing Minow held on network programming.

"They had shot five or six and had shelved them," said Berger. "Paley remembered it. He had liked it and he thought maybe that was something they could testify about without embarrassment. And so he pulled it back off the shelf and decided to put it on."

The decision did not please CBS president James Aubrey, who never let his own taste get in the way of what he believed the public wanted to see. He had set CBS on a path to record profits with highly successful sitcoms such as *The Beverly Hillbillies, Petticoat Junction,* and *Mr. Ed,* which featured a talking horse. He had become notorious for having a programming dictum that required "broads, bosoms, and fun"—not exactly the formula applied in *The Defenders.* He was also used to autonomy when it came to picking shows. "This is a piece of shit and it's going to die," was his reaction when told to put *The Defenders* on the schedule, according to Berger. Going forward, Aubrey demanded Brodkin and Reginald Rose create love interests for the E. G. Marshall and Robert Reed characters in future episodes.

The premiere episode was titled "The Quality of Mercy" and was truly jarring for television of any era. The Prestons defend a doctor who is charged with murder for having euthanized a baby born with Down syndrome (not a term used at the time—the infant is described repeatedly in the episode as "an imbecile"). While the baby is not shown, it's clear to the viewer that the doctor puts it to death with his bare hands shortly after he delivers it. The Prestons defend the doctor without imposing their own judgments. Every week the show tackled cases with mitigating circumstances: such as killing in self-defense, insanity pleas, and the limits on free speech. *The Defenders* was dialogue-heavy and had little action on screen, making it a direct descendent from a bygone era of television. But viewers responded and it became a ratings hit.

Aubrey was still looking for romance. "Jim Aubrey would call up and say, 'Where are the new scripts?'" Berger recalled. "And Herb said, 'Screw the new scripts. We're going back to the way the audience likes it.' Suddenly when you're in the top ten you have a lot of power. And they couldn't say anything."

The writers on *The Defenders* felt confident in boldly pursuing provocative material because Brodkin backed them up. A tall, brooding redhead with the look of a rugged outdoorsman, Brodkin "was a guy who could stand in freezing cold water up to his waist at the Miramichi River in New Brunswick with black flies biting him on the face and having the best time of his life catching an Atlantic salmon," according to Berger. His imposing physical presence came in handy when going up against network executives. "He intimidated the people who you were happy to have him intimidate," recalled Albert Ruben, a writer for *The Defenders* and other Brodkin shows. "Namely the people from the network who were trying to interfere with the work you were doing. He was not easy to work for. But if you wanted someone on your side, he was the man."

"Everybody was scared of Herb," said Alan Morris, who was Brodkin's longtime attorney.

Berger remembers attending a network meeting with Brodkin and British TV director Herbert Wise. After the meeting ended, Wise said to Brodkin, "I've been to millions of meetings at the BBC and ITV and places like that and it's the first time I have ever heard a producer tell the people at the networks to go fuck themselves."

"The network is used to me," Brodkin told him. "For me to tell them to go fuck themselves is like anybody else saying hello."

But Brodkin was likely given plenty of latitude because, when it came to money, he was the anti-Susskind. Highly efficient and frugal in his productions, Brodkin never went over budget. His hour-long shows were usually filmed in five days. His film crews never spent more than one of those days on location outside of the studio, sometimes to the dismay of the writers. "Herb was very, very nervous about any kind of production costs," said Larry Cohen. "If I wrote a scene for *The Defenders* that happened in a luncheonette, he'd say, 'Well, why can't they play that scene in the back of a courtroom?'"

Brodkin's mandate for the directors who worked for him was to use tight close-ups. "Herb used to say, 'If you give me twice as many close-ups as you think I want, you'll be giving me half as many as I need,'" Buzz Berger said. "The first episode of *The Nurses* that I produced for Herb was directed by the English director Michael Powell, who had done *The Red Shoes*. But Michael was a little bit down on his luck in those days, and Herb was a friend, a fishing friend. So he gave Michael a bunch of shows to do. And I'm this twenty-nine-year-old, and I'm saying to Michael Powell, 'I don't want close-ups like this; I want close-ups like this,' because I had been trained by Herb. I think back on that with such horror." Berger believed that Brodkin's stylistic approach had to do with the TV reception in his New York City apartment in Greenwich Village, located across the street from St. Vincent's Hospital. "In those days, everything was beamed from a big antenna downtown, and the building of St. Vincent's got in the way of the signal," said Berger. "So Herb had ghosts up on the screen. And this was before cable. So the only way Herb could understand what people were saying was if it was in a big close-up."

While Brodkin's shows embodied the liberal values of his writers, the producer himself had his own peculiar set of political ideas. "He was full of contradictions," said Berger. "He would say with total conviction that the solution for crime was if everybody carried arms. I'd say to Herb, 'If everybody carried arms there would be all kinds of people being shot by mistake.' He'd say, 'Yeah, but a lot of bad guys would be shot too.'"

Fear of the FCC interfering with the business of the networks helped get *The Defenders* on the air. But the success of the show led the way for a new kind of television hero, one that embodied the aspirations of the Kennedy administration for public service and progress in civil rights. New shows about a young high school teacher *(Mr. Novak)*, caring college deans *(Channing)*, and psychiatrists *(The Eleventh Hour* and *The Breaking Point)* found their way onto the network schedules and often addressed the social issues of the moment, including race relations.

CBS was looking to develop such a series for George C. Scott. The network had hoped he would star in a series about a crusading newspaper reporter. Scott was one of the most lauded actors around after his mesmerizing portrayal of Bert Gordon, the merciless gambler in *The Hustler.* He was in demand as a movie star, but in 1962 he was looking for a big TV payday so that he could start a regional theater in his home state of Michigan. He signed a deal with CBS and United Artists Television that paid him $150,000 up front, $10,000 per episode, and a 25 percent ownership stake in whatever show he agreed to do.

Unable to make the newspaper concept work, Aubrey called his friend David Susskind. Like NBC and ABC, CBS had shunned Susskind after his scalding FCC testimony, but now Aubrey needed the producer. His network was on the hook to Scott and did not have a program for him. Susskind had success in working with the volatile actor on a number of dramatic specials, including a well-done adaptation of the Bret Harte short story "The Outcasts of Poker Flat" for *Kraft Television Theatre,* and *The Power and the Glory.*

Susskind's office already had been working on a show about a dedicated New York City social worker eager to confront the harsh realities of inner-city life. Robert Alan Aurthur, who was credited as the show's creator, disliked the idea at first. He believed it was too similar to ABC's New York–based police drama *Naked City.* But Aurthur had grown tired of the chaos at Talent Associates and agreed to work on the project if Susskind released him from his contract with the company. CBS bought Aurthur's script and committed to a pilot episode of the series, called *East Side/West Side*. Scott became the star and part owner of the property and had creative input going forward.

OUT OF THE MORE than one thousand hours of television produced by Talent Associates over the years, not one was a drama series built around recurring characters. All of Susskind's dramatic shows had been anthologies and specials. Susskind was at his most engaged when he was making deals and seeking properties or talent for a production. He was always perched and ready to pounce on the next challenge. But turning out weekly-series television was more like running a factory. Susskind's agent, Ted Ashley, believed that Talent Associates needed another executive mind at the top if the company was to have any chance of competing in the current television landscape. Paramount was growing impatient as well. Studio president Barney Balaban was angry that Susskind was spending time in pursuit of Broadway stage and movie projects. In a December 1962 correspondence to Susskind, Balaban made it clear that Paramount took its half interest in Talent Associates to get its expertise in making television. "So far the results of our association have not been encouraging," he wrote. Nor was it profitable. Paramount had lost $500,000 on *The Power and the Glory* and *All the Way Home* was running 50 percent over budget.

Ashley, a counselor to many in the TV business at the time, sought out ABC prime-time programming chief Daniel Melnick to help Susskind get more series on the air. Melnick was known for being a fashionably dressed, highly skilled schmoozer who had risen quickly at ABC, earning him the not so flattering moniker of Nathan Network. But he understood the mechanics of developing and running series TV shows. Under Melnick's stewardship, ABC had one of the most popular new programs of the 1961–1962 season with *Ben Casey,* the gritty, realistic medical drama starring Vince Edwards.

Raised in the Bronx, New York, in the 1930s, Melnick said he developed a passion for art and theater as a child after his father was killed in an automobile accident. "My sister dropped out of Hunter College to take care of me," Melnick said. "She schlepped me to museums, schlepped me to concerts, and gave me a nickel for every real book I read instead of comic books. And then my mother remarried and we moved to Forest Hills. So very upper class." Melnick did not sing, dance, or act, but he successfully applied to enter the High School of the Performing Arts shortly after it opened in 1948. He pitched himself as a producer to the school's admissions board. "I said, 'Listen, if you're going to teach all these people to be actors and dancers and musicians, you better teach someone how to put on the shows,'" Melnick explained.

As a teenager, Melnick managed a weekend children's theater group at the Circle in the Square in New York. After graduation he landed a job in the mailroom at CBS. He enrolled at New York University at night in order to avoid being drafted during the Korean War in the early 1950s. "I was the only working-class kid in the mailroom," he said. "It wasn't a training ground, it was the recipient for the rich kids—the sons of the friends of Bill Paley. These kids were so rich, I think they hired outside messenger services to deliver the mail." Melnick then worked on the TV show staffs of Jackie Gleason and Steve Allen before heading out to Los Angeles to be an assistant producer at the new Television City production facility CBS had opened on Fairfax Avenue. On Sundays, Melnick would visit the home of his CBS boss Ben Feiner Jr. for brunch. It was there that he got to know Feiner's sister Dorothy, her husband, the legendary Broadway theater composer Richard Rodgers, and their daughter Linda. "Here was an employed heterosexual," was how Melnick referred to himself. "What could be better for their daughter?" Linda Rodgers became Mrs. Dan Melnick. The kid from the Bronx had married into show business royalty.

After a stint in the army, Melnick returned to New York and joined ABC (he had first met the network's president at a Rodgers family gathering in Connecticut). He quickly worked his way up the ranks to vice president in charge of prime-time programming in 1962. The network had some ratings successes, but it was still hampered by having fewer affiliated stations than CBS and NBC, a situation that would not change until well into the 1970s. Every day was an uphill battle.

Melnick had long had aspirations to create his own programs. Ashley's proposal to partner him with Susskind, still a quality brand-name producer and a larger than life personality, offered the opportunity to attain immediate credibility on that front. But he was wary of Susskind's vocal protests over the state of their business. "Jim Aubrey and Ted Ashley desperately wanted to be able to give David some shows to produce," Melnick said. "But they can't trust him. He's got no commercial instincts. He goes around knocking the commercial world. Why? Because he gets attention from it. David invented the word 'narcissist.' You attack the establishment that feeds you, you get attention." Melnick had said as much to Susskind when they were both at Aubrey's table at the Polo Lounge in Beverly Hills several months before a partnership was discussed. "I told him he was a total phony," said Melnick.

But Ashley was committed to helping Susskind, as was Aubrey. So many beautiful actresses passed through the doors of Talent Associates that Susskind had been providing a steady pipeline of them to Aubrey when they weren't out seeking action together. "Aubrey would call in every other evening at five thirty," Susskind's longtime assistant Anita Grossberg said. "David would say, 'Get your Rolodex, Anita.' I'd give David the number and he in turn would give it to Aubrey. He did that a lot for Jim. People said to me, 'You know what you are—you're a pimp, Anita.' I didn't even know what that meant." Susskind was one of several TV producers with whom Aubrey mixed business and pleasure. "They were both extremely bright, both had, I think, a lot of regard for each other's smarts," said Jerry Leider, who worked as an agent for Ashley and as an executive under Aubrey at CBS. "But they couldn't keep their zippers closed, so they'd pal around a lot. They just got along very well and did a lot of business that way."

After Melnick balked at the notion of partnering with Susskind, Aubrey added an incentive. He told Melnick that if he joined the company he would always have at least one show on the CBS schedule every year. Aubrey had given similar assurances to other producer pals in return for favors, which ultimately contributed to his downfall at CBS.

Before the papers were signed, Melnick and his wife traveled to Puerto Rico for the Pablo Casals Festival, a major annual event in the classical music world. "After the opening night, we were so wound up," he recalled. "It's 8 o'clock in the morning and we decided to go walk on the beach. In the distance, there's one other person, for two miles on the beach."

As the figure walking toward the couple came into focus, Melnick's wife Linda said to him: "Jesus Christ, that looks like Jim Aubrey." She was shaken at the sight of him. "Although he was the Princeton All-American, and always the perfect gentleman, my wife said to me, 'I'm always terrified by him,'" Melnick said.

Showing up on the shore in San Juan unannounced that morning added to Aubrey's menacing persona. "He wanted to make sure that I made the right decision," said Melnick, who in the late spring of 1963 became David Susskind's new partner at Talent Associates.

9

fter a year in the making, David Susskind was ready to present an
early version of *East Side/West Side,* which Talent Associates staffers had called the social workers show. "It sounded kind of dull,"
said Bob Israel, the music supervisor on the project. As executives from CBS
filed in to a dark screening room in the Pathé Building on East 116th Street in
Manhattan to take a look, Israel noted, "There was tremendous tension because there was a lot of money involved in this thing." The pilot was $24,000
over its $175,000 budget. Susskind had had director Daniel Petrie shoot a few
extra days and the editing needed to be rushed. The pressure to complete the
job was intense for Sidney Meyers, whom Susskind had hired to supervise the
film editing on the show. *East Side/West Side* was an ideal assignment for
Meyers, a Renaissance man who had played in a symphony orchestra before
he became a film editor. "He used to practice the viola while he let me cut the
film," said Pat Jaffe, a New York film editor who worked with him. "That's
how I learned." Meyers was best known for *The Quiet One,* a disturbing portrayal of a ten-year-old black boy rejected by his family and rescued by the
Wiltwyck School, an institution for troubled youths. Shot on the streets of
Harlem, the Academy Award–nominated documentary was regarded as a
masterpiece by critics because of its honest depiction of urban life. But Meyers, angst-ridden by nature, couldn't bear the moment of judgment when *East
Side/West Side* came up on the screen for the first time. The blaring brass and
pounding bongos in Kenyon Hopkins' opening theme music surged through
the speakers. On screen, the main titles rose up over the stark black-and-white
footage of passing subway cars and the grim profile of a trench-coated George C.

Scott as social worker Neil Brock. "All of a sudden Sidney sprang up out of his seat and ran down the aisle," said Bob Israel. "He started to do a wild, crazy improvised dance in front of the projected image. While all that music is going on, he's dancing and waving his arms and going through this Nijinsky thing." Susskind looked around to gauge the reaction to the terpsichorean outburst and popped up from his seat. "That won't be in the final cut," he said, just in case the CBS executives needed assurance.

The pilot episode told the story of a fifteen-year-old Puerto Rican gang member who murders an Italian neighborhood shop owner because he refuses to serve the kid a cup of coffee. The jarring opening scene shows the youth taking out his switchblade and stabbing the shop owner repeatedly. The boy's guilt isn't even a question in the drama. Neil Brock's job is to get the kid tried as a youth so he doesn't get the death penalty. Most of the show was a debate on the effectiveness of rehabilitation. Brock grimly acknowledges that there's a chance the boy will kill again. Before even a single frame of the film had been shown to the network, Susskind's office had already received a complaint from the East Harlem neighborhood—at the time considered one of the most dangerous in New York City—where much of the pilot was shot. "We certainly would not have consented to the use of Franklin Plaza if we knew that the film was going to further the common unfair image of the area," wrote a public relations representative for the city housing project used as a location. Another community group was disturbed that teenagers were showing up to the shoots identifying themselves as juvenile delinquents in the hope it would get them some camera time.

But the show was executed well and certainly fit the network's mandate to bring more social realism to prime time. *East Side/West Side* was picked up by CBS for the 1963–1964 TV season, giving Talent Associates its first weekly network series in two years. Susskind was eager to take full advantage of the recent trend of "New Frontier" dramas: shows that depicted the dedicated Americans who responded to President Kennedy's call to "ask not what your country can do for you—ask what you can do for your country." By the time the show went into production, Elizabeth Wilson, who played Neil Brock's boss Frieda Hechlinger, had a wardrobe and hairstyle inspired by First Lady Jacqueline Kennedy.

Susskind now had a show to take on his New York rival Herb Brodkin, who had gotten headlines, accolades, and even high ratings for *The Defenders*, which had taken on hot-button topics such as abortion and the death penalty.

"If they want controversy I'll give them controversy," Susskind told Don Kranze, an *East Side/West Side* producer who had worked on Brodkin's shows.

Susskind had a willing partner in Scott. The actor and his wife, Colleen Dewhurst, were passionate about liberal causes. Scott proudly played on predominantly black softball teams in the Broadway Show League. He felt that his portrayal of Neil Brock, an angry crusader, was a great vehicle to rally the public's attention to the issues of the day. "He became obsessed with the character in a great way," Bob Israel said. "He felt that something wonderful was happening."

Part of Scott's deal was approval of the other principal actors in *East Side/West Side.* (After the pilot was shot, Scott had Victor Arnold, cast as a protégé of Brock, fired from the show, perhaps not wanting to compete with a younger actor who had the kind of good looks that generated mail from female TV fans.) Susskind used Scott's clout to make history by casting a black actress in the role of Jane Foster, a secretary in the office of Community Welfare Services where Brock worked. Never before had a black performer been given a regular role in a prime-time dramatic series. Diana Sands, a stunning top black actress who Susskind used in his film version of *A Raisin in the Sun,* played Jane Foster in the pilot episode. But when it came time to negotiate a deal for the series, Kranze said the salary demands of Sands' agent were too high. Susskind passed and called Cicely Tyson. Scott wanted Tyson after seeing her in an off-Broadway production of Jean Genet's *The Blacks,* an unusual downtown Manhattan theater experience that became a showcase for every top black stage actor working in the early 1960s. Tyson was surprised when she was first called about *East Side/West Side* because it had already been reported that Sands had the part. "I went on and did whatever it is I was doing, which was the play," Tyson said. "Then I got a call from my agent that George Scott and David Susskind wanted to meet with me. I said, 'What for?' They wanted to talk with me. So I went up and met with them in Susskind's office. They asked me all sorts of questions. And it never dawned on me that they were talking to me about this role because I thought it was already cast. Finally, I think they said, 'Very nice talking to you.' They were noncommittal. I said thank you very much and went about my business. A day or two later I got a call from my agent with the William Morris Agency. He called me and said, 'I need you to come over to the office.' I went up there and he said, 'Well, you got the job.' I said, 'What job?' He said, 'George Scott wants you to do the part of Jane Foster in the television series.' I didn't know what to say. I said, 'Oh.' Whatever they had to do, they did."

Susskind did not have to do much convincing to get CBS to accept the casting of Tyson. At the time, the networks and TV producers were under pressure from the NAACP and civil rights leaders to improve minority representation both behind and in front of the camera. Susskind trumpeted the move to the press. "We chose her because it's real and it's right," Susskind told the *Boston Traveler.* "There is no color line when you're dealing with the truth."

While the move from Sands to Tyson in the role was a financial consideration, the decision heightened the breakthrough integration of the cast. The fair-skinned Diana Sands was known as "the beige Bette Davis," according to her close friend Lou Gossett Jr. Tyson, who did modeling work before she became an actress, was much darker than Sands. It made a difference. "There is no question that Diana Sands was fair and there was no question at all that I was who I was," said Tyson. "The impact of that image on the screen in the midst of those white people was like a bowling bowl. Now I look at it and I go—'God, what it must have done to those people.'"

In 1963, network evening newscasts regularly showed the horrific images in Birmingham, Alabama, of blacks who protested to end segregation being set upon by fire hoses and police dogs. Television coverage was largely credited with bringing national attention and support to the civil rights cause around the country. But the sight of black actors in important roles on prime-time TV shows still brought out the ugliness in those viewers who resisted the societal changes brought about by the movement. Nessa Hyams, a casting director for New York TV shows during the 1960s, remembers the vicious hate mail that came into Herb Brodkin's office after Ossie Davis had recurring appearances as an assistant district attorney in several episodes of *The Defenders.* "I would open the stuff," she said. "If you got it today, you would be scared. Even a Yiddish phrase would prompt people to write in and call the show's writers 'Jew commie bastards.'" White audiences were more comfortable with the black performers on musical variety shows of the era. Black singer and actress Leslie Uggams reportedly got more fan mail than any other regular on NBC's *Sing Along with Mitch,* a show that featured a chorus of mostly white middle-aged men in sweaters performing songs from the first half of the twentieth century.

Hate mail stopped neither Susskind nor Brodkin from casting more black actors in their shows than their Hollywood counterparts did. Louis Gossett Jr. believes it had everything to do with the fact that their productions were based in New York. "We had the honest political confrontation about it being more diverse," he said. "We had to deal with one another every day. We came to that armistice quicker. In Los Angeles, you get to hide behind your car, your house. You sit in booths in restaurants. You don't interface with everyone that's complaining. You can hide more easily."

ONCE *EAST SIDE/WEST SIDE* went into production, Susskind gathered his staff in the conference room at Talent Associates to come up with a list of story ideas. It looked very much like the litany of issues he'd tackle on his talk show: Black Muslims, political demagogues, birth control "with a Catholic angle," welfare cheats, police brutality, the John Birch Society, out-of-control classrooms. Such territory would surely attract writers who wouldn't otherwise go near television. At least that's what they thought. Producer Audrey Gellen contacted author James Baldwin, only to get a quick no from his agent. "[With] his natural distaste for restrictions on what he writes, it does not seem to me likely that he will be very interested in trying his hand at a script for *East Side/West Side*," the agent wrote back.

George C. Scott had read a newspaper account of how the city of New York once refused permits to allow the making of a film by playwright Arthur Miller about juvenile delinquency (city officials had been pressured by the House Un-American Activities Committee, which had been gunning for Miller, to impede the making of the film). The actor dashed off a telegram to Miller, inviting him to pursue the subject on *East Side/West Side*. "We are seriously but not academically attacking every subject from anti-intellectualism to venereal disease—from political patronage to miscegenation," Scott wrote. "If you are not irrevocably averse to having work important to you appear in a television series, I would like to discuss this with you from the standpoint of a two-part story." There was no response.

Scott had better luck when he offered a researching job to a young journalist named Pete Hamill. Hamill had interviewed Scott the year before while working as a reporter for the *New York Post*. He was out of work because of the newspaper strike that had started in December 1962. The job action shut down the city's seven dailies for nearly four months. "The idea was I would find out what would happen in the real world when a social worker was on a case," Hamill recalled. "The work helped feed my then-wife and infant daughter." Asked to research a possible story on political patronage, Hamill pounded out a six-page, single-spaced polemic he titled "The Capital of Corruption." In it, he listed detailed examples of scandals and investigations involving past New York mayors, the police, the state legislature, gangsters, and Tammany Hall. Hamill pounded the manual typewriter keys with such vigor that the paper used for the memo was riddled with holes. He was right at home.

East Side/West Side also had to deal with the tricky politics of confronting the combustible problems of New York while using the city streets as a back lot. Susskind was eager to do an episode about police brutality. Joe Liss, the writer assigned to the script, told Susskind it was impossible to do a realistic take on the subject if the series had to depend on police cooperation when shooting on location. "The real thing could never be done," Liss said. "If we told the real story, the New York City Police Department would drive you off the streets, camera crew and all . . . It's wise to forget it." The idea was scrapped.

Every story proposal for *East Side/West Side* had to get the approval of George C. Scott, who was not shy about rejecting scripts even if they had already been completed and paid for. When the investment was pointed out to him, he noted that 25 percent of the show was his and "he would rather see the money go down the drain than waste time on a story he'd never do." The next step was to meet the standards—or overcome the misgivings—of the network and its powerful chief Jim Aubrey, who was infamous for giving his input to producers before a script could even be written. According to Dan Melnick, who joined Talent Associates when the production was under way, *East Side/West Side* had a higher percentage of discarded storylines and scripts than any other TV show at the time.

In the early going, the slow grind of getting *East Side/West Side* scripts written made Don Kranze, who ran the day-to-day production, anxious. He had lined up directors for the start of filming in May 1963, but had nothing to shoot. He let Susskind know of the situation the production was getting into. "David, I want to make this very clear to you," Kranze said. "We are desperate for scripts."

"Never use that word, *desperate*," Susskind shot back. "We are never desperate. Never use that word *desperate* to me. I never want to hear that." But Susskind knew Kranze was right, and Scott wasn't the only problem. Long past its prime as the most prolific producer of live television specials and plays,

Talent Associates wasn't equipped for the rapid assembly-line pace of making an hour-long filmed series. Susskind needed help.

He turned to Larry Arrick, who had been hired after they worked together to develop a pilot for a series with the Second City comedy troupe. Arrick, whose background was in theater, became a story editor for *East Side/West Side*. His prior experience in television had been in the 1950s, as a front for writers blacklisted for their leftist leanings, which he shared. "If I had been around in the 1930s I would have been a communist in a second," he said. "I felt guilty that I had been born fifteen years too late to be a real member of these groups and be a part of all that." Once he was in charge of the scripts, Arrick hired writers he knew from the blacklist era and gave them the rare opportunity to confront issues they were passionate about. "Most of them were liberal. Some of them were blacklisted," he said. "I told them, 'Okay, I don't know how long this is going to last. Yeah, this is television, but you can write about anything you want, and if I think it's honest, I'll fight for it. I know that George will fight for it.'"

Among those who Arrick brought in was Arnold Perl, a blacklisted writer he had fronted for in the 1950s. Perl was shut out of television and movies because of his alleged associations with communist groups during the 1930s. But he thrived nonetheless with a successful theater company and a hit play, *The World of Sholom Aleichem*. Having bought the rights to Aleichem's stories, he used the characters for another play, *Tevye and His Daughters*, that in turn later became the source material for the wildly successful Broadway musical *Fiddler on the Roof*.

Perl's left-wing call-to-arms ethos galvanized the *East Side/West Side* writing staff. Early scripts had taken a cerebral approach to social problems. Perl wanted the writers to tap into their convictions. "Arnold sat them down and he said to them, 'This is the show you've all been waiting for,'" recalled his niece, Emily Perl Kingsley, who worked on *East Side/West Side* as a researcher. "This is an inner-city show talking about real social problems. Real people. This is going to be realistic. This is going to be gritty. We've got George Scott. Tell me what makes you angry.'" At Arrick's recommendation, Perl took over as executive producer of the show.

As late as 1963, the networks still required actors to be vetted for their alleged political affiliations before they could be cast. While formerly blacklisted actors were slowly making their way back into television by 1960, *East Side/West Side* was welcoming to actors, directors, and writers who had done little or no work for years because of blacklisting. Howard Da Silva, Lee Grant, Joshua Shelley, and Will Geer were among those who were regularly hired again after appearing on the program.

Bob Markell, a producer on *The Defenders,* said his boss Herb Brodkin followed Susskind's lead once he said he was no longer submitting names for political clearance for his shows. "Herb said, 'If David Susskind isn't going to submit names, neither am I,'" Markell recalled. *The Defenders* even did an episode in the 1963–1964 season about a blacklisted movie actor, played by Jack Klugman, who gets cast in his first role in ten years. His activity in a group that opposed Franco during the Spanish civil war had deprived him of work. He ultimately loses the job after a red-baiting organization makes an issue out of his past with officials in the city where the film is being made.

Markell said the original script had the actor getting a role in a television show. But CBS insisted that it be a film. "They still didn't want to acknowledge that the blacklist existed in television," Markell said.

Meanwhile, CBS execs were growing more concerned about the commercial potential of *East Side/West Side.* The pilot scored poorly when it was shown to a test audience. "More viewers rejected the program because it deals with an aspect of life that no one really wants to see," the report said. "Drab" and "depressing" were among the other words used. The one finding that gave the network hope was the positive audience response to Scott. But the network's program execs wrote memos to producers that were long, wordy treatises mostly reiterating the test audience's complaints about the gloominess of the series' subject matter. "Of the 12 outlines I have read," wrote CBS executive Alan White, "two deal with illegitimacy, two with mental retardation, two with rape with more than a subtle indication of incest . . . in at least two of these we are investigating the problem of the Negro in American society."

CBS president James Aubrey was more crudely succinct about his concerns during a meeting with Susskind and Scott in his office. "I am tired of stories coming from you guys about spics and niggers," he said, according to the show's script supervisor George C. White, who was there.

Scott didn't flinch. He was insistent that *East Side/West Side* be a frank, realistic examination of the intractable social problems facing America's decaying urban centers of the 1960s and was willing to use his intimidating presence to get his way. People involved with the show recalled stories, perhaps apocryphal or conflated, of Scott showing up to network meetings with a large switchblade. Michael Dann, Aubrey's second in command at the time, said that during one encounter he had with Scott, the actor pulled the knife out from a slot in the side of his boot and an apple out of his pants pocket. In one continuous motion he started to peel the skin of the apple with the knife.

"He keeps going around and around," Dann recalled. "And I keep talking. I said, 'I respect you and I respect the show, but we must make it more positive.' I give him the reasons. And he keeps his eyes on me the whole time, while peeling the whole apple without breaking the skin. When he was done he said, 'Do you have a basket?' And he dropped the peel in. I knew I had gained a victory without David Susskind's help. I knew I'd gotten to him because he had looked at me and was nodding to me."

Scott got up from his chair, the apple in one hand and the knife in the other. "Mr. Dann," he said. "You have described a perfectly wonderful show. As a matter of fact I wish I had thought of it. But as far as *East Side/West Side* is concerned, I think I will continue to do my show. But you should go ahead and do your show and we will both be satisfied.'"

The other oft-told knife tale took place in Jim Aubrey's office at CBS. Production of *East Side/West Side* had shut down that July partly because Scott refused to work until he could meet with Aubrey to discuss "the series' aspirations and freedom of choice in subject matter," according to a producer's memo. During another meeting, held after seven episodes had already been shot, Aubrey was famously quoted as saying the show should get out of Harlem and tell stories about the problems of people who live on Park Avenue. After some more apple peeling, Scott showed what he thought of the idea by jamming his knife in Aubrey's desk. Melnick's version of the apple story had Scott placing the fruit down on Aubrey's desk and asking if the CBS executive was finished with what he had to say. "And Jim said, 'Yes, George,'" Melnick recalled. "And George was furious. He leapt over the desk and went for Aubrey's throat."

Susskind was happy to have a battering ram of a star do his bidding, and often deferred to Scott. "That's the way George wants it," Susskind would say when CBS suits harangued him about the star's intransigence, according to Dann.

While the temperamental Scott's presence gave *East Side/West Side* latitude in the issues it wanted to pursue, it also made the day-to-day production a minefield for some of those who worked on it. "George Scott is a guy that, if you were to agree with him on every point that he raised in a given conversation, at the first moment you disagree with him, he's ready to explode," said Don Kranze. "And he does. You're dealing with nitroglycerine, and not a terribly happy person. He's serious, no lightness in the man at all. Not that he did anything horrendous. It's just that you don't like to be around nitroglycerine all the time. It's very uncomfortable."

Ed Adler, a taxi driver turned novelist who was still driving his cab when he was hired to write several *East Side/West Side* episodes, remembers when he walked past the doorway of Susskind's office at Talent Associates and saw Scott ripping into Arnold Perl. Scott was angry that Perl had apparently given in to CBS executives about an issue with one of the scripts. "Scott had a hold of his jacket, shoved him against the wall and threatened to throw him out the window," he said. Adler and others remember the sight of Scott grabbing the handles on the bottom of the windows, which were sealed shut in the air-conditioned building.

"Here was Arnold Perl, this old leftist whose left-wing credentials were so great and had been blacklisted for years," said Melnick. "George disagreed with him on something and was convinced at the moment that Arnold was selling out. Arnold wouldn't know how to sell out. I don't remember the issue, but I had to pull him away and say, 'George, the windows don't open.'"

Scott's intensity and self-seriousness rarely wavered. Once two schoolboys from a Bronx YMHA newspaper showed up on the show's set at Biograph Studio to interview the star. "Mr. Scott," said one of the boys, pencil and pad in hand, "how did you get into show business?" Scott took a deep breath as he looked up to the ceiling. "I am not in show business," he said. "Singers and dancers and jugglers and comedians are in show business. I am in the theater, which is quite a different thing." The young interviewer wisely moved on to another question. But Scott never let the front-office battles over the show affect him when he was working in front of the camera with the other actors. "George behaved on the set," said Elizabeth Wilson. "He may have caused problems with the writers and, God knows, with the producers. But with us, we were pretty much in awe of him. That was great because he kind of kept it going."

10

As Talent Associates fought to make the groundbreaking *East Side/ West Side* a success on CBS in the late spring of 1963, David Susskind was engaged in a skirmish on another front. At his previous TV home, WNTA, Susskind had been used to running his talk show *Open End* as a self-contained entity, serving his interests and whims with little interference from station management. But after WNTA was sold to National Educational Television in 1961, Susskind moved *Open End* to another New York station, WNEW, where it found an enemy in Bennet Korn.

Korn was a top executive at the Metropolitan Broadcasting Company, which owned WNEW. His personal taste was a bit refined for someone overseeing an independent TV station. WNEW in 1961 relied on roller derby, wrestling, and cartoons to fill time and compete against network-affiliated outlets. Korn had worked at WQXR, the classical radio station then owned by *The New York Times,* and was married for a time to British concert pianist Moura Lympany. After Metropolitan took over WNEW from the defunct DuMont network, one of Korn's goals was to improve the station's image by adding cultural fare and documentaries. Productions of Shakespeare plays showed up in prime time. "He wanted to class it up," said TV personality Sonny Fox, who had been hired to take over a marathon Sunday children's show called *Wonderama.* Fox had been the host of a short-lived but highly regarded educational show called *Let's Take a Trip.* Each week he traveled to locations outside of the studio—a museum, a zoo, or a dance studio—with a couple of children in tow. He described it as an electronic field trip. After joining *Wonderama,* Fox and the show's producers realized that in the captive world of few channels and almost no remote-control TV sets, kids would sit through almost anything to get to the next Bugs Bunny cartoon. So they tried giving them something uplifting in the show's studio segments. Kids who watched *Wonderama* heard opera singer Roberta Peters perform arias or got an explanation of Einstein's theory of relativity in between their Looney Tunes. The show became immensely popular, capturing as much as half of the New York homes watching TV on Sunday mornings. The waiting list to be a part of the live studio audience was years long. "When a child was born, parents would call the station or write in for tickets to the show," recalled Arthur Forrest, then a staff director at WNEW.

Susskind's *Open End* should have fit in with Korn's high-minded ambitions for WNEW. Fox remembered occasionally standing off to the side of Susskind's set to watch the host tape *Open End* and took pride in being on a station that offered smart discussion to its viewers. Korn, too, appreciated Susskind's show when the subject matter was light. "[He can] conduct a very polite parlor game on the merits of authors, comedians, plays or ballet," Korn once said. But Korn scorned any issue that made waves. Before coming to New York, Korn was in charge of Metropolitan's Washington, D.C., station, which carried *Open End* at the time Susskind famously squared off with Soviet premier Nikita Khrushchev. Korn refused to air the program. ("When a man is out of his element, he's simply destructive," he said at the time.) Korn especially disapproved when *Open End* explored the country's changing social mores. Such forums were alternately informative and titillating. One week, Susskind talked with married teenagers, a growing trend in the early 1960s. On another show, he conducted a panel with striptease artists Blaze Starr and Sherry Britton, who he had once had a dalliance with. Korn hated both, describing the latter as "the whore show." Susskind claimed Korn deleted remarks that Jackie Robinson made during an *Open End* panel discussion on the Freedom Riders, the integrated civil rights activists who challenged segregation laws by traveling together on public transportation systems throughout the South. Korn banned other guests who caused the slightest provocation.

"Norman Mailer had popped off about the Catholic Church," said Jack Willis, a producer on Susskind's show in the early 1960s. "So I went to David and I said, 'Let's get Norman and a Catholic priest to do a show.'" Willis found Father Robert Drinan, an outspoken Boston priest who supported civil rights.

(In 1970, Drinan would be elected to Congress as a peace candidate because of his opposition to the Vietnam War.) Willis then called Mailer to invite him on the show.

"You'll never get a priest to come on with me," Mailer told him. "No priest will come on with me."

"You want to bet?" said Willis.

"Yeah," Mailer said. "I'll bet you a dinner."

"Okay, let me see what I can do," Willis replied, knowing he already had Drinan.

Willis won the bet. "It was a terrible show," he said. "Norman was inarticulate. So he called me about it a month later and he said, 'Let's have dinner. I'll pay for the dinner.'"

The two met at the Carnegie Tavern near Carnegie Hall. "He and I are sitting there and we start drinking and he's belting them down and I'm trying to stay up with him," Willis said. "It was really interesting, what I remember of it, because he had gone off drugs. He was drinking, but he wasn't smoking any dope. And he had writer's block. He couldn't write and he talked about that a lot."

After Willis had four drinks, Mailer came at him with a proposal. "I have a really great idea that I'd like you to produce," Mailer said. "I want to go around the country debating Bill Buckley."

"Well, Norman," the impaired Willis slurred, "I don't think that's going to work because you're really inarticulate."

Mailer angrily stood up, slammed the table, and walked out.

"Left me with the bill," Willis recalled. "And the upshot was, he went and debated Bill Buckley in Chicago, got written up in *Playboy*, and then they came and did it at Carnegie Hall."

Mailer and William F. Buckley were a hit on the lecture circuit later that year. But Mailer wasn't going to be on *Open End* as long as Bennet Korn was in charge. Mailer was added to a long list of banished people and topics that included abortion, homosexuality, Rudolph Nureyev, American students who studied in the Soviet Union, jazz, and the FBI.

Most of the rejections seemed capricious. But keeping Susskind from probing the FBI may have been due to the station's own cozy relationship with the agency, which Korn encouraged. When agents attending a Communist Party function heard that New York party leader Gus Hall was to challenge Richard Nixon to a debate on Susskind's program, the bureau asked WNEW executives to look into it. Susskind had no plans for such a program, but the agents were assured that they would be tipped off.

Longtime WNEW employee Paul Noble said that during the 1960s he showed FBI agents videotape of the station's talk shows on occasion if they requested it. At that time, most Americans were unaware of the bureau's excesses. "It was just okay to do it," he recalled. "It was the FBI, after all. We were very patriotic. We weren't hiding anything. Generally, it came to the legal department and they would say, 'Do this.' " Noble believed any specific interest the FBI had in Susskind was largely brought on by right-wing newspaper columnists, including Jack O'Brien, who wrote for the *Journal-American*, the conservative Hearst-owned paper in New York. "The FBI's chosen in the media—they were the ones that instigated it," Noble said. "I don't think David was far afield from the middle of America as far as his show. If anybody was responsible for the FBI's curiosity about David it would have been because of those press items that were either planted or responded to. The right wing had its targets. They put a pink tinge on anybody who didn't think their way." FBI files showed that right-leaning newspaper columnist Walter Winchell passed on to Hoover a postcard from an angry reader that noted Susskind's attendance at the October 5, 1960, reception at the Soviet embassy where he invited Khrushchev to appear on *Open End*.

The FBI was already monitoring Susskind's talk show and other TV appearances in 1959 when his liberal leanings and stated support of the civil rights movement became apparent. Based on Susskind's personal FBI file, the bureau monitored him for fifteen years. Memos were written describing and criticizing any on-air reference to Hoover or the bureau made by Susskind or his guests (the only mention of Susskind's personal life was one of his extramarital relationships with an actress, not exactly top-secret information). In June 1964, the bureau conspired to undermine a viewer call-in show Susskind was trying to sell to independent New York TV station WPIX. The show, called *Hot Line*, featured Susskind with Gore Vidal, Yale chaplain Rev. William Sloane Coffin, and newspaper columnist Dorothy Kilgallen taking questions that came in by a video TV phone set up at Grand Central Terminal. (The technology, called Picturephone, had been introduced at that year's World's Fair in Queens.) Vidal was not surprised that the show was cited. "We were deeply opposed to Vietnam," Vidal said of himself and Coffin. "I guess they thought we were ganging up on the FBI. Which we were." The panel criticized the FBI's handling of civil rights cases and bombings in the South.

Susskind called for Hoover's retirement. In his closing remarks on the pilot program, Susskind told viewers to write in if they wanted *Hot Line* to return on a regular basis. Hearing that, agents in the FBI's New York office planned a letter-writing campaign that complained about the show (without identifying themselves with the bureau). The effort failed, as WPIX added *Hot Line* to its schedule that fall.

Jean Kennedy said she had no knowledge of the FBI's interest in Susskind's show during the many years she produced it. There were numerous times in the 1960s and 1970s that she, Susskind, or one of the show's associate producers invited Hoover to appear on the program to discuss organized crime or other various aspects of the FBI's operations. Hoover (and his successor, Patrick Gray) declined each time, and a bureau file about the request and the subsequent rejection was written up. "I would rather appear with a 'skunk' than with Susskind," Hoover scribbled on one such memo. Susskind was repeatedly described in the files as a figure that "catered to the pseudo-liberal quasi-intellectual left." The memos continued well into the 1970s, and even included a detailed account of a Susskind panel with comedian Godfrey Cambridge and Pete Hamill, called "Does the FBI Have a File on You?"

SUSSKIND'S CONFLICTS with Korn over subject matter for *Open End* reached a breaking point in the early part of 1963 with the taping of a panel about the "American Sexual Revolution." The participants included *Playboy* magazine founder Hugh Hefner; Arthur Kinsolving, the president of the Protestant Council of Greater New York; Dr. Albert Ellis, a psychotherapist; Maxine Davies, a medical columnist for *Good Housekeeping* who had written several books about human sexuality; and Ralph Ginzburg, who had founded *Eros,* a new magazine about sex. Ginzburg recently had been indicted by a federal grand jury for sending through the mail a book called *The Housewives' Handbook on Selective Promiscuity.*

The panelists calmly debated whether American society had become too obsessed with sex and whether the country's puritan ethic was perhaps a contributing factor. Oddly enough, it was Ginzburg, an outsized character with horn-rimmed glasses and a bushy mustache, who stressed the romantic ideal that sex was best enjoyed in a loving relationship. (Several years later, Ginzburg was convicted of obscenity charges for mailing the *Housewives* book and eventually served eight months in federal prison.)

When premarital sex was discussed, Ellis suggested the best advice that Susskind could give to his own daughters, then aged nineteen and sixteen, was to provide as much information as possible about contraceptives. As he often did, Susskind responded with enough appropriate outrage to satisfy the conventional thinking of most viewers. But Ginzburg took Ellis's point even further, saying he planned to instruct his daughters to live with a man before marrying him. The comment was all Korn needed to reject the program. For the first time an entire *Open End* episode was banned from the airwaves, despite the overall tepid nature of the discussion, even by 1963 standards. When the transcript of the show was sold as an article to the woman's magazine *Mademoiselle,* its managing editor Barbara Kerr told Susskind, "it seems rather innocuous compared with so much that is on the newsstands."

Korn's ban deeply angered Susskind. The executive tried to placate Susskind by allowing him to do another show on the civil rights movement, a topic that dominated the news every day at the time. Efforts to get blacks registered to vote were under way in Mississippi, and Martin Luther King Jr. was leading protests in Selma and Birmingham, Alabama, to end segregation. Under the benign title "The American Negro Speaks His Mind," Susskind booked actor and singer Harry Belafonte and novelist James Baldwin as guests for a program to air on May 12, 1963. Belafonte was a friend and one of the most highly visible celebrity allies of Dr. King. Baldwin had emerged as a powerful voice on the state of race relations in America thanks largely to *The Fire Next Time,* his manifesto on the issue first published in *The New Yorker.* The writer eventually led a cadre of prominent black Americans in a meeting with Attorney General Robert F. Kennedy. Baldwin warned Kennedy that northern cities could be faced with "an explosive situation" equal to what was happening in the South if President Kennedy's administration did not move faster on battling desegregation and discrimination. Korn balked at the pairing of Belafonte and Baldwin. He believed having two high-profile names at the forefront of the movement "would not offer a broad enough base of enlightened opinion" and demanded that Susskind add more voices to the program. There is no record of who Korn had in mind to balance the panel. Nevertheless, Susskind refused and girded himself for a fight. "David never backed away from these things," said Jean Kennedy. "In fact he rather relished it."

The dispute came to a boil at the end of April 1963, two months before Susskind's contract with WNEW was set to expire. If Susskind sensed or knew that *Open End* was going to be dumped by the station, he was not going to give Korn the satisfaction of announcing it. Susskind called reporters on a weekend to tell them he was not going to renew his deal with WNEW because he was tired of Korn's constant editorial interference. He presented a litany of examples, including the demands Korn imposed on the panel with Belafonte and Baldwin.

Korn fired back the following day. At a press conference at his WNEW office, he claimed he had planned months before to drop *Open End*. He said he had "lost all confidence in Susskind" as a moderator and had fired him. "I told him last March that the show would not be renewed," Korn told reporters. "Out of courtesy, we refrained from announcing this until he had found a new home. But his discourtesy and inability to accept this separation with grace and his attacks on our programming compel us to speak." He showed a clip from the banned *Open End* episode with Ginzburg's remarks about premarital sex. Ginzburg was sitting among the reporters at the press conference. He stood up and lambasted Korn, calling his action "one of the most outrageous instances of censorship by a businessman." A security guard led him out of the office. In response to Korn's statements, Susskind described his former employer as "a delicatessen proprietor. He should sell liverwurst, not entertainment."

After the relationship with WNEW was severed, Susskind was ready to go ahead and tape the panel with Belafonte and Baldwin. The discussion would air on the twenty stations that carried *Open End* outside of New York. But the two men wanted no part of the circus going on around Susskind's program and backed out. "Under the present climate of charge and countercharge involving a personal controversy between you and [WNEW], we are convinced that the importance of the subject of the American Negro speaks his mind would become obscured," Belafonte and Baldwin jointly wrote in a telegram to Susskind. "Therefore, we both feel that we have no alternative but to withhold indefinitely any commitment to you or Channel 5."

An upset Susskind felt abandoned. "Let's get one thing straight," he wrote back to Belafonte. "My only quarrel with Channel 5 involves your appearance and the right of you two men to speak forth, and their insistence upon watering you down and minimizing your militancy. Your wire and your attitude can't shake my ideals, but they do feed a growing cynicism about human beings and their lack of guts."

Korn considered himself a victor over Susskind when he had lunch with the FBI assistant director Cartha "Deke" DeLoach on May 3. They were out

to celebrate the station's production of "Wonderama Visits the FBI," in which
Sonny Fox toured the bureau headquarters with a group of children. But, as
DeLoach reported in his memo about the lunch, Korn talked incessantly
about Susskind and how his talk show "persisted in depicting the American
people in the worst possible way." Korn presented a fuller and perhaps embel-
lished version of the recent events that led to the announcement that WNEW
had dropped *Open End*. He told DeLoach that he didn't want Baldwin and
Belafonte on the program because he believed they would "use the racial
problem to enhance their own prestige." He boasted of standing up to Susskind who, he claimed, threatened to "march upon [WNEW] television studios with a large bunch of Negros" in protest.

A copy of a newswire story reporting how Susskind was dropped by WNEW
landed on the desk of Hoover. "Good riddance to bad rubbish!!" the director
wrote at the bottom of the dispatch before it circulated through his office.

The aftermath of the conflict left Susskind without an outlet for *Open End*
in New York, the city where it mattered most for him to be seen. Once the
program was gone, even the critics who were exasperated by the host's occasional pomposity and long-windedness missed the weekly window into American society seldom offered elsewhere on television. "No one can match his
particular virtuosity in framing a question of such intricacy that *Open End*
looked as if it had five moderators and one guest," Jack Gould wrote in *The
New York Times*. "But nonetheless, *Open End* is not without virtue. . . . Even
his curiosity about the more superficial aspects of contemporary life, such as
giving two hours to members of the jet set, can be a revealing commentary on
existing mores. The value of Susskind is not always understood: in many ways
he is a remarkable mirror of the nineteen sixties."

Susskind climbed out of the wreckage and went on to deliver one of the most
compelling and important talk shows he ever did. Leaders in the civil rights
movement expressed growing frustration that President Kennedy was slow to
respond to the exploding violence between police and black protesters in the
South. Dr. Martin Luther King, who had been traveling around the country
with his message, accepted an invitation to sit for a one-on-one interview with
David Susskind on *Open End*.

Jean Kennedy doesn't recall any elaborate negotiations to get Dr. King to
appear at such a critical juncture of his movement. He had been a guest on *Open
End* several times before and was said to be wary of Susskind's penchant for
provocative questions. "I just called him and he said he'd come in," she said.

She believed the show's length, then two hours, was the draw. "For someone like that, it was probably a plus," she said. "I also think David was very sympathetic to him. David was not supposed to be taking sides, but he often did." Susskind was friendly with many of the star performers, such as Paul Newman, Sidney Poitier, and Shelley Winters, who supported King. Susskind's call sheet indicated that Belafonte and King invited him to a meeting at Belafonte's apartment on March 29, 1963. It was to discuss King's move into Birmingham, "where he expects to be arrested," the message said. When Dr. King was sitting in a Birmingham jail that April, Susskind was one of many prominent Americans who sent a telegram imploring President Kennedy to step in. Susskind's wife Phyllis had enrolled herself, her husband, and their children as lifetime members of the NAACP. She eventually went to Jackson, Mississippi, to help in a voter registration drive.

On June 6, Susskind taped a full two-hour program with King. When Susskind wasn't puffing on a cigarette, his clasped hands remained on his lap instead of chopping the air as they often did. His questions were pointed and cogent and he allowed King time to give expansive answers without interruption. Susskind introduced King as a great man, but his deference didn't keep him from making the type of inquiries that might have been on the minds of fearful whites.

"Is the Negro community aflame as never before?" Susskind asked. "Is the suspicion or the fear of some that we are on a collision course between the patience of the Negro and the procrastination of the white community?"

King skillfully steered clear of any antagonistic language, using such words as "discontent," "impatience," "despair," and "frustration" to describe how black Americans felt in regard to the lack of progress toward ending segregation and discrimination. They were not going to give up. "There will be no stopping point until there is justice and freedom," he said, adding that if his nonviolent approach did not succeed, more militant groups will see it as an opportunity to come in. Susskind asked about white fears over miscegenation, to which King quipped, with a straight face, "the Negro wants to be the white man's brother, not his brother-in-law."

Dr. King saved his toughest words for President Kennedy, whom he believed had not lived up to his campaign promises. "If we don't get a strong civil rights message and proposal from the president . . . we will see ourselves in a deeper situation of chaos," he warned. When Susskind asked him to compare the current White House's performance on civil rights to the Eisenhower administration, King said Kennedy had substituted "an inadequate approach for a miserable one." That remark landed the interview on the front page of *The New York Times.*

Near the end of the program, Susskind calmly asked King if he considered it "a miracle" that he had not been murdered. The question sounded shocking and sensational on the surface. But in light of the turmoil, intense emotion, and violent death that embroiled the civil rights movement, it was totally appropriate. King calmly recounted the daily threats on his life that he received and admitted to having pondered why there had been no actual attempt to kill him up to that time. "I'm religious enough to say that this is the grace of God," said the leader who five years hence would die from an assassin's bullet.

King appeared relaxed but restrained throughout the exchange. After the interview ended and the credits rolled on-screen, he remained seated and looked straight ahead while a fidgety Susskind bounced up from his director's chair, flipped another cigarette in between his lips, and unclasped the lavaliere microphone from around his guest's neck. King was completely still, as if he knew the audience was evaluating his every move.

Just hours after the taping, Susskind sold the King show to Fred Thrower, who ran WNEW's main independent TV station competitor, WPIX. It's not likely that Thrower, an extremely conservative man, was sympathetic to King or his movement. TV host Clay Cole said Thrower often gave him and his producer Kenny Johnson a hard time about booking many black music artists on the station's teen dance show and demanded to inspect photos of them in advance. "He described them as pinhead niggers," said Johnson. But the King interview was the chance for Thrower to steal some thunder from a market rival.

Susskind received $500 from WPIX for the King interview and was promised a portion of the ad revenues from the program. WPIX aired the interview on June 9 with the rest of the stations that carried *Open End.* Shortly afterward, Jean Kennedy received a telephone call from Malcolm X, then still aligned with the Black Muslims and increasingly critical of King's adherence to nonviolence. The conversation reflected the rivalry that existed between the two leaders at the time. "He called me to tell me how many girlfriends Dr. King had," Kennedy recalled.

But King's message on *Open End* echoed over the dramatic newspaper images of Governor George Wallace facing off with federal marshals over the admittance of black students to the University of Alabama. Two days after the civil rights leader's appearance, President Kennedy gave a 16-minute televised address in prime time. The nation faced a "moral crisis," he declared, unless it addressed the need to end segregation and discrimination. He announced his plan for sweeping civil rights legislation. Congress passed it into law that same month. Not long after that, WPIX announced that it would start carrying Susskind's *Open End* on a weekly basis in the coming fall.

11

East Side/West Side premiered on September 23, 1963, with an episode called "The Sinner." George C. Scott, playing Neil Brock, fights to help Layna Harris, a prostitute and unmarried mother (played by Carol Rossen, wife of director Richard Rossen), keep her baby when the father's mother tries to get custody. Judged harshly by her hausfrau neighbors, Layna is unapologetic about her profession and defends her fitness as a parent. "It helps support me and the kid. You see my baby's furniture . . . that's paid for." She is not presented as a misunderstood saint. When Brock first calls on her, she initially thinks he's looking for her services, and their scene together is played with a bit of flirtatiousness that would be inappropriate between a social worker and his client. He leaves impressed by the pleasant, well-lit nursery Layna has set up for her baby in the dreary walk-up apartment building and agrees to take up her case. But later, when Brock brings a family court judge to the apartment for a surprise visit, they find Layna in the hallway, drunk and with a john (played by a young Alan Alda). She pounds on doors and lashes out at her cruel, disapproving neighbors. Brock expresses his rage that Layna's behavior has destroyed her chances to keep her child. During his rant, he violently pulls a blond wig off Layna's head (again played with a hint of sexual suggestiveness). In the episode's final act, when Brock and a family court matron remove the child from Layna's apartment, the woman's plaintive cries asking for another chance echo through the stairwell of the tenement.

Within days, Susskind's office received letters from social workers across the country with detailed critiques of nearly every aspect of Neil Brock's behavior in his job. Overall, they were not happy. "If someone on my staff walked out on a human being when her emotional turmoil was at such an impossible pitch, I would have fired him," wrote one social service director. "At the point the prostitute mother needs him most, he leaves her screaming, tortured, and possibly suicidal."

"Caseworkers never touch a client except in cases of hysteria, epilepsy, or clearly indicated violence," was the message from the Essex County Welfare Board in Newark, New Jersey.

"We have a difficult time as it is," said two graduates from the Columbia University School of Social Work. "So don't compound the misery."

The dramaturgy in the early episodes, written before Arnold Perl took over, was clunky. There were long and often didactic dialogues between characters about the sociological causes and bureaucratic insensitivities that created or worsened the circumstances of those Brock tries to help. Episodes frequently ended without clear resolution. Still the show lived up to its commitment to confront social problems head-on: mental illness, alcoholism, welfare, gambling addiction, caring for the mentally disabled and the aged, and juvenile delinquency. Scott was particularly proud of a show about a longtime grocer forced to relocate his business and his family because the city wants to build a new playground on the property he leases and manages. (The show had a thinly disguised depiction of New York Planning Commissioner Robert Moses and his role in destroying stable, functioning city neighborhoods in the name of urban renewal.) The actor wrote and paid for his own newspaper ads soliciting viewer responses. "The establishment of a direct avenue of communication between creative people in television and a potentially creative audience is of vital concern to me," Scott's ad earnestly stated. "I assure you I will read your letter."

Most of the early reviews for *East Side/West Side* were positive, praising its attempt at realism. "In certain scenes last night the squalor was so real you could smell it," columnist Harriet Van Horne wrote about the premiere episode. Even those critics who didn't love the show, such as Cleveland Amory in *TV Guide,* cheered the courage of the producers and CBS for putting it on. "You owe it to your conscience not only to see it but also to see that it stays on," he wrote. Any weaknesses in the stories were mitigated by the compelling performances of George C. Scott, who played Brock with a relaxed, naturalistic acting style. He took his time on screen, displaying idiosyncratic tics and a vocal range that could quickly shift from a gravelly rumble to the menacing holler he delivered in *The Hustler.*

"To have an actor of George's caliber on the screen every week was extraordinary," said Alan Shayne, who handled the casting for *East Side/West Side* and numerous other Talent Associates productions. "We had all the best actors in New York working on the show. They were very real. They were wonderful."

While the casting of Cicely Tyson was heralded as a breakthrough, her character was given little to do on most of the shows. As a secretary, Jane Foster was largely a gatekeeper for the other social workers in the office. But Tyson broke through in the small moments she was given. She was allowed to play the part as sexy and knowingly smart-mouthed when necessary, when dealing with blacks and whites alike. Her elocution was flawless. Not for a moment was she ever subservient. She was an equal. A production memo instructing the show's writers on her part said, "She is by no means the house Negro." America had never seen a black woman like her on television. Scott constantly hounded the producers and the network to expand her role. He even wrote a detailed outline of a two-part story where Jane Foster attends New York University at night to get her master's degree in social work and leads a clean-up drive in her East Harlem neighborhood. Scott often had well-intentioned ideas for the series but was unable to turn them into compelling drama, and, like many, this one never made it to the script stage.

One aspect of Tyson's TV presence was stirring debate in the black community—her natural hairstyle. Short, kinky, and unprocessed, it enhanced the perfect roundness of the top of her head. She was beautiful by any standard, except perhaps by the one set by white America at the time. Her look began to change that.

"My hair started the whole natural trend in this country," Tyson said. Natural hair had long been a subject of debate in the black community and the black press, and Tyson got bags of mail on the topic. Half of the letters came from beauty salon owners and hairdressers who complained that Jane Foster's look was bad for business. After seeing Tyson on *East Side/West Side,* customers wanted to emulate her look by cutting off their hair and no longer straightening or chemically processing it.

Others criticized her choice by saying she misused the tremendous platform she had been given on a TV show watched by millions of people—most of them white—each week. "They said I was in a position to extol the beauty of black women and instead I was destroying it by wearing my hair in that fashion," she said. She understood the sentiment. "We had been brainwashed to believe that we had no worth at all unless it's ratified by whites," she said. "It's taken us a long time to recognize our own beauty. We were brainwashed to believe our beauty was minuscule in the scheme of things. That included our nappy hair. So we were to follow the pattern of straight hair. That was the model for us to follow—and I dared not to."

Wearing a natural was a decision Tyson had made in 1959 when she had been hired for a play performed on one of CBS's Sunday morning programs. She had the role of a traditional African woman married to an upwardly mobile African man during a time of social and political upheaval in the continent. "I wanted to stay with the old customs, the old culture, very happy living there with my family," she said. "He was progressive, he wanted to move on. Countries were becoming independent. All during the time I was rehearsing, my hair was rather long and I straightened it. And I didn't feel comfortable because it was not true to the woman."

The night before the live show was scheduled to air, Tyson traveled up to a barbershop in Harlem. She asked the barber to cut off her hair. "He cut it short," she recalled. "He took the wrap off and said, 'How do you like it?' I said, 'No, that's not what I want. I want you to cut my hair to its natural state and then wash it so that it goes back.'" The stunned barber sat down in a chair to catch his breath and asked Tyson to repeat what she had just told him. She did.

"Are you sure that's what you want me to do?" he asked. Tyson assured him that it was and sat with her eyes closed as he continued to cut. When he was done, he led her to the sink and washed her hair. As she looked at herself in the mirror, the barber said, "Now you know what a beautiful woman looks like with her hair cut off."

Tyson showed up at the studio the next day for the live telecast with her hair wrapped in a kerchief. After getting into costume and makeup, she took her place on stage and revealed her new look. The director walked up to her. "Cicely," he said. "You cut your hair." He stared silently for a moment at her head before he added, "I wanted to ask you, but I didn't have the nerve."

Tyson's hair was never an issue when she signed on to *East Side/West Side*. "I asked them, 'What do you want me to do with the hair, and they said, 'The hair? Leave it that way,'" she said.

No matter what they thought of her hair, black Americans saw Tyson's presence on the show as a source of pride. Fans frequently stopped her on the streets of Manhattan to tell her so when she was traveling from Biograph Studio in the Bronx to the off-Broadway theater where she was still appearing in *The Blacks*. "I wasn't making any money," she said. "I was still doing my show at night. It was very exciting. It was fun."

Tyson felt nothing but affection from Scott, Elizabeth Wilson, and the show's producers. Whenever she was in the Talent Associates offices, Susskind and Arrick would gently needle her about her relationship with jazz trumpet legend Miles Davis, whom she would marry years later. "It was my first time around with Miles and they all knew him," she said. "They used to tease me all the time."

For the most part, Scott protected her from hearing any of the discussions with network brass about how large a role Jane Foster should have on *East Side/West Side*. But she was aware it was a source of acrimony. "I knew there was constant battling between Jim Aubrey and George," she recalled. "It was every single day. I could feel the tension." Admittedly naïve about the world of ratings, advertisers, and network affiliates, she had no idea her role ultimately endangered the show's existence. The network's concerns heightened when they saw the seventh episode, titled "Who Do You Kill?" Written by Arnold Perl, the episode was the most trenchant dramatic depiction of discrimination and urban poverty ever shown on network television up to that time. Racism was frequently tackled on dramas during the 1963–1964 TV season, but the villains were almost always misguided individuals or bigots. "Who Do You Kill?" focused on the systemic problems that led to the misery experienced by a young, attractive black couple living in a rodent-infested tenement in Harlem. Diana Sands was Ruth Goodwin, who worked as a waitress at a seedy neighborhood tavern. James Earl Jones, in his first TV role, was her husband Joe, who went to a trade school and took care of their infant daughter on the nights Ruth worked.

While they quarrel in the tenement hallway about the state of their lives, they hear their daughter's piercing screams from inside the apartment. The child had been bitten by a rat. The little girl eventually dies and the episode's denouement is whether the devastated and despondent Ruth will pull herself together for the baby's funeral.

East Side/West Side producer Don Kranze said that during his career of forty-five years he had only seen a few scripts that were as good as "Who Do You Kill?" When he had first read it that summer of 1963, he commanded the crew to give the show every possible chance to succeed. His instructions were: Don't worry about overtime. Build extra sets. Don't cut corners. "I consider it to be the very best television script I have ever read and I want to give it that sort of treatment," he wrote to the show's production designer. Bob Israel had Kenyon Hopkins compose a loping, jazzy closing theme especially for the episode.

Rather than just shocking the viewer, Perl's script showed the harsh realities of the Goodwins' lives. No car or taxi stopped to pick up a terrified Joe Goodwin as he stood in the center of a Harlem street holding his bleeding child. Brock, Freida Hechlinger, and Jane Foster seek a way to lift the Goodwins out of their decayed surroundings. They attempt to get Joe Goodwin a job that would be better than "cleaning toilets at Grand Central Station," an opportunity that his wife says is readily available but unacceptable to him. But the social workers were stymied as union apprentice programs were closed to black men such as Goodwin.

The title referred to a speech Neil Brock gives when trying to explain Joe's simmering rage at the hospital where he has brought his daughter. "He didn't say anything, but it was written all over his face. Who do I kill? My baby's been bitten by a rat. Who do I strangle?" While some of the lines in the script were a bit relentless in driving home the show's message, the subtle performances of Scott, Sands, and Jones made them work. Director Tom Gries shot on the streets of Harlem in a documentary style, showing children playing on sidewalks where trash is piled high and young men gathered aimlessly on building steps. It was a searing glimpse of urban blight beamed right into America's living rooms.

Sands and Jones played the Goodwins as emotionally complex characters rather than earnest symbolic victims. There is even a scene that suggests the couple found time to comfort each other in the midst of their daughter's medical crisis by having sex.

Jones believed the story accurately depicted racial anger as a form of depression. In the penultimate scene, a neighborhood preacher comes to the Goodwins' apartment to see Ruth. He pontificates about the struggles of Harriet Tubman, in an effort to convince Ruth to show up at the baby's funeral. "As he droned on and on, meaninglessly, she got more enraged," Jones said. "You could see it in her body and in her face. She began to explode in a very slow and quiet and scary way."

The anguish that Jones instilled in his character resulted in the production being shut down at one point during the shooting. In the shattering moment in which the Goodwins discover what had happened to their daughter, Jones grabbed a broom and started slashing it inside the crib. "I was caught up in the hysteria and Diana had gotten in front of me and picked the baby up," he said. "The baby panicked and wouldn't stop crying all day." The film crew had to stop work.

After the script for "Who Do You Kill?" first came to CBS execs, they expressed their misgivings (the original title was "The Gift of Laughter," perhaps a clever ploy by Perl to keep its uncompromising content under the radar for as long as possible). Larry White of CBS dismissed the script as a way for Perl to get rid of his own "social guilt." But Dan Melnick said the network agreed to give the episode a go-ahead if the producers could prove that anyone in New York was actually dying from rat bites. Hundreds of city residents, many of them infants, were bitten each year, but fatalities were rare. Emily Perl Kingsley was responsible for checking the accuracy of the situations portrayed in every *East Side/West Side* script. She succeeded in getting the New York Department of Health to supply her with information on a rat bite–related death in Brooklyn that occurred several years earlier.

More than 20 million people watched *East Side/West Side* the night "Who Do You Kill?" first aired on November 2, 1963. While critics had been lauding the series for its good intentions, the episode was hailed as its first true dramatic triumph. Even Jack O'Brien, the columnist who had taunted Susskind for years in the pages of the *New York Journal-American,* heaped praise on the episode.

Cicely Tyson, who grew up in East Harlem, remembers how incredulous people were after the episode aired. "They didn't believe that people lived like that in these United States, in the city of New York," she said. "They thought it was made up. I never thought of it as something that was a television show, because it was real to me. If anything crossed my mind it was that people will see how other people, the poorest blacks, live in this city. The story was very familiar to me. Not in Harlem but in the area in the East Side, from 96th Street to 106th Street east of Fifth Avenue. My whole life was spent in that area. I knew the story. It was very real to me."

Viewer mail for the episode was overwhelmingly positive too. "It is gratifying to see the plight of the Negro portrayed in such a seemingly realistic light," wrote a viewer from Morristown, New Jersey. "The program dramatically and graphically made believable and immediate the protests we have heard before only in speeches." The show may have even motivated the city to act on its rodent problem. Two months after it aired, New York mayor Robert

Wagner approved a massive $1 million extermination program aimed at ridding slum tenements of rats. Most of the buildings were targeted in Harlem, where thousands of tenants went on rent strikes—withholding payments because of the deplorable conditions.

But viewers in some parts of the country never saw "Who Do You Kill?" The CBS affiliate in Atlanta felt the episode would inflame racial tensions in the city and chose not to air it. Stations in other southern states refused to carry the show as well. At the time, network-affiliated stations had the discretion on what they would show in their markets. (*East Side/West Side* never aired on the CBS affiliate in Connecticut, where the Ku Klux Klan was still active at the time.) It was a sign of the troubles ahead for the show.

SUSSKIND AND TALENT ASSOCIATES aspired to make a show that spoke truthfully about the real world, and that commitment made the traumatic events of November 22, 1963, all the more difficult to handle. The *East Side/West Side* crew was shooting a particularly grim episode on location in the lower Manhattan neighborhood of the Bowery. George C. Scott had insisted on authentic locations, the grittier the better. The story centered on a vagrant, played by Maureen Stapleton, who begs Neil Brock to help her get her Bowery derelict boyfriend to stop drinking wood alcohol. Rather than go to a liquor merchant, the man had taken to scrounging enough change to get a can of paint thinner from the hardware store to satisfy his fix. In one of the location shots, there was an actual derelict lying on the sidewalk.

Shortly after 2:00 p.m., news from Dallas, Texas, circulated among the cast and crew. There were reports of gunfire at President John F. Kennedy's motorcade traveling through Deeley Plaza. Within half an hour, they would learn that the thirty-fifth president of the United States, whose idealism inspired the series they were creating, was dead. Stapleton started crying hysterically. The production manager on the set called Larry Arrick at the Talent Associates offices. Arrick told them to stop shooting even though there were several more pages of the script to finish. "I went into David's office and said, 'Listen, I just shut down *East Side/West Side*,'" Arrick recalled. "David said, 'Of course.'"

But Susskind could not afford to stop another production that day, a TV play for NBC's *DuPont Show of the Week*. He had already paid for the rental of NBC's Brooklyn studio for the weekend and there was no time to reschedule the taping before the show's airdate. His decision to go ahead with the program over the next few days reflected the fragile state of Talent Associates' finances.

The play by Nicholas Baehr, called *Ride with Terror*, told the story of two hoodlums who terrorize a group of disparate passengers during a late-night ride on a Lexington Avenue subway. As each passenger is subjected to cruel harassment and at times violent treatment at the hands of the thugs, the others stand by and watch helplessly. The frightening ordeal goes on until a soldier from the South traveling with his Brooklyn buddy uses a heavy plaster cast on his arm to subdue the thugs after he gets stabbed by one of them. One critic described the play as a parable on a modern American society, where too many people are unwilling or unable to stand up to the extremism of a few.

Tony Musante, a young Italian-American stage actor from Connecticut with a mass of dark curly hair, was cast in the lead role of Ferrone, the more menacing of the two subway punks. The show marked Musante's first time performing in front of a camera. He later learned that economics had everything to do with his big break. "I know that Susskind's operation was in trouble financially because that's the reason the script came to me," Musante said. "I was an unknown and most of the people in the cast, if not all, were little-known New York actors (including Gene Hackman and Ron Leibman). They couldn't do a big-budget show. That's how I got the chance. It was very lucky for me that it was staged as a play being shot with a camera, because that's very similar to working in the theater, which was my only background at that point."

Musante had met Susskind earlier that week during a rehearsal held in the space above Ratner's Delicatessen on Manhattan's Lower East Side. The producer's watchful eye made some members of the cast, especially Musante, a bit nervous. "We were not accustomed to having David Susskind there. I mean, you realize David Susskind was very important. His operation may have been fragile at that point economically, but the weight he carried as a producer was monumental," Musante said. "He's observing the show for the first time and he starts following the cameraman around, plotting his shots. And I was wearing contact lenses, and one of my lenses slipped. But I felt—just keep on going, because this is a run-through. And at a certain point, as I was accosting one of the passengers on the subway. I looked up, and there's David Susskind's face, not more than twelve inches from mine. He's studying my emotional output, right? And here I am, thinking, 'Oh my God, I hope he doesn't see my lens floating around in my eye.'"

On the day of President Kennedy's death, Musante left his apartment on Horatio Street in lower Manhattan with his neighbor and fellow cast member Ron Leibman and took the subway to Brooklyn. They were several hours into a rehearsal when an NBC News radio report being fed into speakers in the studio revealed the news. "Everybody was shocked and stunned and we stopped," Musante said. As they waited for more details, a rumor started circulating around the set that it was two hoodlums who had shot Kennedy. "Well, of course, that was not true, and I don't know where that rumor started," said Musante. "But here we are in this show, two hoodlums on a subway, terrorizing a group of passengers. It immediately had another emotional effect on us."

The show's director, Ron Winston, told the actors and crew to take a break for a couple of hours while he talked with Susskind, who instructed him to continue. When the cast and crew reconvened, Winston asked that they walk through the rest of the play before resuming work in the morning. "One thing that Ron Winston said that I have never forgotten," Musante recalled. "He said, 'I know this is difficult, but nobody will know what you have to go through this weekend. The only thing that matters to the audience is the residue, which is what they see on the screen. So I want you all to go home and try to pull yourselves together. Because when we come in tomorrow, we have to work as though nothing has happened.' And I've never forgotten that. Because I've been in many situations since where there's been all kinds of conflict or problems in the production of a project. And I've always remembered Ron saying, 'It's the residue that counts.'"

Musante believed that the events of the weekend added to the raw emotion that came out in the performances in *Ride with Terror*. But the process was torturous. The rest of the Friday rehearsal was useless as the actors, cameramen, and boom microphone men were weeping over the horrific news about the president. Taping began Saturday morning at 8:00 a.m. and wasn't completed until 3:30 a.m. the next day. The worst part, according to Musante, was when the cast sat idly by while the crew tried to fix a faulty camera. "We'd have waits of an hour, an hour and a half, while lights had to be adjusted, cameras had to be removed from where they were and put in different positions because it wasn't working, one way or another," he said. "The times of not actually being in the performance were devastating, because it took us back to what was going on in Texas, and in D.C. By the time it got to midnight, everybody was tired. Everybody's emotions were on edge. And we had to keep going."

Reality collided with the show again a few days later. William Safire, working as a public relations consultant for the New York World's Fair, had already asked NBC and Talent Associates to put a disclaimer on *Ride with Terror,* saying it was not based on an actual event. Safire said out-of-town visitors coming to the fair might get the impression that the subway system was unsafe. That impression was more likely to be reinforced by an actual incident that occurred two days before the December 1 airdate for the show. Three teenagers were charged with killing a New York City police detective on a Brooklyn subway. Susskind and Melnick refused to put up the disclaimer and NBC backed them up.

When *Ride With Terror* was complete, the cost overruns amounted to $12,480 on a show that was budgeted at $70,000. Looking for a way to cover the loss, Susskind tried to convince NBC that the overruns were caused by the pained state of the cast and crew on hearing news of the assassination. "I am well aware that we are dealing in the most nebulous of all areas when we try to evaluate how human emotion can affect the efficacy of a production," he wrote to an executive at the network. "I am also aware that this was an exceptional circumstance." It's unlikely that Susskind got much sympathy or a reimbursement, since NBC had already likely lost hundreds of thousands from preempting commercial programming for several days to cover the assassination and President Kennedy's funeral.

But the request further revealed the dire straits that Susskind's Talent Associates was approaching. He noted in his letter to NBC that he had not been making a profit on any of the eight DuPont shows his company produced for the network that season. "I do not mind not making a profit," Susskind wrote. "But I cannot endure by actually losing money."

As POWERFUL AS "Who Do You Kill?" was, it also highlighted the basic flaw in *East Side/West Side.* No matter how angry or outraged Neil Brock got, no matter how much empathy he conveyed, there was only so much a social worker could do. "They had, as a star," said Larry Arrick, "George C. Scott. Dynamic. Passionate. The next John Wayne. Craggy, but really good-looking. But just rough, gruff. And they give him a job in which the best thing he can do is prescribe a Band-Aid. He couldn't be the powerful, ruthless, idealistic George C. Scott who gets it done. And if he doesn't get it done, make a little bit of a mess in the office, throw a chair through the window. That was his reputation, those were the kinds of roles he played his whole life as an actor, except on television," Arrick said. "*The Defenders* was so interesting compared to *East Side/West Side*. At the end of fifty-two minutes, there was a decision. It was resolved. Guilty or not guilty. There's a winner and there's a loser. If you're a social worker, there's nothing. You've got this great macho guy. He should be the sheriff. He should be in a western. He should clean up the town and ride away into the sunset. But instead he was a glorified clerk. 'Fill out these papers and I can get you a doctor's appointment in six months, maybe. I can help you pay the rent.' He couldn't really be effective. There's a lot of George standing around in the series." Even Bertram Beck and Harold Weissman, the real-life social workers who consulted on the show, agreed that Brock's occupation didn't easily lend itself to creating satisfying drama.

Arrick proposed that Brock leave the Community Welfare Service office for a job with a congressman, whose district in New York City included constituents of varying social and economic backgrounds. Scott's character was made into an assistant to a young, handsome legislator, Congressman Hanson, modeled after John V. Lindsay, the future mayor of New York. Congressman Lindsay was representing the Silk Stocking District on the Upper East Side of Manhattan. Linden Chiles, a thirty-year-old square-jawed actor, was cast in the Hanson role. Neatly coiffed and tanned, he was the polar opposite of the rumpled, rugged look Scott had developed for Neil Brock. The story called for Hanson to hire Brock away from the Community Welfare Service to work in the congressman's office. Once Brock became part of the team, he'd have a natural adversary—Mike Miller (played by John McMartin), a smooth and cynical public relations adviser to the congressman who challenged the former social worker's idealism. Once the show took a new direction, Arnold Perl, the executive producer who had infused the show with passion and honesty about the issues of the city streets, was gone.

Scott approved of the changes. From the start of the show, he had always pushed for a novelistic approach to *East Side/West Side* in which Neil Brock would evolve over time. "Look at me," Scott said to *TV Guide* at the time. "I'm not the same person I was three years ago. Everybody else changes, why not a TV character?" Scott counted Brock's new job as a small victory after the network had thwarted his intention to serialize the show early on by choosing the order in which the episodes would air. In the first few decades of television, networks were firmly opposed to having any kind of continuing storylines in their series. The thinking was, once viewers knew how a series ended, the rest of the episodes would have no value as repeats. The most extreme example of that came in the final episode of *The Fugitive,* in which the wrongly convicted Richard Kimble catches his wife's killer, a one-armed man, after a pursuit that lasted four seasons. ABC ran the finale in the dog days of August 1967, well after the traditional TV season had ended, so as not to diminish the viewing audience for the show's reruns that summer.

As the new plan for *East Side/West Side* moved forward, Elizabeth Wilson's character was phased out. Cicely Tyson remained on board, possibly because Scott had special plans for her character Jane Foster and Brock—network television's first interracial marriage. "George and I had one of our brief discussions," Kranze recalled. "He said, 'You know, I'm not going to stay in one place in this series. This thing has to change. I have to grow. The characters have to grow. And I'm not going to play the same guy over and over again.' And he says, 'Now, in the second year, I'm going to marry Cicely Tyson.'"

Kranze was dumbfounded that Scott was so disconnected from the reality of what was happening to the series. "I think I told my wife that very night, when I came home," he recalled. "I said, 'We're not playing in the South, as it is. And George says he's going to marry Cicely Tyson in the second year.'" In the East, people might have watched. Amid the storm over *East Side/West Side,* Susskind did a panel on *Open End* with two interracial married couples and the daughter of another mixed marriage. More than 1 million viewers in the New York area tuned in, the biggest audience the talk show ever attracted in the market.

The uneasiness of the network and sponsors of *East Side/West Side* only intensified after an episode called "No Hiding Place." It examined the illegal real estate tactic known at the time as blockbusting. Preying on the prejudices and fears of homeowners, speculators scared whites into selling their homes below market price and then resold them to black buyers at a premium. Ruby Dee and Earl Hyman played the Marsdens, a well-educated, middle-class black couple who moved to an all-white middle-class suburban tract in Long Island, next door to Neil Brock's college pal Chuck Severson, portrayed by Joseph Campanella. (Much of the episode was shot on location in the Lake Success neighborhood of Great Neck.) Real estate brokers create a panic in the area, looking for fearful residents to sell their homes cheaply. Enlisted by Severson, Brock tries to get the neighborhood to resist the effort. He suggests his friends throw a party where the skittish neighbors can meet the new couple. The scene was originally filmed with Scott and Dee dancing together at the party. But viewers never saw it. CBS demanded that their dancing be cut.

Many of the internal squabbles inside the production of *East Side/West Side* stayed out of the press. This one did not. Scott called newspaper reporters to express his anger over the excised scene. (CBS defended the edits with the claim that it was unlikely dancing would occur at such a party. But the edits couldn't completely keep the dancing of the other white couples out of the shot.)

It was around this time that CBS president Jim Aubrey had seen enough. He called a meeting with David Susskind and informed him that if he wanted to see a second season for *East Side/West Side,* Cicely Tyson could not be a part of it. CBS affiliated stations throughout the South were not airing the show, and advertisers were growing more uncomfortable with the controversial content. While the show's main sponsors, Philip Morris and Whitehall Pharmacal, had stuck with it, other commercial time was going unsold. CBS was said to be losing $80,000 a week on *East Side/West Side.*

Arrick recalled that Susskind had summoned him to his office after the meeting. He explained the situation to Arrick, who sensed that Susskind was willing to go along with the decision if it meant keeping *East Side/West Side* on the air. "His rationale was the show was too important to sacrifice over an actor. I said, 'David, it's not an actor. It's an issue. It's an issue that we, because of the nature of the program, should be sensitive to.' It's a particularly ugly kind of censorship because it's racism." Others who worked for Susskind at the time said it was highly unlikely he would have even considered firing Tyson. Even Melnick, who did not look back fondly on his partnership with Susskind, said he did not think it was possible. "I don't think David would have gone for it," he said. "He could never have figured out a way to live with the publicity."

Susskind ultimately did not go for it. But he did instruct Arrick to present Aubrey's demand to Scott because of the actor's ownership stake in the program. Perhaps he knew how his volatile star would react.

"So I went to George," Arrick said. "And I said, 'Listen, there's a good chance we can get renewed for a whole season. There's only one thing they want, George. They want me to fire Cicely Tyson and hire a white secretary for you.' And George said, 'You know, I don't feel well. You'll get a call from my doctor.' And he went home." The next day Talent Associates received a letter from Scott's physician saying the actor was ill and unable to work.

Susskind and Melnick had no idea whether Scott would return, so they had the producers draw up plans on how to continue the series without him. They considered building the show around the Congressman Hanson character. But within a few days Scott returned. Tyson had not been fired (although her role was minimized in the Hanson episodes), and the cancellation axe continued to hang over the show.

The *East Side/West Side* writers weren't happy with the new direction of the show. Allan Sloane sent the producers his thoughts about the new format in a memo he titled "The Three-Dollar Bill," a screed about how the show had sacrificed its authenticity and principles. The writing staff had also grown tired of Scott's interference, which wasn't always constructive. "George respects the craft of acting," story editor Arthur Singer told Susskind. "So do I. But I have very deep respect for the craft of writing and for structure in the medium in which I'm working. George doesn't." Sloane nearly came to blows with the actor during the first reading of his script for an episode called "No Wings At All." Theodore Bikel played a shoe repair shop owner who had trouble caring for his mentally retarded son. Bikel's character lectures Brock about how there is no way the social worker can truly empathize with the endless daily struggles raising the boy, who was turning into an uncontrollable man-child. "Can you conceive of living your life with a child one of you has to be with every minute?" Bikel's character says. "With the two of you never alone except in bed—and even then you're afraid you'll make a mistake and bring another one into the world?" Scott wanted the line out. "It's a line the father would never say," Scott said. "Nobody would ever say that." It was the most offensive criticism you could give to a writer about a character he invented. Sloane knew the line had truth. "Not only would the father in the story say that line, but a father did," he told Scott. Sloane's own son was autistic and emotionally disturbed. After Sloane held up the script and threatened to shred it in half, Scott backed down.

The chances of *East Side/West Side* being renewed dimmed with each passing day in December 1963. Susskind and Melnick pulled out the stops to try to save the series by soliciting public acclaim. They sent letters to more than a hundred politicians, White House cabinet members, college presidents, writers, and other opinion leaders, pleading for their comments and support. The list included Secretary General of the United Nations U Thant, Richard Nixon, John Steinbeck, Isaac Stern, and every liberal and moderate member of the U.S. Senate. But politicians and cultural leaders in 1963 had no need or inclination to show a hint of familiarity with TV or any aspect of popular culture. Only the office of then attorney general Robert F. Kennedy offered a commendation of the program. Most of the respondents—and there were few—said they hadn't seen the show or were simply unwilling to take a stand on it. The most bizarre response came from Harry J. Anslinger, the retired commissioner of narcotics for the Treasury Department. As the country's first drug czar, he was best known for his zealous warnings about the dangers of marijuana. "I was not much impressed with the program I saw," he wrote to Susskind. "The actor Scott has a fine voice, very similar to Adlai Stevenson. As a suggestion, you might include a program on medical quackery. The Food and Drug Administration has many dramatic cases on this racket. Don't forget to include the use of marijuana, which leads to heroin and its destruction."

The New York Times ran a story on December 27, 1963, about the new format for *East Side/West Side* with the headline "George Scott, TV Social Worker, Changing Job." Dan Melnick tried his best to spin the plan. "We feel restricted," he told the paper. "All the welfare agency stories have been used. With Scott in a new job, we will have a wider choice of stories. Scott will be involved in social welfare work in the congressman's office, but he will also have many new opportunities. Maybe he can be an influence in changing some social patterns through legislation."

The episodes with Congressman Hanson were set to start airing on February 3, 1964. But CBS canceled the show in late January, before the audience could even weigh in. Susskind and Melnick had production manager David Golden send a memo to the cast and crew explaining the network's decision: "Many stations refused to carry the show because it had a running part for a Negro actress and because it dealt with some of the problems facing minority groups, especially the Negroes. The second reason was that many sponsors felt they could not buy the show because it was not a 'happy' show and that its mood might affect the sales of sponsors' products."

In the second week of March 1964, Scott shot his final scene in the last episode of *East Side/West Side,* called "Here Today." Inspired by the closures of big-city newspapers across the country (three New York dailies shut down after the 114-day strike that led to Pete Hamill's brief employment on the show's production staff), "Here Today" told the story of the demise of a fictional New York broadsheet called *The Light.* "But it was really about the loss of *East Side/West Side,*" said Arrick.

The script by Allan Sloane included some not so subtle references to the tensions between CBS and the producers of the series. In one scene, Brock and Congressman Hanson take the editor of *The Light* to a meeting with a bank executive in the hope of rescuing the financially strapped publication. The banker suggests it would be possible if the lending institution could set conditions about editorial content for the paper.

The editor, played by Will Geer, interpreted the offer for Brock and Hanson. "Steer clear of anything controversial like issues. . . . Just turn the sheet into a comic book, a coupon clipper's paradise. Turn your back on all that garbage about rats, tenements, and juvenile delinquency and let's have some laughs."

In the final act, *The Light* is shut down. After learning of the paper's demise, Brock enters the men's room—a scene shot in the actual men's room at Biograph Studios. A porter, played by dwarf actor Michael Dunn, was at work inside. "We had such a hard time finding a mop for him," Arrick recalled. Dunn went into a speech about how the reader is never consulted when a decision is made to kill a newspaper. "They never asked me," the tiny porter said as he mopped the floor and emptied the trash cans that were as tall as he was. "You buy a paper year in and year out and you like it . . . so then one morning or one afternoon you go in and put down your money and boom. No paper. No *Sun*. No *American*. No *Mirror*. No *Light*. I mean, nobody ever asked me. They didn't ask anybody. . . . Why should they? I'm just a lousy reader. Nobody ever asked me. Numbers. Where do they get those numbers? Who does them? Who are *they*? Nobody asked me." Dunn's porter, a heavy-handed representation of the little guy, was really talking about the viewers of *East Side/West Side*.

"It really was on the nose about what we were saying about losing a voice," said Arrick.

No one took the end of the series harder than Scott.

After the porter exited, an anguished Brock went to the sink to wash his face and hands. The script called for Scott to look in the mirror and throw a punch. Scott's hand was to stop just short of the mirror while a camera shot facing him would show the glass being shattered. "Very corny," said Arrick. "We were all very emotional."

But Scott lost control. He started laughing maniacally and put his fist into the mirror, smashing it for real. The camera wasn't set to capture the moment of impact, but it kept rolling and the final image of the series was a dazed Scott with his bloody fist embedded in the shards of broken glass. "George was supposed to fake that," Arrick recalled. "Blood was spurting all over the place." After the director cut, Scott stormed off the set knocking over a crab dolly with a 35-millimeter film camera on his way out. The stunned crew watched as the actor exited Biograph Studios as Neil Brock for the last time. A few hours later, Scott's wife, Colleen Dewhurst, called Arrick from the couple's Riverdale home. "Where's George?" she asked. "He hasn't come home." Arrick said Scott didn't show up for several days. "He had gone on a colossal bender," Arrick said.

When the 1964 Emmy Award nominations were announced, *East Side/ West Side* was nominated for seven categories, including Best Drama Series. Scott was nominated for Best Actor in a Drama. That year, CBS and ABC were unhappy with the voting procedures and the categories used by the National Academy of Television Arts and Sciences to determine the winners. As a result, executives at both networks announced their employees would not participate in the May 25 awards ceremony. In a move that was surely calculated to curry favor with CBS, Susskind and Melnick said their company was boycotting the Emmys as well. They had already sold another series to the network for the 1964–1965 season and were looking to move on from their *East Side/ West Side* experience.

Disdainful of industry awards, George C. Scott had already skipped one Academy Awards presentation in which he was nominated. He would famously go on to sit out another one in 1971, when he won the Oscar for Best Actor in *Patton*. But Scott proudly showed up at the 1964 Emmy Awards ceremony at the Texas Pavilion at the New York World's Fair. He sat at a banquet table with Diana Sands and James Earl Jones, both nominated for their performances in "Who Do You Kill?" They watched and applauded as director Tom Gries went up to the lectern to accept his trophy for his work on the episode.

12

By 1963, David Susskind had split up with his wife Phyllis and moved out of their home at 1125 Fifth Avenue. He lived in apartments at 132 East Seventy-second Street and then on Sutton Place South, where he had a live-in male servant. The Susskinds were not legally separated until January 1965. When the decree from the judge came down, he was ordered to pay his wife $750 per week in support, at the time believed to be the largest amount ever granted by a court in New York state. "I used to hear about that once a week," said Herb Bloom, a producer who worked on *Open End* at the time. But Susskind did not hesitate to agree to the terms or the continued funding of his children's private school and college tuitions.

The demise of the twenty-four-year marriage can be traced to a wintry day in December 1960, when David Susskind and Art Carney were in Chicago to visit the ad agency that handled Sara Lee Kitchens. "You make great cakes, I make great films," Susskind had told the company's executives as he sought their sponsorship of a TV special that starred Carney. After their pitch, they headed back to the airport, but a heavy snowstorm all along the East Coast kept their plane on the ground. No flights were leaving that night, so Susskind and Carney headed back into town with Carney's agent, Bill McCaffrey, for an evening at the Trade Winds nightclub, where Vic Damone was singing. Others have said they went to the Pump Room, the famous restaurant on the city's Gold Coast where there was always a heavy celebrity clientele. Whatever the location was, there is agreement on what ultimately happened that night. While sitting with his party, Susskind spotted a petite blonde with smooth, pastel skin and blue, jewel-like eyes. "Across the room I saw one of the most beautiful women I've ever seen in my life," was how Susskind described to Johnny Carson the moment he first spotted Joyce Davidson. In Canada, Davidson was a TV personality as well known as Susskind was in the States. Her introduction to Susskind that night was the start of a twenty-five-year relationship that included a twenty-year marriage.

Canadian newspaper headlines simply referred to Davidson as "Joyce." She was one of the first female stars on Canadian television. Her breakthrough was certainly helped by her stunning looks, but it also required tireless will and determination. Davidson was born Inez Joyce Brock in 1931, in a farm town outside of Saskatoon, Saskatchewan. Her British father entered a veterans' home after World War II, while her Norwegian mother worked in a Firestone tire factory in Hamilton, Ontario, until a heart condition slowed her down. While still a teenager, Joyce had to get a job to help support her three younger siblings and never graduated from high school.

Around that time, Joyce met Dave Davidson, a metal-lathe operator and amateur hockey player. "She ended up getting pregnant with me and got married," according to Shelley Stallworth, Joyce's oldest daughter, who was born in 1949. Her younger sister, Connie, was born two years later. The young family settled in a working-class neighborhood in Hamilton. Connie remembered her mother's relationship with her biological father as being turbulent and even physically violent. "He had cut one tooth and instead of having it fixed, he just had all his teeth shaved down, so that when he bit into something it was like he was tearing," she recalled. "He was just that kind of roughneck. . . . Shelley and I were in the middle of a lot of the hostility there."

Joyce Davidson's life was set on a new course in 1950. Her parents entered her into a competition to become a model for the commercial artist Jon Whitcomb, known for his romantic, alluring renderings of women used in magazine advertisements. Joyce was selected. She won $400 and a trip to New York, where she posed for some of Whitcomb's paintings. Shy and a bit ungainly as a child, Joyce Davidson learned she was at ease with the attention that came with becoming a beautiful woman.

When she returned to Hamilton after the trip, she took a job soldering condensers in a Westinghouse factory. She left the job because her male supervisor made a habit of kissing the women who worked on the line. She taught herself how to type and applied for an office job at the new TV station that opened in town in 1954. It led to an on-camera role assisting the host of the station's cooking show. While at home, she studied the live commercials Betty

Furness did for Westinghouse appliances on the show *Studio One.* She eventually started to handle sponsor pitches on her station. Her work in front of the camera led to commercials for a Toronto station as well. It was during a Toronto trip in 1956 that Davidson auditioned for *Tabloid,* a breezy half-hour evening news and talk show on the CBC that once billed itself as the "nightly habit of nearly everybody." The program's signature segment was a lengthy weather forecast from Percy Saltzman, the first face ever seen on Canadian television. Wearing eyeglass frames without lenses, he wildly scrawled barely legible subzero temperatures and drawings of clouds and sunrays across an enormous blackboard map of North America. His signature move was flipping his chalk up in the air when he was finished. Joyce Davidson was hired to be an interviewer on the program, replacing Elaine Grand. With her new job in hand, she split with Dave Davidson and moved with Connie and Shelley to an apartment building in Toronto that catered to unmarried female tenants.

Davidson was not quite ready for such a high-profile TV position. "She was very quiet at that time, shy, insecure and frightened," a CBC producer told *MacLean's* magazine in 1960. "She would sit in a corner and watch and learn everything." Her reserved manner early on may have given the impression that she was cold and led some CBC colleagues to dub her "the Snow Goddess." Ross McLean, the executive producer of *Tabloid,* took Davidson under his wing. Together they analyzed films of her segments and corrected flaws in her enunciation and on-air manner. Over time she became more confident. She stood up for herself when confronted with the condescension and hostility that TV women interviewers frequently faced at the time. When tough-guy actor Robert Mitchum gave her trouble on the air, she told him, "Look, you be nice to me—I'm nervous." Her perseverance paid off. Davidson did not possess a remarkable intellect. But she developed the fearlessness and versatility required to succeed on a daily live-television program. She suited up and went stunt-flying with the Blue Angels, clowned with comic Harpo Marx, and went blonde to blonde over childrearing tips with Jayne Mansfield. Connie and Shelley even made occasional appearances on the program. "People always like me better when they meet my children," Davidson once told a reporter.

"We'd be on set with her," Shelley recalled. "She'd say, 'Shelley is going to say a few words about what she liked about camp.' And Connie would say 'how much longer do we have to do this?' My mother would say 'just 30 more seconds Connie,' and Connie would go, 'Okay—thirty, twenty-nine, twenty-eight, twenty-seven . . .'"

The audience embraced Davidson, and she became a major star, appearing on other CBC shows as well as *Tabloid*. "People in Toronto still tell me how they rushed home from work to watch her," said Shelley. An annual income of $50,000 enabled her to move with her daughters to a house in Rosedale, an old-money section of Toronto. Show business types who came on *Tabloid* often dropped by afterward. "I remember walking into the house and Sammy Davis Jr. was at the piano in the dining room," said Shelley. "She had a lot of friends and they partied. She was young." Connie recalled when Miriam Makeba, the South African singer who was then married to black activist Stokely Carmichael, came to the house, and taught her "The Click Song" before singing her to sleep.

But Davidson had trouble adjusting to fame while being a single working mother still in her twenties. According to Connie, Davidson had a problem with alcohol. "She was lonely. Her career was taking off. She had no preparation for success. I think success can be hugely difficult to deal with, and frightening. Just think how young she was, with two children. And every man, because she was so beautiful, of course, and, I think, talented at that time, was very interested in her. And so were a lot of women. Everybody looked at Mom. If you didn't, I think there must have been something wrong with you. . . . I think she was just desperately lonely and scared. So she'd smoke and she'd drink and she'd make us sit on the bed. She'd keep us up all night, and then we'd have to go to school the next day."

By the late 1950s, Davidson regularly traveled to Hollywood to do commercials on Jack Benny's CBS TV show. Her biggest opportunity came in the fall of 1959 when she landed a weeklong guest spot on NBC's morning program *Today*, as "Girl of the Week," sitting next to host Dave Garroway. During the stint, Davidson was asked for her opinion of Queen Elizabeth's upcoming royal tour in Canada. "I, like most Canadians, am indifferent to the queen's visit," she stated bluntly.

The comment caused immediate outrage back in Canada. The switchboard at CBC headquarters was flooded with calls demanding that Davidson be fired from *Tabloid* (where she had rarely, if ever, presented a strong opinion). As the reports on the remark spread, Connie and Shelley had to be rushed home from school by their grandmother. Frenzied reporters and photographers looking for family members to comment surrounded the house. "I remember sitting in the house that evening, and it was the first satellite feed that ever came from the United States," said Shelley. "It was Mom with her picture up there. I sat in front of the TV set with my legs crossed, really close to it, and I was watching her face on the screen and it was all fuzzy. She was trying to explain to the Canadian people what she had meant."

Davidson was contrite, saying that her remarks were "the mild little opinion of a mild little girl" and that she planned to take her daughters to see Queen Elizabeth in Toronto. While Davidson was becoming tough and opinionated as she matured, she could retreat into being a soft, demure female when convenient or necessary. She later described herself as "a cactus in a velvet glove."

Public anger lingered for days after her comment. When Shelley and Connie attempted to return to school the next day, classmates welcomed them back with defaced photographs of their mother. The girls returned home. "We had to stay home for quite a while until all of this was sorted out," Shelley said. "I remember pictures in the newspapers of my mom getting her bags back in Toronto at the airport."

When Davidson arrived home, she said she was taking a break from *Tabloid* to spare the CBC any further embarrassment over the incident. But the notoriety she gained immediately led to talk of a broadcast job in the United States. She was eventually invited to cohost *Today* during the 1960 Democratic National Convention in Los Angeles. After a few weeks off, she returned to *Tabloid,* but her candor got her in trouble again. She made the front pages when she said that having children raise money for UNICEF on Halloween was spoiling their fun on the day. The final straw was when she gave an interview to a journalist and said that any woman who was still a virgin at the age of thirty was "unlucky." She left the CBC in February 1961.

By that time, Davidson had started an intense romantic relationship with David Susskind. "Life changed abruptly for all of us," said Shelley. "I was around ten years old the first time I met David. It was already pretty serious by then as far as I recall. There were numerous phone calls. He'd be traveling somewhere. She would go into a room, close the door, and I'd hear laughter and talking. He came to Toronto to meet Connie and me. We had on our little plaid coats and hats. We met him and I knew this was a guy my mom was nuts about. I remember I had a butterscotch sundae and my sister had a strawberry sundae. It was the four of us meeting. David was wonderful with small kids."

By the spring, Davidson and her children moved to a nine-room New York apartment on Central Park West. She landed her first full-time stateside television job as cohost of the syndicated late-night talk show *PM East* with Mike Wallace. A few years off of becoming a sensation with his hard-hitting interview program *Night Beat,* Wallace hated the celebrity chitchat he had to engage in on the program. He marked time on *PM East* as he was plotting his way back to CBS News. He also didn't think much of Davidson, and it showed in the duo's lack of rapport on air. But many TV critics believed she was a skilled interviewer, and she was certainly easy on the eyes.

PM East aired out of the WNEW studios where David Susskind did his talk show at the time. He appeared occasionally as a guest on the program, but he also made a habit of showing up unannounced in the control room to offer advice to the director on the best angle to shoot Davidson. "Everybody was afraid to throw him out because we were afraid we'd need a job from him one day," recalled Marlene Sanders, who worked on *PM East*. "The executive producer eventually put a stop to it."

Susskind continued to pursue other women for casual liaisons during his courtship with Davidson. But their commonality was clear. As TV performers, they understood each other's worlds. They both expressed opinions freely. He had the nerve to defy public opinion and put Nikita Khrushchev on his talk show. She withstood the pressure that came her way after speaking her mind about Queen Elizabeth. "Master of Controversy Weds Controversial Gal" read the headline of the New York *Daily News* report on their marriage. They had sharp tongues in private as well. "We were once talking about someone who had left his wife and Joyce asked, 'Who's the woman?'" recalled comedy writer Larry Gelbart. "I said, 'There is no woman.' She said, 'Nobody leaves his wife on spec.' I thought it was a brilliant line." But Davidson was clearly the more tactful of the two. "I used to think of David with a razor blade and my mom with the styptic pencil to stop the bleeding," Shelley said. "Socially, he said anything even if it was hurtful. He did not have boundaries or really understand them."

Gelbart also sensed the intense sexual attraction between Susskind and Davidson when he saw them together. "His reputation was firmly established, so maybe I'm attributing more to it than was actually there, but I always got the feeling that they couldn't wait to pick up where they left off," Gelbart said. "He looked like his clothes were held on with Velcro and he could be naked in a second."

Joyce Davidson inspired one of the more memorable editions of Susskind's

Open End. "They were at a restaurant and Frank Sinatra was there," said Andrew Susskind. "She pointed him out and he said, 'Would you like to meet him?' She said, 'Could I?' I don't know whether David went up to Sinatra or Sinatra stopped by on the way out." When Susskind introduced her, Joyce Davidson put out her hand to the chairman of the board. "Frank said something like, 'I don't want to kiss it, baby, I just want to shake it,'" Andrew Susskind recalled. "It really upset my father. It really embarrassed him."

Susskind responded to the slight by dedicating an entire session of *Open End* to the impact of Sinatra's Rat Pack on the culture. He even invited Sinatra to appear on the show. Sinatra sent him a wire, stating his fee for appearing on television was $10,000. Susskind wired back that he was aware of the fee but believed that was for "saloon singing and ring-a-ding snappy patter. What was his price for intelligent conversation?" Sinatra replied with another wire telling Susskind to "drop dead."

Susskind went ahead with the show anyway in October 1961, booking comedians Ernie Kovacs, Jackie Gleason, and Joe E. Brown, along with journalists Marya Mannes, Lenore Lemmon, and Richard Gehman and celebrity saloon-keeper Toots Shor. Susskind tried to guide them into a discussion about whether the media's glorification of Sinatra and his cohorts was corrupting America's youth. "I wonder if, in a time when the hero symbol is rampant in the country, these are the modern heroes, and that young people think boozing it up, being rude, being wild, and going in for all kinds of bizarre behavior is the way to be important?" he asked. New York *Daily News* columnist Kay Gardella reported that Susskind asked the question with the look of a "wide-eyed Mr. Clean."

Instead of a sociological analysis, the comics toasted their friend Frank—and got toasted on the air after filling their coffee cups with booze. It had turned into a comedy show and Susskind was happy to encourage the rowdy guests after having made his points about Sinatra's clan.

"Tell me, David," asked Kovacs near the end of the show. "What are you going to do now that this series is over?"

"A program like this will keep him on the air," said Gleason. "With a program like this the commercials were just great."

PM EAST LASTED for a single TV season. In the years after its cancellation, Susskind gave Joyce Davidson jobs on his various projects. She was the unit publicist for his theatrical film production of *All the Way Home* and a capable producer for a telephone call-in TV talk show he made for WPIX called *Hot Line*. Davidson booked Malcolm X on the program, which was believed to be the final TV appearance of the black activist before he was murdered, on February 21, 1965. And although Davidson was not an actress, Susskind cast her in at least one of his shows.

Susskind brought Davidson and her children for extended visits on his movie sets as if they were his second family. But the early years of Davidson's relationship with Susskind in New York brought chaos to the lives of Shelley and Connie, who were eventually moved out of the Central Park West apartment to a less glamorous building on Eighty-third Street and Lexington Avenue. Still in their early teens, they were often left alone to fend for themselves. "We were taken from a situation that was very nice and secure and regular when we were in Canada," said Shelley. "All of a sudden we had no family. My mom was with David all the time and we were sort of abandoned in a way. When I look back on it sometimes, it was amazing that my sister and I made it through."

Connie also recalled a bleak existence during those years. "Shelley and I were eating ketchup on top of spaghetti," Connie recalled. "If you went into the kitchen, there was no food. My mother wouldn't give us money. She would forget us. It was out of sight, out of mind. It really was." When Davidson was featured in the 1966 Canadian TV documentary about working single women, there was no mention of her children. Susskind was introduced in the film as her "mentor."

One year Davidson enrolled her daughters at the the Hewlett School, a boarding school in East Islip, New York. Shelley said she was surprised when she arrived to find that Susskind's daughter Diana was also enrolled there. "I had never met Diana," she said. "We all stood there looking at each other with our mouths hanging open. They used really strange judgment when it came to us kids."

The children of David Susskind and Joyce Davidson were given little or no advance word of the couple's marriage on April 22, 1966, just two days after Susskind's divorce from Phyllis had been finalized. There were no family members or friends in attendance when Susskind, dressed in a gray business suit, and Davidson, wearing a pink dress under a pink overcoat, exchanged vows before a judge in Arlington, Virginia. "It was certainly no surprise that they would marry," said Andrew Susskind, who was told about the nuptials a day earlier. "It just seemed like a surprise that they had decided to do it fairly quickly." Shelley said she was informed about the wedding in a lunchtime phone call at school. "I was quite upset," she said.

The Susskinds first activity as husband and wife seemed possible only in a union that included the host of *Open End*. The noon civil ceremony was followed by a visit to the White House for an appointment with Jack Valenti, then an aide to President Lyndon Johnson. He brought them into the Oval Office for a presidential press conference. As Valenti told the story years later, he bumped several reporters out to make room for Susskind and Joyce. The newlyweds were seated a few feet away from the thirty-sixth president of the United States. "I noticed LBJ fixing a momentary gaze every now and then on the rapt face of David," Valenti recalled. "When the press conference was done I asked David to wait in my office because I saw the president beckoning to me. When all departed the president leaned over and he says, 'Is that David Susskind?' 'Yes, Mr. President.' 'Well, he damn near disrupted me . . . he kept staring at me, damn it. I thought he was going to get up and start cross-examining me and I was concentrating so hard on figuring out how to rebut him that I damn near blew a question from the AP.' "

Johnson was probably noticing the new Mrs. David Susskind as well.

THE FOLLOWING MONTH, David and Joyce Susskind moved into a $160,000 duplex cooperative apartment on the thirty-third and thirty-fourth floors of 870 United Nations Plaza, a newly built twin-tower complex off First Avenue in Manhattan. The contemporary-styled buildings had prewar building features such as tiny studios for domestic workers and offered dazzling views of the East River. They quickly became the hot residence of the moment for affluent celebrities such as Robert Kennedy, Walter Cronkite, and Johnny Carson. Truman Capote referred to UN Plaza as "The Compound." Carson, Kennedy, and Cronkite were among those who showed up when the Susskinds threw a bash in the unfurnished space to celebrate their marriage. The guest list also included Sidney Poitier, restaurateur Vincent Sardi, George C. Scott, celebrity hairdresser Kenneth Battelle (better known as Mr. Kenneth), Hume Cronyn and his wife Jessica Tandy, Shelley Winters, Tallulah Bankhead, Alan Jay Lerner, and Artie Shaw. Sunlight from a beautiful day in early May streamed through the floor-to-ceiling windows of the apartments. Guests were given pens and told to write messages for the couple on the blank walls.

Upstairs they lined up to get time with a fortune-teller and a handwriting analyst hired for the party. "People didn't just write their names on the wall— they wrote funny stuff," Andrew Susskind recalled. "It was a great idea. It was really quite a bash."

In December, all five of the Susskind children appeared together on a panel for *The David Susskind Show*. The following month, David Susskind made an announcement at the start of a program taping January 26, 1967. "This past week, I met one of the most extraordinary, miraculous people I've ever met in my life," he said. "She was in fact born last Friday. Her name is Samantha Marie Susskind and she weighed in at six pounds and thirteen and a half ounces. She is not prepared to make her television debut, but she assures me when she does it will be on this program."

13

The blow of losing *East Side/West Side* was softened by CBS's decision to pick up a new Talent Associates series for the 1964–1965 season, just as the network's president Jim Aubrey had promised Dan Melnick. Called *Mr. Broadway*, it starred Craig Stevens, a suave, likable B-movie actor who fancied himself the next Cary Grant. He had become a favorite among TV viewers in 1959 as the lead in NBC's noir detective series *Peter Gunn*.

Mr. Broadway was a charmingly quirky concept that was watered down and ultimately destroyed by network meddling. Garson Kanin, who wrote the sophisticated film comedies *Born Yesterday* and *Adam's Rib*, had accumulated a collection of short stories based on his years working in Broadway theater. "If Damon Runyon had gone to college he might have written them," was how Larry Arrick described the tales. Kanin had shopped them as the basis for a TV series to a dozen producers. No one warmed up to the idea until he presented it to Susskind, who pitched it to CBS.

Already aware that CBS executives were wary of the bleak atmosphere of *East Side/West Side*, Susskind sold *Mr. Broadway* as the antithesis of that series. There would be no tenements or dreary intractable socioeconomic problems endemic to urban life. *Mr. Broadway* would focus on the glamorous side of New York—horse-drawn carriages through Central Park, fancy meals at the Top of the Sixes restaurant, cocktails with celebrities at Toots Shor, and the glittery nightlife of the Stork Club. The city would be portrayed in an alluring upbeat manner. The central character was a slick but well-intentioned Broadway press agent named Mike Bell, who has a pool table for a desk.

Kanin, a gifted raconteur and consummate name-dropper, acted out the parts of a sample script during Talent Associates meetings with CBS executives. They were charmed into ordering a pilot episode. Their only request going forward was that the Mike Bell character have a public relations business and not just be limited to the theater district.

Susskind handed the development of *Mr. Broadway* over to Dan Melnick, who spared no expense in making the pilot a celebration of the city's glitterati. Scenes were shot on location in the Four Seasons Restaurant, Kennedy Airport, the Carnegie House apartment building on West Fifty-seventh Street, fashion designer Oleg Cassini's showroom, and the nightclub El Morocco. Cassini himself, well-known model Nancy Berg, and Leonard Lyons, the newspaper columnist who covered New York nightlife for the *New York Post,* appeared as themselves in cameo roles. Music supervisor Bob Israel hired jazz pianist Dave Brubeck to write the score for the show and the brilliant saxophonist Oliver Nelson to handle the arrangements. The syncopated jazz waltz theme song that played over an animated title sequence of a stylized skyline promised viewers a taste of a rarified Manhattan experience.

Arrick supervised the writing on the series. By the spring of 1964 he had eight scripts in the works. "They were sweet and anecdotal," Arrick recalled. "A little smartass and snobby." Kanin was given an office at Talent Associates where he worked on story ideas. He wanted to use writers outside of the television realm, such as Kurt Vonnegut and Dorothy Parker. That didn't happen, but "things were going along nicely," according to Arrick, until he got a call from Jim Aubrey at CBS.

"I don't like the way this is going," Aubrey told him. "A key thing is missing. Jeopardy. The only successful TV series are the ones in which there is jeopardy."

"You've got Craig Stevens," Arrick said. "He was *Peter Gunn.* You mean this should be *Peter Gunn East?*"

"Exactly," Aubrey said.

"Mr. Aubrey, he's a press agent. You want him to carry a gun?'"

"Right."

Mike Bell was not forced to carry a gun. But after assigning story ideas to writers and getting scripts into motion, Arrick had them all start over. Suddenly, they were working on a show about a press agent who solves crimes. Stevens was dismayed when he saw new scripts. "Mike Bell is turning out to be a cop," he wrote to Melnick. Stevens was still anxious to do the series after spending months on a forgettable Broadway musical written by Meredith Willson called *Here's Love*. It was based on the movie *Miracle on 34th Street*. Every night at the Shubert Theater, Stevens was making an entrance out of a giant toy box.

The network's demands threw the production into disarray and delayed the summer shooting schedule. It meant that Kanin, a calling card for the show, would not be available to direct any episodes. He was already committed to work on the Broadway production of *Funny Girl* that fall. The changes also created havoc with the show's budget. Initially, *Mr. Broadway* was designed to tell stories through dialogue and repartee that could be done on an enclosed set or a glamorous Manhattan location. Instead, the show was shooting expensive chase scenes and action sequences on City Island in the Bronx and at Palisades Amusement Park across the river in New Jersey.

Network censors got in the way of any attempts to make *Mr. Broadway* an adult show. After a script about a rich businessman's romance with a belly dancer, played by Jill St. John, was approved, her entire wardrobe had to be replaced when the original outfits were rejected as too revealing. Dialogue used by guest star Hal March in another completed episode was deemed "questionable" and needed replacing. March, in Massachusetts at the time, went into a studio at a local radio station where he recorded one single new word for the show. The tape was flown and delivered to New York at a cost of $450.

CBS executives also insisted the series have big-name guest stars, and with those stars came demands. When Lauren Bacall was cast in an episode, she wanted a hairdresser from the salon of Jacqueline Kennedy's designated stylist Mr. Kenneth on the set at all times. The show paid $1,000 for the hairdresser, who never once touched Bacall's head. Stevens took his cues from the treatment of the high-profile actors who came through. He was gone for extended lunches, left early when he pleased, and wanted a fully equipped trailer at his disposal at every shooting location. He demanded that his dressing room be redecorated at a cost of $2,000. Arrick remembers one call he received from an agitated Stevens after the first few *Mr. Broadway* episodes were produced.

"I'm very upset with the script," Stevens told him.

"I'm sorry, Craig," Arrick said. "What is it?"

"I never change my clothes."

"The script was a little weak and I wanted to give it some urgency, so it takes place in real time," Arrick told him.

"I'm known for my clothes," Stevens replied. "You notice I always wear a black tie? Cary Grant told me, 'Change your suit as often as possible. But always wear a black tie, so that in a long shot, they'll always identify you.'"

"Do you want me to rewrite the script so you can change your clothes?"

"Larry, at least three times."

The *Mr. Broadway* producers were even accused of racial discrimination. The Congress of Racial Equality office in New York had heard persistent rumors that there was a directive to "go easy on the Negro performers." The charge stung, as many of those who worked on the show had been part of the team that took network fire over making *East Side/West Side* the most integrated series ever on television up to that time.

Mr. Broadway made its inauspicious debut on September 26, 1964. In the premiere episode, Mike Bell is asked by an old pal to keep an eye on his attractive young daughter, Emily, played by Tuesday Weld. Shortly after the young beauty arrives in New York from Cincinnati, Bell discovers he is ill equipped to keep tabs on her. She becomes involved with a shady playboy who turns her into a pill-popping all-night party girl. Bell ultimately gets the man to leave Emily alone, but only after a bizarre confrontation in which he threatens to plant unfavorable items about him in newspaper gossip columns. Such were the weapons of a press agent who doesn't carry a gun.

Critics dismissed the show and viewers stayed away. *Mr. Broadway* was canceled after thirteen episodes, still a rarity in network television at the time, especially for CBS.

"Even I cringed when I read the reviews for *Mr. Broadway*, your worst since the Khrushchev interview," Phyllis Susskind wrote to her estranged husband after the show debuted.

Mr. Broadway was a stinging setback for Talent Associates. But it was not nearly as harsh as the company's actual experience on the Great White Way that was unfolding almost simultaneously with the TV show's run. On February 6, 1965, five weeks after the last *Mr. Broadway* aired, the curtain went up at the Broadhurst Theatre on a musical produced by Susskind and Melnick called *Kelly*. It ran for a single night and lost $650,000, making it the biggest flop in Broadway history up to that time.

Kelly was Susskind's fourth Broadway show. Even after mastering television and producing four laudable theatrical films, he desperately wanted to score a commercial stage triumph. More than one of his colleagues believed he envied David Merrick, the premier Broadway-producing impresario of that time. For Susskind, part of the appeal of producing live television plays was the electric feeling of a Broadway opening night. But in TV, the memory of a critical dud or ratings failure could be quickly erased by the next success. In the case of the prolific Susskind, the next opportunity was never too far off. Mounting an actual Broadway show was a walk on a much higher wire and falling off it was an ugly sight not as easily forgotten.

Susskind tried his first Broadway show in 1956 with *A Very Special Baby,* written by Robert Alan Aurthur. It starred Jack Warden as a thirty-four-year-old man who is the indulged and overprotected youngest member of his family. But he is hated by his tyrannical father, who blames the death of his wife in childbirth on his son. It was the kind of psychological kitchen-sink drama that worked well for Susskind and Aurthur on *The Philco Television Playhouse,* but it was a bit too melodramatic and bleak for Broadway. Susskind scored a casting coup for the play when he landed opera star and actor Ezio Pinza for the role of the father (Talent Associates had packaged Pinza's short-lived TV show *Bonino*). "It was his first dramatic part on Broadway or anywhere, coming out of his great success in *South Pacific,*" recalled Michael Abbott. "And we got Sylvia Sidney to play his daughter."

Having Pinza in the cast helped get *Baby* booked in one of the better Broadway houses operated by the Shubert Organization. Advance ticket sales were brisk. "The theater parties were coming in like crazy because all these little old ladies wanted to see Ezio Pinza," Abbott said. Susskind's good fortune quickly turned. A couple of weeks before the show's scheduled opening, Pinza suffered a brain hemorrhage. The news led to cancellations by the groups that bought blocks of seats. Abbott recalled that he and Susskind were soon called to a meeting with Lee Shubert at his office. "So Pinza's dead," Shubert told them. "Now what are we going to do?"

Susskind and Abbott corrected him. For all they knew Pinza might recover. But Shubert told them they had forty-eight hours to tell him definitively whether Pinza was going to be in the show. If he was not, they were losing the theater.

Pinza did not recover—he died the following year—and *A Very Special Baby* was out of the Shubert house. The show was booked on an interim basis at The Playhouse, where it opened on November 14, 1956. "We got Luther Adler, who was a wonderful actor, but he wasn't Ezio Pinza," said Abbott. "Luther Adler was married at one time to Sylvia Sidney, who was going to play his daughter in the show, and they hated each other because they had a bitter divorce. So, I mean, you can imagine the rehearsals. And scenes with them together, he would push her, she would push him. She always called him noodle head."

A Very Special Baby received decent reviews from the New York critics, but it needed to be a smash hit to justify the expense of moving to another theater. The show closed after thirty-four performances, although Susskind's investment in the show was covered by the sale of the movie rights to Kirk Douglas.

Susskind got closer to a Broadway success with his third show, *Rashomon*. Based on the stories of Japanese writer Ryunosuke Akutagawa, the play, written by Fay and Michael Kanin, depicts the murder of a samurai and the rape of his wife by a bandit as seen through four different eyewitnesses. The production was considered daring, as British director Peter Glenville took the story's tenth-century Kyoto setting and presented it in a contemporary style. Susskind cast Rod Steiger as the bandit and Claire Bloom as the wife. While there appeared to Susskind to be tension between the two actors during the production, they married a few months after the show closed.

Steiger could be an unpredictable character and had a difficult time controlling the instincts he developed as a method actor. When Steiger played the homely butcher in the live TV version of *Marty,* director Delbert Mann had to repeatedly ask the actor not to break into tears during the character's emotional speeches about self-loathing. During the run of *Rashomon* in Philadelphia, Steiger added an unscripted moment when he started slapping at himself on stage. Director Peter Glenville went to Steiger's dressing room afterward to ask if there was a problem with his costume. Steiger explained he was swatting at flies. Glenville said he would have the stage sprayed. No, Steiger said. These were flies he invented in order to give some reality to the forest. (Steiger likely picked it up from Toshiro Mifune's performance in Kurosawa's 1950 film version of the story.) Glenville told Steiger to cut it out. He was upstaging the other actors and confusing the audience.

The following night, Steiger continued to slash away. He even ripped a piece of cloth from his costume and wrapped it around his arm because, he later explained, the imaginary fly's blood had splattered over his arm.

Steiger gave up on his fly swatting by the time the show got to Broadway. Susskind and his partners in the show had reason to be hopeful when *Rashomon* opened at the Music Box Theatre on January 27, 1959. Glenville was getting strong performances out of the actors. The creative staging provided by well-regarded British theatrical designer Oliver Messel and lighting director Jo Mielziner gave the show tremendous promise. "I'm sure that *Rashomon* will be the most successful rape of the season," read one of the telegrams sent to Susskind during the show's out-of-town preview. As had been his custom, Susskind stayed away from the theater and spent the evening drinking at Sardi's. Press agent Arthur Cantor took the reviews over the phone and relayed them to Susskind. *New York Times* critic Brooks Atkinson called the production "a perfectly imagined microcosm of sense, sound and color."

"Is that good?" asked Susskind, who was admittedly inebriated at that point. "Of course it's good," said Cantor, who used the line in the promotion of the show. Abbott, an associate producer on *Rashomon,* believed the highbrow praise doomed the show. "No one knew what the fuck that meant," he said. Abbott was right. The appeal of *Rashomon* was not broad enough to bring in enough ticket sales to cover its costly production values. It closed after a six-month run. "It was not for Broadway and not for that time," said George C. White. "It was a great idea and it was a very good script." (Michael Kanin adapted the play for the poorly received 1964 film *The Outrage,* which set the *Rashomon* tale in the Old West. The killer-rapist was conceived as a Mexican bandit, played by Paul Newman, while Claire Bloom reprised her role as the victim.)

For the next few years, Susskind looked at Broadway from a distance, although he made his presence and opinions known about what he saw. When New York's newspapers were on strike in late 1962 and early 1963, he reviewed plays for radio station WMCA. He managed to pick a fight with David Merrick in one commentary, calling him "a twisted id on a sea of crocodile tears." Merrick replied, "Mr. Susskind is head of Talent Associates. It is obvious the talent belongs to the associates."

Susskind decided to put himself on the line after he received a call early in 1964 from Eddie Lawrence, a writer and comedian with an iconoclastic streak. Lawrence had been a Talent Associates client back in the early 1950s when he was best known for a subtly subversive routine called "The Old Philosopher." Done in a kindly, gather-'round-the-cracker-barrel voice, he mocked the idea that the American can-do spirit could lift anyone who was mired in miserable circumstances. He had also studied painting in France with Fernand Léger for a few years after World War II. Lawrence's partner, Moose Charlap, had written the music for a number of Broadway shows, including the 1954 version of *Peter Pan* that starred Mary Martin and had been a sensation as an NBC TV spectacular. Together they had been shopping a dark musical about life in New York's Bowery in the late 1880s. Called *Kelly*, it was built around the legend of Steve Brodie, a young man who may or may not have jumped off the Brooklyn Bridge supposedly on a bet. Lawrence heard the story as a youth from his uncle, an eyeshade-wearing poker dealer on the Bowery at the time. "He said, 'Most people think they saw him jump,'" Lawrence recalled. "That fascinated me throughout my life. Did he jump? Didn't he jump? What happened?" The event even worked its way into the vernacular, as "pulling a Brodie" became a term to describe a scam or a fraudulent act.

Lawrence and Charlap envisioned taking bawdy characters from old New York and presenting them in the style of Bertolt Brecht and Kurt Weill's *Threepenny Opera*. The songs varied in style from those of Weill to *Guys and Dolls* composer Frank Loesser to Stephen Sondheim (who thirty-six years later designated "I'll Never Go There Anymore," a wistful ballad from *Kelly*, as one of the songs he wished he had written). Lawrence and Charlap presented the Brodie character as an Irish immigrant named Hop Kelly, who had made three failed attempts to jump off the Brooklyn Bridge. Gamblers then try to bring him in on a scheme in which they stage a leap by throwing a dummy off the bridge. Kelly is conflicted. "They don't realize this kid has something inside of him that wants to jump," said Lawrence. The concept was probably better suited to a small theater or cabaret instead, said Anita Gillette, then a petite redheaded ingénue who had become a Broadway fixture after appearing in *Carnival, Mr. President*, and *All American* in the early 1960s. "It was not the kind of thing that was going to make a big deal. The score has a lot of good stuff in it—but it was so odd. The book was weak."

The duo had written the show five years earlier and had gotten close to getting the show made with several producers. Actor Richard Harris was even signed on to star. "It's an allegory of every man who must make the jump someday in whatever he attacks," Harris was quoted as saying in what was probably a planted newspaper column item meant to generate interest in the show. But once Harris's movie *This Sporting Life* took off, he was let out of the deal. Other producers backed away when the intensely earnest authors resisted making any changes to *Kelly*.

But the story and the songs immediately swept Susskind up when Lawrence and Charlap auditioned the show for Melnick and him. "The story had a certain edge to it," said Lawrence. "Susskind wanted that edge. In the beginning, he went crazy. He went wild. A lot of people were afraid of that little edge. He loved it." Lawrence heard Melnick say, "It rings of Sean O'Casey—brilliant." Susskind later wrote in the *Philadelphia Inquirer* that he was "determined that we produce this show or die in the attempt. I was further convinced that if David Merrick ever did *Kelly* I would commit hara-kiri by swallowing a year's supply of Nielsen ratings."

One of Susskind's after-hours avocations was singing at piano bars, and the *Kelly* score became part of his repertoire. "He was crazy about *Kelly*," said Alan Shayne. "He would sing songs from the show."

Melnick did not recall being quite as effusive, but he liked *Kelly* enough to overlook the concerns that scared off the other potential backers. "Eddie and Moose were good storytellers and charming and I liked the Brechtian score," he said. "I had heard the stories about how difficult these guys were because they wouldn't change a word."

Michael Abbott remembered warning Susskind against doing the show. "I wrote him a three-page memo telling him why I thought it would be a disaster," he said. "I didn't like the story. I didn't like the people involved. They didn't have the quality to do the Broadway show."

Susskind was truly passionate about the project. He told Abbott that his criticism "stabbed him in the heart."

"I said, 'David you asked me for my approval,'" Abbott recalled. "'I can't say that I like it. I hate it. I think it's terrible.' I don't think he expected me to be that tough. But I really hated it. I think that enflamed it. He said, 'Hate—what is that? You can hate Hitler, but you don't hate a Broadway show.'"

Melnick's wife Linda also believed going ahead with *Kelly* was ill advised. As the daughter of Richard Rodgers, she had some sense of the challenges the producers faced. "It was one thing to do a couple of plays," Melnick recalled. "But a musical—she didn't want me to get involved."

Nevertheless, in April 1964, Susskind and Melnick announced their plans to bring *Kelly* to Broadway. They had a big money backer in movie producer Joseph E. Levine, who invested $250,000 and received the film rights. Levine was the short, rotund self-made mogul who rose from humble beginnings in Boston's West End to become one of the most audacious and successful film producers and packagers of the 1960s. He expertly marketed both imported genre films (*Godzilla* and *Hercules*) and art house movies (Vittorio De Sica's *Two Women* with Sophia Loren) into box office hits. He had backed *The Carpetbaggers*, a huge success based on the racy Harold Robbins novel, and later produced one of the decade's most heralded movies, *The Graduate*, which catapulted Dustin Hoffman into a major career. But like Susskind and Melnick, he did not have one day of experience making a Broadway musical. "I called them 'The Three Unwise Men—David, Daniel, and Joseph,'" said Don Francks, the Canadian singer and actor who made his Broadway debut in the role of Hop Kelly. Anita Gillette was cast as Kelly's girl, Angela Crane. The other star in the show was Ella Logan as Hop Kelly's mother. The Scottish actress had appeared in the original Broadway staging of *Finian's Rainbow*, and *Kelly* was to be her comeback.

Melnick hired Herbert Ross to direct *Kelly*. At that point, Ross had already won a Tony Award for choreographing Sondheim's *Anyone Can Whistle* and had been brought in to help on *Golden Boy* before it went on to a successful Broadway run, according to Melnick. But he had not directed a show of his own. Looking back, Melnick believed he wanted Ross because he was married to former ballerina Nora Kaye. "I had a crush on her from the time I was a kid," Melnick said. "I used to go to the City Center and sit in the balcony to see Nora Kaye dance. And I never knew she had this terrible Bronx accent. I remember her sitting in my office the first time and she said, 'Herbie, why are we doing this piece of shit?'"

Before rehearsals commenced, the show was announced with a press party on the walkway above the car lanes of the Brooklyn Bridge. Francks, ruggedly handsome with magnetism to spare, did a can-can alongside bodice-clad chorus girls as Charlap and Lawrence sang songs from the score. Levine and Susskind were on hand to show their support. They posed for publicity photos. Cocktail napkins emblazoned with the *Kelly* logo were spread over picnic tables set up for guests and members of the press. Everyone's spirits seemed high. Sandy Stewart, a pop and jazz vocalist married to Charlap at the time, remembered the enthusiasm during an early run-through at a theater in New York. "I was sitting with our lawyer at the time," she said. "He looked at me and said, 'What are you going to do with all your money, Sandy? This is a smash.'"

But Francks and Lawrence recalled another performance before the previews that the producers presented in front of a house full of colleagues and journalists. "There was hardly any applause, hardly any laughter," said Francks. "I said, 'Who are these people?' I was told the producers invited them in. A whole lot of people who are in show business are out there. This was not Mr. and Mrs. Everyday. I thought to myself, 'What's going on? What are these people that they don't want to like us? How come? This is a great show.'" It was dispiriting for the troupe and undermined the confidence of Susskind and Melnick, who had already had their judgment questioned about the show. Francks said from that point forward, *Kelly* started to change and not for the better. When the reviews were mixed after *Kelly* started its three-week run at the Shubert Theatre in Philadelphia, the producers' panic intensified. Patrons were leaving during the intermission. Every night, Francks climbed up a ladder on the back wall of the theater and was strapped into a harness that was attached to a guy wire. He then made his Brodie-like dive. An aged union stagehand who controlled the cable was all that kept Francks from crashing face-first into the floor. "I'd walk off the stage in the darkness and somebody would pour a bucket of water on me," Francks said. After Francks took the leap during a Philadelphia performance, a man in the audience shouted, "I thought that mother would never jump."

Susskind and Melnick began to think a show with an irresolute antihero might not be what the Broadway musical audience wanted. They backed away further from the elements they had initially embraced. "Susskind said, 'Experts told me that this is a balcony show,'" said Lawrence. "Meaning, West Side intellectuals and whatever will love it and it may get a few good reviews, but it's only going to run about a year." Lawrence said a year sounded good to him. But a production on the scale of *Kelly*—a large cast with singers and dancers and elaborate costumes and sets—would have to run longer than that to turn more than a small profit on its initial investment. "Susskind said, 'We want it to be a smash hit that will go on and on—it will still break down barriers, but we want to get the tourists in there too,'" Lawrence recalled. Once again, Susskind's artistic inclinations clashed with the needs of commerce. "I said, 'This is the show you bought,'" Lawrence said. "We wouldn't have minded that much if they told us in the beginning that they wanted to change it and make it more for the people."

As *Kelly* continued its previews, revisions were made at a disconcerting pace. "Things kept disappearing from the show," Francks recalled. "People were disappearing. Dance numbers taken out. Songs were missing. New songs asked for. Suddenly my hair was dyed red. The writers were trying to figure this thing out. They complained bitterly. In Philly, I was handed a song at four o'clock that I had to sing at eight o'clock." Lawrence said he and Charlap attempted to make some revisions, none of which satisfied the producers. "Then they brought in the people to change it further," he said. "It was a disaster." During the course of the show's previews, Ella Logan's role as Hop Kelly's mother was cut from the show while Susskind was out of the country. When he returned, he reinstated her, but more changes led to her being fired again by the time *Kelly* got to Broadway.

Before the production went on to its Boston run in January 1965, Melnick called in a pal, screenwriter David Z. Goodman, to do some script doctoring. Mel Brooks and comedy writer Leonard Stern, a friend from Melnick's days with Steve Allen and Jackie Gleason, were also called in. "By then the show was a remnant of what it had been, not even a mirrored reflection," said Stern. "People were singing songs for which there was no motivation. And it ran originally I think two and a half to three hours. Mel, more experienced in theater than I was, was probably the surgeon. He had to do a lot of work that couldn't possibly be done in the week we were there." Goodman softened the flintiness of Hop Kelly and made him more likable. Brooks and Stern attempted to punch up the dialogue with borscht belt gags that had no place in the earthy late-nineteenth-century New York milieu Lawrence and Charlap created. Angered by the moves, the authors left the show. They went to a New York Supreme Court judge for an injunction to keep *Kelly* from opening. They claimed the rewrites were done without their consent, thus violating the Dramatists Guild contract. But as Guild rules required that such conflicts had to be decided through arbitration, the judge allowed the show to go on. Meanwhile, the producers had burned through the initial funding for the show and needed more money to keep the show going. Levine, sensing trouble, refused to get in deeper. 'He said, 'This is Chicago and I get off in Chicago,' " Melnick recalled. Susskind and Melnick borrowed $100,000 to make it to the February 6 opening at the Broadhurst Theatre. They pressed ahead with the hope that even a hint of a positive notice could be used to promote the show, and maybe get the soundtrack album made by Columbia Records, which was an investor as well.

As the chaos ensued, Don Francks was seeing his shot at stardom diminish by the day. Francks was not a mainstream Broadway player at the time. He had been a jazz musician in Toronto and was transforming with the times from 1950s hipster to 1960s hippie. He chronicled his journey through life with stream-of-consciousness prose that he kept in leather-bound notebooks. He also filled them with drawings of flowers and pictures of his hero Charlie Chaplin. Before the New York opening he wrote: "Welcome once again to Box Canyon, that uncomfortable spot you find yourself in and try to find out how to get out. For your convenience please take notice of the no way out signs posted everywhere you look. . . . Also please realize you're alone here and must figure out how to get by those who block the only exit. You will also observe the thoughtful 'no wall climbing' signs if you want to keep cool, calm and collected. We hope you don't enjoy your stay here far away from where you thought you were going."

Francks was comforted by one of the beautiful dancers in the company, Hanne-Marie Reiner, a stunning Nordic blonde who had been in the Royal Danish Ballet Company. "She looked like she was *en pointe* all the time," he said. Late one night, there was a knock on the door of her studio apartment, located just a few blocks north of the theater district in Manhattan. "Come quickly," she told Francks after she looked through the spyglass in the front door. "There was David Susskind," said Francks. "David had taken a shine to her and thought maybe at two o'clock in the morning it wasn't a bad thing to do. Needless to say, neither of us was home."

Throughout the turmoil, Susskind always told the cast he believed the show was a hit. "He was determined to get this done and I think he blinded himself to the facts," Anita Gillette said. "You wanted to believe him when you worked that hard." Gillette was grateful for Susskind's enthusiasm and support until one night in Philadelphia when they shared a ride back to the Drake Hotel. "That I was in the cab alone with him I don't know why," said Gillette, who was married and had an infant son at the time. "Before I could get out he was all over me. It was frightening. Afterward he flirted and insinuated if I gave him an invitation we could do it the right way. I mean, that's no special place. He did that with everybody."

Kelly made it to opening night in New York, and critics, aware of the show's problems, were ready to pounce. To Francks, it appeared as if none of them wanted Susskind, Melnick, or Levine to have anything to do with Broadway. "That's how it felt," he said. "It was like, 'Why are you fuckers in our wonderland when you're in the boob tube and making Steve Reeves Hercules movies?' There was an unwelcoming committee out. Rusty swords cut us down and the reason they were rusty was they were drawn a long time ago. They had unsheathed these swords and if they had the chance they would have cut it down while we were still rehearsing."

"Let's put it this way," said David Z. Goodman. "The critics were happy to kill it." The Associated Press called it "a monumental bore." The *New York Herald Tribune's* Walter Kerr said the show was "a bad idea gone wrong." The review from Howard Taubman of *The New York Times* congratulated Ella Logan for being fired from the show before it opened.

"Was it that bad? Nothing's that bad," said Goodman. "Did it deserve to run? No."

Leonard Stern recalled how the following day Susskind walked through the Talent Associates offices with his accountant, asking how much would it cost to keep it open. "He was not getting an answer," Stern said. "I think they were trying to stay open longer, but the accountant never came up with a number that gave them any concrete evidence of what it might cost to extend it a week." The following day only four people showed up at the Broadhurst Theatre box office—and they came to get refunds for their advance tickets. Anita Gillette remembered calling the theater on Monday to find out what time she needed to show up for what she hoped would be the second performance. "They answered, 'Broadhurst House of Hits,'" she said. Gillette was told to come to the theater that night to hear some parting words from David Susskind.

"We couldn't come and collect our things and get away before his speech," she said. "It was like a night in which we were in performance. We were playing audience to David Susskind. We sat in the audience and he did another big long speech and as he's talking—I'll never forget—they were hauling the set away. They were taking the costumes away. We're sitting there and he really needed to deliver this. In the background, they are taking down the set and removing the costumes. I saw my beautiful dress with the pink rose on the ass—it could have been a Fellini movie. It went along with the whole experience of doing that show. I was left stunned and exhausted."

Francks learned the news of the closing when he showed up at the Broadhurst that morning. He didn't stick around for Susskind's speech. He headed to the Stage Delicatessen, where he had become a regular and a favorite of the staff. The waiter came over to Francks with his regular order and a piece of paper with a poem written on it. He saved the poem, attaching it onto a page in his black leather notebook.

Though the show's a bomb,
In spite of labor so stout,
The name of Francks will go on,
If only with mustard and sauerkraut

"It was New York on a platter," Francks said.

Never in the history of Broadway had a production the magnitude of *Kelly* closed after a single night. Susskind and everyone else involved would relive the pain of the public failure two months later. Susskind had been so confident of the show, his press agent Jack Perlis approached *The Saturday Evening Post* with the idea of having a journalist go behind the scenes with the producers during three months leading up to opening night. Lewis H. Lapham got the assignment. As Lapham stood in the back of the theater and observed rehearsals, Melnick offered to set the journalist up with the chorine of his choice. The proposal did not soften Lapham's twenty thousand-plus-word opus, called "Has Anybody Here Seen Kelly?" which presented the disaster in vivid detail. The piece cemented the legacy of Broadway's biggest bomb.

Just a few weeks after the spectacular failure of *Kelly*, Talent Associates had another Broadway show open. Susskind, Melnick, and Levine had brought over Bill Naughton's *All in Good Time*, a British comedy about a young man and his new bride who are forced by economic circumstances to move in with his parents. At one point, the show was almost done before it started. Susskind and Melnick had arranged to bring over the set from the original production at the Mermaid Theatre in London. But a 1965 longshoremen's strike kept the scenery locked up in the hull of a ship docked in Baltimore. According to Andrew Susskind, a bartender at David Susskind's favorite East Side watering hole, The Centaur, used her organized-crime contacts who had influence in the longshoremen's union to solve the problem. The scenery was retrieved in time for *All in Good Time*, which opened on February 18. It ran for forty-four performances.

The *Kelly* experience clearly left Susskind in the wrong state of mind to receive a call shortly afterward from writer Dale Wasserman. In 1959, Wasserman had sold a TV play to Susskind about the imprisonment of Miguel de Cervantes by the Spanish Inquisition. For his defense, Cervantes tells the story of the knight-errant Don Quixote, the character in his novel *Don Quixote de la Mancha*. Susskind produced it as *I, Don Quixote* on *The DuPont Show of the Month*. "David never understood it," said Wasserman. "But he trusted me when I said, deceitfully, 'Yes, it's about Don Quixote.' I found it too difficult to explain that in actuality it was about a few hours in the life of a playwright, Miguel de Cervantes. I don't know how he sold it to DuPont—David was a hell of a salesman—but I'm sure he said it was an adaptation of the novel, not the cockamamie idea it really was."

Wasserman was grateful to Susskind for having taken a chance on *I, Don Quixote*, which over the next few years he developed into the musical called

Man of La Mancha. He offered Susskind the chance to produce it on Broadway. "He had been burned in the production of *Kelly* and declined to participate," said Wasserman. "It was the greatest mistake he ever made." *Man of La Mancha* had its Broadway opening on November 22, 1965, and ran for 2,328 performances.

14

In the spring of 1965, it looked as if David Susskind was going to have to shut down Talent Associates. The company was reeling from the costly and embarrassing Broadway failure of *Kelly* and the quick cancellation of *Mr. Broadway*. It no longer had any programs on network television. There was also bad news from the CBS corporate suite. Network president Jim Aubrey, who guaranteed David Susskind's partner Dan Melnick that he would always have a show on his schedule, had been fired.

After years of being the number one network, CBS had lost 11 percent of its audience during the 1964–1965 TV season and was neck and neck with NBC and the once lowly ABC. The decline was due largely to the ratings performance of programs Aubrey had picked up from another producing crony, Keefe Brasselle.

Brasselle was a journeyman actor best known for playing the lead role in the 1953 film *The Eddie Cantor Story*. He had been pals with Aubrey since the 1950s, when he was a local TV executive in Los Angeles. A number of people around at the time say Aubrey was indebted to Brasselle after a situation with a woman with organized-crime connections got out of control. "Aubrey got very rough with women during sex," said Larry Gelbart. "And he broke someone's arm. And that someone had a very powerful boyfriend who took out a contract on Aubrey. Keefe Brasselle was wired with the underground guys, the mob guys, and he intervened apparently. All I know is, one season he had three series on the air, and he used to lay down in front of 485 Madison Avenue in his limo and tell his driver to go get Mr. Aubrey to get his ass down here so we can go out and do whatever—whoever's arm they wanted to break that night. It was pretty shocking and obvious that there was something going on out there." Marc Merson, who worked under Aubrey at CBS, said Gelbart's assessment was accurate. While Susskind had long enjoyed partying with Aubrey, he too had expressed concern over his bizarre activities. Asleep one night in his apartment with Joyce Davidson, he woke up and found Aubrey standing at the foot of their bed looking for a ménage à trois. Aubrey had let himself in unannounced.

Brasselle's reward for protecting Aubrey from mob retaliation was the scheduling of three new shows from his company Richelieu Productions on the 1964–1965 CBS schedule. All three forgettable shows—*The Cara Williams Show, The Baileys of Balboa,* and a drama series with Harry Guardino called *The Reporter*—were picked up, even though no pilot episodes were shot for any of them. All were ratings losers. Aubrey's bosses at CBS suspected something was amiss. But until that season Aubrey was untouchable, as the network's financial performance under his stewardship had been stellar. Profits had gone from $25 million in 1959 when he took over the presidency of the network to nearly $50 million in 1964. Yet at the first sign of a ratings downturn, Aubrey's seamy personal life could no longer be ignored and he was gone.

Meanwhile, Paramount had grown impatient with Talent Associates. After seeing no financial benefit since taking its position in the company, the studio was ready to cut off any further support. Susskind and Melnick staved off the action by slashing the weekly operating cost of Talent Associates by more than half and cutting staff. They also deferred 25 percent of their salaries. Susskind agreed to allow the studio to have its own comptroller on the Talent Associates premises to watch over expenses. He also promised the Paramount board that his company was on track to success with the development of more commercial programs. "It would be both tragic and ironic if Talent Associates were to go out of business at the very moment in time when it gives every indication of profits and success," Susskind wrote to Paramount studio chief Paul Raibourn in a letter that detailed the fiscal measures he was taking.

Michael Campus remembered Susskind calling a meeting in the office to explain the dire situation. "We've got to do stuff we'd never even consider before," Susskind said. Like game shows. Susskind hated them. But he wanted ideas. One Talent Associates staff member mockingly suggested doing a show called *Whose Is It?* "Each week a different celebrity's shit would be brought out on a dish and a panel would have to guess 'whose is it?' " he said. "The celebrity would say where they had dinner and why they were in town."

Everyone in the meeting laughed. But it surely did not seem as funny when Susskind and Melnick bought an idea that was well out of the realm of the classy programs on which Talent Associates had built its reputation. An ad agency executive had told the partners about a soft-drink company promotion that had given contestants a chance to race through a supermarket while jamming as many items as possible in their shopping carts. Susskind and Melnick had veteran game-show producer Jerome Schnur develop it into a program. Schnur was a highly cultured man and a talented live-TV director. Later in his career, he staged ballet performances for PBS and produced a special on the Sistine Chapel. But in 1965, he designed the program called *Supermarket Sweep*, "the show that lets you run wild in your supermarket." The game required contestants to play a game, not unlike *The Price Is Right*, already popular at the time, in which they guessed the retail price of various products. The players were rewarded with minutes to race through supermarket aisles and accumulate items from the shelves. The player with the highest total value of items at the checkout counter was the winner. Unlike every other game show, *Supermarket Sweep* would not be in a studio, but on location in actual supermarkets. "We had a lot of jokes about it," said Ed Vane, an executive at ABC at the time. "But just imagine going to a different supermarket every week and trying to get the camera locations and everything. Technically it was a very difficult thing to do. Only true professionals could make it work."

Vane had recently arrived from NBC to take on the unenviable job of head of daytime programming for ABC. Still a weak number three in the ratings at the time, ABC's daytime shows were not even carried in about 15 percent of the country. "That was a major handicap and we had to scramble and do all sorts of different exciting things to get sampled," Vane recalled. He also remembered the advice he received from the man who gave him the job, ABC's president Tom Moore. "Now, remember, boy, in daytime we ain't improving the breed," he'd say in his Mississippi drawl. "Don't you bother your little head about quality or Peabody Awards. Just go get the money, kid." It was with those instructions in mind that Vane bought *Supermarket Sweep* from Talent Associates. "Perhaps it was too literal a translation of Tom's guidance," he said, looking back.

Schnur and the Talent Associates staffers assigned to the show needed to perfect the game format before ABC could put it on the air. "Little by little the format developed and we'd go out into real supermarkets and try it out," said Emily Perl Kingsley, who worked on the series. "In those days supermarkets were not open on Sundays. We'd come in Saturday night and we had to rig the place. We had to hang lights, set up bleachers for the audience, and have all those cameras, and so on. It wasn't like it is today with all this handheld stuff. There was huge equipment." A game-show casting expert went out into the community to find what the producers called "happy worthies." Kingsley described them as "cheerful people who needed the food" given away on the show.

The notion of people humiliating themselves on television for money and prizes was hardly novel in 1965. ABC had been running *Queen for a Day,* which started as a radio show back in the 1940s. Female contestants told sob stories before a studio audience about some pitiable life circumstance, such as caring for a physically or mentally disabled child, or having an out-of-work husband. An applause meter measuring the response determined the winner, who was crowned and showered with prizes. "The one who would go on to win *Queen for a Day* was the one who had the saddest story," said Bill Chastain, who was Schnur's longtime partner. "So it was not something that's totally foreign." But *Supermarket Sweep* was an optimistic glorification of consumerism set in the brightly lit shiny palaces where Americans celebrated it every day. "The only thing that makes *Supermarket Sweep* sort of impossible to believe was that it was the product of David Susskind and Dan Melnick," said Chastain.

From the start, Susskind tried to distance himself from the show. Susskind was known for his ability to hold a room spellbound when he pitched a program proposal, but he was nowhere in sight when Schnur and Ashley Famous agent Sy Fischer first presented the concept for *Supermarket Sweep* to Vane at his ABC office. "Even in the first meeting there were some giggles to explain why he wasn't there," said Vane. "It just struck me as unusual that the head of a production company would sort of disown his presentation." Fischer wasn't surprised. "David Susskind would never admit to having food from a supermarket," he said.

Campus remembered when Susskind journeyed out to a store in Paramus, New Jersey, to watch one of the early *Supermarket Sweep* tapings. "He was crushed," Campus recalled. "He was saying, 'I don't care if we close the place down, I can't do this.' He walked off to his car. I guess someone else was driving him. And he left because it was too much for him."

After a few test shows, the producers decided that the average woman watching TV at home during the day didn't want to see herself portrayed as a crazed harridan scrambling through supermarket aisles. So the female contestants would play the pricing game and have male runners, either a relative or friend, race through the store for them. One runner in a test show had a heart attack. After that the runners had to be forty or under and have a note from a physician certifying they were healthy enough to participate. "The designated runner actually made it better because they were faster and greedier and there was more action," said Vane. "And when they collided—we always hoped they would—it made for good television."

As the weeks passed, the producers worked the kinks out of the program during the trial runs. ABC executives knew they had a potential hit. In test showings held at movie theaters, *Supermarket Sweep* received the most enthusiastic reaction the network had ever seen for one of its daytime shows.

But supermarket owners were put off by how the game disrupted their stores. Five weeks before *Supermarket Sweep* was scheduled to make its debut on ABC in December 1965, Talent Associates still didn't have a commitment from enough store chains to make a five-day-a-week show on location. Susskind, who was used to wooing the likes of Laurence Olivier and Ingrid Bergman for high-toned television specials, steeled himself to get on the telephone and use his persuasive powers to convince store executives to participate. So did Melnick. The survival of Talent Associates depended on it.

Over much of the same period, Susskind and Melnick struggled to launch a situation comedy. It was another genre in which Talent Associates had no expertise. They found inspiration on the list of box office hits listed each week in the Hollywood trades. In 1964, *Goldfinger,* featuring Ian Fleming's secret agent character James Bond, was one of the year's biggest hits. Another major success at the time was *The Pink Panther,* featuring Peter Sellers as the clueless detective Inspector Clouseau. Melnick believed there was a series idea in combining the elements of both films. He presented the idea to comic writers and performers Mel Brooks and Buck Henry.

"It was so-and-so meets so-and-so, one of those combo pitches that are famous and awful in the movie business—'Lassie Meets Superman,'" Henry said. "But this one was the clearest and best I've ever heard. He said it separately to Mel. I know he said it to me. He said, 'There are two things out there that are making a big deal right now: Inspector Clouseau and James Bond.' Makes sense? You bet it does."

Brooks and Henry were camped out for the next three months at the Talent Associates office, kicking around ideas while shooting pool in what used to be the conference room at the office. Whether or not writers or directors had a project with the company, they lined up day and night to play at the table. "It was a place to hang out," said Mel Brooks, already an habitué of the room. "It was a good place to order Chinese food from."

Buck Henry met Melnick through his college pal, Bob Rafelson. At the time, Henry was writing for a weekly musical satire show *That Was the Week That Was,* and had previously been in the comedy group The Premise, where he did a bit that lampooned Susskind. Portrayed as "David Unkind," Henry presented him as a long-winded, pompous name-dropper who spoke in long complex sentences. "His point was completely forgotten by the time he'd gotten to the middle of it," Henry explained. "It was great fun to do."

Before meeting Susskind, Henry expected him to be "an endlessly talking semi-asshole who knew a lot of stuff but was irritating." But he ended up enjoying their brief conversations in the corridors of Talent Associates. "If you ran into him in the hall and you said, 'The show last night—what about that guy?' You would get an interesting story and some good information," he said. "Socially, he was friendly, pleasant, and giving, I thought." Susskind effectively used the egghead perception he projected to hustle Brooks and Henry at pool. "The irritating thing about that was we were both better pool players than David and he always won," Henry said. "We were always intimidated by him. There was just something about him walking around the table, talking about some deep thought about the political system and—whack! He talked us out of a living. We thought he was a terrible player and we thought we were going to beat him every goddamned time he came into the room. And we never did."

Brooks and Henry eventually came up with *Get Smart.* Their early notes for the show envisioned the Bond character, named Maxwell Smart, as self-absorbed and inept yet supremely confident as he forged ahead against foreign enemy forces on behalf of a Washington-based government surveillance agency called CONTROL. His female partner was just known as Agent 99, a beautiful linguist, judo expert, and crack shot who was "driven by an unquenchable enthusiasm for danger and an inexplicable passion for Max." She often bailed Max out of harrowing situations created by his incompetence. Their boss, the Chief, had a fatherly affection for Max but also a "deep-seated practical wish" that the agent choose another profession not related to protecting the free world.

The show gently mocked government bureaucracy and cold war politics. It was packed with visual gags that parodied Bond's array of gadgets. Smart talked into a phone in his shoe. Agent 99 replied back into a ball of wool, the knitting needles acting as antennae. When Smart asked that a "cone of silence" protect a confidential conversation with the Chief, it was shown as a giant device with two huge clear plastic cones descended around them, making it impossible for one to hear the other. The first villain, named Mr. Big, was played by a dwarf.

"Our intention was very clear and straightforward and noncomplex," said Henry. "It was to make sport of a level of the government and of our relationship to it and of a style of melodrama. We never considered doing it as a sitcom. Neither Melnick nor I would have known how to do it. I was almost always happy dealing with the kind of amiable lunacy of it. But it was terribly hard work."

ABC programming head Edgar Scherick, who bought the idea and ordered a script for $7,500, simply didn't get it. A spy spoof was fine as an element of a variety show. But no one had ever tried such a concept as a weekly series. He decided against making the series and even asked for the network's money back. Henry remembers the words "un-American" attached to the rejection. Melnick and Susskind had to get the money together to refund ABC and send their agent, Dick Dorso, out to shop the script again.

Dorso found a prospect in NBC, which had been looking for a series for Don Adams, a nightclub comic who delivered lines in an exaggerated version of actor William Powell's *Thin Man*–style clipped speech. Adams had played a house detective in an NBC sitcom, *The Bill Dana Show*. The series had been canceled and the network still had Adams under contract and wanted to use him. NBC executive Grant Tinker liked the *Get Smart* script and got Talent Associates to agree to cast Adams as Maxwell Smart in the pilot. His delivery was perfect for conveying the character's lack of self-awareness. For Agent 99, Talent Associates wanted Barbara Feldon, who had become a favorite at the company. A tall sultry-voiced model for Revlon and former nightclub dancer, Feldon had been an extra for a party scene on the *East Side/West Side* series. She had once been an acting protégée of George C. Scott's wife, Colleen Dewhurst, who recognized her when she saw her on the set of her husband's show. After introducing Feldon to Scott, he cast her as the girlfriend of his character Neil Brock in an upcoming episode. Feldon later played a glamorous industrial spy in a featured guest role alongside Craig Stevens on *Mr. Broadway.*

The part essentially became the template for Agent 99. Ed Platt, a solid character actor regularly seen in authoritative roles on TV, was a perfect fit as the exasperated no-nonsense Chief.

"It was remarkably put together," said Leonard Stern, a veteran comedy writer who was brought in by Melnick to run the production of *Get Smart*. "Don with his vocal qualities was perfect casting. It was a fortuitous happening. They couldn't have found anybody better. Then there was something genteel and sensual about Barbara. Barbara was definitely David and Dan's discovery and belief." Stern's first of many contributions to the show was the signature title sequence in which Adams walked through a seemingly endless series of clanging automatic doors that opened in time to the brassy marchlike theme.

The sight gags on *Get Smart* appealed to children, while adults enjoyed the show's irreverent satire. In the days of baby boomers growing up and watching TV with their parents, that was an ideal formula for ratings success, which came almost immediately after its premiere on September 18, 1965. At first there were complaints from the network that Adams' vocal delivery was too strident. But several weeks into the show, a catchphrase that succinctly expressed Smart's well-meaning but hapless nature—"Sorry about that, Chief"— was impersonated on TV by someone at NASA ground control during coverage of the *Gemini 7* space flight. It was in response to the news that a urine bag had broken inside the cabin. TV viewers were captive audiences to the nation's space program at the time, and the massive exposure *Get Smart* received in that moment helped make it a pop-culture sensation. "That was exhilarating," said Stern. "We kept going for catchphrases. Fortunately, a number succeeded, but there were infinitely more that didn't."

As the confident and capable Agent 99, Feldon became a cool role model for girls while not being a threat to male viewers who were still years away from understanding or appreciating the concept of equality for women. "I think she was an amalgam of the 1950s, when women were meant to stand back and let the guy take credit for everything, and what was about to happen with the women's movement in the later 1960s, when women got really aggressive with men," Feldon said. "As part of the movement toward a better life for women, it was probably a natural and necessary stage to go through. Just like adolescents go through a certain stage, I think that was the adolescence of the women's movement. But 99 happened just on the cusp of that. Mel Brooks and Buck Henry, being artists, were envisioning what was to come without the edge in it. They were envisioning it happening—a woman being capable and smart and really getting credit from the Chief, certainly, but still retaining that respect for the male's ego."

Feldon was able to pull off every mod fashion look of the moment on the show and in magazine spreads. Andy Warhol did a pop art portrait of her for the cover of *TV Guide.* "99 was like a line drawing with all these little neat clothes," she said. "I grew up with those neat little cutout books. You cut out the dresses and there's the little cardboard figure and you put the little dresses with the tabs over the shoulders. That was sort of 99. It was all style infused with a human element, and a real communion with Max."

While the show was a parody of cold war paranoia, the producers and stars learned during and after the series that the government was watching them carefully. At one point early in the show's run, the FBI made an appointment to see Leonard Stern at the Paramount lot where the show was filmed. "They wanted to know where some of our ideas came from," Stern recalled. "And from their questioning, it was easy to infer that we were touching on things that existed, but the general public didn't know of. And they wanted to see whether there was any leak. They visited two or three times. The last time, when they were relaxed enough to accept that we had nothing but our imaginations feeding us information, they started to admit that they were fans of the show." (Years later Feldon was invited to CIA headquarters in Langley, Virginia, for an exhibit on spy paraphernalia from TV shows. She was told that caseworkers at the agency would try to imitate the gadgets seen on *Get Smart.* "It was life imitating art," she said.)

While the ratings for *Get Smart* were strong enough to give Talent Associates its first filmed hit series, the company did not see any immediate improvement to its balance sheet. A major reason was Don Adams, whose personal quirks posed challenges to the efficiency of the production. "With Don we were always behind schedule," recalled Jay Sandrich, a producer on the first season of the show. "Don always wanted to make it as exciting and as close to a feature film as he could. That's not a bad thing. But we weren't a feature film. We had to make this half hour in two and a half days. It was frustrating in many ways to Don. He wanted to get out there and do stunts and exciting car chases and things like that."

"Don wanted to be an action hero," said Buck Henry. "One day in the second year he insisted on doing his own stunt and got his jaw broken. Bang. He got fanned out. Busted his face. We had to do a show in which he is completely in a bandage, which of course isn't him, but it's his voice."

The more troublesome issue for the production was that Adams had a serious gambling habit. When he played Las Vegas lounges as a stand-up comic, he often took the $100,000 or so he earned in a week and then lost it gambling in the casinos. *Get Smart* shut down production more than once over its run so that Adams could go back to Vegas for more dates to cover his losses. "The first or second day we were back shooting I'd get a call, 'Don wants you down in his dressing room,'" Harry Sherman, a production manager on the show, recalled. "I would go down and he would suddenly be my pal. He would say, 'Harry, I'm in big, big trouble. I lost everything I made there. Dorothy is going to kill me.' That was his wife at the time, a very pretty gal who had been one of the June Taylor Dancers [the sexy female dance troupe best known for its work on *The Jackie Gleason Show*]. The only way, I guess, to keep him away from the tables was if Dorothy were to go with him and stay there."

It wasn't just Vegas. Adams had a regular poker game that often kept him up until four or five in the morning, just a few hours before shooting was set to start. "He would be wiped out," said Sherman. "It would take him a little longer to get up to speed." There was even action on the set. "He bet on everything," said Barbara Feldon. "He would bet on whether Ed Platt would forget his lines, or get tangled up in his lines, which drove Ed crazy. Because the more pressure that was on him, the harder it was for him to get the words out right. He always had these complicated things that he had to say, technical things in describing something to Max. So there was a lot of fun about that. But I don't think Ed was very comfortable with it. He'd put the radio on, and if there were games on, he bet on the games with the crew."

Buck Henry got a close-up look at Adams' obsession when they went together to the racetrack at Santa Anita. Adams gave him $100. "We're going to pool our bets," he told Henry.

Adams and Henry arrived in time to put money on the third race, which they won. They won the fourth, fifth, sixth, and seventh races, at which point they were up to $3,000. They had to make a decision on the eighth.

"Are you with me?" Adams asked.

"Of course I am," said Henry.

They lost it all. "But it was a great run," Henry recalled. "I was very fond of him."

Talent Associates stood to earn some money from its share of the series once there were enough episodes of the show to syndicate on local TV stations, but that was years down the road. In the short term, the production kept running up deficits. In November 1965, Dan Melnick went to Paramount president Barney Balaban and asked the studio to cover a greater share of the costs. "We were in terrible deficit and we tried to get them to give us more money," Melnick said. "Per episode we were going into the hole. It was explained to them the value of each half hour. And I couldn't budge them." Melnick came back with an offer in which he and Susskind and Stern, who had become a minority partner, would buy back Paramount's half of Talent Associates. "I made the offer in an attempt to get them to give us more money for *Get Smart,*" said Melnick.

But Balaban took him up on it. "I'm going to let you do this to get those sons of bitches off my back," he said, referring to two board members who were giving him trouble over the studio's stock price. The partners of Talent Associates could buy back the Paramount's 50 percent of the company for all of $1.

Melnick, Susskind, and Stern made the deal. Shortly afterward, Talent Associates finally got *Supermarket Sweep* up and running at ABC and it was an immediate sensation. *Sweep* tripled the size of the audience of the show it replaced. When the Allied Van Lines trucks arrived outside of a supermarket with the sets and technical equipment used to set up the game, overflow crowds showed up. Unlike *Get Smart, Sweep* was lucrative for Talent Associates as soon as it went on the air.

While *Supermarket Sweep* saved Susskind's company, he made sure the press was aware that he was not involved in the show. "I have nothing to do with it," Susskind told *TV Guide.* "We have given it a home and provide necessary facilities to put it together. But that's all. These programs are produced by people who know and love them. But I couldn't get within a mile of it as a producer. I wouldn't know how." Susskind occasionally visited Schnur and Emily Perl Kingsley in the office they shared at Talent Associates. "Once a week David would sort of stick his head in the door sheepishly to find out how much money they'd made," said Chastain. "He was embarrassed about doing the show, but he loved the income."

15

While David Susskind and Daniel Melnick had to focus on creating more commercial series so that Talent Associates could survive, they never gave up on the idea of bringing prestigious serious drama back to television.

In the spring of 1963, Susskind attempted to create a TV home for stage plays through a deal he made with Videotape Productions, operated by former CBS executive Howard Meighan. Meighan's facility, known as the Videotape Center, had been a busy hub for TV and commercial production on the Upper West Side of Manhattan. Susskind convinced Meighan's company to put up $15,000 and provide the studio space at the center for the pilot of a one-hour series that would present the works of contemporary playwrights such as Harold Pinter, Eugene Ionescu, and Samuel Beckett. In return, Videotape Productions was to share in the revenue generated by the program, which was to be sponsored and then syndicated to TV stations.

The first play Susskind selected for the program was *The American Dream* by Edward Albee. At the time, the playwright's best-known work, *Who's Afraid of Virginia Woolf?*, was a few months into its first successful run on Broadway. Albee had yet to have a play produced for television and was pleased when his agent at William Morris told him Susskind wanted *The American Dream* for the new series he called *Command Performance*. "I remember being very enthusiastic about it," Albee said. "And I remember being delighted that they were willing to give me a Dramatists Guild contract. You get director approval, cast approval, and not a word of the play can be cut without the author's approval."

The cast included Ruth Gordon, Celeste Holm, Ernest Truex, Sudie Bond, and George Maharis, who had been in the original off-Broadway stage production of Albee's *The Zoo Story*. Susskind also pleased Albee by hiring David Pressman to direct. The show was one of his first jobs after being blacklisted for ten years.

After reading the script, Meighan immediately expressed concerns about its commercial prospects. Getting sponsors to buy into an hour of theater of the absurd was going to be tough enough. But the scatological and sexual references in Albee's play—which Meighan referred to as "questionable material" in his correspondence to Susskind—was going to make it an even tougher sell. "I would be the first to eliminate myself as a judge of scripts or indeed any theatrical literature," Meighan wrote to Susskind. "I do however have a modest experience in the field of client reaction and audience reaction." By the time the play went into production, several pages of dialogue and a few phrases were excised from the script.

Albee was not aware of the edits until he attended the rehearsals of the play at the Videotape Center. He let Susskind know right away that he wasn't happy. "I don't like these cuts," he said. "They go against contract. This is not my entire play." Susskind told Albee not to worry and wait for the finished product. As the rehearsals proceeded, it was explained to Albee that cuts had to be made to fit the play into an hour-long broadcast. "Okay, so it goes over an hour. Cut some of the commercials," was the reply from the self-possessed writer, already on his way to a Pulitzer Prize–winning career. Albee was not about to give in. But Susskind went ahead and taped a performance of the play.

"I remember thinking that David was making a mistake," Albee recalled.

Jack Willis, an associate producer on the project, said it was typical for Susskind to press on with his plans even after being given a reason to stop. "David thought he could charm anybody," he said. "And I can imagine him thinking Albee wouldn't dare pull the plug after they went to the expense of taping it." Maharis believed Susskind took the typically low-key Albee for a pushover. "Edward Albee wasn't very explosive about it or aggressive about it," said Maharis. "That's the kind of human being that he is. Somebody like a David Susskind, who was a lot more aggressive, would not take him as seriously and felt he could manipulate him or control him or do what he wanted. What I heard from Susskind is that he had bought the property and he could do what he wanted with it."

Susskind was wrong. After Albee watched the finished *Command Performance* pilot that featured *The American Dream,* he refused to approve it for air. He did not even read the final contract, let alone sign it. Susskind and Meighan had a pilot, but no rights to Albee's play. Meighan was not even aware that Albee had the right to sign off on the final version until after the program was taped. He had also learned the day before the taping that Susskind received a letter from the producers of *Route 66,* the CBS series that Maharis had recently starred in. They maintained Maharis was still under contract to them and was prohibited from doing any other television work, even though he had left the series the year before because of a bout with hepatitis. "They were threatening anybody that came near me because that's what they did in Hollywood back then," said Maharis.

Still, Meighan was stunned that he wasn't informed about either development until after *The American Dream* had been taped. By the time Meighan was notified, Susskind was flying back and forth to England. He spent much of the early summer there with his daughters at a twenty-three-room Windsor manor in Berkshire, shuttling around London in a chauffeur-driven Humber and looking for theater properties to produce in the United States. The British press lapped up Susskind's delicious quotes during the period, such as his description of Elizabeth Taylor as "overweight, over-bosomed, overpaid and under-talented."

Meighan eventually reached Dan Melnick, who tried to smooth things over. He promised to reshoot the pilot in September with a script that would be approved by Videotape Productions. But Albee refused to approve the existing pilot even for use as a presentation to attract sponsors or stations in the interim.

By September 1963, Susskind and Melnick were consumed with work on *East Side/West Side* and the pilot for *Mr. Broadway.* Meighan could not even get a phone call returned from Talent Associates. "You have abandoned the project without even consulting us," Meighan wrote to Susskind. He asked for his money back and was ready to call his lawyer if he didn't get it.

Susskind could not dodge Meighan much longer, since his talk show *Open End* was scheduled to start taping at the Videotape Center in October of that year. He apparently settled with Meighan and announced that he was scrapping plans for *Command Performance.* Susskind blamed closed-minded advertisers for the show's failure to launch. "Sponsors Reject Top Playwrights," the headline read in *The New York Times* on November 18, 1963. Susskind told the reporter that "after spending five months crossing the country with *The American Dream,* dozens of ad agencies and sponsors felt the project was frankly too egghead, frankly too cultural." While there were discussions with at least one potential sponsor for the program, the pilot episode never made the rounds. It never left the building where it was produced. Susskind's hyperbole about advertiser resistance covered what was ultimately his own mistake. He was credible because the press had seen and heard the scenario in so many other similar situations regarding sensitivity over program content that was the slightest bit provocative. But the incident may have added to a growing belief within the TV industry that Susskind was no longer a dependable producer.

As the turbulent 1960s progressed, prime-time television remained timid. It became apparent to some members of the new generation of executives in corporate America that it was time for television to grow up. It can be argued that it finally did in the spring of 1966, when CBS aired the Talent Associates production of Arthur Miller's *Death of a Salesman.*

Susskind had long wanted to do *Salesman* for television. (If Susskind felt any personal connection to the play because of his own father, a salesman who committed suicide, it wasn't something he shared publicly.) During the 1950s, he proposed it for *The DuPont Show of the Month.* The idea was nixed, as the company did not want its messages inside the searing psychological drama that depicted delusion, depression, and death. Miller also was not eager to sell his work to TV, saying he did not want to run the gauntlet of compromises necessary to please sponsors. Susskind's chances to make the show improved after his representatives at the Ashley Famous Agency absorbed several agents and clients from Music Corporation of America. Citing antitrust concerns, the government had ruled that MCA could no longer have a talent agency in tandem with its movie and television studio. One arm had to go and it was the agency business. As a result, Ashley Famous Agency picked up some former MCA business, which included Miller. Dan Melnick remembered how Ashley Famous wanted Talent Associates to produce the works of the more literary playwrights handled by the agency's "blue-haired ladies," as he called them. Melnick said the company was given what amounted to a free option on several plays, including *Death of a Salesman.* It meant that Susskind and Melnick did not have to bid on the rights to secure the properties for a period of time while they sought a network to agree to produce it. While the networks had become wary of Susskind, his discussions about culture and politics on his talk show had secured his reputation as a serious producer among the esteemed literati. "I know the ladies in the corridor felt very comfortable placing their clients with David," Jerry Leider recalled. "His talk show gave him a cachet that other guys didn't have. He was deemed to be an intellectual, which was very impressive to an Arthur Miller, a Tennessee Williams, or a William Inge. It helped that we represented them."

An opening came in the 1965–1966 television season. Socially conscious drama series had faded with the memories of the Kennedy era. Producer Herb Brodkin, who had the most success with the genre with *The Defenders* and *The Nurses,* saw both shows canceled in 1965. The networks were giving viewers a heavy diet of situation comedies (thirty-two half hours a week in 1965, including Talents Associates' own *Get Smart* on NBC—up from twenty-one half hours two years before). Even a Nazi prisoner-of-war camp was played for laughs on the CBS hit *Hogan's Heroes.* The high ratings gave the network executives every reason to believe that viewers wanted lowbrow escapism, especially after Kennedy's assassination on November 22, 1963. *The Beverly Hillbillies,* the slapstick CBS comedy about a family from the Ozarks that moves to America's glitziest neighborhood, was already a top-rated series when the president's tragic end stunned the nation. But the show's numbers surged to stratospheric heights in the months that followed the mourning period. There were weeks when Jed Clampett's clan was watched by more than 40 percent of the nation's TV homes, accounting for some of the biggest audiences up to that time.

During the 1965–1966 season, FCC chairman E. William Henry was making enough noise about the lack of program diversity to get the network executives to nervously take note, just as they had a few years earlier after Newton Minow's "vast wasteland" speech. Henry sent letters to all the networks inquiring about their scheduling decisions, following a number of inquiries from viewers upset about the cancellation of their favorite programs. The chairman started making public speeches about the decline of drama on TV and proposed curtailing network ownership of prime-time programs (a decree that went into effect five years later). Susskind claimed the unhappiness expressed at the time by government and civic groups sent the networks hunting for high-minded fare. He went to CBS with a proposal to make *Death of a*

Salesman, along with several other dramatic specials based on literary classics, with the assurance "that all of them would be productions of distinction and would reflect great credit on the network and sponsor." He also said he could get Lee J. Cobb, then a TV star on NBC's western *The Virginian,* to reprise the Willy Loman role he originated in the 1949 Broadway production.

Dick Dorso, who represented Talent Associates at the time, said CBS wanted *Salesman* without Susskind. "He had lost credibility as a producer," said Dorso, then an agent at Ashley Famous. "In this business, reputation is repetition. And enough people were saying that David didn't have it anymore." Michael Dann, CBS programming chief at the time, said the network was tired of losing money on Susskind's projects. But Dorso told him CBS was in "an impossible position" in regard to *Salesman* because Susskind had the option on the play. The reply from Dann was: options expire.

"David, they're determined not to have you produce this," Dorso told Susskind. "You better do something about it. Because they're going to wait till the option expires and then do it without you." According to Dorso, Susskind exercised the option himself, paying $250,000 for the TV rights to Miller's play. If CBS wanted *Salesman,* Dorso said, they had to make it with David Susskind. Dann bought it as a special with Talent Associates as producer.

Dan Melnick agreed that the networks were becoming image-conscious at the time of the *Salesman* deal. But he believed there might have been another issue involved at CBS. "I think Mike Dann bought it to impress his wife," he said. Dann, who had great commercial success as an executive at CBS in the 1960s, often acknowledged that his first wife hated television. "My greatest triumphs had largely been celebrated alone," he wrote in his memoir.

"Mike Dann's wife being bugged," Melnick said. "Don't discount that."

As promised, Susskind lined up Cobb and his former Broadway costar Mildred Dunnock to re-create their roles of Willy and Linda Loman. George Segal was cast as the troubled, underachieving Biff Loman, and James Farentino played Biff's sexually compulsive brother Hap. Gene Wilder, who idolized Miller's play as an aspiring actor growing up in Wisconsin, was cast as Bernard, the serious-minded childhood friend of Hap and Biff.

Susskind hired the strong-willed Alex Segal to direct. A veteran of many Susskind TV productions and the theatrical film *All the Way Home,* Alex Segal was known for his vein-bulging temper tantrums. "This was a guy who would go purple when he got angry," said George Segal, who is not related to the director. Susskind often yielded to the judgment of Alex Segal, one of a few directors who held that distinction.

Staged at CBS Television City in Hollywood, scenic designer Tom John created a circular set for *Salesman* that allowed Alex Segal to make the pace of the program faster and more fluid than past televised play productions. It retained the stage version's revolutionary technique of moving to different periods of time and locations without closing the curtain or changing the scenery. "We shot it an act at a time," recalled George Segal. "That gave you the feeling of watching a theatrical production. We shot one act and then we would shoot it again. And then we would go to the next act. We did that over a couple of days. This was after rehearsing for a good three weeks, which was unheard of at the time. They got things that they never got before on that show."

Alex Segal and John effectively used color for the shifting time sequences in the play. When showing the dreary present-day existence of the Lomans, the set was decorated and lit to bring out heavy earth tones. The flashback scenes were saturated with vivid, bright hues of light green, light blue, violet, and pink "to evoke spring flowers," Alex Segal explained at the time.

Alex Segal worked closely with Miller on making cuts from the play for time. Although Miller was quoted as saying he did not have to make any compromises, Melnick recalled how he and Susskind deliberated with the network over language and content issues. George Segal remembered a debate over the scene when Willy Loman is with a woman while traveling on the road in Boston. "He pats her on the ass there in the bathroom," Segal recalled. "The network censored it and said they had to cut above the pat on the ass." A reference by Linda Loman to her son Hap about "going out with whores" was also removed.

But the TV script was considered less sanitized than Columbia Pictures' 1951 theatrical film version of the play. Miller was said to be happy with the final product (although years later he described the production as "condensed"). CBS was confident enough to put out a press release saying the playwright was moved to tears during a private screening before it aired.

For a while nobody knew when the viewing public would see the show. CBS scheduled the show for April 4, 1966. As that date approached, not a single advertiser could be found who wanted to be a part of a first-class TV presentation of one of the most celebrated American plays of the century. The themes of despair, madness, and suicide in Miller's story kept potential sponsors away, until one emerging company finally stepped up.

The Xerox Corporation had become skilled at making opportunistic advertising buys as it rapidly grew during the 1960s. Xerox was managed by the first post–World War II generation of graduates coming out of Harvard Business School. They were young, aggressive, and not afraid of sponsoring programs that were considered a little dangerous.

"The programs that Xerox wanted to do were letter-provoking, thought-provoking, annoyance-provoking stuff," said Fred Papert, then chairman of Papert Koenig Lois, the ad agency for Xerox. "The company chairman Joe Wilson's take was the more letters you get—even hate mail—the better off the country is. His main take was if the society is going down the tubes we're not going to get any business anyhow. That's why they wanted to do good programming. The image of the company was one that cared about art, culture, and discourse."

"They wanted to be Medicis and it worked for them," said William Murphy, an executive at Papert Koenig Lois. "It benefited them in the educational community and Wall Street." That was no small matter, as all those school mimeograph machines were ready to be replaced by Xerox's dry-copying process. The company's stock was one of the high-flyers of the mid-1960s.

Xerox executives wore controversy as a badge of honor. Two years later, in 1968, when the company sponsored a CBS News series called *In Black America,* it received a letter from the Grand Wizard of the Ku Klux Klan requesting the service on his copy machine be terminated. Frank Marshall, who worked as an advertising consultant for the company at the time, said he made sure every major newspaper and wire service in the country knew about the request from the KKK.

Xerox became the sole sponsor of *Death of a Salesman* for a bargain rate of $250,000. CBS had paid Susskind $580,000 for the production. When the actual cost of the airtime was figured in, the network's net loss was $630,000. But it was able to set an airdate.

The only public backlash Xerox received for its participation was a written protest from an organization called Sales Executive Club of New York. The executive director wanted the show to have a brief epilogue called "Life of a Salesman" that would cite "modern customer-oriented selling methods." The aim was to "dispel the idea that the rewards of a selling career are often disillusionment and death." The proposal was virtually a replay of what Columbia Pictures attempted when it released its movie version of Miller's play. At that time the studio produced a short called *Career of a Salesman,* intended to run before the movie. The short extolled the sales profession and had Stanley Kramer, the film's producer, stating that the "Willy Lomans of the world are largely extinct." It essentially mitigated the downbeat message of the film. "It was cultural McCarthyism and it occurred just about the time the play was being attacked in this country as a time bomb set by Communists to blow up the country," Miller later told writer Ronald Hayman. The playwright claimed he got the short pulled from theaters.

Xerox and its ad agency had no desire to soften the message of *Salesman* for television. After the program aired on May 8, 1966, the company's executives looked like geniuses. The production drew raves from nearly every TV critic across the country. Congratulatory telegrams and letters for Susskind and Melnick piled up in the Talent Associates office in the days after it aired. After sitting through a TV season with few nutritious calories, critics were stunned by the feast presented before them that evening. "Like a drowning man in a last gasp for air, the medium came alive with *Death of a Salesman*," *Newsweek* wrote. "*Death* was so superior to most things available on TV in recent memory it gave this viewer a strange feeling to see something so good appear on a glass screen," said the *Chicago Tribune* review. But even more impressive to the networks was the 30 percent share of the viewing audience the special garnered against TV's number one show at the time, NBC's *Bonanza*. The number of viewers who watched *Salesman* that night—17 million—was twenty times that of the attendance for 742 performances of the play's original Broadway run.

Salesman aired too late in the season to be eligible for the Emmy Awards presented on June 4, 1966 (it won the following year). Still, the glow of Talent Associates' recent triumph was in full effect during the televised ceremony. Xerox had been given the National Academy of Television Arts and Sciences Trustees Award in recognition of its sponsorship of quality programs. Susskind and Melnick won the Emmy Award for Program of the Year for the production of *The Ages of Man,* which featured Sir John Gielgud performing soliloquies from Shakespeare plays. They had sold the show to CBS around the same time as *Salesman,* but it had been relegated to running on a Sunday afternoon in January. The victory was sweet. "In this moment of pleasure and recognition I can't help but remember we also produced *Kelly* and *Mr. Broadway,*" a humbled Susskind said from the lectern in the Americana Hotel ballroom as he held his winged statuette. "David has said it all," said Melnick. Looking splendidly prosperous in their tuxedos, you would never know how close the company came to oblivion. *Supermarket Sweep* was ringing the cash register for ABC. *Get Smart,* which also won an Emmy that night for comedy writing, was a top fifteen show in the Nielsen ratings. At the same time, the partners could bask in the spotlight and kudos that came from bringing Arthur Miller and Shakespeare to the masses. They successfully launched a new syndicated program, *Esso Repertory Theatre,* that featured works by the regional repertory companies sprouting up around the country in the mid-1960s.

The ratings for *Salesman* made it almost fashionable for networks and sponsors to pursue ambitious dramatic productions through the rest of the 1960s and well into the 1970s. Original plays and restaged classics were in demand, as the networks saw that it was possible to amass both critical accolades and large audiences. Talent Associates was a major beneficiary of the trend. Almost immediately, Xerox signed on to sponsor Susskind productions of Miller's *The Crucible* and Tennessee Williams' *The Glass Menagerie* for the 1967–1968 season. Susskind and Melnick were also hired to produce shows for *Stage '67,* ABC's first dramatic anthology series in a decade. *Variety* summed up the Talent Associates comeback with the headline "David & Dan: TV's 'Play' Boys."

When Susskind's rebound was chronicled in *Newsweek* in the fall of 1966, two photos accompanied the story. One was of Cobb and Dunnock in *Death of a Salesman.* The other was of three T-shirted men behind shiny steel shopping carts ready to go crashing through the aisles on what the magazine called the "daytime greed-fest," *Supermarket Sweep.* After several years of being in serious professional peril, Susskind had no trouble justifying his motley stable of productions. He had gone from being an idealist to a realist. "If I stuck just to my mold," he said, "I'd be out of business."

16

With Paramount no longer in the picture, Susskind and Melnick controlled the destiny of Talent Associates. The two partners wanted to remain in New York, but Melnick, who had brought Leonard Stern on to oversee *Get Smart,* wanted to develop more shows on the West Coast. "Dan said, 'We need somebody in California because neither David nor I want to live there, and I recommended you,'" Stern said. "The three of us met. And we talked. And we had rapport. I think we were all intellectually compatible. Our precepts of life and concepts of living were harmonious. We were different in how we expressed ourselves." Stern, who sported a Mephisthophelean beard and stood well over six feet tall, remembered one specific request from Susskind before the partnership was sealed. "Will you do me a favor?" he asked. "When we're talking, will you sit?"

As a partner, Stern had to adjust to Susskind's habit of inserting himself into a project at the last moment. In 1966, Stern created a series for NBC called *The Hero,* which starred Richard Mulligan as a TV western star who is invincible on screen but has difficulty managing his suburban home life. Before Stern's finished pilot was delivered to the network, Susskind did his own edit on it. When Stern looked at it again, he was aghast at how Susskind had cut the film down to twenty-three minutes, about four minutes shorter than the typical program running time for a half-hour sitcom of that period.

"David," Stern said. "You cut to the bare bones."

Susskind told him the executives at NBC would never notice that it ran short. "He was so right," Stern said. "When it was over they said, 'That was a fast half hour.'" NBC bought the show and put it on the 1966–1967 schedule.

Susskind mostly weighed in from New York about the costs on *Get Smart.* Some of the money NBC put up for the production of the series went back to New York to help finance Talent Associates' more highbrow projects. Stern fought for the dollars he believed he needed to make *Get Smart* work. "David would be upset over that when he saw the statements," said Harry Sherman, a producer on the show. "Leonard very much wanted to see that it was a success financially. But he also would insist upon perfection with certain gags, and sometimes we had to reshoot them because they didn't come off as well as they should have. And he was right. There's nothing worse than a badly executed gag." Stern's persistence paid off, as *Get Smart* won seven Emmy Awards during its five-year run, including two for outstanding comedy series.

The success of *Get Smart* did lead the networks to order more sitcoms from Talent Associates. One of Academy Award–winning screenwriter Marc Norman's first jobs was as a $65-a-week assistant to Stern. He took copious notes as Stern formulated show concepts out loud in his office. "I could take his rough ideas for a pilot and turn it into a ten-page treatment that was more than just kind of an operator's manual of the series," said Norman. "I'd make it look like it was an ancient document, or in Middle English. I'd make it a secret government paper that was a report on something. I would put some spin on it that made it interesting."

Out of those sessions, Stern came up with a series called *He & She,* about a young married couple living in New York City. "Our stories are of the first year of life together . . . of their adjusting and coming to terms with each other . . . those years of discovery when you learn you are living with someone you hardly know and that someone is you," the proposal said. The couple would have no children, but quirky childlike friends and oddball associates who came through their apartment. One was a firefighter who walked across a plank from the firehouse next door and entered through the couple's window. "There are more doors in their apartment than a French farce," Stern wrote in a proposal that was illustrated like a children's storybook.

In 1967, CBS was eager to do a series for Paula Prentiss, a long-legged Texas beauty who had worked steadily in films after having debuted in *Where the Boys Are.* CBS programming chief Mike Dann said Talent Associates could produce the show if Stern came up with a suitable idea. "She was sensual, tall, beautiful figure, and funny," Stern recalled. "I didn't know Paula Prentiss. I dismissed it."

Meanwhile, Stern's wife Gloria, an actress, had recently been in Chicago, where she had seen a road company staging of Neil Simon's *Barefoot in the Park*. "I just saw a performance and I'm going to tell you the name of the person because I think he's so much your type of actor," she told her husband. "His name is Richard Benjamin." Stern filed the name away in his head.

A short time later, Stern was at his weekly poker game where he was seated next to a player who was filling in for one of the regulars. It was Paula Prentiss's agent.

"I have an idea for Paula," Stern told him. "May I send it to you?" The agent said sure and soon had the proposal for *He & She,* which had been shopped around for a couple of years by that time.

The agent liked it. "But there's a kicker," he told Stern. "She will only work with her husband." Prentiss was tired of long stretches away from home while working on film sets.

"Who's her husband?" Stern asked.

"It's not somebody you will know," the agent said. "His name is Richard Benjamin."

Trusting his wife's judgment about Benjamin, Stern did not have to wait a beat before agreeing to attach him to the show as well. He called Dann to say he could get a commitment from Prentiss to do a series. Using the agent's words, he added, "There's a kicker. She wants to work only with her husband."

"That's okay," Dann said. "Make the deal."

Two weeks after Talent Associates signed the couple to the show, Stern had a message from Dann to call him in New York.

"Leonard?" Dann said. "Did you make that deal with her husband?"

Stern said that he did. There was a pause on Dann's end of the line before he asked, "Is her husband an actor?"

The fully realized *He & She* had Richard Benjamin and Paula Prentiss playing Dick and Paula Hollister. He was a cartoonist whose character Jet Man had been made into a TV show (a nod to the *Batman* series that had turned the comic book hero into a pop culture phenomenon at the time). Paula Hollister was an earnest volunteer aide to foreign travelers at a New York airport. Jack Cassidy was Oscar North, a foppish, narcissistic actor who had the role of Jet Man on TV. It was a perfect piece of casting, Melnick believed, as Cassidy was "a guy who couldn't pass a mirror without looking into it."

After *He & She* was added to the CBS schedule for the 1967–1968 season,

Susskind touted the show with his customary fervor. "Smooth, polished sophisticated comedy in the tradition of Cary Grant and Irene Dunne . . . Doris Day and Rock Hudson," he raved to a *New York Times* writer. Early on, critics dismissed *He & She* as a copy of *The Dick Van Dyke Show*. But in a short time Stern's series was recognized for its own distinctive voice. Benjamin played Dick Hollister with a sardonic New York attitude that suggested the world was conspiring against him. Prentiss softened him perfectly with her character, who was big-hearted, buoyant, and sexy. The banter between the Hollisters was always playful. It never devolved into the putdowns that had become standard in domestic sitcoms. "A comedy based on love—and I really believe this one was—is harder to sell and harder to sustain," said Stern. "Why? I don't know. But comedy writers generally can do deprecating humor much more readily and easily than they can humor that is loving and caring."

Benjamin and Prentiss were committed to the show's approach, and their genuine affection for each other as a real-life couple came across on the screen. Benjamin wanted their relationship off camera to be respected as well. He refused to discuss producers' notes about his wife's performance unless she was present. "I'm an actor," he would tell Stern.

Yet directing Prentiss and Benjamin did require some skillful navigation. Jay Sandrich, who directed most of the episodes, remembered one about the Hollisters' agreement to put a five-dollar limit on birthday gifts. Dick ignores the edict and buys his wife a beautiful coat. Paula abides by the rule and gives her husband a small rock that fell on him during their first date in the Adirondacks. She tells him she plans to have it made into a key chain. Dick is dejected as he stares at his spartan gift, in spite of the agreement. Paula is hurt and a bit angry that he's so sad about it. Dick then loses the rock. The story ended happily, but off camera, Paula Prentiss could not let go of Paula Hollister's bruised feelings.

"She was mad at Richard all week," Sandrich said. "I remember saying, 'Paula, he didn't do it. The character in the show did it.' In her mind she was a very serious actress and this guy that she's living with is the character in the show sometimes."

Cassidy got the biggest laughs on *He & She* as the pompous, hammy Oscar North, but the character made CBS executives nervous. "They were concerned about Jack, who we characterized as a mama's boy," Stern said. "But he was playing the gay end of it." Stern said he was told to "minimize" the role, which was really a subtle suggestion to fire Cassidy. Stern refused.

Harry Sherman, the unit production manager on the show, believed the issue with the North character was a factor in CBS's decision not to pick up *He & She* for a second season. (At first, ratings were lackluster for the show, which was parked right on the schedule behind two of the network's rural comedies, *The Beverly Hillbillies* and *Green Acres*). After the cancellation was announced, there was strong word of mouth for the show and the audience started to grow. In the spring of 1968, Prentiss, Benjamin, and Jack Cassidy were all nominated for Emmy Awards, and the series won in the category of Outstanding Writing in a Comedy. The network wanted to reverse itself and return *He & She*. It was too late, as Prentiss and Benjamin had already moved on and were signed to do the film *Catch-22* for director Mike Nichols.

But *He & She* had a lasting impact, as it paved the way for the more sophisticated, urban-based TV comedies of the 1970s, many of which came out of MTM Enterprises, the company formed by Mary Tyler Moore and her then-husband Grant Tinker. Sandrich says it was his work on *He & She* that led MTM to hire him as the primary director on *The Mary Tyler Moore Show*.

Stern then sold another series to CBS called *The Good Guys*, about two lifelong underachieving pals. Bob Denver was cast in the show after completing his three-year run playing the hapless first mate Gilligan on *Gilligan's Island*. CBS had canceled the sitcom about a motley group of island castaways while it was still popular (it went on to become an iconic camp classic in reruns), so there was a lot of audience goodwill toward Denver. He was paired with Herb Edelman, a tall New York stage actor who played Murray the cop in the film version of *The Odd Couple*. Stern was a fan of comedy teams, especially after having written *Honeymooners* sketches for Jackie Gleason and Art Carney. He described the buddy pairings as "marriage without sex—there's always the fundamental love for one another, but like marriage there's all of the frustrations too." Stern envisioned that kind of dynamic for *The Good Guys*. Edelman's character, a diner owner, was the grounded realist, while Denver played a cab driver who was a bit of a spaced-out dreamer. As it turned out, "Bob was that person, in real life," said Stern. When promoting the series, Denver gave stream-of-consciousness interviews to journalists and suggested he was embedding secret messages in the episodes. He frequently improvised lines during the show's tapings, much to the dismay of the more straight-ahead Edelman.

Off camera, Denver, who played TV's first beatnik on *The Many Loves of Dobie Gillis*, lived a California hippie lifestyle. When Denver's wife showed up at tapings of the show, she brought along a monkey who was fully dressed and introduced to the studio audience as one of the couple's children. The scent of marijuana was always wafting out of Denver's dressing room, eventually forcing the production to switch from shooting with three cameras and a studio audience to using a single camera on a closed set. "I was told by the fire marshal that if you don't go to one camera, I'm going to have to arrest the audience for a contact high," Stern recalled.

NEVERTHELESS, STERN'S ABILITY to get salable shows on the air on the West Coast and renewed interest in dramatic specials by Susskind and Melnick in New York eventually turned Talent Associates into an asset again at a time when many American companies were hunting for acquisitions. Conglomerates had become the new favored route of corporate expansion. Companies were buying other companies at a rapid rate regardless of whether there was any kind of apparent strategic fit. Paramount had been a prime example. Its new parent, Gulf + Western, was a producer of auto parts, zinc products, and fertilizer. Such deals were seen by corporations as a quick fix to boost their balance sheets. Spreading them over the different unrelated industries was a hedge against running afoul of antitrust laws.

Susskind and Melnick found a buyer in Norton Simon Inc., a company formed the year before out of a series of mergers. Norton Simon himself was a California industrialist who parlayed his interest in a small juice company he bought in the 1940s into the ownership of Hunt Foods and Industries. Simon used his profits to take stakes in other companies. "He then began to look around for where to invest the company's excess money," said Gerry Bewkes, a Norton Simon executive in the 1960s and 1970s (and father of Time Warner chairman Jeff Bewkes). "He'd invest as a minority shareholder in companies that he thought were undervalued, and then kind of rattle their cage," and eventually take them over. After Simon gained control of beverage maker Canada Dry and McCall's Corporation, the magazine publisher, dress-pattern maker, and owner of the second largest printing plant in the world, he brought in an executive named Bill McKenna to complete the transformation of his company Hunt-Wesson into Norton Simon Industries. McKenna had overseen Litton Industries, one of the major conglomerate success stories of the 1960s.

Simon remained a major shareholder, but he left the management of the operation soon afterward so he could devote more time to collecting art (in 1974, he brought his growing collection to a financially struggling museum in Pasadena and turned it into the Norton Simon Museum of Art). "I remember my wife and I visited with Simon once and he'd told us how much he paid per square inch for a painting," said Ed Gelsthorpe, who was a senior executive with the company. Once NSI formed, the buying spree continued. It added the holdings of Halston, the designer, cosmetics manufacturer Max Factor, and Somerset, the importers of Johnny Walker scotch.

Talent Associates was a small independent company, not a major studio that could have a material impact on a corporation's balance sheet. Yet Susskind, Melnick, and Stern received NSI shares worth several million dollars when they agreed to sell Talent Associates in August 1968. Susskind's shares were valued at $1.725 million a few months after the deal closed.

Susskind said in a press release that Talent Associates' new parent would be "a powerful financial helpmate, a big brother." His company was able to function as a self-contained entity within Norton Simon Inc. While they welcomed the influx of money the deal brought, corporate life was something new for the three freewheeling partners. They found themselves attending board of directors meetings and shareholder gatherings where they listened to other Norton Simon executives spin out analysis on market share for Reddi-wip dessert topping, the sales potential of Hunt's Manwich sandwich sauce, or revenue growth for the company's glass container manufacturing unit. Susskind's presentations became a celebrity attraction at such meetings. But when asked to make financial projections for his unit's performance, he would say, "I have no clue. I don't know if the networks are going to pick up our shows. I don't know whether the star is going to be in a movie. I have no idea. It's not a predictable business. It's a business that depends in many cases upon the whims of talent, television executives, and moviegoers. I just don't know."

Jay Cooper, who was legal counsel for Talent Associates in that era, said the Norton Simon deal was an early example of how the entertainment industry, dependent on the emotions of creative people, decision makers, and, ultimately, the fickle public, was incompatible with other businesses such as manufacturing and marketing consumer products. "David told them the truth," he said. "A lot of people come into Hollywood because they like the idea of what it represents. They like the visibility and the star power. To mundane businesses like the ones they owned, it was very attractive that we controlled the rights to this show or that show. Executives are seduced by that kind of thing. They were seduced by the names. The projects and David Susskind himself and the things that Leonard was creating and producing seduced them. But I don't think they fully understood it. I don't think much has changed since."

Steve Binder learned the hard way that Talent Associates was not much more than a fancy hood ornament for Norton Simon. As NSI shareholders themselves, the Talent Associates partners were not eager to take risks outside of the realm of television and film. Susskind and Melnick, finally enjoying a financial cushion, were tentative when approached by Binder about starting a record label. Binder had been working out of the Talent Associates West Coast office to oversee taped and live programs, and believed music was an obvious place for the company to expand in 1969. The music business had low start-up costs and, if successful, huge margins, as the baby boom generation came of age and gained more spending power. (When Kinney Service Corporation bought Warner Bros. in 1969, the company's music business was considered the crown jewel and the thinking was that the laggard movie studio would be spun off.)

Binder knew how record industry types were viewed within the social order of show business. "Up to that point, music people were considered sort of second-class citizens to television and film people," Binder said. "They liked all the revenues music people were earning, but they certainly didn't want to socialize with them." Talent Associates would be no different.

"I went to Melnick and said I'd like to start a record company," Binder said. "Melnick basically said, 'That's a great idea but we're not going to risk any of our money in it.' There was no synergy at Talent Associates. Every one of us did our own thing. And everybody was kind of not wanting to spend any of the money, because everybody had stock options and wanted Norton Simon stock to go through the roof."

Susskind also had no interest. He once admitted on his show that he was baffled by the current hits that his children loved in the late 1960s. "They are playing the phonograph and the radio and very strange music is coming out of it—music I don't really comprehend," he said before a panel that included Neil Diamond, Fred Katz of Blood, Sweat and Tears, Frankie Valli of the Four Seasons, and Felix Cavaliere of The Rascals. The names were so foreign to Susskind, he had to do several takes to get the introductions right at the start of the program.

Binder was on his own in a search for talent and financial backing for a record label venture. While he had mostly worked in television as a producer and director during the 1950s and 1960s, he had made plenty of music business connections. He directed *Teenage Awards Music International* (better known as *The TAMI Show*), the explosive 1964 concert film that featured James Brown, The Supremes, the Rolling Stones, the Beach Boys, and Marvin Gaye performing before a wild crowd at the Santa Monica Civic Auditorium. Binder also put go-go dancers in America's living rooms for the first time when he directed the first thirteen episodes of NBC's 1960s pop music series *Hullabaloo.* His most notable credit was producing and directing Elvis Presley's epochal 1968 program for NBC, which went on to become known as "The Comeback Special." The electrifying hour that relaunched the dormant career of the once reigning King of Rock 'n' Roll happened largely because Binder talked Presley's manager, Colonel Tom Parker, out of having Presley sing an entire program of Christmas songs.

The first act Binder found for TA Records was the soft acoustic singing duo of Jim Seals and Dash Crofts. They had been in an early 1960s band called The Champs that once had a number one hit called "Tequila." He remembered going out to the home of one of their in-laws in the San Fernando Valley to hear the act. "I sat in the kitchen while they brought out their mandolin and guitar and they auditioned for me, playing songs like 'Summer Breeze,'" he said. After signing Seals & Crofts, he hired Eddie Rosenblatt, a distribution and promotion man who worked for Herb Alpert's A&M Records. They went to New York to meet with the major labels to solicit help with financing and distributing records to wholesalers and retailers. None of them would bite; they were concerned that a label owned by a company as large as Norton Simon could eventually be a major competitor. They ended up making a deal with Bell Records, still a scrappy independent label at the time, which specialized in Top 40 singles acts such as the Box Tops.

By the summer of 1969, Binder had TA Records up and running. The label adapted the Talent Associates logo seen on the end credits of its TV shows. Binder ran his venture while still producing TV specials out of the company's new West Coast office in Studio City. "Leonard Stern was on one side of the building. I was on the other side of the building," said Binder. "If they looked like they were rock-and-rollers with Levis and T-shirts everyone was sent over to my wing. If they showed up in suits and ties they went over to Leonard's wing."

A songwriting team Binder had signed, Brian Potter and Dennis Lambert, gave the label its first hit, an antiwar anthem called "One Tin Soldier." Binder had a Canadian group named Original Caste record it, and by the winter of 1970, it moved up the Billboard Hot 100 (the song later became better known as the theme for the film *Billy Jack*). A second chart hit in the summer came from a soulful vocal quintet Binder discovered called Five Flights Up. Seals & Crofts released two albums and were even set to perform on *The David Susskind Show* (the TV newspaper listing for the show read: "Rock Music That Sounds Good: Seals & Crofts!"). All seemed to be going well until Binder received a call from Dan Melnick in New York telling him he had to fire his right-hand man Rosenblatt. "He said, 'We're cutting our budget,'" Binder recalled. "I said, 'Dan, it's not your budget. All this money is coming from Bell Records.' I had brought my music attorney into the company, Jay Cooper, to set this whole deal up. And Jay became legal counsel for Talent Associates because of it. I went to Jay and told him, 'This is ludicrous. I'm not going to fire Eddie Rosenblatt. He's got three kids, and he's doing a great job for us with spit to spend on this company. We don't have any promotion money. We don't have any advertising money. I've created this whole thing from scratch, including the logo and the name of the record company and everything else and the artists.' I'd given up the personal management of Seals & Crofts and a piece of the publishing. I felt it was unethical when I went into that job to retain ownership. I gave up 100 percent of everything I had to Talent Associates."

Binder went to David Mahoney, the new chairman of Norton Simon, and told him he was going to leave the company. "I'm being called to let go of my right arm in the company, and we're existing with no manpower or no personnel," Binder told him. "And the reason given is Eddie doesn't fit our caliber of Talent Associates executive material." Melnick didn't budge. Melnick even said that his father-in-law, Richard Rodgers, hated the Seals & Crofts album he played for him.

"Eddie was a good friend and I wasn't about to fire him," said Binder. "I said, 'If Eddie goes, I go.'" Mahoney sympathized with Binder but refused to step in. "We're going to accept the fact that you're 100 percent right and they're 100 percent wrong, but you're not going to win this battle," Mahoney told him. "We want you to stay in this company. We like what you're doing. There is no question about your contributions." Mahoney told Binder that when it came to Talent Associates, all that really mattered was having David

Susskind's picture in the annual report to impress the stockholders. "It clearly wasn't for money," Binder said. "We certainly didn't have a plan to grow the company that I knew about. I was young and really frustrated and I said, 'The hell with this.' So I left."

Binder's instincts about talent were proven correct. After TA Records was disbanded, Susskind sold the Seals & Crofts contract to Warner Bros. Records, where they became a multiplatinum-selling group for the rest of the 1970s. Lambert and Potter were sold off to ABC Records. They went on to be one of the most prolific writer-producer teams in pop music and created hits that revived the careers of Glen Campbell, the Four Tops, and the Righteous Brothers. Eddie Rosenblatt earned millions as one of the top executives in the music business, heading up David Geffen's record label.

DAVID MAHONEY was an ambitious executive who worked his way from a modest Depression-era upbringing in the Bronx to a scholarship at the Wharton School of Business and a series of executive positions before he took over Norton Simon. "Most men play not to lose—I play to win," he would say. He attempted to raise his personal profile by positioning Norton Simon as a socially conscious company, perhaps laying a base for a career in politics. The company became involved with environmental conservation efforts, and its executives testified before Congress to express their opposition to the Vietnam War. Susskind did not involve himself in such corporate initiatives.

"The President's Council is making a study of Norton Simon Inc.'s role in the entire ecological anti-pollution problem," said a 1970 memo from an NSI executive. "In order to determine where we stand with respect to this problem, would you please let us know of any instances of pollution contributed by Talent Associates as well as those anti-pollution efforts you may be taking in the future."

Susskind replied, "As far as I know, Talent Associates has never really made any contributions to pollution, except intellectual, which was both unfortunate and subliminal."

Along with impressing shareholders, Mahoney saw another benefit from having a show business company in the Norton Simon portfolio. "David Mahoney was an elegant gentleman who also had a eye for the ladies, and he loved to be around celebrities," said Harry Sherman. "That was very obvious. And one year I got a phone call, and they said there'll be 'a young lady coming to California and it's very important that you see her and do everything you can to help her.' I said, 'Help her do what?' Well, she wanted to be an actress. I was told, 'Harry, you know, this is really an important thing, so don't blow it.' "

When the woman arrived in Los Angeles, Sherman made an appointment to have her come to the office. "She came and she had a see-through dress," he said. "She was smashing-looking, but she spoke with a terrible accent—German or Slavic or something, And very attractive, but, you know, she was interested in an acting career. And I talked to her about going to dramatic coaches— Milton Katselas and Nina Foch and people like that who had reputations in those days as being able to turn sticks into actors. She was so different from what I expected. I expected sort of a Marilyn Monroe type. She needed a lot of work in enunciation and elocution." Sherman said those kind of meetings happened more than once. "Some of the people in the executive ranks at the corporate office said, you know, 'We're in the picture business—we can set you up,' " he said.

17

John V. Lindsay was New York City's first made-for-TV mayor. Elected in 1965, the six-foot-four matinee-idol handsome Republican was already an admired figure among Manhattan's elite after having represented the Silk Stocking District of the borough for seven years. At a time before it was mandatory that a politician appear comfortable on television, Lindsay was completely at ease trading quips with the panel on *What's My Line?* or bantering with Johnny Carson on *The Tonight Show.* Show people were Lindsay's people, and that included David Susskind and Daniel Melnick, who became a close friend and adviser. Susskind and Melnick had modeled the Congressman Hanson character that appeared in the last few episodes of their series *East Side/West Side* after Lindsay.

Having a friend in City Hall enabled Susskind and Melnick to produce *N.Y.P.D.,* the first TV cop show with the official imprimatur of the New York Police Department. Over the years, many television entities had proposed police dramas with an official association with New York's finest, as Jack Webb had done in Los Angeles with the LAPD on *Dragnet.* Lindsay's predecessor, Robert Wagner, once granted access to New York City's case files to a producer friend who sought to do a show. But Wagner's police commissioner and district attorney refused to go along with it.

It was Lindsay's troubled relationship with the department that led to the creation of *N.Y.P.D.* During 1966, Lindsay's first tumultuous year in office, he pushed a proposal for a civilian review board, an independent body that would investigate questionable police actions. The city's minority communities had complained frequently about police brutality and a perceived indifference to the problems of their neighborhoods. Residents were rising up against the conditions under which they had been living, creating tensions with the uniformed officers charged with keeping the peace. They wanted some kind of system outside of the department that could provide some recourse. The Patrolmen's Benevolent Association, the union representing the department, was deeply opposed to any measure that would allow outsiders to judge its members' actions. The PBA already felt it was under siege from the social disorder of the times and believed the Lindsay administration and much of the public failed to appreciate the daily stress level police officers experienced on the job. (Antipathy for Lindsay among some in the department would run long and deep. During a panel on *The David Susskind Show,* several veterans of the force said they hoped the mayor was successful in his 1972 bid for the White House solely because it would get him out of City Hall.) But Lindsay was serious about making the board happen. He dismissed the sitting commissioner who opposed the idea and replaced him with Howard Leary. As Philadelphia's police commissioner, Leary had developed a reputation as a progressive law enforcement official after taking a hands-on role in quelling the rioting in the northern part of that city in 1964.

Lindsay campaigned vigorously for the passage of the city referendum on the ballot in 1966 that would make the review board law. He even rallied his show business pals for support at a party held at the home of Susskind's longtime friend and agent Ted Ashley. Susskind was a vocal supporter of the review board and was among the show business celebrities in attendance with actors Henry Fonda and Eli Wallach. But voters rejected the referendum that November.

The defeat sent Lindsay into 1967 with a demoralized department. Voters who supported the review board were angry as well. Looking for an opportunity to assuage the force and perhaps create understanding among its critics, the Lindsay administration agreed to allow the NYPD name to be used in a half-hour police drama series Susskind sold to ABC. It starred character actor Jack Warden as Police Lieutenant Mike Haines, with stage actors Frank Converse and Robert Hooks as two detectives in his squad. The pitch to the network said the show would portray "the new cop" or "Leary's kind of cop," one that was mindful of protecting the civil rights of accused criminals and reflected the "racially mixed reality of the city and the police force." The city's contract with Talent Associates granting the department's cooperation on the show clearly stated what was expected—a prime-time platform that would help boost public cooperation and confidence in the police. In return for providing technical advice on the series, Police Commissioner Leary's office had script approval and could even review early versions of episodes before they aired.

The carnival barking that accompanied the show's pickup by ABC created the impression that the episodes would be based on actual police case files. No such permission was ever granted. Even the suggestion that real files were to be used led to a lawsuit by a gadfly citizen attempting to stop the production of *N.Y.P.D.* Susskind had to state in a court deposition that he did not have any such access, which perhaps deflated some of the excitement surrounding the show.

There was little need for actual police files. *N.Y.P.D.* writers got their stories straight out of the city's newspapers. Arnold Perl, the writer-producer responsible for the boldest episodes of *East Side/West Side,* was credited with creating *N.Y.P.D.* with Susskind. Emily Perl Kingsley believed her uncle developed the series by taking the newspaper stories clipped for potential *East Side/West Side* stories and approaching them from the point of view of the police instead of a social worker. One of the writers hired for the show was Heywood Gould, a former newspaper reporter who had no experience in writing for television. "The producers trotted me in to meet David when they hired me," he recalled. "He asked me where I was from and what I had done. I hadn't done anything. I'd been a reporter. He didn't seem fazed by it all." Gould, who covered the police beat for the *New York Post,* was so green at screenwriting that in his very first script he put quotation marks around the dialogue. *N.Y.P.D.* producer Bob Markell made him retype it before showing it to Susskind. But Gould was a font of tales from the seamy side of New York, accumulated from his years of telling grisly yarns for the tabloid. The first story he spun out was based on a real case about a man who buried his girlfriend in a trunk after she had died from a botched illegal abortion. "All the shows I did were based on stories that I covered," he said. "It was easy for me, frankly. I had a thousand of them."

Bob Markell had the ultimate creative responsibility for *N.Y.P.D.* With the blessing of Susskind and Melnick, he convinced ABC to allow him to produce the series on 16-millimeter film instead of the television and movie industry's standard of 35-millimeter. Filmmakers of the late 1960s were still exhilarated by the results director Richard Lester achieved when he shot The Beatles' first feature, *A Hard Day's Night,* in 16-millimeter. "We were trying to cash in on that in television," said Albert Ruben, the story editor during the show's first season. "Use some of that stuff and make it look real, make it look like New York and at the same time make it commercial—and try to beat the problem of not having a lot of money." The show had a budget of $77,000 per half-hour episode, modest even by 1967 standards. Markell equipped the show's film crew with Arriflex cameras that were handheld or quickly set up on a tripod. Instead of using a crab dolly, necessary for moving large cameras, the cinematographers were pulled along on wheelchairs. "It was guerrilla film-making," said Markell. "The cameramen ultimately got so good at using the handheld, they had to be told to shake it a little bit to create the feeling of verité." The lighter equipment allowed the crew to travel quickly around the city in a station wagon instead of the several large trucks typically needed for a location shoot. The mobility was essential, as each episode of *N.Y.P.D.* was shot in two and a half days while using as many as nine different locations. Speed and efficiency were necessary to bring the show in on budget. When filming on Riverside Drive and Seventy-ninth Street, even the rats used in a location shoot had a tightly scheduled call time for their work. The show's fast-paced, street-level point of view was established in the opening titles, in which each of the letters, *N, Y, P,* and *D* came up over the flashing light of a moving squad car in time to the beat of the harmonically jagged theme music. Reza Badiyi, a director, got the shot by strapping himself onto the back of the car. The show borrowed techniques from European art films of the 1960s, using jump cuts instead of dissolves and giving the characters interior mono-logues. Some scenes had no dialogue at all. "Will people buy another cops-and-robbers show à la Alain Resnais?" Rex Reed asked in *The New York Times,* referring to the director of *Hiroshima Mon Amour.* "They'd better," answered Dan Melnick. "If they don't we're in trouble."

The assistance of the New York Police Department gave the show access to helicopters, squad cars, and heavy equipment emblazoned with department logos. But most important, it provided control of the streets. Filmed televi-sion production in New York had disappeared at the end of 1966 when ABC canceled *Hawk,* a police drama that starred Burt Reynolds as a Native Ameri-can police detective. The show died because of low ratings, but the frustration over the kind of day-to-day trials the producers experienced kept other film-makers away from the city. Problems ranged from bureaucratic red tape—producers needed permits from numerous city agencies before they could film—to paying off police officers to keep pedestrians from interfering with shots. The public was often hostile as well. "Wherever we went there were people who would come out of the woodwork and sit down in the middle of the shot," said Paul Bogart, who worked on *Hawk*. "And if you asked them to leave they'd say, 'No. I'm a citizen and I'm going to sit here.' They knew there'd be money if they resisted moving right away. People found that out about movie companies. Just get in the way and they'll give you money to go away. A couple of bucks, or some pastries and coffee. And we had all sorts of things happen to us in the middle of the night. I remember once somebody, some thief, grabbed a can of finished film that we'd just finished shooting. He ran away with it and we had to chase him down. We got it back, but it was those kinds of people who turned up at night."

With *N.Y.P.D.* as an example, Lindsay could encourage filmmakers to shoot in the city again, which in turn would generate business revenue and tax dollars. The mayor's office simplified the permit process for shooting on the streets, and eventually created the first municipal office dedicated to attracting local film and television production. The police department assigned officers to work on locations at no cost to the producers. "We got all kinds of cooperation," said Badiyi. "Prior to that, every time you wanted to shoot, you had to pay money. You had to have it."

The show was a breakthrough in terms of cinematic style for television and provided first-time screen exposure for such up-and-coming New York actors of the day as Al Pacino, Jill Clayburgh, Jane Alexander, and Jon Voight. But it may be best remembered for the social impact of casting Robert Hooks in the role of Detective Jeff Ward. Earlier in the 1960s, Talent Associates had wanted to make a drama series with Robert Ryan and Sidney Poitier as New York City detectives. "ABC said they would only buy it if the black man would arrest black criminals and the white man would arrest white criminals," Melnick recalled. "I said, 'Forget it; I don't have the nerve to tell those actors that.' I never discussed it with another network. I just said, 'Fellas, I can't sell it.'"

At the time, Bill Cosby on NBC's breezy espionage series *I Spy* had been the only other black lead actor on a network drama series. Hooks shattered the color barrier for the cop show genre at a time when tensions were running high between black Americans and their local police, as evidenced by New York's divisive battle over the civilian review board. Frank Converse, a blond all-American boy type, was cast opposite Hooks (the actors knew each other from having worked together in Otto Preminger's poorly received 1965 feature

Hurry Sundown). The two detectives were presented as equals under their gruff veteran boss.

The handsome and dynamic Hooks was a rising stage actor in New York in the 1960s. He also had a personal history with Susskind. They first met in the spring of 1963 through George C. Scott when *East Side/West Side* was ramping up for production. Scott and Hooks played together on the Negro Actors Guild softball team in the Broadway Show League. Before one of the games Scott had to meet with Susskind to talk about their series and brought Hooks along. Hooks hit it off with Susskind, who cast the actor in his first television role, a guest spot as a police detective on *East Side/West Side*.

The two soon became fast friends, with one major common interest being women. Hooks provided Susskind with introductions to many of the beautiful black actresses he knew. "Women liked him, not just the people who were friends of mine. Women," Hooks recalled. "And not just because he was David Susskind. He was a smooth operator. And he was always clean. He was always dressed. David was really into being with two women. I knew a couple of girls who didn't mind. I knew more than a couple who didn't mind. Most of the time we just met and we hung out and David might have gone on with a couple of my friends. Ladies, always ladies. David and I were the only guys."

One time the arrangement went awry when Susskind suggested to Hooks and two female companions that they could party at the Park Avenue apartment of a friend who was out of town. "We went up to the apartment and had a wonderful time," recounted Hooks. "I'm not going to call any names here. But they were friends of mine, actresses and gorgeous women. So, the four of us are up in this apartment on Park Avenue. And we're hanging out, getting high and doing our thing. And one of the girls wanted to take a bath. And she did take a bath. And so we had fun—boom, boom, boom. Next day, I get a call from David. He says, 'What the hell?'"

Susskind was enraged. The woman who used the bathtub neglected to turn off the faucet after she had finished. "The water seeped down into the apartment underneath," said Hooks. "This created a big problem for whoever his friends were. I don't even know who it was. But it was a Park Avenue apartment. And it was a gorgeous place. And the young woman left the water on. David was furious. I said, 'Look. It wasn't me. I didn't do it.'"

The incident put an end to their partying, but not their friendship. "The meat of our relationship was deeper than that," Hooks said. Susskind helped support Hooks's efforts to create opportunities for minorities in theater and film. He served on the advisory board of the Negro Ensemble Company, the theater company that Hooks had cofounded. "He did write a few checks, too," Hooks recalled. "If I needed something, I would call David. I'd call other people, as well. But David was very, very helpful, whenever I called."

NEC was conceived and formed by Hooks in 1965 as a way to provide black people experience in all aspects of the theater, from acting to technical work. It grew out of the Group Theatre Workshop, an acting class that Hooks held in his Chelsea apartment and later in a loft on West Nineteenth Street, off Fifth Avenue. The sessions were filled with dozens of teenagers, mostly minority, many of them poor, and some considered delinquents. "We actually had performances in my living room and my bedroom," he said. "Some of the kids in the Group Theatre Workshop had been in the riots. Some had been dealing drugs. Some were gang members. And we took the kids out of that. We gave them opportunities."

Hooks's experience with the workshop made him a credible ambassador for *N.Y.P.D.*, as the producers did a lot of location work in New York's troubled neighborhoods of the time. When the show set up to shoot in Harlem or the Bedford-Stuyvesant section of Brooklyn, crowds of young people showed up. "They automatically wanted to create problems—until they saw me," Hooks said. "Once they saw me come out of the trailer in my suit, then all of a sudden it changed." Hooks moved easily through the crowds to ensure coopera-tion. "You're going to allow us to shoot in your neighborhood because the stories are good," Hooks would say. "You're not able to read the script, but I'm here to tell you that it's good. It's good for the community." Hooks managed to smooth over even the people who showed up to take advantage of the wads of cash that production companies gave to locals to keep the peace.

"That created problems," Hooks said. "If you're giving money to the leader of the community, a leader of the gang, so to speak, the other people are going to come around. So I was charged with—and enjoyed—dealing with it. I enjoyed talking to these brothers. The fact that there was this cop who was a black guy was not a big problem. Us against them—it was none of that." Over time, kids on the street would recognize Hooks and hum the show's theme for him.

When Hooks did publicity interviews about his character on *N.Y.P.D.*, journalists tried to provoke him with such questions as, "Do you beat up any white people on your show?" He never took the bait. But on the set of the show, Hooks quietly made sure that the portrayal of Jeff Ward was mindful of the concerns of black viewers at the time. "They didn't want to force him to do something he didn't want to do," said Reza Badiyi. "Before the script got to everybody, I heard [the producers] say, 'Give it to Hooks. Let's see if he has any notes and then we'll finalize it.' Robert Hooks never asked that a story be altered. If there was a line he was uncomfortable with, the writers came up with an alternative or gave it to Converse while he was out of the shot." Badiyi directed an episode called "Cry Brute" that dealt with police brutality, the most severe problem minorities had with the New York Police Department. Hooks was completely written out of it.

Hooks pushed for his character to have a family, and with the backing of Melnick, he got one. Denise Nicholas was cast as Jeff Ward's wife, and they had a baby girl who, viewers learned in a throwaway line during one episode, was named after slavery abolitionist leader Harriet Tubman.

The first season of the show was filmed at a studio space on the Bowery and East Fourth Street that ABC had used for *Hawk*. "It was a place where they used to have bar mitzvahs when they were not shooting movies," Markell said. Vagrants used to wander in looking for coffee and donuts from the spread of food set out for the cast and crew. "They would come into the studio and help themselves," said Nessa Hyams, a casting director on the series. "No one ever accosted you. There was an unwritten law that drunks and the people in the Bowery didn't bother you." Hyams believes she may have ensured everyone's safety by giving a bit part to Sandy Alexander, whose Hell's Angels motorcycle gang had its New York headquarters nearby. "According to him I would never have a problem," she said. "I could have gone anywhere I wanted."

Dan Melnick was the executive producer on the show and became known as "the Suit." He never failed to show up in the latest expensive threads from designer Roland Meledandri (often paid for out of the show's wardrobe budget) and shirts from Turnbull and Asser. "Dan always looked great," Gould recalled. "He and David had a competition. If Dan went to Meledandri, David would drop whatever he was doing so he could go to Meledandri's shop. If David showed up in one of those big fat ties, Danny would drop whatever he was doing and go to Meledandri. Just to make sure that they were both spending equal amounts of ABC's money, you know?"

When Melnick showed up for script readings, the staff was treated to a catered meal from The 21 Club delivered by servers in white coats. Melnick was once dissatisfied with his meal and threw his plate against a wall in disgust. The sight was hard to bear for a staff of hungry scribes used to ordering in dinners from Dial-A-Steak, a local takeout joint. "I was going, 'Wait, wait, wait—I'll eat it,'" said Gould. But Melnick was a great supporter of the show's technical experimentation and always backed Markell's effort to navigate the writers into daring subject matter. Markell had been steeped in the social consciousness of the CBS lawyer show *The Defenders,* where he had been a producer. In all his years on that program, the one topic absolutely forbidden by the network was homosexuality. Markell made it the focus of *N.Y.P.D.*'s premiere episode. James Broderick played a gay steelworker who helps the detectives break a blackmailing scheme. The episode was a landmark for television for its portrayal of gay characters without any stereotypical flamboyance or fey behavior. There was dialogue that even suggested that the struggle for gays to openly be themselves in society was akin to what black people had sought during the civil rights movement, a bold statement for prime-time TV in 1967.

For the most part, *N.Y.P.D.* stories reached for social topicality without getting on a political soapbox. Racial problems were presented realistically but without moralizing. When Al Pacino played a southern white supremacist being hunted down by black activists, the character refuses to be questioned by Ward and insists on talking only to a white detective. The most daring episode depicted a rookie white uniform officer who is looking for a black suspect on the roof of Ward's apartment building. Ward, with his gun drawn, goes up to investigate as well and gets shot by the rookie cop before he can identify himself as police. The officer is remorseful, and Ward, who takes the blame for the mistake, forgives him easily. But the episode posed the question of whether the cop would have been as quick to shoot if Ward had been white.

The police department's notes were mostly ones about procedure, which at times seemed to find their way into scripts as turgid chunks of dialogue. Its involvement also filtered out any bad cop stories that may have been pitched.

When New York Police Department officers vetted the scripts, they were likely following Lindsay administrative directives that *N.Y.P.D.* be in line with its efforts to improve the city's dismal image during the late 1960s. "The Central Park setting must be changed to another city park," said one note from Lieutenant James J. Cleary about an episode about a middle-aged man who dresses like a hippie to pick up young girls and ends up killing one of them. "It has been the policy of the present administration through the Park Commissioners [Thomas] Hoving and [August] Heckscher to enhance the Central Park image. Attractions in Central Park include weekend cycling, concerts on the Sheep Meadow, Shakespeare theater, jazz concerts, Goldman Band concerts, swimming, ice-skating and boating. Homicides and hippies are not typical of Central Park. It is urged that Washington Square Park be the setting for this story." The note was ignored.

N.Y.P.D. lasted two seasons, long enough to give the stars a special status among the police force, which could come in handy. "I saved Jack Warden's ass once," said Hooks.

Warden's most successful years as a character actor in the movies were ahead of him. During much of the run of *N.Y.P.D.,* he was miserable over a failing marriage and his loss of a role in the Broadway production of Arthur Miller's *The Price.* One reason it was essential to have the cast and producers do a table reading of every *N.Y.P.D.* script that came in was so a foggy Warden could keep track of when production had ended on one episode and started on a new one. "He loved the alcoholic beverages," said Nessa Hyams. "He was the greatest storyteller in the world and all his stories had to do with being drunk."

One night during the show's run, Hooks had left Elaine's, the Upper East Side restaurant frequented by writers and show business types, when he saw an inebriated Warden urinating in the street. A police squad car stopped and two officers confronted him. "They were going to lock him up," Hooks recalled. "Jack was ready to fight them. They just thought it was a red-faced Irishman pissing in the street. And he was going, 'Fuck you, you fuckin' cop you.' I said, 'Look, guys. I'll take care of him, it's Jack Warden.' And they said, 'All right.' So we had, not carte blanche, but because we were on *N.Y.P.D.,* you know, it was nice. We never abused what we had."

During the production of *N.Y.P.D.,* there were signs of a growing divide between Susskind and Dan Melnick. The two had shared credits on the programs that came out of Talent Associates during the first few years of Melnick's tenure at the company. But by 1967, they were off pursuing their own separate projects. "You knew that the people who worked on David's show were David's people," said Patricia Nardo, a television writer who started her career at Talent Associates. "A lot of Dan's stuff was in L.A. There was that distinction in the office between Melnick and Susskind. I always thought it was silly and funny. David was fiercely competitive with Dan, who was very smart, very handsome, very dynamic. And he was taller than David. And David didn't like men around. He never liked men around."

Albert Ruben sensed a rift two months after *N.Y.P.D.* had gone into production in the spring of 1967. "We developed scripts," he said. "We were rocking and rolling. We were producing scripts and episodes and we had a number in various stages of production. Then Danny decided to go on vacation, which was not the best thing to do. No sooner had he left town than David said to Markell, 'I want to see everything you've got on film.'"

Markell rented a screening room to show some footage to Susskind.

"We ran the stuff for David," Ruben said. "And after we finish, David lights into Markell. Just tears him up one side and down the other about the quality of what he's just seen. It's clear to me that he's been waiting for this opportunity. It's not about the material. It's not about what he's seen. It's not about Markell. It's about his relationship with Danny. I'm sitting in the back of the room as quiet as a mouse. I'm thinking either I get up and walk out or I sit here or I tell David what I think of his performance, which I think is just terrible. Somewhat to my shame, I just didn't do anything and stuck it out. It was such a lesson to me what can happen to partners in the business who somehow get together for reasons I never really understood."

Markell was so shaken by Susskind's tongue lashing that he called his agent and asked to get off the show before it even got on the air. "David was unnecessarily cruel. And that concerned me," he said. "It was a bad time. I wanted to leave. I remember telling Danny, I can't do this."

Markell was persuaded to stay, and, looking back, he believed there "must have been some kernel of truth" in Susskind's criticisms "because Danny really got on top of us after that. I do think the scripts did get better."

The relationship between Susskind and Melnick did not.

Yet Andrew Susskind, along with the people who worked for both men, rarely if ever heard one say anything disparaging about the other. "David felt Dan was a glamour boy who married well and had an easy professional path and was modestly talented," Andrew said. "But he was impressed by the Richard Rodgers connection. And I do think he recognized and probably resented Dan's ease. Dan had all the moves. Dan was smooth and David wasn't. He was a bull in a china shop. I think there was a striving that Dan had and David understood and had some sympathy for. While I think everybody knew David had an attitude about Dan, including Dan, I almost never heard anything. He might have rolled his eyes. It was a little older brother, younger brother kind of thing."

Jon Merdin, who worked in the office as a production assistant in the late 1960s, said it was understandable why there was some professional tension between the two men. "They had to be together because they knew they were good for each other," he said. "As a consequence they hated each other because they had to be together. Nobody with egos that large wants to concede that they need anybody else in their life."

Outside of the office, Susskind and Melnick actually spent a lot of time together enjoying the kind of social experimentation that was very much a part of the show business scene in the late 1960s. One of Reza Badiyi's early assignments at Talent Associates was to monitor the TV broadcasts of a conservative Los Angeles news commentator who threatened to reveal details of a wild Hollywood gathering that Melnick and Susskind attended, which, at a minimum, was clothing optional.

One well-known screenwriter who worked for Talent Associates recalled seeing the partners at such an affair. He could never forget the image of Susskind seated on a banquette in front of a large picture window overlooking Los Angeles and talking about the Vietnam War. "He was naked and sitting guru-style, cross-legged like a Jewish maharaja," the screenwriter recalled.

FOR THE NEW YORK employees who worked at Talent Associates, having two competitive bosses with outsized personalities was exhilarating. "I didn't know of another place like that," said David Z. Goodman. "We who came there were family to slightly dysfunctional parents in terms of interaction with each other. In their way they were good parents. They cared about doing good stuff. It gave people a lot of opportunity to do good work."

Best of all, risk taking was encouraged. "David did set up an atmosphere in which you could throw out ideas and not be humiliated," Judy Crichton said. "I mean, the only way that you ever create anything is to come up with a thousand bad ideas. You need an atmosphere in which someone recognizes that, and you don't get penalized for the bad ones, or the ones other people don't like. But they leave you free to keep concocting, and concocting, and concocting."

Marc Norman, who came to New York after working as Leonard Stern's assistant on the West Coast, remembered how Susskind wanted him to research the idea of a children's version of *Omnibus,* the heralded cultural television show that the Ford Foundation funded in the 1950s. "He said, 'Let's do *Omnibus,* only, let's make it for kids, right? We'll get Balanchine to do a ballet for kids. We'll get Stravinsky to write music for kids. We'll have so-and-so do a movie for kids. Everything will be for kids. Write up a treatment.' So I said okay. I went out and I thought of some ideas. And just for the hell of it, I thought I would call a child psychologist on the faculty at Columbia University and ask him what kids would like to see in a television show for kids. So I found a child psychologist on staff at Columbia who was very cooperative and very willing to talk. And I told him roughly what I was working on. And I said, 'What would kids really like to watch?' And he said what kids would like to watch would be things on fire, things exploding, trains crashing into each other, planes falling out of the sky and crashing—especially if children were responsible for it."

Norman reported his findings to Susskind. "He said, 'Aw, fuck that. Forget all that. Just keep working on this," he recalled. "And I just kept working on it. And I'm sure he sent it off, and it didn't go anywhere. But most of what I did didn't go anywhere. The job for them was the same job I had for Leonard, which was just taking all their spitballs and putting them into some concrete form, and letting them throw it at the networks, and just figuring that if they did it enough times, something would stick to the wall."

Judy Crichton thrived in the Talent Associates environment. As the mother of four children she was surrounded by the rock music explosion of the late 1960s, and looked for ways to make it more accessible to the television audience. She pitched the idea of having a film crew go on tour with a rock band. She attempted to develop a syndicated show in which local TV personalities would present promotional films that record companies had started to make for their acts, an antecedent of music videos on MTV. She eventually sold a game show called *Generation Gap* to ABC in 1969. The concept capitalized on the social and cultural divide that developed between the adults who came of age during the Depression and World War II and their baby boomer offspring. A panel of young contestants was asked questions related to old newsreel footage of events, such as King Edward's abdication from the British throne. An opposing team of parents was tested on current pop phenomena, such as naming each member of the Beatles, or identifying a contemporary artist who performed live on the set.

Crichton had spent most of her professional career working on such game shows as *I've Got a Secret,* and during that time, the casting of black contestants was rare. She wanted to change that. "It wasn't that in other shops people would have been openly racist," she explained. "By the end of the 1960s, nobody expressed that feeling. But you didn't get support." Crichton went to a church in Brooklyn that helped her find minority youngsters for test episodes of *Generation Gap.* "I knew that we would land some of them as our first on-air contestants," she said. "And David was very supportive of that."

Crichton wanted to get out of the game show business and into news and documentaries. While at Talent Associates, she took her first major step toward that goal with a deal that was made through her kitchen window. Crichton was a cousin of Dan Melnick's wife, Linda Rodgers, and had known Hal Prince and Stephen Sondheim since they were all teenagers. When Prince and Sondheim were preparing their original production of their 1970 musical *Company,* Crichton asked if she could bring a camera crew in to film the making of the Broadway cast album. Once they agreed, she set out to find a sponsor.

"I lived on Seventy-first Street, in a brownstone," Crichton said. "And in the brownstone next door, across sort of an airshaft, lived a guy who was from the ad agency Young & Rubicam. Through the kitchen window I screamed at him, 'Hey, you want to sponsor a show on the making of a cast album of Steve and Hal's next show?' And he said, 'Sure. I can sell that.' So I go into Danny Melnick and he says, 'Great, we'll put up the money. And while you're at it, get D. A. Pennebaker as the filmmaker.'" Pennebaker was the premier documentary director of the era, who captured Bob Dylan at the height of his 1960s popularity in *Don't Look Back.* He had also directed *Monterey Pop,* a filmed document of the 1967 rock festival that propelled the careers of Janis Joplin, the Who, Jimi Hendrix, and Otis Redding.

"I wasn't smart enough to know Pennebaker's work," Crichton said. "But I called up Penny and he said, 'Sure.'"

Crichton's neighbor from Young & Rubicam got Eastern Airlines to agree to sponsor the program, which Talent Associates had hoped to turn into a series of Broadway-cast album recording sessions. The recording of *Company* was scheduled for May 3, 1970, at Columbia Records' Thirtieth Street studio. The date followed Broadway tradition, in which cast recordings were made the first Sunday after a show opened.

The plan almost unraveled after representatives from Eastern saw *Company* on its April 26 opening night at the Alvin Theatre. One of the conquests of the show's commitment-phobic lead character Bobby is an airline stewardess named April. In their big song together, "Barcelona," she suggests after their one night of lust that she can miss the flight she is scheduled to work on. That didn't fly with Eastern. Just a few days before filming, Crichton's project lost its sponsor.

"Penny had committed to sixty, seventy, eighty thousand dollars' worth of film," said Crichton, who was married to author Robert Crichton at the time. "We were running three cameras. My husband had just had a bestselling book. I told Penny if we couldn't raise the money, I would write a check. Bob would have divorced me. It was scary."

Crichton did not have to dip into the joint checking account. Just before the close of business on a Friday afternoon, Chrysler-Plymouth Dealers had agreed to go into the show. With three homemade handheld cameras, Pennebaker's crew proceeded to capture a startlingly intimate glimpse of theater performers and creators at work. The climax of the marathon eighteen-hour recording session came when Elaine Stritch, who admittedly had had a few glasses of champagne since her 2:00 p.m. arrival at the studio, was unable to deliver a usable take of her signature number in the show, "The Ladies Who Lunch." The three hours spent on trying to get the song right were condensed to fifteen minutes of the fifty-one-minute film. A clearly dismayed Stritch revealed the kind of vulnerability and frustration that no performer would volunteer to share in front of a camera in the days before reality television. The last scene of the film has Stritch returning fresh on a Wednesday, in full makeup before a matinee performance, and she triumphantly nails her tune. Had it been written in a script, it would have seemed pat. Word got out around the theater community about the film's unflinching look at Stritch, Sondheim, and noted recording producer Thomas Z. Shepard under duress. The final product, called *Company—An Original Cast Album,* was presented on a big screen to two full houses at the New York Film Festival at Lincoln Center before it aired on television stations across the country in October 1970.

Crichton produced several more documentaries for Talent Associates before she was hired at CBS News in 1974. She was the first woman producer in the network's prestigious *CBS Reports* unit and later went on to be the founding executive producer of the PBS documentary series *The American Experience.* "I might never have had a serious career if it wasn't for Susskind," she said.

OTHER CAREERS WERE LAUNCHED at Talent Associates when the partners asked for help when a project was in trouble. In the summer of 1967, Susskind developed an interview program called *Good Company,* in which defense attorney F. Lee Bailey was to interview celebrities on location at their homes. The show seemed jinxed from the start. Before the advent of twenty-four-hour news and live courtroom coverage, a defense attorney who helped free accused murderers turned TV personality was not a concept the public was quite ready to embrace. John Aaron, who had produced Edward R. Murrow's famous *Person to Person* for CBS, initially oversaw the program. But Susskind wanted harder-hitting interviews than Aaron was willing to do, and he fired him just weeks before the show was scheduled to premiere on ABC. In need of a producer, Susskind stalked the corridors of Talent Associates until he fixed his eyes on Patricia Nardo, who was working as Dan Melnick's secretary.

"He comes into my office one day and says, 'You're going to London tomorrow,'" Nardo recalled. "I didn't even have a passport." Nardo had led a sheltered existence in the Bronx, where a fearful mother "raised me to be afraid of everything." She said she was too shy and insecure even to go to college and had worked as a secretary since she was seventeen. She had come out of her shell in the idyllic work atmosphere of Talent Associates. But *Good Company* pushed her to a whole new level. She suddenly found herself flying off to London to do research and preparation for Bailey's interviews with J. Paul Getty, Sean Connery at the height of his 007 stardom, and actress Patricia Neal, who was recovering from her stroke. "It changed my whole life," she said. "I went from being a secretary to being on F. Lee Bailey's private jet. He'd fly himself to Chicago, where we interviewed Hugh Hefner. At one point I remember him reaching behind and asking me to hold his glass of scotch while he's flying the plane."

While occasionally unnerving, the experience gave Nardo the confidence to pursue a new career path. At work, she loved to laugh at Mel Brooks, Buck Henry, David Z. Goodman, and the other writers who hung out around the pool table at Talent Associates. By 1970, she headed out to Hollywood. She worked for producer James L. Brooks and became a writer for *The Mary Tyler Moore Show* and its spin-off, *Rhoda*.

REZA BADIYI HAD BEEN a newsreel cameraman for the shah of Iran before coming to the United States to study film at Syracuse University and then became an assistant to director Robert Altman. He was first hired by Susskind and Melnick to be an associate producer on a Talent Associates sitcom called *Run, Buddy, Run,* a slapstick comic takeoff on *The Fugitive.* Badiyi was called into action when Melnick faced a deadline on a TV project he'd put together for director Sam Peckinpah. Alcohol abuse had made Peckinpah unreliable and untouchable in Hollywood for several years, but Melnick was willing to take a chance on him in 1966 to direct an adaptation of the Katherine Anne Porter story *Noon Wine,* starring Jason Robards and Olivia de Havilland, for ABC's anthology series *Stage 67.* Although he indicated otherwise, Peckinpah was inexperienced at handling the videotape technology used for the program, much of which was shot outdoors on a farm in the San Fernando Valley. Badiyi finished the hour show by putting together a film crew with three 16-millimeter cameras. He did 115 setups in a single day. (The network complained about bad lighting, scratched videotape, and inconsistent skin tones on the portions that Peckinpah directed, but praised Badiyi's uncredited work.) The film was transferred to videotape and seamlessly edited into the show (and first presented the possibility of shooting *N.Y.P.D.* in the 16-millimeter format).

Peckinpah refused to share a directing credit with Badiyi, who was recognized only for his work on the titles of *Noon Wine.* But Badiyi became a hero at Talent Associates. "It was like home to me," he said. Badiyi was put on other projects and was soon a sought-after television director throughout the industry. He helmed more than four hundred episodes of filmed television over a three-decade career. Some of his opening titles (he insisted that his own credit read as "title visualization") became fixtures in American popular culture. When Badiyi filmed the opening for *The Mary Tyler Moore Show,* he convinced the reluctant star to toss her beret in the air, a signature moment that communicated the show's celebration of a single woman living on her own. He was nearly swept away on the north shore of Hawaii after a giant wave broke right on top of him and his long-lens camera while he was shooting footage for the famed opening of *Hawaii Five-0.* "Everything was wet," he said. "I pulled the tripod up, put it in the car, drove, and got on the telephone and called the lab in LA. They said, 'Don't empty the magazine if there's water in it. Just put it in something.' The film was processed. There were six good waves. The one that we used was not the best. The best had a scratch on it. I fixed the one with the scratch and I sold it to a soap company in Germany for a commercial."

Another director Susskind favored in the late 1960s was Ted Kotcheff, who had started out in the early days of Canadian television at the CBC. Kotcheff directed a memorable version of Jean Cocteau's *The Human Voice,* a painful monologue given entirely on the telephone by a middle-aged woman who desperately tries to hold on to her lover who has left her for another. Susskind got Ingrid Bergman to star in the hour for ABC's *Stage 67,* which was taped in London, where Kotcheff was based.

Susskind was so pleased with *The Human Voice* that he wanted Kotcheff to come to the United States to direct a version of John Steinbeck's *Of Mice and Men* for ABC that was to star George Segal and Nicol Williamson.

Kotcheff enjoyed Susskind and was delighted to get another assignment— but there was a problem. "I was banned from entering the United States," Kotcheff said. "When I was seventeen, I belonged to a left-wing book club for seven months. And I'm a Canadian, so I'm a foreigner. And when I tried to enter the United States to go on a holiday when I was twenty-one, they rejected me, and banned me from ever entering the United States because I belonged to an 'organization disseminating literature advocating the forceful overthrow of democratic government.'"

Kotcheff was a teenager working in a diner in Toronto in the early 1950s when a patron who sold *The Daily Worker* convinced him to join the club. "It was the height of the McCarthy period," he said. Numerous efforts to get his name cleared by the U.S. government had failed. But Kotcheff knew of other Canadians with similar political associations in their backgrounds who had gotten into the country. He took the job from Susskind and was able to get past immigration and enter the United States, in 1967. "And I got in once because bureaucracies make mistakes," he said. "They didn't see it. I thought, 'Oh, maybe they've forgotten about this thing,' you know? And I arrived, and I got into the United States."

But before Kotcheff signed the deal, he received a form from one of Susskind's lawyers. "It said at the bottom, 'Have you ever been forbidden entry into the United States?'" Kotcheff recalled. "And I didn't want to lie and get David into trouble. I thought, 'The shit's going to hit the fan now.' So I said, 'Yes, I've been rejected.'"

Susskind was stunned and immediately called Kotcheff to his office and offered his support. He wanted Kotcheff to tell his story on *The David Susskind Show.* "David was amazing. He said, 'We're going to fight this. Come on. You're going to go on my show and you're going to tell everybody what these crazies, these right-wing crazies, are doing. Tell them.'"

Susskind's lawyer, Justin Feldman, told Kotcheff that a public airing was ill advised. "Justin talked him out of it," Kotcheff said, "He said, 'Look, let me see what I can do.' And David said, 'All right, Justin, go for it. But if there's anything I can do. . . . And David paid Justin to represent me.'"

Feldman ultimately could not take the case, but he hooked Kotcheff up with Abba Schwartz, the former head of the Justice Department for the Kennedy administration who was responsible for liberalizing the Immigration and Naturalization Act. "David said, 'Help him in any way," Kotcheff said. "I don't care how much money you spend.' He was an angel, I'm telling you, in this regard." Susskind paid the tab for Schwartz, who made Kotcheff's problem go away. "I owe David a lot," said Kotcheff, who went on to have a long career in Hollywood and New York as a director and producer. "He's my hero."

Susskind called Kotcheff again that year with another job offer, but this was one he could refuse.

"I want you to do *Voice of the Turtle* with Princess Lee Radziwill," he said.

ABC president Tom Moore and his wife had met Radziwill during a trip to London. Radziwill was Jacqueline Onassis's younger sister and was married to a Polish nobleman. Living in London at the time, she had made her acting debut at age thirty-four in a Chicago dinner theater production of *The Philadelphia Story*. Moore thought she could star in a dramatic TV special and asked mutual friend Truman Capote to come up with an appropriate property. Why Capote chose *The Voice of the Turtle,* a dated World War II–era comedy about a single girl looking for sex in the city, was a mystery and, most likely, an act of mischief. Susskind had the TV rights to the play. Friends urged Radziwill to study acting seriously before taking on a high-profile role, but Capote told her too much training would "diminish her star quality," according to reports at the time. "Truman was such a little troublemaker," said Gloria Rabinowitz. "He probably thought it was so funny, that he could get David to say, 'Ah, not a bad idea.'"

Kotcheff tried to warn Susskind. "I said, 'Honestly, David. She can't act. You know, she got panned terribly in Chicago,'" Kotcheff said. "'You're going to put her in a two-handed play, the most difficult thing there is for an actress or an actor? You know, you're exposed. Find another play with her, where there's about ten, fifteen other characters that can carry her, if you're going to try to do it.'" *The Voice of the Turtle* had three characters, with the lead on stage in every scene.

Susskind was insistent that Kotcheff direct the play. Along with *The Human Voice,* he had successfully directed Siobhan McKenna in Doris Lessing's

Play with a Tiger on London's West End. "I got a reputation for being a women's director as a result," he said. Susskind pushed, wheedled, and even dangled a lovely bonus in front of Kotcheff, who played the violin.

"If you do it, I'll buy you a Stradivarius," Susskind said.

"You prick," a tempted Kotcheff said. "Don't do this to me, David."

"I know you like Impressionist painting," said Susskind. "Look, there's a Monet that's on sale. I can get you a Monet if you'd like."

Kotcheff managed to resist, but Susskind did take his advice and found a more suitable piece for Radziwill's limited skill set—a remake of *Laura,* the 1944 noir film that starred Gene Tierney. The main character is believed to be dead and doesn't appear until halfway through the film. "One had, therefore, the comfort and security of half a play without an actress or a would-be actress," was how Susskind described it with some bitterness years later.

Susskind got Capote to go along with the *Laura* idea, and they convinced Moore as well. Capote's friend Thomas Phipps adapted the screenplay. Susskind believed Radziwill only had to be serviceable in the role. While in retrospect Susskind said Capote "dragooned" him into making the project, at the time he knew full well a TV show with the sister-in-law of the martyred President Kennedy would generate massive publicity, and it did. She was billed by her maiden name, Lee Bouvier, driving home the message.

But there was a thin line between brilliant publicity stunt and embarrassing debacle. When the show was in rehearsals in London during the fall of 1967, Susskind and director John Moxey found Radziwill's line readings wooden and her movements stiff. Her costar, Robert Stack, later told writer Lawrence J. Quirk that Susskind wanted him to "scare the hell out of her" in the hope that it would shake her out of her "Café Society cool." During the filming of one scene, Stack said he threw a chair across the room and pounded on a table just to get things going.

Bob Israel, who did the score for the show, said Susskind spent $100,000 on additional music in an attempt to cover up Radziwill's performance. "Every time that woman moved you had to have strings," Israel recalled. "They had marks on the floor to tell her where to go. The mixes were endless. They were a nightmare. David was with me. Every time she did anything we stopped. We looked at it again. 'Let's try this music cue.' 'Put music in.' 'Well, the music wasn't written for this scene.' 'Put music in anyway.' We had no choice. We had to cover her." Moxey depended on tight close-ups of Radziwill, giving the show the look of a live TV drama of the 1950s or a soap opera. Nevertheless,

Susskind never backed away from the notion that it was an event for TV and the New York social scene. He previewed *Laura* in a private screening at his UN Plaza apartment in December 1967, a month before the show aired. Near the TV monitor were easels that displayed sketches of the fashions British costume designer Julie Harris created for the show. They did not help. Johnny Carson and Ingrid Bergman were said to be so appalled by Radziwill's performance that they walked out of the party before the show ended. Other guests smoked and chatted, ignoring the program as it played on. Meanwhile, journalists were getting their daggers ready. *Los Angeles Times* columnist Hal Humphrey wrote a piece that provided "Acting Clues for 'Laura' Watchers" so the average viewer could give his or her own critique. The program was not nearly as terrible as legend would lead one to believe, thanks to a supporting cast that included seasoned pros such as Stack, George Sanders, Farley Granger, and Arlene Francis. Radziwill, her head seemingly large on her boyish, pencil-thin body, was more bland than bad, although far below what people expected from a Susskind production. One viewer wrote to Susskind that she "had all the charm of a block of ice." A *TV Guide* editorial blasted ABC and Radziwill for what it called "a shoddy effort to cash in on America's fondness and sympathy for Jackie Kennedy." She never acted on TV again.

Susskind's instincts about audience curiosity were correct. He took bets with Melnick and the agents at Ashley Famous on what the audience share would be for the program. Susskind came in the highest, with a 43. He won. *Laura* was watched by 38 million people on January 24, 1968, the most viewers ever to watch one of his shows up to that time.

18

On May 21, 1966, William F. Buckley Jr. had David Susskind as his guest on one of the early episodes of his discussion program *Firing Line,* taped weekly at the RKO Studios in Times Square. The topic, "The Prevailing Bias," provided an opportunity for Buckley to espouse the notion that the media was controlled by elite liberals who conspired to squelch the flow of conservative ideas. Susskind was presented as Exhibit A. "He has probably appeared on more hours of television tortures than anyone in the history of television, which may or may not have something to do with the unhappy state of our universe," Buckley said at the start of the program. "He is a staunch liberal. If there were a contest for 'Mr. Eleanor Roosevelt,' he would unquestionably win it."

Susskind calmly replied in kind. "I must say that I regard that introduction as somewhat rude and insulting," he said. "I had hoped, on the occasion of having your own television program, you would abandon your traditional penchant for personal bitchiness and stick to the facts and issues. But evidently your rude behavior is congenital and compulsive. And so I forgive you."

For the rest of the hour, Susskind the Harvard man guest and Buckley the Yalie host squared off in a duel over the issue of media bias. Susskind was hardly on the defensive. He stated that the prevailing "bias" of not just the media but also much of the country was in fact liberal. He cited the last presidential election, which saw President Lyndon Johnson swamp his Republican opponent, Senator Barry Goldwater, and the legislation on civil rights and Great Society programs that was making its way into law. "There's nothing sinister or evil," he said. "We call that progress." (Buckley and Susskind had a $1,000 bet on the 1964 presidential election, which Susskind won.)

Susskind came loaded with statistics about the plethora of media outlets that gave a voice to conservative ideas, although he opined that it wasn't always easy to find representatives of the political right for his own program because he believed most of them were dull. "You can count on twelve that can keep an audience reasonably awake and interested," Susskind said. "And I cry for their slim numbers, as do you." The parrying was friendly throughout. "You are not without charm," Susskind told Buckley at the end of the hour. "You are, in fact, in my view the most elegant anachronist in our country."

While he disagreed with Buckley's politics, Susskind privately envied Buckley's lingual dexterity. "He sometimes fantasized out loud how he wished he could have his polysyllabic exuberance," recalled Sam Szurek, a producer on *The David Susskind Show* during the early 1970s. "He berated the staff for not coming up with comparably clever intros. From time to time David would pore over the dictionary and select Buckley-ish exotic and archaic words and try them out on whoever was in earshot."

Buckley hosted *Firing Line* for thirty-three years, but most of that time was spent in the protected sanctuary of public television stations, away from the pressure of ratings. The kind of spirited but collegial debates Buckley conducted, and Susskind preferred, began to disappear from commercial TV in the second half of the 1960s.

It was the fall of 1966 when David Susskind's talk show returned to its previous flagship New York outlet, WNEW. Bennet Korn, the hostile station executive who drove Susskind out three years earlier, had moved on. WNEW's parent company, by that time known as Metromedia, had installed a new management team at the station led by Larry Fraiberg. His group believed the debates over the cultural, social, and political issues of the day were an opportunity to turn the "sofa and desk" format of the TV talk show into an electronic public square. They wanted the turbulence over the Vietnam War, race relations, and free love represented on the screen. "Everything was going on at the same time," said Paul Noble, a WNEW producer at the time. "There was the sexual revolution, the drug revolution, hawks versus doves, permissiveness in speech and other things. And so the talk shows were a reflection of that."

When Metromedia launched *The Joe Pyne Show* on its Los Angeles station KTTV, it became the first talk program in which guests were provoked and the audience talked back. Pyne was a cantankerous World War II Marine veteran who had lost the lower half of one leg to cancer. He made his name as a brash radio call-in host with a show called *It's Your Nickel* (listeners who irritated him were told to "go gargle with razor blades") and adapted his act to TV in 1964. His image was working-class populist and his invective was aimed at anyone who deviated from so-called mainstream America, whether they were avowed communists, Ku Klux Klansman, hippies, or devil worshippers. Audience members were asked to express their own views from a lectern in the studio called the Beef Box. The copy for one of the show's tune-in ads read: "Have An Argument This Weekend. See The Joe Pyne Show."

"He was a linear ancestor of what became the Fox News Channel at night," said veteran TV executive Alan Bell, who worked for Metromedia at the time. Actually, Pyne was capable of being far more incendiary than the cable news pundits who succeeded him. In 1965, when rioters shook the black community of Watts in Los Angeles, Pyne told viewers he was prepared for them and demonstrated by pulling out a revolver. Metromedia executives suspended him for a week. Other times he showed up on the set with a German shepherd guard dog.

Pyne's show was a ratings winner in Los Angeles and was rolled out to other stations across the country. Metromedia then looked to imitate it. "I learned an important lesson," said Bell. "Make sure you never let the words 'sets' and 'costumes' pass through your lips if you're going to be successful in independent television of that era. We weren't doing news then either. The whole notion that you could make audience success and money out of nonfiction was a revelation. Once you get started on that stuff you realize there is an infinite number of ways in which you can slice that baloney. There's the tough-guy talk, there's the arty-guy talk, and there's the guy who reads your mind." For a short time, Metromedia even had an anti–Vietnam counterculture talk show in the late afternoon hosted by actor Don Francks, called *Coming Around.* Producer Rupert Hitzig replaced the standard talk-show swivel chairs with large boxes painted in bright colors. "We would book guys like the Smothers Brothers and everybody in the audience got flowers," he recalled. "Francks and Joe Raposo wrote the theme song 'Coming Around'— *'It's a whole new world, we're coming around.'* The problem was, Don Francks was stoned most of the time. Sometimes I couldn't get him out of the dressing room. I'd say, 'Tell Don we're ready to go,' and he and Mason Williams from *The Smothers Brothers Comedy Hour* had been smoking weed. I'm rolling tape and the two of them came out and sat on the boxes and giggled.

And I'm thinking, 'I'm not sure this is a good idea.' But Fraiberg encouraged all that."

The best-known New York talk-show character to emerge from the era was Alan Burke, a bearded journeyman radio disc jockey and newsreader with a commanding theatrical baritone delivery. Burke had caught on as an abrasive radio talk-show host in Miami, and Fraiberg brought him to New York to do an East Coast variation of Joe Pyne's format. "Larry Fraiberg was attracted to the idea because it would be a chance to show his boss that if you want to do an abusive show, don't give me something from the other end of the country because their way of abusing people is not the way you abuse people in New York," said Bell. "Burke in private life was an absolutely delightful and charming charlatan. The show was in no way what he was like, whereas with Pyne, what you saw was what you got. Burke decided he would create the persona of a nasty guy on television who would tell you to stick it up your ass if he disagreed with you. He would challenge you and be abrupt. It was an act. He would come into the studio and turn himself into Alan Burke. Then he'd go home and be a perfectly nice guy."

Burke was a dandy who wore a pinky ring and a long coat that looked like it came off the back of a riverboat gambler. He smoked long thin cigars. His interviewing style was first to make a guest feel comfortable with his charm and then launch into a confrontational line of questioning. "We had guests get up and walk out and he would fill the rest of the half hour," said director Arthur Forrest. "He couldn't care less."

A former ad man, Burke did his best to promote the notion that he was the talk-show host people loved to hate. "You don't need talent to be the star of a TV talk show. All you need is an obnoxious personality," he once told a journalist. "And with me it comes naturally."

But Burke was not always able to keep his caustic on-air persona locked in. "We had Joan Baez on the show," said Paul Noble. "At that point, Alan was sort of a raving right-winger, or hawk, and he was attacking Joan Baez by calling her Joanie Phony. The audience was hoping, 'Oh, can't wait to see him get his fangs into her.' And we bring on Joan Baez, and Alan Burke absolutely melted. By the time the interview was over, he asked her to sing 'Scarlet Ribbons' a cappella, which she graciously did. And the audience was in tears." The moment revealed the real Burke, who once released an album called *My Naked Soul*. It was a collection of his romantic poetry read over lush orchestral arrangements.

Burke's best-remembered guest was a nun who renounced life in the convent to become a go-go dancer. Such a sensational subject was a double-edged sword. On the Monday morning after it aired, Noble said, management came in singing his praises. But by the afternoon there were high-level meetings about losing advertisers. "It would be, 'The Catholic Church is having Pan Am pull out,'" Noble recalled. "She said the unforgivable thing on television in 1967. She said that certain nuns had particular friendships and the convent always had to break them up."

Once Susskind returned to WNEW, he tried to distance himself from Pyne and Burke (both of whom scored higher ratings than he did in many weeks). "He would put them down," Bell recalled. "He would say they're vulgarians, that it was a circus on television and they're not interested in serious ideas." Susskind slammed Pyne's audience directly when he appeared as a guest on *The Joe Pyne Show*. "Never in one time and place have I seen such an assembly of slack-jawed, thin-lipped, beady-eyed political morons," he announced. He once opened his own show with a diatribe against Pyne. "Are you tired, down, logy, restless?" Susskind said. "You're probably suffering from that terrible TV virus Joe Pyne-itis. . . . It comes from overexposure to humbug, hypocrisy, rant, cant and foolishness. I wish I could offer a positive cure, but there isn't any. You might make some progress by turning off the TV set."

Off camera, Susskind was cordial to colleagues and crew, but he never exuded much warmth around the WNEW studios. "You almost had to stand up when he walked in the room," said Jim Shasky, a longtime director for Susskind's program. "He was like a general. He meant business all the time." Paul Noble remembered an encounter with Susskind in the station's green room before black activist Stokely Carmichael was set to appear on the show.

"Is this the studio where my favorite show *Rudy Kazootie* used to come from?" Carmichael asked Noble.

"Stokely, that was done over at Channel 4, over at the RCA Building," Noble said. "But I remember the *Rudy Kazootie* theme song. Do you?"

"I do."

"Let's sing it."

Noble was then joined by the militant figure who coined the phrase Black Power, and founded the organization that became the Black Panthers, in an impromptu performance of the classic kid show's opening theme: ''Who is the boy who is full of fun and joy? He's Rudy Kazootie!''

"At that point, David walks in," Noble recalled. "And everything cooled down. I left."

Still, Susskind was willing to adapt to the more pluralistic style of television discourse once he determined it was necessary to keep his show on the air. The executives at WPIX, the New York station that carried *Open End* in the mid-1960s, had complained that his show was dull. By the end of its run there, they cut it back to a single hour. At WNEW, where the program was restored to a two-hour format and renamed *The David Susskind Show,* he added a studio audience to enliven the proceedings.

"It was a time for yellers and screamers," said Herb Bloom. "*Open End* was a discussion with a group who interacted among themselves. On *The David Susskind Show,* the audience affected the whole mood and tenor of the show. They often interrupted what was going on. Some of the questions were inane and worthless." This often led to chaos in the studio. A tense session on race relations, called "Watch Out, Whitey—4 Angry Blacks," became so raucous, a woman in the audience claimed she was mugged and robbed right in the studio after the show. On a show called "Free Love—Free Pot for All," Abbie Hoffman came out of a marijuana smoke–filled green room with a live duck that he set loose. It defecated on the set. The moment exists only in writings about the program, as Susskind's producer Jean Kennedy edited it out before airtime. Bloom believed Susskind much preferred serious issues and important guests such as Israel's deputy prime minister, Abba Eban. "The line he used was, 'My mother and Mrs. Eban will be the only people who watch this show,'" Bloom said. But just as he had done as a TV producer, Susskind the talk-show host needed to respond to the marketplace at that time.

Susskind himself always managed a steady, dignified presence during the tapings, even when the proceedings got wild. He kept the show serious enough that WNEW could list it as public service programming, something which stations needed to show on their schedules during FCC license-renewal time. Like *Firing Line,* Susskind's show was largely sustained in the years that followed by the public television stations that continued to carry it in other markets.

As THE LATE 1960s became more polarized, Susskind's personal politics moved toward the middle of the road. The Democratic liberal tradition he grew up with was under fire by forces on the political left. While he gave

Stokely Carmichael a platform, he was unable to show the same kind of empathy he had with Dr. Martin Luther King Jr. Susskind was opposed to the Vietnam War, yet he publicly criticized Muhammad Ali for his refusal to serve in the military on the grounds that it was against his Muslim faith (a stance that resulted in his being stripped of his heavyweight boxing title).

Susskind was an active supporter of the 1968 Democratic presidential campaign of Robert Kennedy until the candidate was shot by assassin Sirhan Sirhan on the night of his June 5 California primary victory. Kennedy died the next day. Susskind was invited to ride on the train that took Kennedy's body from New York to Washington on June 8. Instead, he fulfilled a commitment to give the commencement speech to the graduating class at Rhode Island College in Providence. He used the occasion to address the unthinkable act of violence the nation had witnessed. He wrote down an addendum to his prepared speech on the back of an envelope of the Sheraton Biltmore Hotel where he stayed. "This hour of your commencement coincides exactly with the funeral mass for Senator Robert Kennedy," Susskind told the audience that day. "It is not enough that we universally feel sad and sick and spent. Mark this as a day of catharsis and change in the American way of life. It is time for love and peace and gentleness each to the other." The crowd of four thousand stood and applauded.

However, Susskind refused to get behind eventual Democratic Party nominee Vice President Hubert H. Humphrey after Kennedy died. He believed Humphrey took too long to break with President Johnson's Vietnam policies. Susskind wagered $2,500—and won—in a betting pool with friends that Humphrey's Republican opponent Richard Nixon would win the November election. After Nixon's victory, Susskind wrote a congratulatory letter to the president-elect, stating that he voted for him.

Even as Susskind's own political views had moderated, he was still open to exploring new ideas and social trends and that allowed his show to give voice to the activism that emerged at the time.

By the fall of 1968, the news that women were organizing to push for greater equality had largely been disseminated through magazine articles, books, pamphlets, and consciousness-raising meetings in big cities. Early press coverage of the movement was provided or encouraged by the few women working in newsrooms at the time. Male TV newscasters typically delivered their stories on the subject with a sarcastic sneer (an early New York TV special on the movement was titled "Women Are Revolting"). On the rare occasions women's issues were discussed seriously on TV, it was often men who were doing the talking. "David Susskind had four men talking about abortion, and should women be allowed to secure abortions," feminist author Susan Brownmiller recalled. "Four men. I remember sitting there watching it and wanting to throw my shoe against the TV screen."

Jane Everhart was working as a fiction editor at *Cosmopolitan* magazine when she handled publicity for the National Organization for Women. After business hours, Everhart and feminist author Kate Millett snuck into the *Cosmo* office to use the Xerox machine to copy handouts for their picket lines and demonstrations. "That's about as close as *Cosmopolitan* editor Helen Gurley Brown came to supporting feminism," she said. But Everhart knew street protests and fliers were getting the movement only so far. Television exposure was necessary to reach critical mass. She tried to get TV producers to book NOW representatives on talk shows, but "they thought we were a bunch of crackpots," she recalled. "We couldn't get anybody interested except for David Susskind and it was because of Jean Kennedy."

By 1968, Kennedy had been producing Susskind's talk show for ten years and was still one of the few women in her field. She met Susskind while she was employed at the Fox Theater in Detroit and he came through town to promote his feature film *Edge of the City.* She stayed in contact with him and later moved to New York to become the producer of *Open End* just a few months after it premiered. Jean Kennedy always had the office next door to Susskind's at Talent Associates. "Jean Kennedy did an enormous amount of work on it," said Judy Crichton. "She had a small staff. She worked eighteen-hour days. It was entirely her life. She read for David. She absorbed the information for David. And she knew how to feed the information to David. He was a quick study." Susskind was said to have a photographic memory and could process clips and background materials quickly.

Kennedy came in each day with a shopping bag filled with newspaper clippings, magazines, and books she was reading that were written by potential guests. Papers piled so high in her office that other Talent Associates employees joked it would be an effective bomb shelter. She appeared to live on cigarettes and coffee, often drunk cold. By the end of each day she filled pages of her long yellow legal pads with proposed shows and guests. "If David wasn't always receptive to an initial idea that she thought was good, she would keep going after him with it," said Herb Bloom. Susskind got most of his ideas from *The New York Times.* Producer Gloria Rabinowitz recalled how Susskind often pulled crumpled-up newspaper clippings out of the pockets of his de-signer suits. But Kennedy's influence on his show was considerable, if only because Susskind's work on producing television programs, films, or plays often left him little time to prepare each week.

Kennedy was guarded and reserved by nature, and Everhart said it was dif-ficult to tell if she was actually sympathetic to the feminists' cause. "Jean came across as pretty tough," Everhart recalled. "In those days you couldn't be too soft and be in a man's job. Jean didn't ever let us know that she was on our side. She never let me know that. I heard from other people that she was." Kennedy maintained that her only interest was putting together a compelling show every week. If the show was anything less, Susskind was capable of rais-ing hell, even if a single guest was a dud on camera. "No matter how success-ful a show, David would never let us forget the occasional nonperformer," Szurek recalled.

By the fall of 1968, the women's liberation movement had made national headlines with the protests held outside the Miss America Pageant on the boardwalk in Atlantic City. The event became linked with "bra burning," even though no undergarments of any kind were set ablaze. But Susskind needed more convincing before presenting the topic on his show. Like most men of his generation, he dismissed it, and he used his pulpit to freely express his disdain. Asked earlier in the year by fellow talk-show host David Frost for an opinion of the American woman, Susskind used the phrase "overly emanci-pated." Could Susskind ever work for a woman? "That would be intolerable," he told Frost. "I couldn't take it."

Despite Susskind's macho posturing, he was fully aware of women's capa-bilities. Jean Kennedy was among the many women Susskind hired in the 1950s, when such opportunities were scant. He developed a reputation for be-ing a supportive boss and maintained an office environment that was hospi-table to women. "There was an absolute assumption in many shops that you would sleep with the boss," said Judy Crichton. "To use an old-fashioned ex-pression, holding on to your dignity in television in the late 1960s and 1970s, as a woman, took real confidence and willpower. It was hard to do. I was a married woman. My husband was a well-known writer. I had four kids. And I was constantly under assault. And so, being in an office where women were respected was a very pleasant experience. The level of casual sex at Talent As-sociates was enormous. But if you weren't a player, you could go in your office and nobody would bother you."

Talent Associates was even mindful of reproductive rights. "The company must have paid for nine abortions that we weren't responsible for," said Dan Melnick. "Women would get in trouble and we would take care of it. We'd just come up with the money. Everybody knew that we were protective. It really was familial."

But the women's movement was about gaining equal rights, not benefactors. The old rules would not stand, even at Talent Associates. "The first day I was there someone comes out to tell me that 'Mr. Susskind does not like women to wear trousers in the office,'" Crichton recalled. "I'm not sure I wore slacks all the time, but the weather was very bad that day. And I said, 'Tell Mr. Susskind that when the weather is bad, I will wear trousers.' And I did."

NEVERTHELESS, JANE EVERHART LEARNED from Jean Kennedy that to get feminist leaders booked as guests on *The David Susskind Show* she would have to take an old-fashioned approach. "I had to have them cast based on their looks because I knew that David was a connoisseur of female beauty," she said. "Although I had to put Kate Millett on the panel because she had a new book."

At Kennedy's suggestion, Everhart arranged for a few of the potential guests to first meet Susskind at his office. One of them was Jaqueline Ceballos. A mother of four children, Ceballos had left her husband to join the movement and had become active in NOW, eventually becoming its president. A round-faced brunette in her early forties at the time, she remembered being told that Susskind wanted her on the program because she reminded him of his first wife, Phyllis. "The story I got was I looked like his ex-wife and they chose Rosalyn Baxandall because she looked like his new wife, Joyce Davidson," Ceballos recalled. "She was blond and very attractive."

Ceballos recalled being quizzed by Susskind about how she could have walked out of her marriage to a wealthy Colombian man to join NOW. "So your husband lives in Bogotá, Colombia, and you live over here," he said. "What do you do for sex? What does he do for sex?"

"I don't care what he does," Ceballos told him. "We have an agreement. We're separated and I'm not interested in my sex life now. I'm interested in the movement."

Ceballos said she watched as Susskind walked out and stuck his head into Kennedy's office to say, "I want her—she'll be easy."

"He was so anti what we were doing that he thought it would be easy to disregard everything I said—that I was doing all of this because of a bad marriage," Ceballos said. "In other words, he really didn't want to interview us as much as he wanted to show us up."

On a night in early October 1968, the show was scheduled to tape. Women from several factions of the feminist movement packed the bleachers at the WNEW studio. Members of the more militant groups, such as New York Radical Feminists and the Red Stockings, sat alongside members of NOW. But they were united in their anger when Susskind announced the panel discussion on their topic would only be a twenty-minute segment. Some of the women started heckling Susskind about giving short shrift to their cause. He cut the taping short, riling them up even more. A dozen of the audience members spilled out of the studio and onto East Sixty-seventh Street, where a limousine was waiting, presumably for Susskind. Some of them started rocking the car up and down. Everhart came outside and calmed them down once she said Susskind agreed to give their issue a longer segment on a future date.

Susskind lived up to his word and reassembled the panel on October 14, 1968. He remained skeptical of their purpose. "He opened the show by saying, 'Why would four beautiful women like you be interested in women's liberation?'" Ceballos recalled. "I'll just never forget it. He was smiling and gracious, but he couldn't get over our answers. He was stunned at everything we said. The women in the audience were getting up and screaming because he was so obnoxious."

After listening to the panel's vision of equality for women, a male audience member stood and said, "'You mean to tell me that when I get married, I can't expect my wife to wash and iron my clothes, to cook my food, keep my house clean, and bear my children?'"

"Sir, what you need is a maid with bedroom privileges," was Kate Millett's reply.

Susskind's resistance turned out to be a small price to pay for the national exposure the women gained for their respective groups during the program. Throughout the hour-long discussion Ceballos repeatedly gave out the address for NOW headquarters in Manhattan. Baxandall's group, New York Radical Women, didn't even have a post office box, so she gave out her home address.

The program aired in New York on December 8, 1968, nearly two months after the segment was taped. It was titled "Angry Women Rap Men, Sex & the System." The response was instantaneous. As the tape of the program made its way to stations for airing across the country, sacks of mail from each city came into the NOW post office box. "Every time a show aired in a market we'd get telephone calls and telegrams," Ceballos said. "More and more and more. We got more members. The movement just grew like mad." Baxandall received thousands of letters as well from women who wanted to join NYRW.

Brownmiller said once Susskind's show opened the door, *The Dick Cavett Show, The David Frost Show,* and other TV talk programs booked representatives from feminist organizations. They quickly gained more followers and clout as a result. Susskind revisited the issue on his show as well. But his public criticism of feminist leaders became increasingly harsh, almost irrationally so, when he appeared as a talk-show guest or gave interviews to journalists. When *New York Magazine* wanted David Susskind and his wife to be among the high-profile couples included in an article called "Living with Liberation," Joyce Susskind asked to be interviewed separately from her husband.

Susskind told the writer he agreed that women deserved equal pay for the same job, but then launched into a bizarre sexist screed. "I have a private theory that the militants are a bunch of overwrought and undersexed ladies!" he said. "I know that Kate Millett. I've had her on my show. Those eyes are unhappy female eyes. They say, 'I'm not fulfilling myself. I have not got a good love life. I am not surging with pleasure two or three times a week. I'm not in love or getting enough love from a man.' None of these goddamn women have had a healthy orgasm in a long time. If they keep up their unattractive militancy, they'll get less and less sex."

Such remarks branded Susskind as a prominent male chauvinist pig and likely cost him some thoughtful female fans who had looked to his program as an oasis of smart conversation on television. Some even suspected he was cynically bashing the women's movement as a way to attract attention to himself. "Since no intelligent human being could truly hold the archaic ideas you seemingly espouse, you must do it for a purpose," a viewer wrote after watching Susskind rant when he filled in as host of ABC's *The Dick Cavett Show.* "Perhaps you want to be controversial and interesting in order to hold an audience."

It could also be that Susskind did not want to let other men in on the great deal he was getting from hiring so many capable women. "He definitely appreciated their intelligence, but he also appreciated that he could fight with them and they wouldn't quit," said Diana Kerew, who joined Susskind's company in 1971 and became one of the main producers on his staff during the ten years that followed. "So he could do whatever he wanted to do. We could scream back, but we weren't going to walk out. Frankly, where were we going to go? He was the only game in town. There was a conscious manipulation of the situation going on. Whatever the negatives were in that equation, you could kind of work with it. You could say things to David that a man could never get away with. You could be on equal footing with him creatively."

David Susskind was certainly not the only intelligent man unable or unwilling to publicly embrace the women's movement. "A lot of people didn't get it," Brownmiller said. "A large part of the male intellectual establishment said, 'We'll weather this little storm and then go on and talk about our serious issues.' They never expected it to become a mainstream issue that would transform the country and the rest of the world."

The David Susskind Show was rarely, if ever, more tempestuous than the night of November 1, 1971, when the topic was "What Have You Done for Us Lately? Furious Feminists." The panel was built around Germaine Greer, who had become a hot ticket on the TV talk circuit. The author of the 1970 feminist manifesto *The Female Eunuch,* Greer was fearlessly provocative, humorous, and statuesque. A fawning press portrayed her as "a feminist that even men could like," according to Brownmiller.

Susskind was not taking her on alone. He booked acid-tongued movie critic John Simon, *New York Times* book reviewer Anatole Broyard, and Dr. Edgar Berman. Berman had been a personal physician and an adviser on medical issues to Hubert Humphrey when he was vice president. In 1970, the Democratic Party had to distance itself from him after he said that physiological factors affected the ability of women to take on leadership positions.

Greer was flanked by Brownmiller and Brenda Feigen, a lawyer who helped launch *Ms. Magazine* with Gloria Steinem. When word of Greer's appearance spread among the feminist meeting groups in New York, their members again packed the studio audience for the taping. Susskind antagonized them immediately with a warning at the start of the show not to "make asses" of themselves, according to Brownmiller.

Greer lived up to her reputation for glib, shocking statements. "Women have very little idea how much men hate them," she said, as a bewildered Susskind looked on. "Otherwise they would not end up beaten, defiled with bottles stuffed up their vaginas in vacant lots all the time."

But it was Simon who stirred the audience into a near frenzy after expressing concerns about the movement's more radical political factions. As the crowd jeered his remarks, he said, "I'm always worried about sexual revolutions initiated by women who are so incredibly homely that no man would look at them." Greer's jaw literally dropped.

Simon's comment prompted a young woman in the audience to stand up and tell the men on the panel she wasn't fighting to make herself more attractive to them. "I am fighting to become a human being and I demand that kind of treatment," she said. Others started shouting "Pig! Pig!" When an exasperated Susskind could not calm the audience members during a commercial break, he told director Arthur Forrest to stop the taping. Jean Kennedy was asked to come down to the set.

Anne Marie Riccitelli was one of the young women active in the movement who was on hand for the taping. She remembered the pained look on Susskind's face as he pointed to Kennedy and said, "This is my producer. I pay her $650 a week. I treat women with great respect. All of the women who work for me, I respect, and I pay them well." Riccitelli said her circle of hecklers in the audience fell silent. "You could have knocked the whole group over with a feather," Riccitelli recalled. "It was like, 'How do we get a job with you?' You know, we're all ready to get down on our knees after that."

From Brownmiller's perspective on the stage, Susskind's display with Kennedy didn't cut any ice. "He didn't like being attacked," she said. "He thought he had perfect politics." Once the taping resumed, the audience did not sound as if they were assuaged by Susskind's plea. The unidentified young woman in the audience who was enraged by Simon resumed her speech with even more passion. She revealed the anguish she felt over being what she considered a second-class citizen because of her gender. Viewers didn't know her name. She didn't have a book to plug. Yet she made the most eloquent case of the night on why the women's movement was vitally necessary.

"I am not a human being because I can be raped on the street," she said. "I am not a human being because I can be refused a job. I am not a human being because when I try and do something that women don't usually do, I am laughed at and questioned."

In drawing the heated show to a conclusion, Susskind chastised the audience one more time like a stern dad: "I assure you I will not have another women's liberation panel for the next year." But the genie was already out of the bottle, and *The David Susskind Show* had played a role in releasing it.

During the rest of the 1970s, men at other companies had to adjust to the influx of women in the workplace that occurred because of class-action suits and the other changes that resulted from the feminist movement. Susskind and Talent Associates did not. "There was no harassment," said Kerew. "He was gender-blind in the workplace. It was a strange paradox to me."

Perhaps no one knew that as well as Margaret Matheson, a young London-based protégée of Verity Lambert who was hired to work on several Talent Associates programs produced in England during the 1970s. Matheson, then married to British playwright David Hare, was eight months pregnant when she supervised an adaptation of George Bernard Shaw's *Caesar and Cleopatra* for the *Hallmark Hall of Fame.* "David Susskind arrived for the taping on December 23, 1974, and he was slightly startled to see me sticking out for a mile with my first child," Matheson recalled. "That was all fine. He had no argument with it."

Susskind liked Matheson's work and was eager to deploy her on more projects he had lined up. "He looked at me and said, 'I'm very visceral about this kind of thing and I know this is right,'" said Matheson. "Nobody here spoke like that. It's so un-English to be that direct." She learned just how determined Susskind could be, when he wanted her to oversee the making of a feature film based on James Herriot's novel *All Things Bright and Beautiful.*

"I had the child a week earlier than expected on Christmas Day," she recalled. "In those days in the public health system in England you would have twelve in a ward. I was in the most beautiful ward in a building across the river from the Houses of Parliament. Literally my bed is by the window, and I'm looking at Big Ben. We're not allowed any phone calls and there [were no cell phones] back in 1974. My husband must have told David that I had the baby, because the next thing I know, a phone is wheeled in on a trolley. Of course, it's David Susskind who obviously refused to take no for an answer. He says to me, 'How would you like to produce a a picture?' I said 'Listen, I've just had a baby and it's Christmas Day. Maybe we should talk in a week.' That was very David. It was sort of gloriously inappropriate."

19

After she and David were married in 1966, Joyce Susskind would tell journalists that she was content with her life as a wife and mother and no longer felt a need to do television. Susskind also said freely that he wanted his wife at home. "I remember meeting you at a party one evening, and you said, 'I don't want my wife to work—one ego in the family was enough,'" Barbara Walters told Susskind during an appearance on his show in 1968.

There was a lot of attention that came with being the new Mrs. David Susskind, and Joyce eagerly filled that role. Susskind loved buying expensive clothes and jewelry for his wife, including made-to-order items from designer Arnold Scaasi, who became a friend. "She was very good-looking, with a beautiful figure," Scaasi said. "She could wear model sizes. She had a lot of style. She had great excitement about dressing. She loved to dress up. Of course, David was very proud of her. And she always had one or two things from each collection. They were very fantasylike and very feminine." Her closet also housed furs from Ben Kahn, and outfits from designers Mollie Parnis, Pauline Trigère, and Oscar de la Renta. Joyce occasionally walked the runways at fashion shows in New York and appeared in shoots for magazine and newspaper fashion sections.

Joyce Susskind spruced up her husband's wardrobe as well. For years, Susskind wore gray suits and knit ties, the uniform from his days as an MCA agent. By 1969, David Susskind was a dedicated follower of designer Roland Meledandri and made the International Best Dressed List. "It's absolutely marvelous," Joyce told *The New York Times*. "It proves that fashion is not just for the young." When Susskind traveled, Joyce carefully packed his clothes with instructions on which items should be worn together.

Over time, the Susskinds turned up on television together. In September 1969, they appeared on a syndicated game show *He Said, She Said,* "the game of marital quotes." Each celebrity couple earned points based on their ability to identify each other's answers to a generic question, such as "What makes her laugh?"

"Me," was Susskind's answer.

When the show's host, Joe Garagiola, read Susskind's response to the question, Joyce didn't press her buzzer to identify it. "He does make me laugh," she said. "You know why I didn't get that, dear? It's too small a word. You know how you talk."

The Susskinds also failed to score on a question about miniskirts. "Incredibly attractive" was David Susskind's answer. He explained by noting his wife's ability to pull off the look: "My wife is incredibly attractive in miniskirts, in anything, but boy, when you can see her thighs . . ."

Joyce identified her husband's answer, but not the reasoning behind it. "David loves women," she said. "And the more he sees of them, the better he likes it. But I will say, he likes to see it on the other fellow's girls. My skirts . . ."

"Wait a minute, honey," an exasperated Susskind said. "Don't go too far . . ."

But occasional TV appearances weren't enough for Joyce Susskind, who clearly missed the self-made stardom she had achieved in Canada. "I think she wanted to do things for herself," Shelley Stallworth said. "My mom had a large ego. I think she wanted to work and I think she needed it."

David Susskind did his best to be supportive of his wife's desire to return to TV. Not to be supportive was to really risk "some serious marital discord," according to Andrew Susskind. An opportunity arose in late 1970 when Metromedia's Washington TV station had developed the idea of launching the first nighttime talk show hosted by women. Feminist leader and writer Gloria Steinem was signed on to do the program with socialite turned Washington journalist Barbara Howar. "It was really a bold idea," Howar recalled. "There were simply no women on the air. There were simply no women reporting the news. It was unheard of." After a labor dispute at Metromedia put the planned show on hold for several months, the project was turned over to Talent Associates. Susskind was eager to do the show but wanted to add Joyce as a third host. (Howar swears that at an early meeting with Joyce she claimed her words to Susskind were, "Daddy, buy me a show.") Steinem wanted no part of Susskind, who was once ranked on her list of top ten male chauvinist pigs. She dropped out of the project and told Howar she would be unwise to stay on. But Susskind was able to get sponsors for the show and get it on the air. Howar, a single mother with two children, needed the income. In her 1973 book *Laughing All the Way,* Howar noted how she should have listened to her mother's advice at the time: "The only way to work a husband-and-wife team is for *you* to be the wife."

Called *Joyce and Barbara: For Adults Only,* the syndicated show was supposed to present two women with different points of view—Joyce Susskind as the traditionalist and more conservative of the two, while Howar was the independent, single mom with a feminist bent. Joyce was ill-suited for the role: her life had been anything but traditional. As an interviewer, she did not possess the confrontational style needed for the planned format, where each week the women hosts would take on a male guest from their own perspective. Joyce's demure approach did not mesh well with the glib, hard-charging Howar.

The show's producer, Rupert Hitzig, said Susskind was desperate for the show to succeed and spent thousands of dollars of his own money to have Arnold Scaasi come to the show each week to dress Joyce. "David loved her," Hitzig said. "He worshipped her." Howar brought up her own clothes from Washington in a shopping bag. During the first episode, taped at a station in Philadelphia to save money, Susskind became overwrought when he didn't think it was going well. It didn't help that he was out drinking before the program with its first guest, George C. Scott, Hitzig said. An inebriated Susskind stood up on the console in the control room and started screaming obscenities at Howar.

"David would say to her, 'You have three of what most men have two of,'" producer Jinny Schreckinger recalled. "And she said, 'Well, if you'd like, I'll lend you two, because you obviously don't have any.' That was the nature of their relationship."

During the pilot taping, Hitzik and director Arthur Forrest threw Susskind out of the control room and locked the door. "David pretty much left me alone after that," Hitzik said. It didn't help, as *Joyce and Barbara* lasted only a few months.

Susskind eventually found a way to revive his wife's TV career. He had been among the first American TV producers to make shows in Canada in order to take advantage of the favorable currency exchange rate at the time. In the early 1970s, he had his business manager Ron Gilbert make a deal with Glen-Waring Studios in Toronto. Talent Associates would commit to using the studios for its TV movies if Joyce could get a program at the parent company's TV station, CFTO. Through the rest of the 1970s and well into the 1980s, Joyce Davidson was a fixture on Canadian television again.

Later, when asked by if she liked being back on the air as Joyce Davidson instead of Joyce Susskind, she said, "Oh sure, especially when I get a higher rating than my husband."

20

The gay liberation movement took far longer than feminism to find its voice on television. Its representatives, mostly members of pioneering gay-activist organizations such as the Mattachine Society and the Daughters of Bilitis, began to show up on local TV and radio talk shows in Los Angeles and New York during the 1950s and early 1960s. In those years, gay people did not reveal their predilections on television without careful consideration. The stigma and prejudice against them was so intense that they would be putting their jobs, their relationships with family members, and perhaps their own safety at risk. For years, gay people who appeared on camera were shrouded in darkness, wore wigs to disguise themselves, and identified themselves by first name only.

Elaine Noble, a gay activist in Boston during the 1970s, said the fear of being outed on the news resulted in understating the reported turnout for gay pride parades and demonstrations. "If it was two hundred thousand they'd say it was fifty thousand or one hundred thousand," she said. "I started one of the first gay pride parades in Boston. By the end there were thirty-five of us because cameras showed up and people freaked out and they didn't want their mothers to see them on TV. Unlike people who moved to San Francisco, most of the gay people I knew in Boston went to school there or moved from Dorchester or the suburbs and had family there. Boston, up until the mid-1990s, was a very parochial little Catholic town. But we got sophisticated about making press kits and I started a radio program and other people started newspapers. We started taking communication devices in our hands to guide and educate. That was a big step forward. Better than letting people define us, we started defining ourselves."

Television talk shows provided the least filtered outlets for the message of the emerging gay rights movement. Susskind's producers had wanted to tackle the subject for years, but station management kept them away until 1967, according to Jean Kennedy. Susskind's first show with a gay panelist—Dick Leitsch, the president of the New York Mattachine Society—is believed to be the earliest TV discussion about homosexuality in front of anything resembling a national audience. (*The David Susskind Show* was on twenty stations across the country at the time.) The program had the unfortunate title in the TV listings of "Homosexuality: Sickness or Perversion," and Leitsch was flanked by two New York psychiatrists. Just addressing the topic drew a severe negative reaction to some of the stations that carried the show, such as WQED in Pittsburgh.

"Educational stations, a couple, got into a lot of trouble by playing the program," Susskind told another panel of gay men who appeared on the program, which did not occur until 1971. "People wrote to the state legislature in Pennsylvania and said if there are going to be homosexuals on educational television they should have their charter revoked."

"But what was your rating that night?" asked Randolfe Hayden Wicker, a Mattachine Society member who had appeared on several TV talk shows at that point. "I'll bet it was very good." Wicker's assessment was correct.

Susskind worked with gay people every day at Talent Associates and he and his wife Joyce socialized with gay couples, often dining with Arnold Scaasi and his longtime partner. On the first show he did on homosexuality, he said he accepted the medical establishment's view that it was a disease. But he was clearly open to alternative views. Throughout the 1970s, *The David Susskind Show* was for the most part a friendly forum for gay people, who could talk about their lives and make viewers who shared their orientation feel less isolated. At the same time, the gay press questioned whether Susskind was exploiting the community for the sake of sensationalism—the subject attracted large numbers of curiosity-seeking viewers. A cartoon in one publication once depicted five David Susskinds being interviewed by a gay person.

In March 1974, David Susskind oversaw what was likely the most compassionate televised examination of gay people up to that time, with a show called "Homosexuals Who Have Come Out of Hiding." David Rothenberg, a well-known New York activist for prisoners' rights, revealed he was gay on the program, after suggesting the topic to Jean Kennedy. It was a bold decision at the time, as Rothenberg had already experienced the power and reach of Susskind's program five years earlier. He was a theatrical publicist on Broadway and an aspiring producer who, in 1967, staged John Herbert's play about prison life called *Fortune and Men's Eyes*. After each performance at the Actors Playhouse in Greenwich Village, Rothenberg and the actors listened to comments from audience members. Many of them were ex-cons who stood up and shared their own prison experiences.

"I was becoming an expert," he said. "So after about six months I brought a few of them together. I said, 'We could educate, inform the public, and change the prison system.' So one night at the theater, I announced that we were starting this group. We were going to call it Fortune, from the play's title. And about eight or ten people gave me two dollars each, because I said we could keep in touch with them. We mimeographed our first couple of newsletters, and we kept people informed. And my office paid for them. I was plodding along until I called Jean Kennedy. I knew she had done programs on Gamblers Anonymous and drug addicts. I asked, 'Have you ever done a group of ex-cons?' She said, 'We can never find any.' So Susskind had them on. And at the end of the program, he took my address. He said, 'If anybody wants to contact these men, they are part of a new organization, the Fortune Society, at 1545 Broadway.'"

The Monday after the show aired, on March 10, 1968, Rothenberg went to his office in the six-story building occupied by theatrical business types at the time. "I got there about nine thirty in the morning," said Rothenberg. "And the stairwells from the sixth floor to the first floor looked like a prison scene in an old movie." Dozens of men who saw the show the previous night showed up at Rothenberg's door to learn more about the Fortune Society. He was not prepared for the response. "They thought they were coming into a thriving new organization," he said. "And it was me alone, Schmuck-o in his office with his *Hair* and Tennessee Williams theater posters on the wall behind me."

The Fortune Society was soon off and running. It became New York's central source for ex-cons looking for help with food, jobs, shelter, and a connection with other people who understood what they had been through in the penal system. Rothenberg, while continuing his work in the theater, gained stature as a prominent advocate for the rights of former prisoners. He was still, as he said, "deeply in the closet" when he was approached to be a part of the National Gay Task Force, a gay-rights advocacy group that was coming together by the end of 1973.

"Somebody recommended me, because they wanted people from different fields," he said. "They had to get somebody from criminal justice. And they approached me. And one of the criteria was that you had to be out, and open. Also, I had just entered into my first adult relationship. Because when you were closeted in the 1950s or 1960s, everything was furtive. So you don't have a relationship, because then they'd think gays were gay."

As the leader of the Fortune Society, Rothenberg had asked ex-cons to step forward and deal with the media as a means of eradicating the stereotypes and prejudices they faced. He believed he had to take the same step as a gay man. "I was very unhappy with the duplicity," he said. Once again, he called Jean Kennedy.

"You've had a couple of programs about gay activism, but there's another story," he said. "People who have lived industrious lives, who have established real careers in a variety of fields, but who are invisible in terms of their sexuality."

"Like who?" Kennedy said. "Can you mention anybody?"

"Like me," Rothenberg said.

Rothenberg tried to help Kennedy line up a panel for the program. "I had approached five other people, all of whom said yes, and none of whom came on," he said. "One of them was Emile Griffith (the former middleweight boxing champion), who eventually came out."

Kennedy and her staff booked Elaine Noble, an Emerson College professor by that time. Even though she was still talking about gay issues on her Boston radio program, she had reservations about presenting herself as a lesbian on television. "It was still quite risky," Noble recalled. "Some of my colleagues were very afraid for me." Noble asked for assurances that Susskind would not focus on the "fitness" of gay people to function in certain jobs. "I was assured that the framework be around who we are or how we're coping and what being gay really means and that it was not going to be demeaning in any way," she said.

Before the program was taped on February 11, 1974, Rothenberg gathered the key members of the Fortune Society together for a meeting in his office.

"I have three things to tell you," he said. "I'm gay. I'm going on *David Susskind* to talk about it. And I'm prepared to submit my resignation as executive director."

Fortune Society member Mel Rivers asked Rothenberg why he felt a need to leave the organization.

"People might have problems with someone openly gay," said Rothenberg. "People might not support us."

"You've stood behind us for six years, telling us to be a man," Rivers told him. "Give us a chance to stand along with you." He also asked the sartorially challenged Rothenberg to find something decent to wear on television.

Rothenberg and Noble were joined on Susskind's panel by Dr. Howard Brown, a former New York City health commissioner who taught at New York University; Carolyn Innes, a registered nurse from Philadelphia; Joseph Norton, professor of counseling at the State University of New York in Albany; and Dr. Adrianne Smith, a clinical psychologist from Chicago. When Susskind presented them he noted that none of them were "hairdressers or interior decorators."

He expressed surprise that there was nothing in the appearance of the panel members that suggested they were gay, especially Noble. "One thing I can't get over as an active heterosexual is that there seems to be no rays being sent out by an attractive homosexual lady," said Susskind. "I would, for example, as a single man make very interesting proposals to you. There would be no sense that that's a waste of time."

"I'll help you over that," Noble shot back.

Later in the show, Susskind was asked how he would feel if he learned his own son were gay. "I would try to discover if there was any medical help that would be brought to bear," he said, leaving his guests a bit perturbed, since the board of trustees for the American Psychiatric Association had recently agreed to drop homosexuality from its list of mental disorders.

But to Elaine Noble, the candid response only helped in objectively presenting the panel's cause. "In many ways he reflected what a host of American fathers would say," she said. "There was no hostility and no evaluative behavior. That's what struck me. Under that macho exterior, there seemed to be a very loving man in a lot of ways. That's what came through. Nobody else would have taken that on. I think it was an important event for a lot of people because it was the first show where gay people appeared to be just like anybody else. And that was the objective of it. It was very important and far-reaching."

Noble sent a letter to Susskind after the taping. "The airing of this show will do more for improving attitudes toward homosexuals than all of the picketing, shouting, be-ins, sit-ins and other demonstrations I have taken part in over a five-year period of time," she wrote. Noble said the show helped her father deal with her coming out. By the end of 1974, she became the first openly gay person elected to political office when she won a seat in the Massachusetts State Legislature. She later met a fan of her TV appearance at a Democratic Party gathering. "Warren Beatty, the actor, came over to me at a Democratic Caucus and remarked on how much he liked *The David Susskind Show*," she recalled. "We became friends and still stay in touch. Warren could not believe I had not had psychoanalysis."

Rothenberg said he received nearly six hundred letters about the program, an overwhelming number of them supportive. His mother watched it at her home in Miami. "When she called after the program, she said not only that she liked it; she said one of her friends commented, 'How wonderful that he's so secure with your love that he could do that,'" Rothenberg said. "That was in the early 1970s. This is pre-AIDS, so people were not coming out because they were dying. When I look back, it was an act of courage on my part."

21

In 1963, Dan Greenburg was a twenty-seven-year-old writer from Chicago working for *Eros,* a slickly directed hardcover magazine about sex. He often dined out for lunch with his editor, Ralph Ginzburg. It was over one of their meals that Greenburg had a life-changing revelation that had nothing to do with sex.

"He was a bit overweight and I was always underweight," Greenburg recalled. "It turned out we essentially had the same Jewish mother urging us to eat. He responded by eating too much and I responded by eating too little. All of the things that each of our mothers told us turned out to be the same in terms of instilling guilt for not eating. Instilling guilt in general. I said, 'My God, where do they get this? They must have some kind of Jewish mother's handbook.' It suddenly occurred to me that I ought to write one."

Soon after that conversation, Greenburg ran into Roger Price, the writer and TV comedian who was part owner of the publishing house Stern Price Sloan with Talent Associates partner Leonard Stern. Built off the wildly successful series of *Mad Libs* game books, Stern Price Sloan marketed other titles as novelty items in gift shops and other locations that didn't typically carry books. "They were called nonbooks," said Greenburg. He told Price he wanted to do a snob's guide to status cars.

"I don't know anything about cars," said Price. "Do you have anything else?"

"Just a title," Greenburg said. "*How to Be a Jewish Mother.*"

Price didn't need to hear another word. "I'll buy it," he told Greenburg.

The image of the overbearing, manipulative, and emotionally suffocating

Jewish mother was familiar to most first-generation Americans with European immigrant parents. In October 1964, Stern Price Sloan published Dan Greenburg's *How to Be a Jewish Mother: A Very Lovely Training Manual,* and the archetype was launched into new heights of notoriety. The back cover showed a photo of an adult Greenburg being spoon-fed by his own mother, Leah, which means "the weary" in Hebrew. It was a re-creation, some twenty-five years later, of a photo of Greenburg's mother feeding her son when he was a toddler. Leah Greenburg also received credit for providing "technical assistance." The book's bone-dry text offered instructions on "how to administer the third helping" and "the technique of basic suffering." The glossary included definitions of such terms as "unmarried surgeon: the answer to a mother's prayer." Three months after its release, *How to Be a Jewish Mother* was in its fourth printing.

"Word of mouth suddenly exploded that book," Greenburg said. "Everybody was reading it. It outsold everything in fiction. Everything in nonfiction. It outsold the *McCall's Needlework Treasury.* It was hundreds of thousands in hard cover. In soft cover there were several editions and it went into the millions."

Greenburg's book was adapted into a stage show in 1967 and a bestselling comedy album performed by Gertrude Berg of *The Goldbergs* fame. But at the time, humor that dealt overtly with the Jewish experience was still largely exposed through comics doing short bits on television variety shows.

In the big-city TV markets that showed *The David Susskind Show,* the Jewish mother was a natural topic, even though Susskind himself wasn't completely comfortable with it. "I think David liked to stay away from Jewish things," said Jean Kennedy. "When we first had Jewish mothers on, he said, 'Get some Italian and Irish ones.' Not the same. David was a little self-conscious about these things."

"I think he was, like most of us, insecure and afraid of not measuring up to a certain Anglo-American ideal," said *Susskind Show* associate producer Sam Szurek. Szurek was the son of Polish and Austrian Jews who had immigrated to Bolivia to escape persecution during World War II. "I believe David resented having grown up in a Jewish household of relatively modest means," Szurek said. "He joked that he couldn't possibly be his mother's son; at the maternity ward an incompetent nurse exchanged babies and his real mother was Rose Fitzgerald Kennedy. I remember him saying with pride that his parents never spoke Yiddish." Susskind did not deny his Jewishness, nor did he embrace it. When Susskind had a group of nuns on his talk show in 1966, he told them he was always glad to have one on an airline flight. "The minute I see a nun I figure that I am traveling with the Lord and that I'm relatively safe," he said. "Is that an old wives' tale?"

"You mean you can forget your own rabbit's foot and leave it at home?" one of them replied.

Szurek and the other producers wanted to do another show on Jewish mothers by approaching it from a new angle—having successful Jewish men come on and talk about them. They all thought it was a brilliant idea. Susskind did not. "The staff repeatedly pressed, until David relented," Szurek said.

Dan Greenburg, who at the time was developing screenplays for Susskind, signed on as a guest. "The whole examination of Jewish mothers from that point of view had not really gone on before on television," said Greenburg. "It was very much time to examine that phenomenon. A lot of people had mothers who were born in Europe and had that sensibility."

Susskind then enlisted Dan Melnick to put in a call to Mel Brooks, a regular in the Talent Associates offices when he and Buck Henry were developing *Get Smart.* "It was Danny who called me," said Brooks. "He said, 'You know David's talk show?' I said, 'Good show. I watch it all the time. I'm waiting to see Senator McCarthy.' I loved the show. 'Well, he wants to do something called sons of Jewish mothers.' 'Ooh,' I said, 'Dan Greenburg?' Dan Melnick said, 'Yeah, it's based on the book.' I said, 'Who do you have in mind?' 'We thought about you, we thought about David Steinberg, we thought about George Segal and Greenburg himself.'" Brooks's second directorial effort, *The Twelve Chairs,* had just been released, while his first movie, *The Producers,* was still building its cult status with bookings in small theaters around the country. He was happy to show up to plug his films.

Another call went out to George Segal. The actor had grown up in Great Neck, a town on the North Shore of Long Island with a large Jewish population. Segal, who had been in the Talent Associates production of *Death of a Salesman,* was headed into his most successful years as a major film star. He had just made *Where's Poppa?,* a bizarre, raunchy comedy in which he played a tortured lawyer whose addled but indomitable Jewish mother keeps him from getting on with his life. (Ruth Gordon, who in one scene kisses Segal's bare buttocks, played the mother. The studio nixed the movie's original ending, which had the two of them in bed together.)

Susskind also wanted David Steinberg, a hot young comic at the time.

Steinberg was the Canadian son of a rabbi who infused a 1960s counter-culture sensibility into a traditional stand-up comic style. He already had secured a place in television history with his rabbi's sermon routine, which included some mildly risqué wordplay and closed with the admonition, "Let's put Christ back into Christmas and *chah* back into Chanukah." After Steinberg performed the bit on *The Smothers Brothers Comedy Hour* in defiance of the CBS censors, the network canceled the show in April 1969. CBS executives were already gunning for the program, which they hated for its overt criticism of the Vietnam War.

Steinberg was reluctant to appear on Susskind's Jewish sons show, but it had nothing to do with the topic. "I was very un-self-conscious about talking about Jewish things," he said. "My approach on television, even when I did anything Jewish, was anything but self-deprecating, it was sort of militantly Jewish. So this was fine for me. But I thought I was on TV so much, I didn't want to do the show. At that point I was already guest-hosting *The Tonight Show* and *The Dick Cavett Show.* I had cohosted Mike Douglas." Once Susskind was committed to doing the show, he would not give up. The day before the taping, he asked Brooks to take Steinberg to lunch at the Russian Tea Room in the hope of convincing him to come on.

"Of course I remember the lunch," said Brooks. "I paid." Brooks clowned with Steinberg. He told the young comic that his experience studying for rabbinical school would be great material for the discussion.

"He said, 'Come on, it will be fun. It will be good for me,'" Steinberg recalled. "Whatever it was, you can't say no to Mel."

The producers added Larry Goldberg, a comedian turned entrepreneur who was writing a humorous diet book and had founded a successful restaurant chain, Goldberg's Pizzeria. "We had food covered," said Szurek. But Susskind wanted one more panelist who could guarantee some controversy.

Stan Herman was a hot designer in the 1960s and president of a dress company called Mr. Mort. "I used to do what they call 'fashion for a price,'" said Herman. In those years, Herman was a go-to guest whenever fashion was a TV talk-show topic. He remembered having first been booked for a Susskind show appearance along with designers Donald Brooks and Geoffrey Beane. "I went up to the office and was interviewed by one of his lackeys up there," Herman recalled. "I left, and the next day she called and said, 'You're too good to be wasted on a show that just has to do with fashion. We're doing another show that we think you'd fit into very well.' So they booked me for this show that was going to be famous sons of Jewish mothers. I was Jewish and I was famous at the time."

Shortly before the show's scheduled taping, Susskind asked Herman to stop by the Talent Associates offices for a brief conversation about it. When Herman got there, he remembered how Susskind looked at him with a "sly-boots look in his eye" and said, "Most designers are gay, aren't they?"

"Yes," Herman replied.

"Are you?"

"Yes."

"Would you be willing to talk about it on the show?"

Herman's sexual preference was known among his friends and in the fashion industry, but not far beyond that. He was on the verge of transforming his status as a big name on Seventh Avenue into the highly lucrative business of designing company uniforms. He had just completed a job for Avis Rental Car and had secured a contract from the fast-food giant McDonald's, a potentially huge source of income. He wondered how his new clientele would react to having its image shaped by a New York Jew who announced to the world on television that he was a homosexual. Herman went home and discussed Susskind's proposal with his partner, a novelist, who told him, "You have to be true to yourself. You have to say what you want to say." Herman called Susskind back and said he would discuss his sexuality if it was handled properly and not sensationalized.

Herman put the show out of his mind until the day of the taping on November 12, 1970. Earlier that day Herman had presented his new Avis uniform at a fashion show at Maxwell's Plum, the art nouveau–designed restaurant and bar considered one of New York's swinging hot spots at the time. A limousine waited outside the restaurant to take him to the WNEW studios just a few blocks away on East Sixty-seventh Street. "I was in a state of shock," he said. "They rushed me over to the show and there in the green room were Mel Brooks and George Segal, who was a very hot actor at the time, and Dan Greenburg and David Steinberg."

On top of his anxiety over the prospect of coming out as a gay man on a nationally syndicated TV talk show, the diminutive Herman had a wardrobe malfunction. His knit slacks in the rust color that matched the Avis uniforms were not fitting properly. "When you make knit pants, if the fabric doesn't have retentiveness, the crotch drops down eight inches," he said. "I looked down at my crotch before I went on and I said, 'Oh shit, man.' I must have had my legs crossed the entire time."

Susskind himself still had his doubts about how the Jewish sons show was going to play, even as he headed over to WNEW with Jean Kennedy. "He said, 'Do you think this is going to be any good?'" she recalled. "I would have said yes regardless, but I said, 'Of course, it's going to be wonderful.' After about five minutes he realized he had gold."

He had it even before that. A half hour before the taping started, Mel Brooks went into the bleachers in the studio and warmed up the crowd. It was as if he was back to his days as a tummler working the crowd in a Catskills resort. "He was in the audience doing shtick," Greenburg remembered. "He was so on it was unbelievable." Laughter rumbled through the set by the time Susskind started his introductions at the top of the program. Usually unflappable, Susskind was breaking up as George Segal lovingly blew thick clouds of cigar smoke into the host's face.

Within moments, Brooks went into overdrive. He announced in all the years he lived with his mother, he had never seen a piece of furniture. Sheets to keep the dust off had always covered it. "But what's criminal is that my mother has four great paintings that we've never seen," he proclaimed.

When Goldberg talked about how the small Jewish population was dispersed in his hometown of Kansas City, Brooks said: "I bet they all get together for pogrom—gathered in one big Jew cellar while the Gentiles go thundering by!"

Susskind started Steinberg off by asking if his mother was still alive. The comic stared into space as if he were trying to remember. He then described a dream in which they were in a ballroom on a luxury liner. "We danced until dawn," he said. "I'm three and she's fifty-two and I'm just about to get her into my crib—and I wake up."

Brooks topped him later by claiming he had left the Jewish faith because the sign of the cross was easy to make in a time of panic. He demonstrated how a Star of David would require both hands. "Two triangles," he said. "That's a lot of work!"

The show became a joyride powered by a relentless, unpredictable Brooks, who could fill any pause in the conversation with a routine or a song. That was nothing new for anyone who had spent time with the comic in a TV show writers room. When his colleagues on the 1950s sketch program *Your Show of Shows* were stuck without a funny line or a joke "Mel would say, 'Got it! Listen to this,' and he'd stand up and sing a chorus of 'All of Me,'" Larry Gelbart once told Susskind. "We'd all watch and then sort of applaud and go back to work."

The performance had the technical crew in the show's control room rocking with laughter. Even Jean Kennedy had shed her typically reserved demeanor and was doubled over in a corner. Jim Shasky said the camera operators on the studio floor laughed so hard they were unable to keep their shots steady. "The live audience really set the tone," said Herman. "I remember one of my assistants, a redhead, was the only person not laughing. She was a nice non-Jewish girl from California. I don't think she knew what was going on."

"It was anarchy," said Segal, who sent the studio audience into convulsions when he got up from his chair to do a song from his days as a Dixieland jazz bandleader and stepped on the cord of the lavaliere microphone that hung around his neck. He started to choke when the cord tightened like a noose. When Susskind got face to face with Segal to help him, the actor looked in the host's eyes and said softly, "What are you doing later?"

But it was Brooks who kept on taking command. He thought of the rest of the panel as straight men, and they knew it. "They were all funny," he said. "As far as I was concerned they were very, very good, but I was better. It was just give me the mike and stand back and I'll take care of the evening."

"Mel has got that streak in him, that 'I'm taking this over no matter what,'" Segal said. "Welcome to the Mel Brooks Show. But that was okay. He was being Mel and that was the best part of him really. I don't know what you call that kind of aggression, but it certainly worked on that show. Mel was totally comfortable with David Susskind. David kept giving him rope and Mel kept advancing."

"Mel and I were sort of discovering each other there," said Steinberg. "You could see me half improvising and finding material I didn't even know I had on the show. At some point I realized all I wanted to do—whatever subject David Susskind hasn't found, I wanted to find another one for Mel." Brooks did not let anyone, even Susskind, slow down his momentum, at one point dismissing a ponderous question from the host with a playful "Shut up, David!"

"It was my favorite moment in the whole show," said Greenburg. "Everybody wanted to say 'Shut up, David' for years. People roared with laughter." So did Susskind.

Stan Herman remembered being uneasy during the show's early moments as he wondered how Susskind would approach the subject of his sexuality.

Less than ten minutes into the discussion, the host zoned in on Herman. Susskind asked how Herman's mother viewed his choice of profession, positing that mothers "don't rear their sons to be fashion designers."

Herman rambled on a bit with a story of how his Jewish stepmother removed many of the doors of his Passaic, New Jersey, family home to make it look larger.

"That's so you don't do private things," Brooks said, once again cracking up the panel and the audience.

There was no lock on the bathroom door, either. "It tended to open all the time at the most embarrassing moments," Herman said.

"So you never had a normal boyhood?" a persistent Susskind asked.

"No," said Herman. "No doors. No locks."

He came back at Herman a few more times, asking about his mother's attitudes toward the "idiosyncrasies" and "lifestyles" in the fashion world, but never directly asked the question about being gay. Brooks and Steinberg kept on using Susskind's dead-serious inquisition as setups for jokes.

"Mel was very good to me," Herman said. "He saw how nervous I was at the beginning. There was one point where he wanted to get me to sing. Then I realized David wasn't going to ask me about the homosexual thing, so I relaxed a little more."

The humor of the show allowed the famous sons to offer glimpses into how they dealt with assimilating and their cultural identities. They revealed their neuroses, such as Steinberg admitting he owned a Volkswagen until he was overcome by his childhood fears that the cars would be used to drive Jews back to Germany. They talked about the modest circumstances of their immigrant homes (Brooks recalled using old jelly jars for drinking glasses), and how they had to explain the kind of big money they currently earned to their disbelieving parents. They talked about introducing their parents to non-Jewish girlfriends for the first time (Steinberg's advice was to bring home a black girlfriend first). Steinberg believed it was the first time the term "Jewish princess" was ever used on TV. They explored the need for some Jews to alter their names and noses. "If you're really funny, you get a lot more truth than talking seriously about the same subject, so the themes start to come up out of the woodwork whether you want them to or not," Steinberg recalled. "Once you start saying, 'Okay, we're talking about Jewish mothers,' you start to talk about what we were proud of, what we were ashamed of. You notice that Mel is probably first-generation like I was. My parents came over from

Russia, as did his parents. What you start to get is the outsider feeling. Jews weren't as assimilated then as they are now. Right now my daughters wouldn't understand any of the stuff we're talking about."

For Segal, the show was remarkable for having such an unfettered and intimate TV discussion about being Jewish when the notion of being "too Jewish" for Hollywood was still fresh in his mind. "Just a few years before this time there were all those Warner Brothers shows like *77 Sunset Strip* with all these cute guys," said Segal. "I went up for a thing that took place in a tobacco field and it was going to be shot in Connecticut. The casting director for Warner Brothers at the time—I believe Jewish with quite a honker on him—said to me, 'That was a very good reading, but you can't be in film unless you change your name and change your nose.' That was out there still." (Despite his being a devoted Anglophile, Susskind never considered changing his name and advised others in show business not to, even in the 1950s. "The only advice he ever gave me was not to change my name," recalled screenwriter Larry Cohen. "He said, 'Keep your name. If you change your name, you'll always be ashamed.'")

Whenever Susskind realized he had a good show, his body seemed to stiffen up, an almost reflexive action that kept him from interfering with the moment. It was especially true on this night. As the session went on, he minimized the wording of his questions, sensing that all he had to do was raise a subject for Brooks or Steinberg to run with. "You can't be that brilliant without someone like Susskind right next to you eating it up and laughing at it so you feel like you're in secure territory," Steinberg said. "That was remarkable in him, how he at one point was going to Mel and going to me for another idea, just enjoying seeing what's coming out without a plan."

Oddly enough, Greenburg, the man responsible for catapulting the Jewish mother into a pop-culture icon, got lost in the crossfire. "I was completely inundated, by Mel especially," said Greenburg, who told the stories of his mother in the deadpan style of his book. That dry wit did not sync with the more outrageous performers on the panel. "There was a period there when I didn't speak for an entire hour. I was afraid to say anything because these were some very funny guys."

Segal did not personally connect with the Jewish mother concept. While his mother was the daughter of Russian immigrants, she was reserved and distant. "It was contrary to me because I had a very Victorian mother who grew up in Philadelphia," he said. "It was mythical to me." After being peppered with questions about his relationship with her, Segal decided to turn the tables on Susskind. With mock outrage, he asked how often Susskind saw his own mother. (Susskind quickly calculated that it was one and a half times per week.) Susskind attempted to move on, but Segal didn't let him off the hook. Segal accused the typically detached Susskind of pursuing his inquiry of the panel as if he himself did not have a Jewish mother. Susskind said, with great pride, that he did.

Brooks piled on, wanting to know about financial support: "What do you give her, David?" ("I was so rude," Brooks said looking back.)

David Susskind's mother, Frances, was an outspoken and often overbearing woman who recognized her son's abilities early on and reveled in his success. As Susskind ascended in the television and film industries, his mother frequently bragged about "my son, the producer." She was also the subject of the most repeated personal anecdote about her son. Frances Susskind once brought a group of her friends to a guided tour of the Talent Associates offices, which she treated as her son's personal fiefdom. At one point, she opened the door to a small office that had been provided to writer Robert Alan Aurthur, who was at work on a novel. "And this is where my son David keeps his writers," she boasted. For years afterward, visitors who met with Susskind needled him by asking to see the office.

Frances Susskind frequently gushed over her news-making son's fame, not least of all when she had her hair done regularly at a beauty parlor in Queens. "That's my son David," she announced during each visit. Over time the boasting got on the nerves of one regular patron at the shop, the mother of Ely Landau, who ran WNTA, the TV station that aired Susskind's talk show in New York at the time. "Ely's mother said she was holding her tongue for months," Landau's widow, Edythe, recalled. "And finally she went up to her and said, 'Excuse me, Mrs. Susskind, I just want you to know that *your* son works for *my* son.'" When the maternal showdown was recounted to Ely Landau, he said, "You didn't do that," to which his mother replied, "I certainly did."

In the years when *The David Susskind Show* had a studio audience at the WNEW studio, Frances Susskind frequently attended the tapings. Once she was on hand for a show in which Susskind questioned four cleaning women who worked in city office buildings. He asked if any of them had walked in on employees having sex in the office after hours, an activity with which the host himself was familiar (Susskind's executive assistant, Michael Abbott, remembered how he once walked in on his boss and a pretty young production assistant having a late-night tryst at Talent Associates). The union representative for the cleaning women stood up from the audience and angrily chastised Susskind for bringing up the subject of sex. Always looking out for her David, an upset Frances Susskind telephoned Jean Kennedy afterward and pleaded with her to edit out the exchange before it aired.

Kennedy never bowed to such requests. But Susskind always indulged Frances Susskind whenever she arrived unannounced to show off her son's workplace to friends or the ladies from her Hadassah chapter. He was by all accounts a dutiful son. When Frances Susskind's brother Eli Lear was sent to prison for armed robbery, David Susskind honored his mother's requests to visit his uncle while he was incarcerated and provide financial support during the times he was out. After the non-Jewish Joyce Davidson became Susskind's second wife, she learned how to bake challah bread to please her new mother-in-law. David Susskind made sure Frances lived out her years comfortably until her death in 1980. Yet in press profiles, he reflected only on the childhood time he spent with his father Benjamin and the erudite Sunday afternoon lectures they attended in Boston. Frances was not part of the public image he wanted to convey. When Segal brought her up on the Jewish sons show, the inquiry momentarily unsettled Susskind. "He didn't want to be a participant," said Segal. "He wanted to be above the battle and yet he was central to it. The question he was asking, I think, was how he felt about his mother. He had the Jewish mother of Jewish mothers on that panel. There was the irony I guess."

After Susskind said good night to his guests and the credits were rolling, director Arthur Forrest told the technicians and producers in the control room that they had just seen a classic in the making. "This is going to last forever folks," he said. "It's never going away." Over time, Forrest was proven right. "How to Be a Jewish Son—Or, My Son the Success!"—as it was called in the newspaper television listings—first aired on November 29, 1970. The following day the switchboard at WNEW lit up with calls from many viewers who were not amused. "Vile," "vulgar," "disgraceful," "the most insulting thing Mr. Susskind has ever done," were among the comments that came in. Brooks was denounced as an apostate not only for his Star of David gag but also for his answer on whether he asked his wife, actress Anne Bancroft, to convert to Judaism ("She don't have to convert, she's a star!"). One caller who described herself as a Jewish mother said, "This is how Jew-haters are made." Susskind received an angry letter from a representative of the Anti-Defamation League who called the show an example of Jewish anti-Semitism. "The reaction was, how dare you show the worst aspects of us," said Szurek.

The callers turned out to be an infinitesimal minority. Brooks, Steinberg, and Segal saw their status only rise in the eyes of the public and the entertainment industry after the show aired. "The center of the television power at the time was still in New York," said Steinberg. "So everyone was aware of this show. You couldn't miss it. You had five stations to watch. Everybody talked about it the next day. I remember the experience of walking down the street in New York after that show. They went nuts. 'That was great.' 'The funniest show I've ever seen.' This was bigger than doing *The Tonight Show.* Everywhere I went people were talking about the Susskind show. Not just show business people. Everybody. My career took off after that."

Steinberg recalled his initial doubts about showing up. "This is an example of how little you know about your own career," Steinberg said. "I remember sitting in the bleachers before the audience came into the studio and pouting because I thought the show was such a dumb thing for me to do, when I don't want to be one of those people that's just on TV all the time. I did the show and I felt I had done fine. I enjoyed Mel so much and George Segal and I became good friends and saw each other a lot after that show in Los Angeles and in New York. And after a year or two, I had the feeling that the show was the thing that moved my career to the next place. Somehow it was the subject, Mel, me. I don't even know, when I look at it now, why it did that, but it did. But the thing for years that people always mentioned to me was this Susskind show."

Brooks didn't recall any immediate response to "How to Be a Jewish Son." After viewers clamored for Susskind to run it again, the show was repeated annually around New Year's Day. Its popularity and legend grew along with Brooks as he became a major comedy box office attraction as a director and performer during the 1970s with *Blazing Saddles, Young Frankenstein, High Anxiety,* and *Silent Movie.* "Suddenly I'd hear about the show from one person and another," he recalled. "It was very much like *The Producers*—it made an explosion when it opened, and it was kind of quiet and little by little it gathered its own steam and its own force and moved forward. It got to be legendary. The same thing happened with this show. You never know what's going to happen. Who knew that this little roundtable interview show, certainly not a great forum for my talent, would be one of the best things I ever did in my life? It would launch me as a first-rate comic personality. Who the hell knew? It was amazing." Jon Merdin, a Talent Associates staffer at the time who was on the set the night of the taping, said it was clear Brooks's on-camera madness was a revelation for the audience. "He didn't have a public face outside of being a performer, and then suddenly you realized that he was as nuts as a person as he was as a character," he said.

George Segal said for years fans praised the Jewish sons show as part of his body of work. "There are certain movies, like *Blume in Love* or *Touch of Class,* and they shake your hands with two hands because it meant so much to them. It was seminal for them," he said. "They're thankful in a certain kind of way, and those are the same kind of looks I would get from that Susskind show. There is a kind of chicken soup warmth in it." Greenburg may have gotten lost on the panel, but *How to Be a Jewish Mother* was a gift that kept on giving. His series of paranormal adventures, *The Zack Files,* launched him into a new career as a successful children's book author. But he was still getting residual checks from Europe for stage performances of *How to Be a Jewish Mother* more than forty years after he wrote it. What struck him the most was how the experiences described in his book and on the Susskind show were universal. "As I said in the book, you don't have to be Jewish or a mother to be a Jewish mother," he said. "I would meet Korean guys, Japanese guys, certainly Italians, who said, 'You're talking about my mother.' You're talking about a specific type of behavior that isn't only Jewish, like wanting to control the child a lot and using various devices like guilt. I don't think there's a culture in the world that doesn't use guilt to control children."

The lasting legacy of Susskind's Jewish sons show did not make everyone happy. Stan Herman's story about the missing doors and locks in his house angered his stepmother for years. "When Susskind replayed the show every New Year's she kept thinking I was on again, repeating the same remark," he said. "I'm not kidding."

Susskind soon found out the show was an inspired, lightning-in-a-bottle type of event that could not be easily duplicated. After a story about Jewish princesses appeared on the cover of *New York* magazine in March 1971, he jumped at doing a show on the subject. "David loved the idea, some might say probably because it was demeaning to Jewish women," said Szurek. "We spun our collective wheels for the longest time trying to book it. But no self-respecting, accomplished, smart woman would do it. So we ended up with a panel of non-entities. A terrible show was taped and I don't believe it ever aired."

AFTER THE JEWISH sons panel, *The David Susskind Show* entered a period where it became a funhouse mirror of the 1970s—although no distortion was necessary in order to present some of the bizarre social trends that emerged during that decade. Jinny Schreckinger, then a young production assistant on the show, remembered fielding a phone call from Deborah Hartin. A navy veteran, she was known as Buddy Hartin before undergoing a gender reassignment operation (then simply called a sex change) in Casablanca. The she who used to be a he sent over pictures of herself before and after the transformation. "I remember showing them to Jean Kennedy, who turned beet red, which she always did at the drop of a hat," Schreckinger said. "Then David came in and he thought it was the best idea imaginable." Hartin was invited on the show along with two other women who had recently undergone the procedure.

"The panel included a striking brand-new woman," said Sam Szurek. "She was so new that I had to fetch her from the hospital room where she was recovering. It was exhausting—an hour before tape time I was still at her bedside trying to convince her to appear on the show. She finally agreed. We caught a cab and raced to the studio." Schreckinger remembered that the woman, Diane (formerly David) Fadool, was still hooked up to an IV drip when she arrived at WNEW. Her face was glamorously made up and she wore a low-cut dress that showed off the results of hormone treatments she had been undergoing for years. During the show she apologized for squirming in her seat, as she was still in pain from the surgery.

Throughout the decade, *The David Susskind Show* needed to occasionally resort to the sensational, as the host now had competitors entering the boundary-pushing territory the program once ruled. Empathetic host Phil Donahue made taboo topics of the moment easy for housewives to digest on his syndicated daytime program. In New York, a high-strung, self-involved host named Stanley Siegel was getting attention by lying down on a couch once a week on his show for a session with his analyst. Radio was also getting more adventurous. In 1972, Susskind did a show with the first generation of "shock jocks"—which included a young Don Imus—who talked about how female listeners were willing to call in to their shows and talk about their sex lives on the air. Gary Dee, a well-known host from Cleveland, told Susskind, "What we're doing in radio is what you've been doing for years."

Susskind, for the most part, was up to the challenge of exploring the wild side of the 1970s, if that was what was necessary to maintain his hold on the broadcast real estate that served his curiosity, business interests, and ego. The show plugged into every trend and subculture that came along in the era—group encounters, communes, cryonics, midi- and miniskirts, underground movies, transcendental meditation, disco, and Elvis Presley impersonators. One topic always worked. "Anything with sex got ratings," said Jean Kennedy. "People said, 'Why don't you do more serious subjects?' Well we did some very serious subjects and they'd be excellent shows. We'd take great pride in them. But the ratings wouldn't be as good as if you did homosexuals, drag queens, or people who change partners."

In the fall of 1972, Susskind once turned over an entire show to a simulated two-hour sex-therapy session conducted by psychologists Phyllis and Eberhard Kronhausen. They talked to two couples, who were masked to conceal their identities. "David just introduced it and then he wasn't really involved in the interviewing or anything," said Jill Gelbach, a production assistant at WNEW at the time. "What happened on that show would be tame now. But apparently nobody cleared it with the powers that be at WNEW. All of us in the control room got into a bit of trouble because nobody alerted them to what was going on. The show never aired. But no one had really touched on anything like that. We were just coming into an era when women were allowed to wear pants at work. It was indicative of how groundbreaking David Susskind was, but this show came up against a brick wall."

The program presented the Kronhausens talking to the couples just as they would have in an office interview. "People are anxious to be informed today," Susskind told the New York *Daily News*. "There's no psychological reason why people can't enjoy sex."

Susskind was never salacious in his approach to talking about sex on his show. Much of the discussion with experts or subjects was clinical in nature. He cleverly played the befuddled everyman when a guest said something particularly outrageous. Some who worked with him had a hard time reconciling the real Susskind with his on-air persona, which occasionally required a certain naiveté to work. "I hardly ever watched because it wasn't the man I knew," said Diana Kerew. "David was a very no-nonsense man, and very focused on the work, and just very professional, for want of a better word. When he was sort of the fumbling dumb guy who has to ask the stupid question to provoke the answer it made me crazy, because that wasn't David in conversation. That was not anybody I recognized. So I really couldn't watch it." (However, the show did offer advantages for everyone in Susskind's circle. When Kerew had trouble finding a rabbi who would perform a marriage ceremony for her and her non-Jewish husband-to-be, Jean Kennedy came up with the name of a rabbi who had appeared on a show about intermarriage.)

As the topics and guests became more provocative and outlandish along with the times, Susskind became concerned about his reputation. He did not want the sideshow aspect of his program to overshadow his image as a serious producer and businessman who hobnobbed with politicians and corporate executives. A serious segment with Gore Vidal or a senator could balance out the madness. But Susskind pressured his staff to give his show a veneer of respectability at all times. "The sleazier the show, the more legitimate the guests had to look," said Larry Strichman, who worked on the program in the mid-1970s. "So you were in this impossible position of finding male strippers who looked like accountants."

Strichman remembered when he and Jean Kennedy took a trip to Plato's Retreat, the notorious sex club in the Ansonia Hotel in Manhattan, in search of people who would agree to appear with Susskind to talk about their adventures. When they walked in the club, the first thing that struck Strichman was a small swimming pool, with water so cloudy you couldn't see the bottom. "It looked kind of like a sheep dip to me," he said. "Except in this case you'd catch something instead of getting rid of it." There were rooms for dancing and canoodling but only one place to have sex. It was called the Mat Room. The floor was completely covered with the sort of exercise mats you'd find in a school gymnasium.

Guided by Plato's owner, Larry Levinson, Strichman and Kennedy wandered into the low-lit room in search of prospective guests. "Well, how about these?" Levinson said as he pointed to a writhing couple on the floor. Kennedy looked down and said, "No, I don't think so." Smartly dressed in a tailored suit, the proper looking middle-aged woman was focused and businesslike as she stepped over sweaty half-clothed bodies in search of two that she could picture looking respectable enough to sit next to David Susskind on TV.

"She was absolutely professional," Strichman recalled. "Clearly the only thing on her mind was the necessity of who would make good guests. I was just stunned. It reminds me of one of those shows like *CSI*, where someone has a body on the table and all that's on their mind is getting the job done."

"Oh God, that was so seedy," Kennedy said when she recounted the trip. "It was so awful. It was probably the most unsanitary place in the world. The lights were low, and I thought if they ever turned the lights on you'd want to scream. We went to some real dumps and dives, let me tell you."

Kennedy found a couple from New Jersey and had them up to the office for an interview before the taping. "She asked them how many times they had been to Plato's Retreat," Strichman recalled. "They said sixty-nine times. When they were asked how many kids they had, there was a disagreement. They didn't know how many kids they had, but that sixty-nine was out of their mouths in a flash."

The stature Susskind had built up over the years actually made it easy to convince uninhibited guests to come on, according to Dan Berkowitz, whose first day working on the show required him to find men who used prostitutes. "You would put in a call to whorehouses and they'd go, 'Oh, *The David Susskind Show*,' and half of them would still hang up, but the other half would go, 'Well, you know, let me ask a few of the guys,'" he recalled. "Because it was the kind of thing that everyone knew what it was. And it did have that feeling of, you know, this is a prestige show where you do get famous writers and actors and so on, but you also get the common man because he gives a side to that as well."

It was the common man or woman who did uncommon things that occasionally turned *The David Susskind Show* into great theater. In 1973, Susskind devoted half of his show to a man who identified himself only as Joey. He claimed to be a contract killer. He was the author of a book that chronicled his life and times, including thirty-eight murders he said he was hired to commit. Before the taping, he disguised his identity with a black ski mask. The control room had his voice patched through a phone line so that it could be electronically altered.

In grave tones, Susskind questioned Joey about the murders he took credit for. Joey gladly obliged, even recounting the joy he felt in the killings he committed out of revenge.

"Killing has never made you sick?" Susskind asked.

"No," Joey replied.

"Has it ever made you question your sanity? Do you think you're sane?"

"Yes . . . I had a psychiatrist study me during a murder trial and he told me I was the coldest person he ever met."

"Do you like that?

"In my business, I like it. It makes me different than other people. I am different than other people. Just like you're different than other people, and you like it."

The producers and crew wondered if Joey was what he claimed to be. "I know that there was a real sense that there was something underhanded about this. Something that may not be all aboveboard, something that we don't trust," recalled Don Roy King, who directed the show. "The more he talked and the more he dealt in detail, I remember thinking, 'Man, I'm glad I'm in the control room and not out on the floor.'" Still, the notion of a hit man promoting his profession on TV, even for a book, seemed dubious. Once the show aired, its authenticity was no longer an issue. Anyone who saw the dramatic exchange was talking about it the next day.

In any case, Joey certainly knew how to stay in character. Jinny Schreckinger was assigned to escort him out of the WNEW studio after the taping. They stepped into an elevator together and as it descended, Joey reached under his jacket and pulled out a handgun. He had it drawn toward the door until they reached the lobby level. Along with seeing Joey out, Schreckinger was charged with the task of getting the ski mask back from him so it could be returned to the store where it was purchased for a refund. When they reached the exit, she asked him for it. Joey just looked at her and then walked out onto East Sixty-seventh Street.

As the decade moved on, Susskind became more of a talk-show icon than a truly vital media figure who influenced the national conversation. Still, he enjoyed that role, satirizing his show on *Mary Hartman, Mary Hartman* (where the housewife played by Louise Lasser had a nervous breakdown on *The David Susskind Show*). He played himself in the movies *Network* and *Simon*. Bill Murray impersonated Susskind on *Saturday Night Live*. Rick Moranis parodied him on Canada's *SCTV*. He stayed on public TV stations by having wealthy friends and acquaintances make contributions with the contingency that they air the program. He had Jean Kennedy write the solicitation letters. *The David Susskind Show* was the toy he refused to put away.

22

The financial stability provided to Talent Associates by its new owner, Norton Simon Inc., got David Susskind back into the movie business again in the late 1960s. More than five years had passed since his last film, *All the Way Home*, a well-crafted, sensitive rendering of James Agee's *A Death in the Family*. The 1963 film, which starred Robert Preston and Jean Simmons, had a modest budget of $600,000. Susskind completed it at double that amount, $1.2 million. The film failed at the box office, maybe because it was released only a few weeks before the assassination of President Kennedy. Susskind believed the film was pulled early from theaters because it was too bleak for moviegoers traumatized by the president's death. The moviegoing public was likely not in the mood for Agee's anguished tale about the sudden loss of a loved one.

As part of NSI, Susskind offered Talent Associates' services as an independent producer and did not put the company at any financial risk. Talent Associates put projects together and then took them to studios, which would put up funding. In return it received a production fee and a minimum of one-third of a film's profits.

Stylistically, Susskind's previous films had been dialogue-driven adaptations of television and stage plays. In television, no one was better than Susskind at getting TV networks to take established literary classics that had big-name stars attached. He sold Tennessee Williams' *The Glass Menagerie* with Shirley Booth to CBS in 1967 and then later to ABC with Katharine Hepburn in 1973. But to get back in the movie business, he needed a younger executive to help him keep up with the new filmmaking style of the era, which reflected a more personal vision of the director and welcomed experimentation. In 1969, he found one in Anthony Loeb, who joined Talent Associates from the United States Information Agency, where he made documentary films for President Lyndon Johnson. Loeb felt compelled to write to Susskind about a job after watching his talk show. "The show gave me the sense of his elegance, and that he really stood for something," he said. "The quality, the quiet kind of dignity—to me, I thought it was beautiful. I didn't watch that much of it, but I liked the person I saw on it. " A native of Chicago, Loeb saw Susskind as "a quintessential New York guy" and began a correspondence with him. "I wanted to make some features, the dream that many of us have," he said. "He asked to see my work, and thereafter there was a seduction, so to speak, over six months. He would give me material to read. I loved him because he took a chance with me and was generous."

Loeb eventually moved up to New York from Washington and was assigned the task of helping Susskind gauge the transitory taste of the movie audience at the time. "I remember going to a screening at Columbia with him, and we looked at *Easy Rider*," he recalled. "And I knew that this thing was really powerful. But David was from another generation and another ethic. He looked at *Easy Rider* and he didn't relate to it. But the point that he made to me was that I was to search out, to be his eyes and ears. I was fairly cocky and I was young. And he was looking to me as an entrée to a new kind of filmmaking that began to be going on at that time."

Susskind's taste for classics and traditional storytelling prevented him from mustering much passion for some of the original material that came his way during the period. He passed on such properties as *Shaft* and *Dirty Harry,* both of which went on to become genre-defining films of their time. Susskind was hardly the exception among the executives from his generation who had trouble grasping the new film styles and culture. But Loeb believed Susskind had gotten in the habit of reacting to the marketplace rather than attempting to break new ground as he once did. "He really didn't have a rock bottom point of view," said Loeb. "It was more the approximation through other movies of what might or might not sell. And that ultimately wasn't a very consistent compass for him."

Loeb believed he could develop a noisemaking contemporary film out of *Shoot It,* a 1967 novel by Paul Tyner about an alienated white police officer who pointlessly kills a black purse-snatcher in cold blood. Susskind had the rights to the book, but the project was languishing after Roman Polanski, Sidney Lumet, and other directors and producers passed on the initial script written by the author. Loeb reworked the screenplay with writer Ed Adler so that the cop was sympathetic up to the moment when he pulls the trigger. He thought they could turn it into a story that spoke honestly about racial tension in the nation's urban centers.

Loeb's enthusiasm grew when Susskind sent him to a production of Tennessee Williams' *Camino Real* at the Vivian Beaumont Theatre to see the actor he had lined up for the lead role. It was Al Pacino, before he had broken through as a movie star in *The Godfather*. "He was extraordinary," Loeb said. "We had him for the movie." The script went to George C. Scott, who was working in London at the time and was interested in directing *Shoot It*. Having Scott attached would have likely made the low-budget project salable to a studio. "You're going to London," Susskind told Loeb. "I want you to continue to work on the script with Scott."

The package appeared to be ready to go, when Susskind received a call from Scott. "This is a great script," he said. "Only the cop can't kill a black man, he has to kill a white man." Scott's choice to remove the racial element in the story was baffling to Loeb, who was devastated. He knew the project would no longer have the social impact needed to break through. "The whole point was we've got something really ahead of its time here, you know?" he recalled. "The country is in turmoil and we've got a story here. I said, 'David, this will not work.' And he agreed. And that was the end of the project. I think he had something else going on. I mean, he was in perpetual motion and always onto the next deal."

Susskind did have success on the first movie he produced during the new era. Martin Baum, a longtime agent who became the head of ABC Pictures, the theatrical movie operation started by the TV network, enlisted him to make *Lovers and Other Strangers*. Based on a short-running Broadway show by the husband-and-wife team of Joe Bologna and Renee Taylor, *Lovers* focused on the state of matrimony and courtship in America at a time when traditional values were being challenged by the generation that was growing up with rock music, coed dormitories, and the birth control pill. The wedding day of a young couple already living together, played by Michael Brandon and Bonnie Bedelia, became the nexus of several relationships in a variety of stages.

The interwoven vignettes effectively conveyed how baby boomers were going to demand more out of life than what their parents often settled for. It had a funny script (doctored by David Z. Goodman), and Susskind and his casting director, Alan Shayne, put together a solid group of New York actors, including Bea Arthur, Richard Castellano, and Diane Keaton (in her first film role).

Larry Gelbart was Susskind's original choice to direct *Lovers*. Gelbart, who was living in London at the time, believed it was a done deal after getting the script and having several discussions with Susskind. "David said, 'How'd you like to direct a film?' And he was the first person who asked me to do such as thing," he said. "I was incredibly complimented and willing to give it a go. I talked to him about my ideas. I loved the script. I loved Joe and Renee."

Gelbart was then shocked during a dinner at the Savoy Hotel on July 20, 1969—the day *Apollo 11* astronauts walked on the moon—when Susskind offhandedly mentioned that Cy Howard, another comedy writer far less gifted than Gelbart, was directing the movie. "He just pulled the rug out from under me and said that and didn't say boo about the fact," Gelbart said. "I didn't either, which was my fault, of course. I should have said, 'You fucking cocksucker.'" Gelbart was so upset he could not get the dinner off his mind hours later at home while watching the historic broadcast of the moon landing. "I remember Neil Armstrong climbing down and I'm thinking, 'Fucking David Susskind,' and the other part of me saying, 'Why are you worried about David Susskind at a moment like this?'" he recalled. "But I couldn't help myself."

Lovers would likely have been a better experience for Susskind if Gelbart (who went on to develop the hit TV series *M*A*S*H*) had been at the helm. Howard, a close friend of Baum's, who got him the job, had never directed before. He had trouble setting up camera shots. During the filming in New York, Susskind called Leonard Stern in Los Angeles and had him give instructions to Howard over the phone. Susskind believed Howard's inexperience was driving up the cost of the $2 million film. He tried to get Howard replaced in the middle of the production. "At one point, David called me up, and he said, 'Do you want to take over this movie?'" said Loeb, who had no experience as a feature director. "I mean, there was that much conflict." But Baum would not consider firing Howard. "He could not be dislodged and his loyalties were not to David," said Loeb. The situation sent Susskind into a rage. "Why you wish to delude yourself about his extraordinary lack of talent is your affair except as it threatens to damage the result of the movie," Susskind wrote about Howard in a memo to Baum. "He is good-natured, well-intentioned, but a hapless, hopeless incompetent." Aware of his protected status, Howard tweaked Susskind when the producer showed up on the set to complain. "You know what your problem is, David?" Howard said. "You wanted to be tall and they turned you down."

Susskind was also incensed over how Baum allowed one of the film's stars, Gig Young, to sit in on discussions about the final edit. Some of Young's scenes and lines had been cut from the film because he had been drunk or hungover during the production. "There were many days during the shooting process when (putting it mildly) Gig was not up to his best form—days when he photographed poorly and performed consistent with his appearance," Susskind told Baum. But Young was also a former client and close pal of Baum from his days as an agent. Young used his influence to restore some of the dialogue and close-ups that had been cut.

Despite Susskind's concerns, he believed *Lovers* had the potential to be a hit. He was right. The film earned $6 million at the box office in 1970, making it one of the twenty top-grossing films of that year. Despite Howard's ineptitude, the film had a number of honest and affecting performances, especially from Castellano, who was nominated for an Academy Award for Best Supporting Actor and went on to greater acclaim in *The Godfather*. The film's "For All We Know," written by Fred Karlin, James Griffin, and Robb Royer (the latter two from the soft-rock group Bread), was honored for Best Original Song.

Susskind was far less successful with his next film, *The Pursuit of Happiness,* which was a more blatant play for the youth market made for Columbia Pictures. Directed by Robert Mulligan, *Pursuit* starred Michael Sarrazin as an alienated college student from a wealthy WASP family who drops out of society after he hits and kills a female pedestrian with his sports car. There was joint rolling, nude frolicking in a lake with Barbara Hershey, and an apartment decorated with Milton Glaser's Bob Dylan poster and antiwar messages. But with lines like "There's a nervous breakdown going on out there and I don't want to be a part of it" and "Relax, I'm under thirty, you can trust me," the film already felt dated by the time of its release in February 1971.

Around the same time, production was under way on another film that ultimately broke Susskind's already strained relationship with his partner Dan Melnick. In the summer of 1969, ABC Pictures purchased the rights to a book called *The Siege of Trencher's Farm* by a Scottish novelist named Gordon M. Williams. Baum wanted Susskind to produce it as well. The plot revolved around an American professor on sabbatical who seeks a tranquil escape from the violence and turmoil that had engulfed 1960s America. He relocates his wife and daughter to a farmhouse in a village in the English countryside. A series of events leads to his having to protect himself and his family from an attack by several brutish locals in a savage showdown inside his home. The plot of the novel was wafer-thin, but the tale of a coward who finally stands up to the bullies was a proven formula. The story also provided an entry point to make a statement about how no civilized man was safe from the violence that was saturating society at the time. Susskind and Loeb developed two scripts based on the story, neither of which they believed could work. "I tried to reset it in Appalachia to give it a more American reality," Loeb said. "They didn't go for it." Susskind gave up on the property and handed it over to Melnick. "I made the deal with David and then for some reason he gave it to Melnick to produce," said Baum. "I was surprised when David suggested Danny produce it. He didn't want to do it."

Melnick, who had recommended bringing in David Z. Goodman to work on *Lovers and Other Strangers,* had the writer take a crack at a script based on *Siege.* They brought it to Sam Peckinpah. The troubled director's career had rebounded after Melnick used him in the TV production of *Noon Wine.* By the time Peckinpah received *Siege,* he was bankable again, thanks to the success of his ultraviolent action-adventure feature *The Wild Bunch.* On the surface, the mayhem level in that film made Peckinpah the right choice for *Siege.* But it was his complete reworking of the story that turned the final result, called *Straw Dogs,* into a cinematic jolt to the system.

Shot on location outside of Cornwall, the film starred Dustin Hoffman as the milquetoast professor named David Sumner. Susan George was cast as his young, flirtatious, and often braless English wife. The roughneck locals that Sumner has his standoff with are workmen who had been making repairs to the farmhouse, one of whom had had a previous relationship with the professor's wife. The film became notorious for its rape scene in which George's character, after initially resisting, enjoys the assault by her ex-beau, until one of his crew walks in on them and takes his turn. "Only one rape was mine," Goodman noted. "The second was Sam's."

When *Straw Dogs* was released at the end of 1971, it generated far more controversy than what seemed possible from Williams' novel. It challenged attitudes about virility, manhood, and primal instincts in an age when many Americans wanted to give peace a chance. While depicting the growing anxiety over violence in the culture, the film elicited cheers from the audience when the professor and his wife blow the hooligans away with shotguns during the spectacularly brutal farmhouse siege. Reactions from critics were visceral and polarized. *Newsweek*'s critic Paul D. Zimmerman called the rape sequence "a masterful piece of erotic cinema." Judith Crist's harsh review in *New York* magazine ran with an illustration of a dog standing over a pile of excrement in the form of celluloid. "For the first time in my life, I felt concern for the future of cinema," Dilys Powell wrote in London's *Sunday Times.* What mattered to Melnick was that the world was talking about *Straw Dogs,* "A Dan Melnick Production." After being in the shadow of his larger-than-life partner David Susskind, Melnick showed that he too could provoke the public and the press and gain notoriety. The large antique bear trap that Hoffman is seen carrying in the opening scene of *Straw Dogs* (and later snaps on the neck of one of the intruders) was proudly displayed in Melnick's office at Talent Associates. Unlike most projects that came out of the company, Susskind was not effusive about the movie. "He never spoke well of it," said Andrew Susskind. "I don't know whether he didn't think it was a good film or whether he was jealous."

The success of *Straw Dogs* suggested that Melnick had deciphered the code to the new movie making, and he was rewarded with a ticket to Hollywood. Old friend James Aubrey had been brought into MGM to turn around the financially strapped studio and offered Melnick a job as head of production. It gave Melnick an exit strategy from Talent Associates, which no matter what he did would always be a reflection of Susskind. "I think that basically Dan was overwhelmed by a rock-solid situation, a family that he wasn't part of," said Loeb. "He was a visitor at the table, so to speak."

There was a lot of shouting between Susskind and Melnick as they convened behind closed doors in the days before Dan's departure in early 1972. But the executives at Norton Simon agreed to release Melnick from his contract. What followed for Melnick was a long tenure as a highly successful creative studio executive at MGM and Columbia, where he oversaw the development of such memorable films as *Network, Kramer vs. Kramer,* and *The China Syndrome.* As an innovative film producer his credits included *All That Jazz, Altered States,* and *Footloose.* By the end of his life in 2009, Melnick was using an Emmy Award trophy as a doorstop in his Hollywood duplex apartment that was filled with extraordinary art pieces he collected.

"It was a very lucky break for him that David wasn't interested in *Siege* and just handed the book over," said Loeb.

Shortly after Loeb left in 1971, Lawrence D. Cohen joined Talent Associates as a "reader." The low-level job required sifting through manuscripts and screenplays—"a slush pile," as it's called in industry parlance—and then providing a synopsis with an opinion on whether any of them were worth pursuing as a movie or TV project.

Cohen was an aspiring screenwriter who had graduated from the University of Wisconsin in 1969. He had been immersed in the new filmmaking culture, writing about it for *The Saturday Review* and the show business trade paper *The Hollywood Reporter.* He took the job at Talent Associates because he needed the money and was not looking to rise within the company. "I think the kind of kid I was in the 1960s, producing to me was anathema," he said. "I was a bearded, jeans-wearing, card-carrying hippie." He occupied a small windowless office at Talent Associates that was filled with scripts and books, just as Bob Rafelson had more than a dozen years earlier. Out of the pile, Cohen pulled a script called *Alice Doesn't Live Here Anymore.*

Robert Getchell, a college literature professor, had written *Alice* after seeing a succession of actresses go on *The Tonight Show with Johnny Carson* and complain about their status in Hollywood. "The 1970s were a big, male-dominated decade in movies," he said. "And so many women would come on the Carson show, cross their legs, and say, 'There are no parts for women.' I thought, 'Hmmm. There's an opening that I could take advantage of.' So, part of it was cold-blooded. I thought I'd write a movie about what I thought was a really great part for a woman and would have a chance of getting made." Getchell's screenplay told the story of an insolvent but self-sufficient widow who hits the road with her wisecracking twelve-year-old son to pursue her dream of becoming a lounge singer. Along the way she escapes from a violent relationship and settles in Tucson, finding a job as a waitress. She meets a rugged, handsome, and nice rancher. But she considers her desire to become a singer before making a long-term commitment to him.

Cohen was sold after reading the first five pages of the script. "I went, 'Let's do this,'" he recalled. "'This is an incredible piece.' So I wrote my glowing coverage that Getchell had an amazing, original voice, that it was a vehicle for an actress who would win the Oscar—the basic pronouncements of being twenty-two, ridiculously cocky, used to having my opinion written down, and not having any fear particularly."

Cohen brought the script to Susskind, who was circumspect at first. But Audrey Gellen Maas and other women working for him at the time responded strongly after reading it and urged him to take a chance on it. "It was radical because a woman leaves home," recalled Diana Kerew. "An abused woman says, 'I'm not taking this anymore,' packs her bags, and goes and makes a life for herself. And that was a shocking idea." Susskind had always said he hired women because he trusted their response to material, and *Alice* was the best example of that. "Audrey really pushed him into it," said Andrew Susskind. "She said to him, 'You don't get this. This is a woman's thing.' I think he listened to that. He listened to her passion. He also liked Getchell as a writer." David Susskind took an option on the script, which Getchell recalled as being around $2,000.

Susskind recognized Cohen's acumen and invited him to attend the weekly staff meetings to review the status of the company's current projects. During the summer of 1973, *Alice* came up and was discussed as a feature film or TV movie with names such as Shirley MacLaine, Jane Fonda, Dyan Cannon, Diana Ross, and Bette Midler cast as the lead. "I would go, 'Has anybody read this?'" said Cohen.

Both Cohen and Getchell said they suggested Ellen Burstyn, who had been in *The Last Picture Show*. "Ellen Bernstein, who's that?" Susskind said mockingly to Cohen. If *Alice* could be made into a feature, Susskind wanted Anne Bancroft, an established movie star he adored.

But executives at Warner Bros. were excited by what they saw of Burstyn's work in the dailies for *The Exorcist,* set for release later that year. They believed she was on her way to an Academy Award, or at least a nomination. The studio was looking for a movie she could star in. Burstyn had read *Alice* and was eager to do it. "They were keen to make whatever movie Ellen wanted to make next," said Cohen. "As long as it cost under $2 million. That was its caveat."

Susskind got a call from Burstyn's agent, who told him Warner Bros. wanted to make *Alice* with the actress. By that time, Susskind had paid Getchell $4,000 for a second option on the script that was soon going to run out.

"He came trotting down to my closet," Cohen recalled. "He said, 'I'm on the phone with an agent at William Morris named Tony Fantozzi. He represents that Ellen Bernstein woman. And she wants to do *Alice Doesn't Live Here Anymore.*' I said, 'Say yes.' In his inimitable way, he tried and made three calls over the weekend to see if we could set it up elsewhere without her, because he wasn't anxious to partner. Having failed to hustle it somewhere else, David agreed, and we progressed with Ellen."

Once Warner Bros. became involved, Susskind no longer had much clout. He went along with the studio's decision to give Burstyn approval of the director. She wanted to go with Martin Scorsese, who had just done *Mean Streets,* his dark independent film that had been purchased by Warner Bros. about small-time mobsters in Little Italy. After completing the *Alice* casting, which included Diane Ladd, Harvey Keitel, and Kris Kristofferson as the rancher, Susskind assigned Cohen to be the conduit between the filming in Tucson and the Talent Associates office back in New York. Cohen had quickly gone from reading a slush pile of scripts in a closet to being a production executive on a major studio feature.

With Susskind at a safe distance in New York, Cohen allowed Burstyn, a major advocate of the Actors Studio style, and Scorsese to experiment on the film. Actors were given the freedom to improvise during rehearsals. Cohen and Scorsese's girlfriend, Sandy Weintraub, an associate producer on the film, listened to tapes of the rehearsals and had some of the improvised lines integrated into the script. "Larry Cohen would call me every day and tell me what was needed," Getchell said. "I would write it and call him back and dictate it over." But after a few weeks, Getchell stopped participating in the process.

Burstyn was intent on infusing the film with her own response to the feminist movement. "It caught the wave of what was happening then," she said. "There was an awakening in women at the time and there was an awakening in me. I put in that line, 'it's my life, it's not some man's life I'm helping him out with.' That was my realization at the time. I had just gone through a marriage and I was learning from all the women like Gloria Steinem to come into my own wholeness."

David Susskind never had an issue with the sexual politics of *Alice,* which were, in retrospect, very mild. It was Warner Bros. that insisted Burstyn's and Kristofferson's characters remain together at the end of the movie in spite of Alice's yearnings for independence. Susskind's major concern was that less of the screenplay he had originally bought was turning up on the screen. "Why are you doing this?" he would ask Cohen after seeing new script pages coming in every few days. Several weeks into the filming, Audrey Gellen Maas and Susskind came out to visit the set in Tucson. The lore among Talent Associates employees was that Susskind had a physical altercation with Scorsese during the visit, but Burstyn said that was not the case. However, he was asked not to come back again.

Susskind certainly believed it was his prerogative to discuss an aspect of an actor's performance. Burstyn said Susskind ran afoul of Scorsese because he made a remark directly to her. "He gave me some direction or he made a comment on what he saw in the dailies," she said. "I told Marty what he said. He stepped on Marty's toes as a director and so Marty told him not to come around. There's a protocol on the set that only directors talk to actors about performance. Producers don't, and he stepped over that line." In this new era of filmmaking in which the director's personal vision ruled, Susskind's input was especially unwelcome.

Susskind later met with Cohen on what may have been the same trip. At a restaurant in Tucson, Cohen said he sat for more than two hours listening to Susskind express his unhappiness over the footage he had seen. "Look. You just don't like her acting style." Cohen told him. "You don't like Actors Studio, particularly. And there are a lot of people, for example, who don't like Kim Stanley"—referring to one of the Studio's most famous early practitioners.

Cohen recalled that Susskind pounded the table and said, "Kim Stanley! I fucking hate Kim Stanley!"

"He just didn't get it and I think it made him mad," Cohen said. "It just pissed him off. I think David was the last vestige of that particular period of television-as-movie sensibility. And we were just full-out lurching into some other thing that happened to be coinciding in time with another movement altogether. And that was just its serendipity. The piece was truthful and charming, irrespective of the women's issues that it also was about. He honestly believed it was an unreleasable picture. He just looked at it, and everything about it that made it 'now' he hated. The taste was different. The acting styles drove him insane."

Cohen also angered Susskind by showing the film to Warner Bros. chief

John Calley first. Susskind wanted Cohen fired from the movie. But Calley, who had been aligned with Burstyn and Scorsese throughout the production, never cared for Susskind's impolitic style, and refused.

If Susskind was as unhappy with *Alice* as Cohen said he was, he did not reveal the full extent of those feelings back in New York. Diana Kerew's impression was that Susskind remained supportive of the movie. "He recognized the talent," she said. "He recognized something good was coming out of it all. So it wasn't like, 'Oh, God, I hate every frame of this film.' It wasn't like that at all. In spite of the personal clash on the set between Marty and David, I don't remember that as a terribly, horrifically, difficult time. I really don't. Because it was a good movie, and we all knew it was a good movie. And we knew it was a good script. It was way ahead of its time. It got made by accident." Cohen acknowledged that the main source of Susskind's unhappiness was "resentment that a movie was getting made, but it was so not his movie. And the control, because of Ellen's in with Calley and the way it was set up, was very different than how he would have chosen it."

Released at the end of 1974, *Alice* opened to mostly positive reviews and further advanced Scorsese's stature as an auteur. Even with the movie's watered-down politics, Burstyn's character became a symbol for the feminist movement. Burstyn did not get an Academy Award for *The Exorcist,* but she did win the Best Actress trophy for *Alice.* She has talked about *Alice* as being her film and maintained that Susskind had little to do with it. But Getchell believed that Susskind's role as a producer who decided to take a chance and put his money on a project with no guarantee that it would reach fruition should not be discounted.

"Every picture, in order to get made, has to have a first step, a first plank to be put down to make the journey," Getchell said. "And David Susskind reached his hand in his billfold—twice. So I remember him fondly because of that." *Alice* was not a smash at the box office, but Susskind reaped the financial benefits from the highly successful situation comedy based on the movie's characters that ran for eight seasons on CBS (he received an executive producer credit early on, but had no direct involvement in the show).

Nevertheless, Cohen was fired from Talent Associates. After his departure, he wrote the screenplay for the seminal 1976 horror film *Carrie,* based on a short story from another English teacher, this one by the name of Stephen King. It was another property that Cohen had found in his Talent Associates slush pile.

While Susskind may have had trouble embracing the new style of movie-making, he still had an innate feel for stories set in New York City. Around the same time *Alice* was being produced, Heywood Gould, one of the writers who worked on *N.Y.P.D.*, sent Susskind a bold script about cops in a South Bronx precinct ravaged by drugs and poverty. He loved it and told Gould, "I'm going to make this movie."

DAVID SUSSKIND
14 Claflin Road

C.   Modern Language
N.   Dave
I.   Finding a college
A.   College, fortune, fame
S.D. None, I never suppress any
"Sagamore" '35, '36, '37, '38; News Editor '36, '37

Susskind as a graduating senior in the 1938 Brookline High School yearbook. (Courtesy Brookline Public Library)

ABOVE LEFT: David Susskind, Anita (Zang) Grossberg, and Al Levy at Talent Associates, circa 1954. (*TV Guide Magazine*).

ABOVE RIGHT: Sidney Poitier and Hilda Simms in the 1955 *Philco Television Playhouse* presentation of "A Man Is Ten Feet Tall." (Photofest)

Rosemary Harris and Richard Burton in "Wuthering Heights," adapted for *The DuPont Show of the Month* in 1958. (Photofest)

With Richard Nixon on *Open End* in May 1960. (Photofest)

With Premier Nikita S. Khrushchev on *Open End* in October 1960. (UN Photo/Martin Bolotsky)

Above Left: Susskind and Sidney Poitier during production of *Raisin in the Sun*, 1960. (Photofest)

Above Right: Susskind's first wife, Phyllis, in 1960. (*New York Post/Splash News*)

With Harry S. Truman at a 1961 press conference at the Waldorf-Astoria in New York where plans to turn the former president into a TV star were unveiled. (*New York Post*)

Susskind is delivering his testimony to the FCC in June 1961. (*New York Post/Splash News*)

Above Left: With Laurence Olivier during the filming of *The Power and the Glory*, 1961. (Photo by Shel Secunda courtesy of Renée Valente)

Above Right: Susskind, Maureen (Hesselroth) Berger, Renée Valente, and Audrey Gellen Maas on the Brooklyn set of *The Power and the Glory* in 1961. (Photo by Shel Secunda courtesy of Reneé Valente).

With Roald Dahl while filming an opening for *Way Out*, 1961. (CBS)

CLOCKWISE: Richard Gehman, Lenore Lemmon, Joe E. Brown, Susskind, Jackie Gleason, Marya Mannes, Ernie Kovacs, and Toots Shor pondering the social implications of Frank Sinatra's Rat Pack on *Open End* in October 1961. (*New York Post/Splash News*)

ABOVE LEFT: Joyce Davidson, circa 1962. (Photofest)

ABOVE RIGHT: Susskind and Rod Serling on location for *Requiem for a Heavyweight*. (Photofest).

Susskind, Audrey Gellen Maas, and Bob Israel at the recording session for the *East Side/West Side* soundtrack in late 1962. (Photo by Shel Secunda courtesy of Bob Israel)

ABOVE LEFT: At the recording session for *East Side/West Side* soundtrack. (Photo by Shel Secunda courtesy of Bob Israel).

ABOVE RIGHT: Cicely Tyson, George C. Scott, and Richard Dysart in *East Side/West Side*. (CBS)

ABOVE LEFT: With Dr. Martin Luther King on *Open End*, June 1963. (Wisconsin Center for Film and Theater Research)

ABOVE RIGHT: Diana Sands and James Earl Jones in the *East Side/West Side* episode "Who Do You Kill?" (CBS)

Tony Musante, Kathy Dunn, and James Scheller in *The DuPont Show of the Week* episode "Ride with Terror." (Photofest)

Don Francks and friends on the Brooklyn Bridge at a press event for the Broadway musical *Kelly*, 1964. (Photo © Henry Grossman)

Susskind and Dan Melnick offer their support to Anita Gillette on the Broadway opening (and closing) night of *Kelly* at the Broadhurst Theatre, February 1965. (Photo © Henry Grossman)

Susskind makes friends with a chorine backstage at *Kelly*. (Photo © Henry Grossman)

Get Smart stars Don Adams and Barbara Feldon, 1965. (Courtesy *TV Guide Magazine*)

With Craig Stevens and guest stars Liza Minnelli and Eduardo Ciannelli on *Mr. Broadway*. (CBS)

Bill Malone prepares to launch three "runners" on *Supermarket Sweep*, circa 1965. (Photofest)

ABOVE LEFT: With Arthur Miller at a screening of *Death of a Salesman*, 1966. (CBS)

ABOVE RIGHT: Mildred Dunnock and Lee J. Cobb in *Death of a Salesman*. (CBS)

Dan Melnick (right) and his then father-in-law, Richard Rodgers (left), circa 1968. (Photo by Shel Secunda courtesy of Bob Israel)

ABOVE LEFT: Susskind and Joyce Davidson on their wedding day in Arlington, Virginia, 1966. (Photofest)

ABOVE RIGHT: Talent Associates partner Leonard Stern with Barbara Feldon and Gloria Stern. (Courtesy of Leonard Stern)

Richard Benjamin, Paula Prentiss, and Jack Cassidy of *He & She*. (Courtesy of *TV Guide Magazine*).

Robert Hooks, Jack Warden, Mayor John V. Lindsay, and Frank Converse on the set of *N.Y.P.D.*, 1967. (Photofest)

With Lee Radziwill during the making of *Laura*, 1967. (Everett Collection)

With director Cy Howard on the set of *Lovers and Other Strangers*, 1970. (Photofest)

With producer Gloria Rabinowitz on the set of *The David Susskind Show*, circa 1970. (Courtesy of Gloria Rabinowitz)

With Germaine Greer and John Simon on *The David Susskind Show*, 1971. (Wisconsin Center for Film and Theater Research)

CLOCKWISE FROM UPPER LEFT: director Daniel Petrie, producer Harry Sherman, Edward Herrmann, and Jane Alexander, in *Eleanor and Franklin*, 1976. (Photofest)

With Paul Newman on location for *Fort Apache, The Bronx*. (Wisconsin Center for Film and Theater Research)

David and Joyce Susskind attending a party for Yves Montand at Luchow's, September 1982. (Photo © Ron Galella)

With Carmen Dell'Orefice, circa 1987. (Photo © Eric Weiss)

23

After the departure of Dan Melnick in early 1972, series television became less of a priority at Talent Associates even though it was the surest way to bring in steady income. Leonard Stern continued to run the company's West Coast operation. Joining him in the office was a young aspiring actress from Chicago named Sherry Lansing, who decided to change her career course and try her hand at developing TV movies (ultimately a successful transition: by 1980 she was the first female studio president, at 20th Century–Fox). Stern never came up with another hit comedy to follow *Get Smart*, but he did sell the breezy husband-and-wife detective series called *McMillan & Wife*. When Stern first pitched the idea to NBC there was little interest. Once he got Rock Hudson, a longtime friend, to agree to star in the pilot episode, the network made a deal without seeing a script. The show ran for six years as part of NBC's *Sunday Night Mystery Movie.* But Susskind showed little interest in the West Coast activities, "probably because they were too commercial," Stern said. There was no acrimony when Stern left Talent Associates in 1974 to continue producing shows on his own.

As Talent Associates continued its steady output of long-form television projects, Susskind was no longer the angry showman railing against mediocrity in the TV industry. There was no reason to be. Network television was flush with cash throughout the decade and there was less fear about taking risk. ABC had successfully developed *Movie of the Week,* producing twenty-five original movies for television each year. They regularly tackled social issues of the day, such as race, homosexuality, drug abuse, the Vietnam War, and feminism, and often delivered big ratings. Their success encouraged bigger and more lavish productions in which stories were told over several nights as "miniseries" or even high-mindedly dubbed "novels for television." The typically prickly editorialists in *TV Guide* were thrilled with the trend. "These forms should provide a great deal more variety in programming and less straining for inane plots to keep characters busy week after week," they wrote in 1973.

"They were like the movies and they were really high-quality," said Diana Kerew. "Wonderful actors were willing to be in them and you could deal with social issues, you could deal with political issues. And then that became fashionable for a while. 'Let's have programming that's so titanic, that are real events that the nation will stop for.' It was what we now call 'appointment TV.' Everyone will have to be there. Remember, no TiVo, no VCRs, none of that existed. So you had to be there. And those big shows didn't tend to get rerun, or if they did they got chopped up into pieces and rerun three years later." The era brought the dramatizations of the Holocaust and slavery to massive audiences in prime time. The final night of Alex Haley's *Roots* was watched by more than 50 percent of the nation's TV households. Susskind acknowledged that the television industry had matured to a level of aspiration that no longer required his chiding. Part of it was pragmatism as well. "I've grown up," he would say. But in retrospect, Susskind's stubborn willingness to take chances and push the networks into airing bolder fare had helped pave a way for such shows.

THE KANSAS CITY greeting card company Hallmark, which had been sponsoring classy TV fare since the early years of the medium, turned to Susskind as a regular supplier during the 1970s. He provided a number of elegant productions, including Arthur Miller's *The Price,* with George C. Scott and Colleen Dewhurst, and Royce Ryton's *Crown Matrimonial,* starring Greer Garson, a compelling play about King Edward VIII's abdication. Both were taped in London. Susskind became a major supplier of television films as well.

"We did big, political sagas," said Kerew. "We did important moments in American history. We did family dramas that had something to say. And almost all of our movies aired as specials. Unless it had a pedigree, we didn't do it." The networks' specials departments, as they were called, remained based in New York, and were generally more open to prestigious projects that could be supported by a single advertiser. Susskind could pitch a special to all three networks without leaving the Avenue of the Americas.

IBM became a supporter of Susskind's programs when in 1973 it sponsored *The Glass Menagerie,* with Katharine Hepburn, the legendary actress's first television role. Susskind had hotly pursued Hepburn for the role of Amanda Wingfield over a number of years, even though she didn't think she was right to play the vulnerable, alcoholic Southerner of Tennessee Williams' play. She finally relented when Susskind agreed to shoot in London with the director of her choice, Anthony Harvey. After twenty-five years of deal-making and producing, Susskind still thrived on such acts of mountain-moving showmanship. But by this time, colleagues occasionally began to see moments in which Susskind's excitability went beyond the boundless energy and willfulness he was known for. Mike Dann was advising IBM on its television shows at the time. After visiting *The Glass Menagerie*'s set and watching some of the filming, Dann and his wife joined Susskind at the White Elephant restaurant in London. Dann initially had doubts about Hepburn in the role, but was pleased with what he had seen. "I said, 'I just can't believe she can do this role,'" he recalled. "I made the mistake of using the present tense. And David grabbed me and said, 'How the hell could you ever question my judgment?' And he went into a tirade, screaming. Here I had brought IBM in to sponsor it. I didn't question anything about the budget. It was a terrible scene. My wife had to get hold of our server. She hated David from then on, and if he ever came around she wouldn't have anything to do with him. I was used to it, but at that given moment I wasn't. I was damned scared."

British TV producer Verity Lambert had a similarly harrowing experience with Susskind in London a couple of years later when the two worked together on a production of *The Norman Conquests.* While dining at Harry's Bar, Susskind "just lost his temper in a major way, for no reason," Lambert said. "I can't remember why he was so angry. It might have been about the restaurant. But he was horribly angry and very, very unpleasant. And the next day we were at the White Elephant and he apologized to me profusely. In a way he didn't need to apologize—I didn't think it was normal behavior. I thought this man is behaving in a very peculiar and irrational fashion."

THE CONFRONTATION did not keep Dann or IBM from doing more business with Susskind, as the company sponsored what became the producer's signature programs of the decade. Susskind made two TV films based on the intimate biography of Franklin and Eleanor Roosevelt by Eleanor's close lifelong friend, journalist Joseph Lash. The 765-page opus, called *Eleanor and Franklin: The Story of Their Relationship, Based on Eleanor Roosevelt's Private Papers,* topped the nonfiction best-seller list after its publication in 1971. The book was considered extraordinary at the time for its candid insights into President Roosevelt's complex relationship with his wife. It examined her vital role in his rise to political success and his policy decisions. Susskind was surrounded by strong women in his professional and personal life, so it was easy to understand how he connected with the story, which also focused on the powerful force that was the president's mother, Sara Delano Roosevelt.

Susskind had the project set up at CBS, but the network backed away after company chairman William Paley objected. As a capitalist who had an emerging business in the 1930s, Paley had a lingering disdain for Roosevelt and his New Deal policies. According to Diana Kerew, "We developed *Eleanor and Franklin* at CBS, and then Mr. Paley said, 'I'm not putting a film about that man on my network.'" ABC picked it up once it became available.

Susskind wanted actress Jane Alexander to play the role of Eleanor Roosevelt. ABC agreed, as she had already won a Tony Award and received her first of four Academy Award nominations for her performances in *The Great White Hope.* It was far tougher to sell the network on Ed Herrmann, then a lesser-known stage actor, for the role of Franklin. The six-foot-five Herrmann had a patrician air and was a dead ringer for the thirty-second president of the United States. But none of his supporting film roles had elevated him to the kind of marquee name that was considered necessary to bring in viewers to a major television event. When Susskind brought Herrmann's name up to Ed Vane, the ABC executive expressed his doubts. "David, I don't know. This is a three-hour program, prime time, and the lead character is a no-name," Vane said. "I'm very worried about that. I just don't know that he can handle it."

After persistently pleading for Herrmann, Susskind came up with a proposal. "Tell you what," he said. "I'd like you to meet Ed." Vane set a date for Susskind to bring the actor to ABC headquarters in New York. Shortly before their scheduled arrival time, Susskind called Vane and asked him to leave his office for five minutes and then come back. "I said, 'Wow, that's an unusual request,'" Vane recounted. "But I did it. I went upstairs and chatted with my friend, an ABC executive named Jim Duffy, for a while. I came back down and walked into my own office and there was David and Ed Herrmann. But Ed Herrmann was sitting in a chair with that FDR cigarette holder with the cigarette in it. He had it in his mouth in that jaunty manner. He looked exactly like him. I said, 'Okay, David, you win.' It was beautiful staging on his part."

Herrmann did not remember coming in with a cigarette holder. "Maybe David gave it to me," he said. But the actor did recall Susskind's instruction that his wardrobe should bring out the FDR in him. He went with the yachtsman look. "I came in with a white button-down and a boatneck sweater that I had worn in college, and one of those little tennis hats that has a little floppy cotton brim that goes all the way around," Herrmann said. "And apparently it was exactly what the doctor ordered. I thought it was a little odd that David should ask. But I was not daunted. He was very sweet. So we walked in, and they saw it immediately."

Talent Associates did not get a usable script out of the first writer suggested by ABC, leading Susskind to turn to veteran Emmy Award–winning playwright James Costigan. He was best known for the play *Little Moon of Alban,* which debuted as a TV play before its Broadway run in 1962. The delay in getting the script done was hard on Herrmann, who depended on doing commercials to pay the bills between his stage and film roles. "I didn't want to do any commercials while this was pending," Herrmann said. "I didn't want to be the toilet bowl man if I had a chance to be Franklin Roosevelt."

As Costigan toiled, the network began to get antsy about the cost of the project, which kept going up. "We took a location scouting trip," Susskind recounted. "We realized that we had to go to Hyde Park and we had to go to Warm Springs, Georgia, Washington, D.C., and Campobello, Maine, and we realized that authenticity dictated being at these places and that was a considerable expense involved, much greater than we had anticipated when we laid out a budget in advance of the script being written. And so we reassessed the cost elements and came back to ABC and said we need more money to do it well. We should only do it well or not do it at all." To keep the project on track, Susskind agreed to mortgage it to the network. ABC would get the receipts from overseas sales of the *Eleanor and Franklin* movies to cover any costs that went beyond the license fee the network initially agreed to pay.

The added expense of Costigan's work, location shooting, and careful attention to period costume and hair design that spanned sixty years paid off handsomely. More than 30 million viewers watched the quietly stunning production of *Eleanor and Franklin: The Early Years* over two nights in January 1976. The show earned eleven Emmy Awards, including one for the year's Best Special Program. Jane Alexander was nominated in the Outstanding Actress category. Ed Herrmann's performance as FDR opened a virtual side business for him. For the rest of his career, he was often cast as a powerful politician (including FDR again in the film version of *Annie*) and as a narrator for various presidential-themed documentaries that sought his comforting but authoritative vocal tones.

For the sequel, *Eleanor and Franklin: The White House Years,* the Talent Associates producers believed it was essential to film on the grounds of the White House. But the federal government rejected repeated requests to do so. "We had applied through the park police, the Secret Service, all the normal channels, and had been turned down constantly over a period of months in preproduction," recalled Harry Sherman, who served as production manager on both *Eleanor and Franklin* films. Sherman eventually found an inside connection during the later stage of President Gerald Ford's hard-fought 1976 election campaign against Democratic nominee Jimmy Carter. President Ford's political team had hired Don Penny, a onetime nightclub comic who ran an advertising production house. "He was brought down to Washington and lived in the White House, where he was training Gerald Ford," said Sherman, who knew Penny. "Don Penny had these mirrors put in a room there and rehearsed the president constantly and gave him jokes to say and attempted to loosen him up. And I called Don and asked if he could help me in any way, and he said, 'Well, let me work on it.' And over a period of time he kept being rejected. Then as Ford was doing better in his campaigning, Don went to him again and said, 'Look, this friend of mine is doing this project about the Roosevelt years and they would like very much to be able to film outside the White House in the grounds.'" Director Dan Petrie had started shooting *The White House Years* on a soundstage in Los Angeles when Sherman received good news from Penny. "He caught Ford when he was in a good mood because the polls were up and Ford said to him, 'When it happens I don't want to know about it,'" said Sherman. "Don called me right away and said, 'Get your ass on a plane immediately and come right to my office in the Old Executive Office Building.'"

As Sherman and Penny worked out the details, Petrie was told to shut everything down in Los Angeles and head to Washington with the cast and a crew. "Two days later we were shooting at the White House," said Sherman. "We did entrances and exits of the inaugural limousines coming into the grounds and a few exterior scenes of Eleanor driving around Washington and George-town, and we duplicated Marian Anderson's performance at the Lincoln Memorial. We started shooting at about six thirty in the morning and shot until we couldn't get any more light, and then the next day we did the same thing."

BY THE MID-1970S, there were signs that Susskind's relationship with his wife Joyce was beginning to fray. Susskind was not a faithful husband the second time around. Even though he was far more discreet around the office than he had been in years past, Joyce Susskind decided at some point that before her husband hired a new female employee, she would get to meet the woman first. Susskind agreed to this arrangement, according to Jane Deknatel, who recalled having to have dinner with the couple before she could sign on to work for him.

Joyce Susskind was not the type to talk openly about any problems she had with her husband. "I don't care what happens here—you put on a happy face when you go out in public," was how Shelley Stallworth described her moth-er's attitude, a by-product of her Norwegian upbringing. When there was marital conflict, it could put the people who worked with Susskind in the line of fire. Harry Sherman and Dan Petrie were in such a situation when they presented Susskind with an early version of *Eleanor and Franklin* at a studio screening room in Los Angeles. "David had, you know, strayed from the path a few times," Sherman recalled. "He and Joyce had come out and they were at the Beverly Wilshire and they had apparently had a real knock-down, drag-out fight. We were going to run the rough cut for him. We went into the projection room at Fox and we ran the first two hours and David was sitting between Dan and myself and the yellow pad came out. He had one of those pens that had a little light at the bottom so that you could write in the dark. And so I saw David writing constantly. And when the lights went up I thought, 'Oh boy.' We sat there and David was brutal. 'He said, you guys have just destroyed the best piece of material we've ever had.' Oh, I mean he just called us every name in the book. And it was pretty debilitating. He thought certain things were wrong and some of the cuts were wrong. But there was another reason behind all this, which was he was having serious domestic prob-lems. And he went on for about twenty-five minutes."

Sherman had been with Susskind for nearly ten years, but it was the first time he was on the receiving end of such a display. "I had never been the subject of an attack before," he said. "And Dan was pretty upset and David left. And the two of us had lunch and went over all the notes and we were both a little taken aback by the severity of the attack. David had the good sense that night to call Dan Petrie at home and apologize to him, and Dan called me right away. Now David called me but he did not apologize. He said, 'You better get this thing right.' And then he and Joyce left for Acapulco, I think for the holiday season."

After the vacation, Susskind returned to Los Angeles while Joyce headed directly back home to New York. "He came back to California for two or three days," said Sherman. "And we went through the same thing again, running the picture for him. When the lights came up he stood up and said, 'You guys are geniuses. This will take every award.' He raved on and on and it was like 180 degrees difference. Well, we didn't really change that much."

24

A s Andrew Susskind was heading toward graduation from Harvard in the spring of 1976, he was undecided about his career path. He had a major in government, just like his father, David, and considered a career in politics. But like many college students of his generation, he experimented with drugs, and at the time he figured any scrutiny of his personal life would disqualify him. He dreaded the idea of going into the kind of business-school trainee program where his friends were headed. He had been a camp counselor and liked working with children, which led him to consider taking a teaching job at the private Allen-Stephenson School he had attended in the 1960s. Or perhaps he'd put his summer bartending experience at Maxwell's Plum to work and open a restaurant. He and a friend had begun to scout possible sites in Manhattan.

On one of those trips down from Cambridge, Andrew met with his father and talked about his future plans. Susskind listened until he could find an entry point for a suggestion of his own. "Look," Susskind said. "Have you ever considered television?" Andrew had thought of it. But he never wanted to deal with the daunting task of following in his famous father's footsteps.

Susskind, always the persuasive negotiator, made his case. He was still feeling the loss of Audrey Gellen Maas, who had done much of the heavy lifting on his productions. After suffering from years of alcohol abuse, she had died of a brain aneurysm at the age of forty-one. "I am really short-handed," Susskind said. "I could use the help. Would you consider coming into business with me?" He even suggested that Andrew could be running Talent Associates himself one day. "I spent thirty years building a business, and it could be yours," Susskind told him. "And you can eat in any restaurant you want."

It was the best offer out there, Andrew said, "although had I been smarter than I was, I would have realized that it's the kind of business you can't hand over. It's not like there are inventories and factories."

But there was another issue at play. At the age of twenty-two, Andrew still didn't feel he knew his father very well. "I knew he was the kind of guy for whom the work was really the most important thing," he said. "I thought it was the best chance he and I had to get to know each other better. I had the sense that it would really make a difference in my life, if not literally, then down the road with my relationship with my children. I just had the sense that knowing each other better would be a good thing."

Andrew had yearned to get closer to his father throughout his childhood and even ran away from the apartment he shared with his mother after his parents split up. He was eight years old when David and Phyllis Susskind separated, although it happened months before he was told. "In the summer of 1963, I was away at camp and they visited me separately," Andrew recalled. "In some tiny visceral way I thought that was weird."

When Andrew returned to the city in late August, his mother called him and his sister Diana into her room. "She said my father and she had separated," Andrew said. "And I really didn't know what that meant. But I kind of knew, and I remember I started to cry." Andrew and his sister were then told to meet their father for lunch at the Plaza Hotel. "He said, 'You know I love you and everything is going to be fine,'" Andrew recalled. "And then a really weird thing happened. My mother rented a car and wanted to take me for a drive. I had never seen her drive. She rented a red convertible. We went for a drive through Central Park and she pulled over somewhere and started to cry." Andrew was surprised, as he always saw his mother as tough, smart, foul-mouthed, and not very maternal. Given the choice, he would have preferred to have lived with his father, but it hadn't been discussed. Then came her pre-emptive strike. "She said, 'Your father wants you to live with him and I want you to live with me and you'll have to decide, and whatever you decide is okay,'" he said. "She's crying. And it was like—what choice do I have? I would have chosen to live with my father. So I said, 'Oh mom, I want to live with you.'"

It led to a desperately lonely existence for Andrew. Despondent over the split, Phyllis Susskind became a recluse in the family's apartment. "She lived in her bedroom," Andrew said. "She had double doors. There was a door and four feet of space that looked like a foyer and then another door and that was the bedroom. Both doors would be closed. She wouldn't come out." Andrew spent many afternoons after school by himself, bouncing a rubber ball against a wall in the apartment. With his sisters away at college and boarding school, "I was really alone. Not just alone with my mother. I'd come home and she was not available."

Andrew missed his father terribly, and became especially anxious when he traveled out of town on business. By the time he was ten, Andrew was actively lobbying to live with him. "And my mother said absolutely not," he said. "I think it had to do with the fact that my father was seeing or living with Joyce Davidson. I think they were very careful that it not appear that they were living together, at least to my eyes."

But in their conversations, the message Andrew got from his father was, "Look—I love you. I would love you to live with me. I cannot do anything to encourage you to live with me. But I would never turn you away."

During the summer of 1966, several months after Joyce Davidson and Susskind married, twelve-year-old Andrew went to his sister Diana and announced he was leaving to live with his father and his new wife. He waited for his mother to go to the neighborhood beauty parlor, when she could be counted on to be out for several hours. Andrew had already been accumulating personal items at Susskind's UN Plaza apartment. He packed the remaining things he wanted and took a taxicab over. Susskind took his son in. But that night he had Andrew call his mother on the telephone. She said to him, "I don't have a son." He never spent another night under the same roof with her again.

Andrew lived at UN Plaza along with his new half-sister Samantha and Joyce's daughters, Connie and Shelley. Diana also joined the newly blended family. Susskind wanted to adopt the Davidson girls, but their birth father would not allow it. Susskind always referred to them as his daughters and to himself as "Daddy David." He paid for their private school and college educations and walked them down the aisle at their weddings. Susskind threw a spectacular celebration for Shelley when she married her college boyfriend, Michael Andreas, whose family owned the agribusiness giant Archer Daniels Midland.

The Susskinds' beautiful duplex apartment was put to good use by Joyce Susskind, who was active on the New York social scene, thanks to her husband's fame. Joyce and daughter Samantha were featured in the fashion pages of the city's newspapers and in magazines. One photo in *The New York Times* showed David, Joyce, and Samantha looking through one of the large floor-to-ceiling windows of the apartment and out at the extraordinary panoramic views of the East River and the Queensborough Bridge. A curved staircase connected the two floors of the beautifully appointed apartment. The walls were decorated with oil portraits of Joyce, a young Andrew, and Samantha as a toddler. A large Georgia O'Keefe painting hung over the mantle in the living room, along with works by Grandma Moses and American portrait artist John Singer Sargent. "I know that he was very proud of that apartment," said Shelley. "It was very prestigious for him. He was proud of having a home and proud of having a lot of kids."

Joyce Susskind enjoyed entertaining and threw lavish dinners and parties with guest lists as varied as *The David Susskind Show*. Paul Newman, Sidney Poitier, Shirley MacLaine, Gordon Parks, and Chuck Connors were regulars. Some nights Johnny Carson set up his drum set and jammed while the other guests danced. "I still have a drawing of me and my mother that Louis Nizer did on a napkin at dinner," said Shelley. Russian interpreter Viktor Sukhodrev, who remained friendly with Susskind after they met when Khrushchev appeared on *Open End,* was an annual dinner guest. When the UN General Assembly was in session, there was a "Sukhodrev night" at the Susskind household. Each year, Sukhodrev brought Samantha a doll dressed in the native garb of a different Soviet republic. KGB agents stood in the lobby of the building as the festivities went on.

Andrew was not particularly fond of Joyce Susskind. But Andrew said having his stepmother as a stand-in for the often contentious Phyllis Susskind was a relief in some ways. "Joyce was a more pleasant presentation of a mother whenever there were functions at school," Andrew said. "When my mother would go to my school and help out at the book fairs, she would get into fights with the other mothers. She fought everybody in front of people a lot. She was backstage at a Gilbert and Sullivan production and decked a kid because he was mouthing off to her. I mean, she was wild. Joyce never did that. Joyce was lovely-looking. She would show up and she would be helpful."

Connie and Shelley remembered David Susskind as a strict father, who was perhaps attempting to compensate for the years when they had little supervision from their mother. But there were ways to handle him. Susskind once came home to find Connie and several long-haired male friends in denim jackets (including her future husband, writer and poet Nicholas Christopher) in a marijuana-induced haze. Susskind recognized the pungent smell of cannabis and threw up his hands. "What's going on here?" he said. "This is unacceptable."

"He was really pissed off and was on the verge of throwing us out," Christopher said. "Connie waited for the right moment and interjected, 'These are my three friends from Harvard.'"

Harvard was a magical password for Susskind. He immediately calmed down and no longer saw three pot-smoking degenerates in his living room. "All right, have a good time," he said. "But go on the roof if you want to smoke anymore."

Connie was grateful for Susskind's parental involvement. "He's the only person who ever did my homework with me," she said. "He was very supportive toward my education. And I wouldn't be with my husband Nick if David had not been my father. They both went to Harvard and that was a huge deal."

Shelley and Samantha said it was not easy growing up with the expectations—real or imagined—of a man who was famous for setting high standards for his work and highly critical of those who failed to live up to them. "He had great expectations that half the time I didn't know if I could live up to," said Samantha. "When your father is David Susskind and your father is a success, and your father is brilliant and then he says he wants you to succeed, it takes on a whole different meaning. I never realized until he was gone that what he wanted was for me to succeed *for me,* not to succeed according to his standards of what success should be. But at the time, that's what it felt like."

"David made me nervous a little as a kid," said Shelley. "I always wanted his approval, and I always tried to look gorgeous and act certain ways to make him proud of me. He had an energy that was so palpable. He had a great laugh. He loved a good joke, and if I could make him laugh, that was my happiest time. I felt a little lost in the whole thing with David and Joyce. It was all about them."

ALL OF THE SUSSKIND children, with the exception of Shelley, who was married by the time she was twenty, worked for their father at some point in their lives. (Shelley later became a casting director in Chicago and worked on a number of major studio films.) Susskind's oldest daughter, Pamela, was an assistant in casting at Talent Associates and eventually became an associate producer on several projects. Diana started out as a production assistant on the game show *Generation Gap.* They were expected to deliver. "They did not have joke jobs," said Jon Merdin, who also worked on *Generation Gap*. "Diana came into work every day and did not stroll in at eleven and leave at two. She had the same long hours as everybody else." Connie asssisted Jean Kennedy on *The David Susskind Show*. But it was Andrew who Susskind hoped would one day lead Talent Associates and create a show business legacy. Diana Kerew had heard him express that desire from the time Andrew was in boarding school at Phillips Exeter.

Of course, once Andrew decided to sign on to work at Talent Associates in 1976, Susskind set some boundaries. "There are a couple of things," he said. "I will invite you into meetings from time to time, on one condition."

"What?" Andrew asked.

"That you don't speak," Susskind said.

"Well, why not?"

"Because you have nothing to contribute."

But Andrew loved it. He spent the first six months to a year reading scripts and going to editing and mixing sessions for shows. Susskind was known for his inability to get along with other male executives. As Susskind's adoring son, Andrew's status was different. "He had to love me," he says. "He was great to me. He was a great teacher. He included me, not all the time, but a lot. And I didn't speak for quite a while. . . . I think to be honest, at a fairly early point he came to the conclusion that I wasn't an idiot. I think he was really pleased and relieved by that."

They also grew closer personally. One day early in his employment, Andrew asked his father to come into the office at 747 Third Avenue on a Saturday morning so they could talk privately. He started by saying how much he enjoyed working with him. "My father said, 'Me too, it's great,'" said Andrew, who then recounted a story from his childhood that occurred shortly after David and Phyllis Susskind had split.

"When I was about nine, I said to my mother one day, 'Gee, Mom, isn't it interesting that both Grandpa Aaron [Phyllis's father] and Grandpa Ben both died of cancer," Andrew said. "To which my mother replied, 'What do you mean? Grandpa Ben didn't die of cancer, he hanged himself in the bathroom.' That's how I learned at age nine that my grandfather committed suicide. And I remember so powerfully thinking at that moment that a nine-year-old is not supposed to be told that kind of information that way. I also knew that because I'd been led to believe something else I wasn't supposed to know that."

Susskind had always described his father as an intellectually curious man who helped shape his own passion for learning. There was never any discussion about any battles with depression. Faced with Andrew's knowledge of the truth about Ben Susskind's death, Susskind talked to him for the first time about the guilt he felt over not being able to save his father. He expressed his regrets over giving in to Ben Susskind's pleas to sign him out of a hospital after an earlier suicide attempt. Susskind's eyes began to well up with tears. Up to that moment, Andrew Susskind had never seen his father cry.

25

I used to say David Susskind could sell anything," Leonard Stern said. "I didn't realize at that time it would often be Talent Associates."

By 1974, Talent Associates was generating about half of the revenue it did in the late 1960s and just a minuscule profit. The executives at Norton Simon Inc. could no longer justify keeping it around. After being a high-flying conglomerate since its inception in 1968, the company saw its first decline in earnings during the recession of 1974. NSI chairman David Mahoney decided the company needed to be focused on its high-margin businesses of food, liquor, cosmetics, and soft drinks.

David Susskind never liked having to come up with the financial projections and five-year plans that came with having a corporate owner. Whenever NSI brass expressed dissatisfaction with Talent Associates, Susskind offered to buy the company back. In July 1975, they took him up on his offer. Susskind owned his company again for the price of $1.

Going it alone again was a tall order. As productive as the company was, Talent Associates had trouble taking in enough money to cover its overhead, which included expensive headquarters on a high floor in a shiny new office tower at 747 Third Avenue.

"David was spending a lot of money," said Ron Gilbert, who started out as an accountant at Talent Associates in the early 1960s and became Susskind's partner in the firm after the buyback from Norton Simon. Gilbert spoke with a raspy voice and thick Brooklyn accent that made him sound like he could be a Damon Runyon character. He managed the budgetary end of many of

Talent Associates productions and was widely known as the guy who watched Susskind's back on financial matters. It was not an easy task.

"Our [operating] budget was $2 million a year," he said. "If you looked at us in that office we were in seventh heaven at the time."

While the television output of Talent Associates remained strong in those years, Gilbert said Susskind continued to pursue feature film projects and Broadway shows. Many of those projects did not come to fruition and led to carrying more employees than the company's revenues could sustain. "It should have been a leaner operation or I needed more development," he said. "But there were so many people doing so many things. He hired a lot of people. We were fine for two years. But when it started to escalate I said, 'David, where are we going?' We had to find somebody to buy it."

In 1977, Talent Associates was on the block again. The company's outside counsel at the time, Richard Barovick, also represented Time-Life Films, a Time Inc. subsidiary that sold educational movies, documentaries, and BBC shows to television. Bruce Paisner, a Time Inc. veteran who started as a correspondent at *Life* magazine and was working his way up the corporate ladder, ran the unit. "Barovick came to me one day and he said, 'Well, if you want to expand, I've got a real thing you ought to look at because TV movies are hot, TV series are doable, and I represent a guy who's had a nearly flawless track record at making stuff work,'" Paisner recalled. "He has a reputation as a big spender, but I can tell you, and you're a friend, he's really not, at least when it comes to controlling his productions. You'd get along with him and I think he'd fit in here.' So I said, 'Who is it?' He said, 'Well, it's David Susskind.' I said, 'I don't want to touch that.' Because everybody knew David and he was rather flamboyant and controversial and tough. He had a reputation for temper tantrums. I think he had a reputation for being difficult to work with. But Dick said, 'C'mon, just meet with him.' So I said okay. As anybody could have predicted, he charmed the pants off me."

Acquiring Talent Associates would give Time-Life Films a running start into the TV and film production business. Susskind had commitments for a number of upcoming television films, including *Blind Ambition,* a miniseries based on the book by Nixon White House counsel John Dean, and an order from CBS for *On Our Own,* starring Bess Armstrong, a half-hour situation comedy about two young women working in a New York advertising agency. The company also had the rights to develop a number of other projects.

Talent Associates was sold once again for around $1 million in Time Inc. stock. But the relationship differed from the setup Susskind had with his previous corporate partners Paramount and Norton Simon. Both companies allowed Talent Associates to operate independently and ultimately had trouble keeping it under control. At Time-Life Films, Susskind would be an employee working under contract. Talent Associates, the company name that had come to represent his ambitions and achievements, would no longer exist. It was a hard concession for him to accept. "He really was the measure of his work," said his daughter Samantha. "His work was so integrally tied to who he was that by selling his company, he was essentially selling a piece of him. And I think it was very hard. It was hard on his ego. It's not even an issue of whether or not you're prosperous. It was an issue of the integrity of your work." Samantha remembered seeing her father at home with tears in his eyes as he discussed the sale with Joyce.

Susskind understood the deal was financially necessary. Yet he tried to back out at the last minute. "We had a deadline we had to meet in order to get all the paperwork in," said Gilbert. "He kept going, 'Well, maybe we shouldn't, maybe we should.'" Gilbert was determined to get the deal through, even working through the New York City blackout in the summer of 1977 to complete the transaction on time. "I had to go in," he said. "And I walked up thirty-three flights. It was hot. It was unbelievable to put all the papers together. I couldn't see. I used a flashlight. There was nothing going to stop me from going into that building."

The contracts were to be signed on August 5, 1977. The night before, Gilbert got a call from an extremely distressed David Susskind. "He said, 'You know what, I don't think I want to do this,'" Gilbert said. "I said, 'There is no way that we're not going to go through with this. You can't make the kind of money you spend, David. We can't exist anymore without it. We're going through with it. We're going to do this.' He didn't say anything. He might have been drinking that night or I don't know what."

THE DEAL WENT THROUGH as planned and David Susskind's operation became a part of Time Inc. It was not an ideal fit. Publishing was still the main business at the company. It owned HBO, but cable television was in its infancy and HBO was years away from making its first original movie or series. Its program line-up in the 1970s was mostly uncut Hollywood movies, boxing matches, and an occasional special such as coverage of the Pennsylvania Polka Festival from Allentown. Still, it was a subscription business that relied on fees from consumers, something the button-downed corporate executives at Time Inc. understood. They did not have the stomach for the guesswork and risk taking that revolved around a brash personality such as Susskind. "Time was still run by people who were not entertainment-oriented," said Michael Fuchs, a longtime executive at HBO. "So they were suspicious."

As part of his employment deal, Susskind insisted on keeping his car and driver. Andrew Heiskell, the chief executive of Time Inc. at the time, hated such extravagances. He prided himself on taking the crosstown bus to the Time-Life Building at Rockefeller Center. Like Susskind, he also lived at UN Plaza. When both men left their apartments for work in the morning, Susskind's car was waiting for him. "They would often leave the building together and they'd come out the door and David would say, 'Andrew, we're going to the same place—why don't you let me give you a ride?' Andrew would say, 'No, David, I like to take the bus,'" Paisner said. "And you know, every once in a while Andrew would call me or see me at something and say, 'I don't know about your David Susskind—he makes good movies, but that car and driver, it's driving me nuts.'"

But Susskind was able to dazzle the Time Inc. types when he swung into action to pursue a book property he wanted for a TV project. Early on in his tenure at the company, a call came in from Irving "Swifty" Lazar, the agent whose clean-shaven head was once described by author Joseph Heller as resembling an inverted teardrop.

"David, I've got some good news and bad news," said Lazar. "The good news is, I've got a new book from Arthur Schlesinger about Robert F. Kennedy and the Kennedy family thinks you should make the movie."

"What's the bad news, Irving?" asked Susskind.

"The bad news is, the rights will cost $500,000 and you can't read it," Lazar said. "If you want to read it, the price is $1 million."

"Irving," Susskind said. "Can you at least tell me what's in the book?"

"David, it's Arthur Schlesinger. It's Robert Kennedy. What more do you need to know?"

The Kennedy family had been particularly impressed with Susskind's *Eleanor and Franklin* films. But Susskind was no longer in the position of saying yes to what he wanted without worrying about how to pay for it. Paisner controlled the purse strings of his productions. When Lazar asked to discuss the book over lunch, Susskind said Paisner had to come along. Fine, Lazar said. "But don't tell him I called and asked for the meeting," the agent added. The three met the following day at Lazar's elegant Fifth Avenue apartment overlooking Central Park. After they finished their meal, Lazar turned and said, "Okay, David, let's get down to it. I've got Arthur's book. I want to sell it as a miniseries."

"Well, where's the manuscript?" Susskind asked. "I could read it overnight."

"No," Lazar said. "I've decided that nobody's going to read the manuscript. It's going to be bought without reading the manuscript. David, you don't need to read the manuscript. It's Arthur Schlesinger. It's Robert Kennedy. What more do you need to know?"

This was all new to Paisner, who was slightly dazed by the proceedings. He sat there thinking, "So . . . this is how the business operates at these levels." Then he heard Susskind say, "Irving, you know I'm part of Time-Life now. I can't make those decisions anymore, but Bruce here can." They both turned to Paisner. "So Bruce," Susskind said, "what do you want to do?"

"I don't know, David," Paisner replied. "I think I want to go off and talk to you and we'll get back to Irving."

"Well, all right," Lazar said. "But you've got twenty-four hours. It's a very simple decision, and if you don't want it there are plenty of people who do. Although clearly, David Susskind is the person to do this."

Paisner remembered that he felt a bit queasy when he and Susskind returned to their offices at the Time-Life Building. "Don't worry about it," Susskind told him. "Here's how we're going to handle it. We're going to go to CBS tomorrow and skip all the programming people. We're just going to go to Gene Jankowski." Jankowski had just been named president of the network. Susskind predicted that CBS would put up the money for the RFK project without reading the manuscript. A few minutes later, Susskind stopped by Paisner's office again to tell him they had an appointment with Jankowski for 10:00 a.m. the next day at CBS headquarters.

Paisner marveled at the way Susskind had coolly wrangled a meeting with a network chief while under the gun of a slick superagent. But the best was yet to come. "We go into the meeting," Paisner recalled. "There's a bit of chitchat and then I hear David say, 'Gene, suppose we had a project that was really important for CBS but so special and unusual that no individual drama or movie department head could understand its implications? Where would we go?' Jankowski—I'll never forget this—points to himself. I'm thinking, 'Aha, dummy. It's taken you a while but finally you see what David's strategy is.'"

Susskind goes on. "Well, then, I'm very glad we're here, Gene, because we've got just that kind of thing. Arthur Schlesinger has written a new book on Robert Kennedy."

"Sounds great," Jankowski said. "We'll keep it here right at my level. I'd like to read the manuscript overnight."

Paisner gulped. Susskind didn't miss a beat.

"Gene," he said. "Irving Lazar has a policy on this that he's not putting the manuscript out to be read. But really, what difference does it make? It's Arthur Schlesinger. It's Robert Kennedy. What more do you need to know?"

Paisner heard Susskind repeat word for word what Lazar said at lunch. And it worked.

"You're right," Jankowski said. "We'll buy it."

Later, Robert Daly, then the head of business affairs for CBS, called Paisner. "'I work here so I've got to go forward on this," he told him. "But just before I do, I want to make sure I understand it. We're going to pay $500,000 for a book without ever reading the manuscript and all we know about it is that it's Arthur Schlesinger writing about Robert Kennedy?"

Paisner, a little incredulous himself, said, "It sounded that way to me."

David Susskind's first two years at Time-Life Films were profitable as well as productive. *Blind Ambition* was the only television project to run up a significant deficit while under the new corporate auspices. The production of the eight-hour miniseries based on former White House counselor John Dean's book culminated with a standoff between Susskind and CBS over the script's use of expletives taken from President Nixon's taped Oval Office conversations during the Watergate scandal. Even though the networks generally were sticklers when it came to the veracity of docudramas, CBS censors demanded that "Jesus Christ," "bastards," "son of a bitch" and "God damn" be excised. Susskind held firm. He believed sanitizing the language of the Watergate coconspirators would be tampering with history. Over the network's objection, Susskind delivered the final cut of the film with the language intact. The network took the bizarre step of bleeping the words out in *Blind Ambition* when it first aired in May 1979.

But most of Susskind's TV projects for Time-Life made money.

Paisner managed to control Susskind's spending and got along extremely well with his charge. A Harvard graduate with a beautiful French wife, Paisner had been a Washington correspondent and was worldly enough to converse about politics and international affairs with Susskind when the two men traveled together. Paisner was often reminded that he was in business with a major celebrity. He would marvel at how women of a certain age would stop Susskind on the street and want to touch his white tufts of hair. He admired the royal treatment Susskind received when arriving at customs in Kennedy Airport after trips to London. "There was never any wait," he said. "Somebody would essentially greet him as he got off the plane and he'd get whisked through. I remember the first time it happened, I turned to him and I said, 'That's nice when it happens this way.' And he said, 'It should always happen this way for me. It's my town.' And the fact is that whatever kind of figure he was in the rest of the country, he really was a central cultural figure for New York. It was his town. He bestrode it and liked that, cultivated that. He was in a way the quintessential New Yorker who made good."

Over time, Susskind had built up enough goodwill with Paisner to convince him to make feature films for Time-Life. Time-Life sold its TV movies to networks and stations in packages, and having a few recognizable theatrical titles would help. "The studios weren't going to give them to you," said Paisner. "We felt, 'Well, here's a perfect opportunity. We'll make a certain kind of movie and we'll get a couple of them a year, and that's all we need.'" In late 1979, they landed an agreement with 20th Century–Fox: it would finance up to twelve projects over the following three years at an agreed-upon price. Time-Life would have to cover any cost over the agreed-upon budget. Fox would get theatrical distribution rights, while Time-Life would get the TV revenue, some of which would come from HBO. David Susskind was back in the movie business.

WITH THE FOX DEAL in hand, Susskind acted on the promise he made years earlier to screenwriter Heywood Gould. He wanted to produce Gould's script *Fort Apache,* about two cops who worked in the hellish 41st Precinct in the South Bronx.

Producers Marty Richards, Gill Champion, and Tom Fiorello had first developed *Fort Apache* at their New York casting company in the early 1970s. During the days of hippies, long hair, and beards, Champion said they often hired real cops to play in such films as *Three Days of the Condor* and *Death Wish.* "I once got criticized because I think I gave more cops in New York Screen Actors Guild cards than anybody else," he recalled. "I said, 'I can't find guys who talk like cops. I can't find guys who walk like cops. And I can't find guys who dress like cops. So I'm giving it to these guys to make the movie look better. It's part of adding realism, particularly in that time, to the movie. It was also helpful that they could wear guns on the set. So if there was ever a problem, whether you were shooting on Broadway or anyplace else, they would at least be able to assist you in some emergency."

Fiorello was from the Bronx, where he had become friendly with two

NYPD members, Pete Tessitore and Thomas Mulhearn, who had spent four years in the 41st Precinct in the 1960s. At the time, the crime-infested precinct was compared to an embattled outpost in the Old West and earned the nickname "Fort Apache." Through the first half of the twentieth century, the South Bronx had been a solid enclave of Jewish families who rose out of the squalor of the Lower East Side of Manhattan. But they fled in the 1950s and 1960s, frightened by the influx of indigent Puerto Rican immigrants and blacks. Landlords were paid above market rents by the city's welfare department to house poor families. Poverty and weak family structures led to drug abuse, youth gangs, arson, and a sense of hopelessness. Newspaper stories about the South Bronx inevitably contained the description "rubble-strewn." Few minority cops served in the neighborhood at the time. Many of the officers had been transferred to the 41st because they had become problems in their old precincts. An assignment in the 41st Precinct could be used as pressure to get bad cops to quit, and many did.

In the early 1970s, Mulhearn and Tessitore had taken Fiorello, Champion, and Richards on tours through the beleaguered area and regaled them with tales from their four-year rotation. "There was one block, I think, if I remember right, in the four-one, where there was only one apartment standing out in a whole burned-down block," Champion said. "And the one sector car just had to ride around that block, and that one building kept them busy pretty much during the course of an eight-hour shift. So it was a very strange world in those days. It was bleak. It looked like bombed-out Berlin during World War II."

The producers believed that the battleground Mulhearn and Tessitore once navigated could be the backdrop for a gritty, realistic film—if they could find a writer capable of turning the cops' stories into a screenplay. But running with the pair was not for the faint of heart.

"They were bigger-than-life personalities," said Champion. "I remember, we brought one writer up to a cops' bar in the Bronx, and we're sitting there all night, drinking, and all of a sudden these guys pull out their guns and they are shooting holes in the ceiling of the building. I mean, the days were very different. It's three o'clock in the morning. You know, we were drinking pretty good in those days. You couldn't do that now. That writer, he took off. I never saw that guy again." Two other writers failed to make it through the night, with one ending up inebriated and lying in a heap outside the entrance of the Bronx Zoo, a gathering point for neighborhood prostitutes at the time.

Heywood Gould also had to run the gauntlet of a night out with Mulhearn and Tessitore. "I went up to the Bronx for the ritual writer-bashing with these two guys," he said. But Gould had practically been in training for them. In the early 1970s, he worked as a bartender and was drinking a quart of Hennessy cognac a night before he walked home to his apartment in upper Manhattan at the end of his shift. "I was a seasoned professional," he said. They could not outbooze the six-foot-four Brooklyn native. "They said, 'Okay, this guy can write our story,'" Gould said. "So then I started to hang out with them. They were legitimately tough Bronx cops ready for anything."

Gould described himself at the time as "an angry rebellious guy who had trouble with authority." But he developed empathy with the police during his years covering them at the *New York Post*. "I kind of knew who the cops really were," he said. "And I liked them. I didn't have any illusions about them being heroes, that's for sure. And I also knew that they were kind of looking for what they could get out of life, as is everybody else. But at the same time, they did have a certain innate respect for law and order and stability. They lived in a stable word, and a hierarchical world. And they didn't place themselves at the top of the hierarchy; they knew where they belonged. They gave respect to the people above them. The people below them—you better toe the line."

Gould's script for *Fort Apache* told the story of a cop named Murphy who, after fourteen years in the 41st Precinct, had developed his own unorthodox but often compassionate style of dealing with prostitutes, pimps, suicidal drag queens, purse snatchers, and knife-wielding lunatics. He is cynical about police department politics. On the street, he finds ways to cheerfully manage the mayhem that surrounds him, until he witnesses a member of his squad throwing an unarmed teenaged Puerto Rican boy off the roof of a building during a riot. The plot then centered on the dilemma over whether to turn the cop in and possibly put an end to his own career. The script was filled with intense depictions of urban brutality and chaos. In the opening scene, a black strung-out hooker stumbles across the street and shoots two rookie police officers sitting in their squad car. She is later killed by two drug dealers, who roll her up in a carpet and dump her body in one of the many vacant lots in the neighborhood.

Susskind loved the script when Gould first showed it to him in 1973 and gave the writer other assignments to keep him going. After a number of studios had passed, Susskind persuaded Richards, Champion, and Fiorello to let him take over the rights to the property. With Susskind's record of making realistic films and TV shows on the streets of New York, they knew he was their best chance of getting the film produced.

Time-Life gave Susskind the green light to proceed with *Fort Apache* once he got Paul Newman to sign on for $3 million and 15 percent of the gross earnings beyond that figure. Still a major movie star, Newman had been on a bit of a cold streak. His previous box office success had been *The Towering Inferno* in 1974. Steve McQueen, already stricken with the cancer that would take his life, passed when he was offered the role. A call went to Nick Nolte, but he did not want to do location work in New York during the dead of winter.

Newman wanted some support on the marquee and Susskind tried to land John Travolta for the role of Carelli, Murphy's younger swaggering partner. Instead, the producers ended up with Ken Wahl, a virtual Travolta double who had starred in *The Wanderers*. Ed Asner, then a major TV star on the CBS series *Lou Grant,* signed on as a martinet of a commanding officer sent in to boost the precinct's performance. The producers went with a total unknown for the role of Murphy's girlfriend Isabella, a streetwise nurse with a taste for heroin, when they hired Rachel Ticotin. The dark-haired actress grew up in the South Bronx, the daughter of a Puerto Rican mother and a Jewish father. She had only one previous small film role and was one of one hundred actresses to answer an open call, making her a great New York story of a local girl made good. Danny Aiello played the belligerent racist cop who murders the boy.

After signing on, Newman expressed concerns about the unrelenting intensity of the urban horrors depicted in the script. The roughhewn Murphy was darker than the smooth, likable characters Newman tended to play. "He was conflicted about it," said Gould. When Gould and the film's director, Dan Petrie, had their first meeting with Newman at a restaurant in Malibu, the actor came with a set of notes with changes he wanted. "Dan Petrie was looking at me like, 'Don't queer the deal,'" Gould said. "So I didn't say anything." At the end of the evening Newman announced that all of his notes on the script had to be followed or he was not doing the movie.

Gould went back to his hotel room and stewed over Newman's suggestions, which he believed would soften the harshness and black humor he envisioned for the film. He called Susskind at home in New York where it was 4:00 a.m. "These are the notes he's given us," Gould told him. "He's kind of taken out the guts of the movie."

"Go to sleep," Susskind told him. "Don't worry about it."

Gould heard nothing about Newman's notes again. "Somehow it all blew over," he said.

Susskind had been friendly with Newman for years and was able to keep him in line. Later, during a rehearsal, Newman weighed in on a scene be-tween Ken Wahl's character and his girlfriend, played by Kathleen Beller. "Paul was sitting there, because we had just rehearsed a scene that he was in," said Gould. "And he started giving me notes on this scene that Ken Wahl was in. And David said, 'Paul, I'm paying you three and a half million dollars to be in this movie. Please don't give notes on scenes you're not in.'"

Still, Gould remained anxious that Newman might back out until the filming started in early March 1980. "Once we started to roll, or once we had some press, I knew we were going to do the movie," he said. "And that's be-cause of David. David was not going to let this movie get stopped."

However, as shooting began, a force emerged that did try to stop it. As the 1970s progressed, the South Bronx had become a national symbol of urban blight. President Jimmy Carter had made a surprise visit there in 1977, calling for increased aid for housing and jobs. Presidential candidate Ronald Reagan, Mother Teresa, and Pope John Paul II all made high-profile appearances in the neighborhood over the next three years. The press coverage of promises for help gave community activists hope that the area could be revitalized (an ambition that was realized in the 1990s). Once they heard about the production of *Fort Apache*, they assumed it was based on a recent book of the same name, written by a former cop named Tom Walker. Walker's tome presented a harsh portrayal of minorities through the eyes of the police. Putting those images on the screen would set back the rehabilitation efforts, the community activists claimed.

Walker claimed that the movie, renamed *Fort Apache, The Bronx,* was substan-tially similar to his book, and sued unsuccessfully. By the time activists had got-ten a copy of an actual movie script, they had already revved up an organization called Committee Against Fort Apache. Represented by high-profile attorney William Kunstler, they filed a suit in New York State Supreme Court to stop the movie on the grounds that it was unfair to minority groups in the area.

A judge dismissed the suit without even reading the script, as its intent disregarded the right to free speech. But the committee wanted to galvanize the community, and what better way to do it than tossing a big-time movie production into the cauldron of New York City politics. It held Stop Fort Apache marches and a Stop Fort Apache Arts Festival. Its members offered to debate Susskind and Newman on a local TV show hosted by Bronx borough president Herman Badillo. Newman, a staunch liberal and civil rights advo-cate who once earned a spot on President Nixon's enemies list, had to give a press conference to say the film was not racist. "It is tough on Puerto Ricans, blacks, and the neighborhood," he said. "But the two villains are Irish cops who throw a Puerto Rican off the roof."

The police were also not pleased with what they heard about the film. "The cops hated me," said Gould. "We didn't shoot in front of the Forty-first because the streets were too narrow. So we shot in front of the Forty-second for the big riot scene. And the captain came out. And he kind of came over and he gave me the gimlet-eye cop look. And he says, 'Where did you work?' And I said, 'What do you mean, where did I work?' 'What house did you work in?' He thought I was an ex-cop. I said, 'I was never a cop, Captain.' He says, "That's not what I hear.' I said, 'Well, you heard wrong. I was never a cop. You can check me out.' They were convinced that I was a renegade cop who had written this bad stuff about cops throwing guys off roofs and frightening people, and all this kind of stuff. So everybody had a gripe against the movie."

Gould said narcotics officers investigated the set looking for a movie star bust after Newman was photographed on the set wearing a razor-blade necklace, the jewelry of choice at the time for serious cocaine users. Newman did not use drugs. There were other people working on the movie who did, including some of the off-duty cops who provided security. "I mean, the cops on the film would literally get coke that they'd picked up off the street and bring it down to the crew," said Susskind's stepdaughter, Connie Christopher, who worked as a production assistant. "During the wrap party, I sat in a detective's car on Broadway outside. You know the cups where you put your coffee? The whole thing was filled with coke. He never did that much coke. He'd do a line or two. But he was dealing the coke."

Even the neighborhood junkies and derelicts taunted the filmmakers. While a daytime street scene was being shot, one of them wandered in and settled down onto the sidewalk. "He wouldn't move," said Gould. "The assistant director didn't know what to do. Dan Petrie came over and the man started calling him a racist pig." Petrie, who was the gentlest of souls, tried to correct him. "I'm not a racist," he said. "I'm a liberal. I did *A Raisin in the Sun*."

The man just looked at him and said, "You want to put a raisin in the sun? What do you want to do that for?"

Petrie's pleas actually were effective in their own strange way. "This guy thought Petrie was nuts," Gould recalled. "He got up and walked away." Less amusing was when angry residents gathered on the elevated subway platforms above the street and threw trash down at the actors and crew while they were shooting on the sidewalks.

Susskind mitigated some of the community's anger by getting waivers from the unions so he could hire neighborhood people as production assistants and for other low-level jobs on the film. Children were brought in from a local day-care center to be used as extras. A little showbiz exposure went a long way when dealing with civilians. "It was a thrill for the children in being part of this process," the day-care center's executive director wrote to the producers. "They enjoyed meeting and talking with Paul Newman, a real live movie star." Susskind's threshold for such controversy was high by this point of his career. "He loved it," said Gould. "It was good for the movie. It stirred things up. It provoked discussion. That's what he liked to do." Gould was not the conciliatory type, but he was sent to meet with the activists. At one meeting, a nun threatened to chain him to a desk until he made changes to the script. He stood his ground and came with a Puerto Rican detective who worked in the neighborhood who insisted the screenplay was an honest depiction of South Bronx life. But Gould was instructed by Susskind to come up with a disclaimer to run at the start of the film. He reluctantly wrote, "Because the story involves police work it does not deal with the law-abiding members of the community, nor does it dramatize the efforts of the individuals who are struggling to turn the Bronx around."

Still, the Committee Against Fort Apache never stopped beating the drum against the movie. It passed out literature over the summer after initial photography had ended and showed up that fall in front of the Grand Hyatt Hotel in Manhattan where Susskind was to be honored by the Chamber of Commerce for helping to revitalize the film industry in New York. David Susskind did not attend and sent Andrew Susskind to accept the award. A committee member managed to get inside the film's publicity tour in Atlanta and pepper Newman with questions about the community's concerns during a press conference. Some theater chains held off on booking the film, fearful that picketers would show up outside.

The protesters were out in force behind sawhorses near the movie house on East Eighty-sixth Street where David Susskind took his daughter Samantha to see the film when it opened in February 1981. "He looked pretty proud of himself, walking in there," she recalled. "And the people protesting were screaming at him, 'Hey, David!' And he just had this little smirk on his face, walking in." The headline in the February 9 edition of *Variety* read, "Fort Apache Biz Brisk in Spite of New York Protest."

The major reviews for *Fort Apache, The Bronx* were mixed, but none of them suggested the film was racist. "The movie takes a liberal attitude toward its milieu," wrote *Time* magazine's Richard Schickel. Most critics agreed that Newman had broken new ground as an actor with his raw and honest portrayal of Murphy. The performance clearly whet the appetite of audiences and critics for his next two roles, in *Absence of Malice* and *The Verdict,* both of which earned him Academy Award nominations.

AT THE START of 1980 there was a change at Time-Life Films. Bruce Paisner lost a power struggle with the executives at HBO, which was emerging as a force in the television business. He was ousted and replaced by a Time Inc. and HBO veteran named Austin Furst. Susskind may have groused privately about Paisner when he prevented him from spending money on certain projects he wanted to pursue. But under his watch, Susskind had a safe corporate home with a boss who recognized his ample talents and knew how to manage his sizable ego. "I really respected him," Paisner said. "I thought in terms of television he was a creative genius. He was the kind of person, and there were few of them, who could just look at a book and see the movie and get you from first to second. And that's hard. He had an ability to cast. He had an ability to get creative people to do things that they never thought they would do. He had the ability to go acquire things from people who never thought they would sell those kind of rights. I kind of celebrated that. I celebrated it to the management of Time and I celebrated it with David, because I believed in him. I think maybe he bought into all that and then it was pulled away one day, quite suddenly."

Paisner said once he departed Time Inc., Susskind was treated as "another producer on the lot" by Furst. Susskind described his new boss as "a six-foot-five calculator with no showmanship and no flair." Paisner also believed that Time Inc. agreed to change the terms of the favorable film production deal it had with Fox after he left.

As soon as Paisner was gone, Time-Life Films started losing money. A TV movie based on John Hershey's *The Wall* that was being shot in Poland ran nearly 50 percent over budget. "The government was collapsing while that was going on," Diana Kerew recalled. "That was during the Gdansk shipyard strike, and a number of our Polish coproduction people were imprisoned."

While *Fort Apache, The Bronx* eventually made money, the film showed a $2 million loss for Time-Life Films in the year after its release. *Loving Couples,* a contemporary romantic comedy that Susskind made with Shirley MacLaine and James Coburn, cost $6 million to make, and took in only $3 million at the box office. Susskind was also initially involved in Peter Bogdanovich's ill-fated New York–based caper *They All Laughed,* with Audrey Hepburn. He lost control of the film to the maverick director and relinquished his role as executive producer on the doomed project. Bogdanovich had cast his *Playboy* centerfold girlfriend Dorothy Stratton in the film. After filming was completed, Stratton died at the hands of her jealous ex-boyfriend in a heinous murder-suicide. Fox refused to release the film and Bogdanovich tried to finance its distribution out of his own pocket in 1981, a move that led him into personal bankruptcy.

But it's likely that Susskind's overall film strategy looked less appealing to Time Inc. after the emergence of such high-gloss blockbusters as *The Empire Strikes Back, Raiders of the Lost Ark,* and *E.T.* He was not going to turn out the kind of movies that would make Time-Life Films a major studio. Susskind left Time Inc. nine months after Paisner's departure.

As Susskind got older, he became more resistant to adapting to popular tastes. Samantha remembered a conversation she had with her father when she was a teenager about the Thomas Harris novel *Red Dragon.* It was the thriller that introduced the character of serial killer Hannibal Lecter, who went on to become a major screen villain in the film version of *The Silence of the Lambs.*

"He had the book on his nightstand, and I said to him, 'Are you looking at this?' And he says, 'No. Go ahead and read it.' Well, I started reading it. I couldn't put it down. I read it in three days. I did not leave the house. It was one of those types of books. And I come back up to him, and said, 'You have to make this movie. This is the scariest book. I couldn't stop reading. I was on the edge of my seat.' So he said, 'Okay, okay; I'll read it.' And he used to blow through books. He read it in a day and a half—or at least he said he read it. When I said, 'Did you finish that book?' he goes, 'Oh, yeah. I finished it.' And I said, 'What do you think?' And he goes, 'It's drivel and it's sensationalism and it's gore. I would never make a movie [like this]. I don't know why they are even sending this thing to me.' And I said, 'Are you crazy? This is the coolest book. It would make a great movie. People would go see it.' He goes, 'Yeah. Your people would go to see it. But my name would be on it. I'm not making that movie.'"

By the end of 1981, Time Inc. shuttered Time-Life Films and was out of the movie business altogether until it merged with Warner Communications to become Time Warner in 1987. Once again, David Susskind was going to be his own boss.

27

Near the end of 1980, David Susskind founded the Susskind Company, with headquarters at the corporate offices of MGM in Manhattan. The movie studio's chief, David Begelman, was an old friend who had survived a massive forgery scandal during his tenure at Columbia in the 1970s. He gave Susskind's new company a film and TV production deal and a West Coast office in the Spencer Tracy Cottage at the MGM lot in Culver City. Andrew Susskind, along with several producers and story editors, had joined David Susskind at the new company. Jean Kennedy and the staff of *The David Susskind Show* followed him over as well.

The Susskind Company immediately went to work pitching projects to the commercial broadcast networks. But the made-for-television movie business had started to move away from the kind of work Susskind favored. "The nature of the movies of the week started to change," Andrew recalled. "They really became disease of the week. A little more tabloidy." The Susskind Company would only end up selling one TV movie to the commercial networks, a workmanlike Rita Hayworth biography with *Wonder Woman* star Lynda Carter in the lead role.

Susskind had better luck with public broadcasting, which became a steady customer for his brand of drama specials that matched up proven material and classic literature with serious stage performers. He reunited Jane Alexander and Ed Herrmann for a presentation of *Dear Liar,* and signed British actor Sir Ian McKellen to perform Shakespeare soliloquies in front of an audience. The company developed one-man shows that featured actors portraying important historic or cultural figures, such as Charles Durning as New York Yankees manager Casey Stengel.

But there was another issue at play in Susskind's career at the time. He had long had a reputation for being kinetic, capricious, and even volatile. Sometimes those characteristics made him charming, other times infuriating. Even with his quirks, he had developed what appeared to be an unfailing survival instinct in business. That instinct began to fail him in the years after his split with Time Inc., as he entered a behavioral state he was unable to control.

The signs were subtle at first. Veteran screenwriter Loring Mandel recalled how he flew from New York to Los Angeles to join Susskind for a meeting at CBS. They had pitched a drama series to the network and were trying to take the project to the next phase. Before a three o'clock meeting at the network's Television City headquarters, Mandel had lunch with Susskind and one of his employees at the Polo Lounge at the Beverly Hills Hotel. "We were about done," Mandel said. "And we had to go over to CBS, and David said, 'I've got to go to the can. I'll meet you at the maître d's desk.' We went over to the desk and we waited and we waited. No David. It's getting really late." Mandel finally started to walk around the restaurant to look for him and found him sitting with a group of diners he had never met before. "He just sat down with strangers and started talking to them," he said. It was unusual, as Susskind did not dawdle and was always punctual. He acted strangely at the meeting as well, Mandel said. "There's something wrong with him," a friend at CBS told him as they headed out.

Other bizarre incidents occurred that were more alarming. Jane Deknatel, who worked for the Susskind Company in Los Angeles after a few years as a vice president of movies and miniseries at NBC, remembered how Susskind had lined up the TV rights to the 1981 feature *The Four Seasons* and was able to package it as a series with the original cast. "He asked me to sell it," she recalled. ABC was interested and called for a meeting. "They were young network executives and they had never met the great David Susskind," she said. "So I said to David, 'You have to get on a plane and come out and seal this deal.'"

Deknatel and Susskind drove separately to ABC's Los Angeles offices located behind the Century Plaza Hotel in Century City. They met in a nearby parking lot. "David was acting a little spacey," said Deknatel. "I thought, 'Oh, he's jet-lagged.' And we get to the meeting. He lies down on the sofa, and he goes to sleep. We can't wake him. I am mortified and also worried. I think, 'Should I call an ambulance? Is he having a seizure?'"

Once the incident occurred, the pitch meeting was over. "It didn't matter whether he was having a physical issue or if it was behavioral," said Deknatel. "All the ABC people saw was a man who wasn't capable of walking into a network and commanding the presence of all these young network executives and who they were about to give some vast amount of money to. So the deal went away."

Susskind eventually got on his feet and he and Deknatel left the ABC offices. "What the hell is going on?" she asked once they were outside. Susskind told her he wanted some pizza. The request was unusual, as it was still morning and no die-hard New Yorker in his right mind would ask for pizza in Los Angeles during the 1980s. They wandered through the mall of shops and restaurants located below the ABC office building and found some. Once in the parking facility, Deknatel told Susskind that he was in no condition to drive and offered to take him back to the hotel. She would have his car picked up later. "He said okay," Deknatel recalled. "He gets in my car and we drive toward the exit." As the car approached the one-way traffic spikes on the ground surface of the parking lot, Susskind put his arms in front of his face and shouted for Deknatel to stop.

"David started to freak out," Deknatel said. "I said, 'What is the matter?' He said these spikes were coming out of the ground twenty feet tall and enclosing the car. I stopped the car and waited for him to calm down." Deknatel stepped out of the vehicle and went to find a pay phone to call Joyce Susskind, to alert her to what was happening. "I left her a message," she said. "I said, 'David is ill. I'm going to take him to the hotel. Just call me back.'" When Deknatel arrived back at the car, Susskind was asleep again. She got him back to his hotel room. When Joyce Susskind finally called Deknatel back, she said, "He's fine, don't worry about him."

But he was not fine. Back in New York, another Susskind Company employee had brought a young Nathan Lane up to the office to discuss some script treatments he had worked on with his writing partner. "His ideas were good so I said, 'Let me grab David while you're here,'" the former executive said. "Lane wanted to meet him. Most people wanted to meet him. And it was just a bad day. Poor Nathan did his song and dance and David was practically asleep on the couch. He just sat there completely stone-faced. I said, 'Omigod, how can I make this stop?' I just wrapped it up as fast as I could."

At one point, Deknatel wondered if Susskind was under the influence of drugs, which were flowing openly in the entertainment industry at the time. While Deknatel was at NBC in the late 1970s, one of the secretaries in the area where she worked at the network's Burbank office had measuring scales on her desk. Deknatel, a single mother with two young schoolaged children at the time, innocently asked what the scales were for. "My secretary told me the man she works for provides everybody with cocaine around here," she said.

Deknatel confronted Susskind and he admitted to her that he had been going to a "Dr. Feelgood" in New York who provided him with prescription drugs. Such doctors usually provided amphetamines such as Dexedrine and painkillers. Susskind was also on medication for other health problems. But his bizarre behavior—the expansive sociability, extreme mood swings, ravings and hallucinations—indicated that he was in the throes of something that went beyond any excessive pill popping. He suffered from bipolar disorder. "His doctor told him he had it," said his daughter Samantha.

Alcohol was prevalent throughout the marriage of David and Joyce Susskind and it had become particularly problematic during their last few years together. Samantha believed both her parents had developed drinking problems—her mother eventually went into an alcohol rehabilitation program and stopped drinking completely. By 1980 Joyce demanded that the family move to an apartment on Park Avenue, leaving behind the UN Plaza apartment that Susskind adored. "I think he felt very diminished by that," Andrew recalled. "I think that apartment represented a lot for him." Samantha also recalled her father's anger over the move. "When they split up, it was still coming up as an issue," she said. "He said, 'The one place I absolutely loved.' He would always bring it up."

The couple's arguments had escalated to the point that led to the late spring day in 1983 when Susskind packed a suitcase and moved into a suite at the Wyndham Hotel on West Fifty-eighth Street, where many show business types stayed for extended periods. Joyce Susskind filed for divorce that summer and hired Raoul Felder as her attorney. The separation sent Susskind into a deeper tailspin.

Susskind's bipolar condition affected his business decisions—he often described grandiose plans around the office. Andrew became alarmed after a dinner with his father in which he started going into delusional rants about forming a multibillion consortium to take over the entertainment industry.

"He'd say, 'I am Eisenhower—I am Napoleon,'" Andrew recalled. "'I told him, 'You are nuts. You need help.'"

Susskind had papers drawn up to be filed with the Securities Exchange Commission to take the Susskind Company public with shares traded on the stock exchange even though the MGM affiliation had ended and business had dropped off. He violated one of his own strongly held business precepts by investing his own money in a Broadway show. As a way to get a stake in the Nederlander Company's production of *La Cage aux Folles,* Susskind put $750,000 into Anthony Newley's musical based on the life of Charlie Chaplin. The project never made it to an opening night in New York. Susskind indulged in other wild personal spending, purchasing Rolls-Royce automobiles on his American Express card. He told staffers to look into purchasing a private jet that he could use for regular trips to London. He had gone into advanced negotiations for a new production agreement with Group W Productions, part of Westinghouse Broadcasting, which would have paid for the Susskind Company's overhead for the next three years. Ed Vane, who headed up Group W at the time, had thought it was virtually a done deal in June 1983 before he suddenly received new and more extravagant demands from Susskind. "He was irrational and very erratic in what he said," Vane recalled of their last telephone conversation on the matter. "It sounded to me as if he had been taking drugs." The deal was called off. Later that year, Susskind entered serious talks about spending more than $500,000 of his own personal funds to buy the Mermaid Theatre in London. He then caused a stir in Los Angeles when he was fired from a small acting role, playing himself on the ABC sitcom *Oh Madeline!* He had gone into a volcanic rage on the set of the show because he believed the director was treating him rudely.

Susskind started hiring people he met on the street, on an airplane, or, in the case of a woman named Marvlous Harrison, a restaurant. Harrison was out celebrating her fifty-first birthday with friends at an East Side bistro when Susskind sat down with her party. He invited her to come work for him. She said in a lawsuit that she showed up at Susskind's suite at the Wyndham Hotel the next day and took notes and phone messages for him. But when Harrison, who stood five feet tall and weighed two hundred pounds, showed up at the offices the following Monday, Susskind told her she could not have the job unless she lost some weight. Months later she filed a $500,000 breach-of-contract suit against him. Harrison's lawsuit was covered in the New York *Daily News,* one of the few incidents covered in the press that indicated that something was deeply amiss with Susskind. Employees at the Susskind Company said the random hirings happened with alarming regularity. "You'd come into the office the next morning and these strange faces would be sitting there," said Anita Grossberg, who rejoined Susskind as an assistant at his new company. "He hired them off the elevator. I would ask, 'David, who is that person?' 'Well, he's going to read scripts for me.' They didn't last, of course."

Other civilians were randomly pulled into Susskind's life as well. Around the same time as the hiring spree, Dr. Lewis Gordonson, an ophthalmologist from Great Neck, New York, was driving with his wife in a gray Buick sedan out of a parking facility and onto West Fifty-eighth Street in Manhattan. As he waited for people to pass before pulling onto the street, a man tapped on the window of the car. Gordonson recognized him as David Susskind. "You look like nice people," Susskind told them. Unable to get a cab, he asked for a ride over to the WNEW studio on East Sixty-seventh Street. Dr. Gordonson had never met Susskind before, but by coincidence, he had performed cataract surgery on his mother years earlier at Long Island Jewish Hospital. They made small talk as Susskind got in the backseat of the car.

While the vehicle sat in traffic, the Gordonsons chatted with Susskind about his mother and their own children. "Between the time he got in the car and Sixty-seventh Street, he had found out that my son worked for an electronics company and that the CEO of the company was separated from his wife," Dr. Gordonson recalled. "That our anniversary was coming up that weekend and that we had reservations for dinner in Manhattan for our anniversary. And he said to us, 'Here's what I'm going to do for you—I'm going to take you to the Four Seasons. I'm going to take you to a surprise and we're going to finish at the Algonquin.' So Saturday comes and we don't cancel our dinner reservation because he sounds crazy."

The couple took a chance and showed up at the Four Seasons restaurant and learned that Susskind would be meeting them there. "Yes, Mr. Susskind has called," they were told. "He'll be a little bit late. He wants us to seat you at the best table near the fountain." Susskind walked in ten minutes later with his divorced sister, Dorothy, and the chief executive officer of the company that Gordonson's son worked for. He had set them up as dates for the evening. "Can you imagine?" Dr. Gordonson said. "The CEO got this call—'This is David Susskind, what are you doing tonight?' " After dinner Susskind took them all to a small theater space where a play based on the life of Tallulah Bankhead was being showcased. "They were looking for investors," Dr. Gordonson explained. "In the audience were Eli Wallach and his wife. A couple of Rocke-fellers. After that we were at the Algonquin." The Gordonsons saw Susskind on a regular basis after that night.

Despite his erratic behavior, Susskind was somehow able to host his talk show every week. "Some days he would be perfectly fine and be the old David," said Dan Berkowitz. "Other days he would walk in with his head hanging down and shuffling. And then other days it would be like when the day he came in and he pointed at me and yelled, 'Get the pope on the phone. I want him on the show this week.' And you go, 'Oh-kaaay.'" Kennedy said she would have to put a call in and leave a message for such requests.

Before tapings, Jean Kennedy coached guests based on Susskind's moods. If he was morose, she'd tell them to jump in, keep talking, and not wait for his questions. If he was contentious and aggressive, she told them not to be afraid to push back. "It was basically preparing them for whatever was going to walk off the elevator," said Berkowitz. "If David came moping out, we'd go into the guests and say, 'We think he's probably going to be quiet today, so just re-member to keep talking. With very few exceptions, you wouldn't know that he was crazy."

"You had to make sure you took the camera off him at times," Kennedy said. "You'd try to save him from himself, and I guess we did to a certain ex-tent. It was a very difficult time. I would breathe a sigh of relief when we fin-ished taping. We'd get him to the station hoping he didn't go off on some tangent. It was not easy. He liked to think he was in charge. You had to be careful. People in that condition don't have any objectivity."

Before a show he taped in June 1983, Susskind informed his staff that he was discussing a topic that was so important he would not be pausing for com-mercial breaks. After Kennedy told him that would violate the contract with the show's originating station, WNEW, he said, "Just tell them to put them all at the end. I'm not going to stop." Once the taping began, he barreled through the discussion for ninety-six minutes straight. The interview was with the author of a book about tennis. It was perhaps the only time Susskind had ever been on television without a tie on.

Andrew Susskind was appalled when he saw the show on the air. His fa-ther's condition had started to put tremendous pressure on their professional and personal relationship. While working out of the West Coast office, he was often at the receiving end of Susskind's abusive phone calls from New York. "He started to treat me badly and had no respect for anything I said," Andrew recalled. "He just belittled me." Bills were going unpaid. Both Andrew Susskind and his sister Diana had been putting their father's name on shows they produced to protect his revered reputation. As the situation became worse, Diana summoned Andrew at the Los Angeles office to come to New York on short notice to join in an intervention. They intended to get their father some kind of psychiatric treatment. At some point Susskind had been prescribed lithium, but people who worked for him at the time said he often did not take it or consumed alcohol when he did. Andrew Susskind took a red-eye flight to New York and went straight to his father's suite at the Wyndham Hotel. When Andrew, Diana, and his oldest sister, Pamela, arrived at the door at 7:30 that morning, Susskind dismissed their concerns and angrily turned them away. "He was very smart," Andrew said. "I could see what would happen if we tried to take him before a judge. 'Your honor, I've spoiled them. They've lived a very comfortable life. They don't understand the rough-and-tumble of the real world. They worry for me because I have to make some investments.' What judge was going to commit David Susskind? It just wasn't going to happen."

Andrew Susskind theorized that his father resisted psychiatric treatment because of the anger and mistrust he felt over Ben Susskind's suicide. "I know it had to do with what he felt was a terrible betrayal of his own father," Andrew said. "When they said, 'Yes, you can take him home, he'll be all right,' and he wasn't." But David Susskind's condition was likely causing him to have suicidal thoughts as well, according to Dr. Gordonson.

The Gordonsons had been seeing Susskind regularly since their first night out at the Four Seasons and the Algonquin. "We were very excited," Dr. Gordonson said. "In retrospect, we asked ourselves what kind of person knocks on the window of a person's car? But at the time we were going with it. Now let's answer the question, Why does he want to be friends with me? What could I do for him? He asked me many times to supply him with drugs so he could kill himself."

Dr. Gordonson, who had worked in psychiatric wards, said the suicide discussions were another textbook symptom of Susskind's condition. "It was said in his manic phase," he recalled. "When he said, 'I want to kill myself,' the affect was all wrong. He was David. He would just bring it up. I never saw the deep depression." Dr. Gordonson never acted as Susskind's physician but urged his friend to get help.

Andrew Susskind never feared that his father would take his own life. But he was deeply concerned that Susskind was forever destroying his ability to work and create, the things that made him feel most alive. "I was worried that he would burn his personal and financial bridges," Andrew said. "Other than his children, I didn't see who would be there emotionally. I didn't think it would have been enough for him."

Eventually, Andrew Susskind decided he could no longer protect his father's image and had to think about his own future. "I couldn't influence him or control him in any way," he said. "I wasn't going to go down emotionally or professionally with it." In November 1983, he resigned from the Susskind Company.

"I didn't know what I was going to do or where I was going to go, but I thought, 'This is not healthy,'" Andrew said. "I hated coming in. I hated the decisions he was making. I couldn't influence him or control him in any way. He asked me not to go. He asked me to stay. But he wouldn't really own up to anything. I feel bad in retrospect only because he really wasn't well." After a few months, Andrew took a job with Norman Lear's production company in Los Angeles.

Susskind was out of control for much of 1983 and 1984. Business at the Susskind Company waned as he maniacally worked the phones to pitch projects based on his past successes. The notes from his meetings and phone logs of the period had him discussing new versions of *The Power and the Glory*, *The Moon and Sixpence,* and even *The Glass Menagerie,* which he had already produced twice. He attempted to relive his Khrushchev interview and proposed sitdowns with Soviet premiers Yuri Andropov and Konstantin Chernenko. He dictated letters to Viktor Sukhodrev with a request for him to interpret the meetings. In the letter, Susskind said, "I hope you remember me," even though the two men had been friends for years. Susskind asked old associates to join the Susskind Company and approached Howard Cosell, who had recently been dropped from his announcing job at ABC's *Monday Night Football,* about coming to work for him.

As the situation became dire, Diana enlisted Norman Lear to step in and implore her father to get help. By that time, Lear had cemented his status as a television industry legend, as the producer of many of the biggest comedy hits of the 1970s. He had begun a second career as a political activist and a Hollywood statesman, forming People for the American Way, which he set up as a response to the emergence of Christian conservatives. David Susskind had deep admiration for his cousin and proudly introduced his colleagues to him whenever he had the chance. Perhaps, the Susskind children believed, he was the one person who could get through to their father. "I knew he had great affection and respect for me," Lear said.

Dan Berkowitz remembers Lear walking into the Susskind Company headquarters at 650 Fifth Avenue. Wearing his signature porkpie hat, Lear went behind closed doors to confront David Susskind about his mental illness. According to Andrew Susskind, Lear told his father that he cared about him and asked him if he was aware of what he was doing to himself. Susskind sheepishly told him no. It was the first time he acknowledged the turbulent state of affairs he created.

There was a change in Susskind's condition after the meeting with Lear. By all accounts the extreme highs and lows he experienced had ended. He took steps to manage his illness. "He didn't crash-land," Andrew said. "But it wasn't a soft landing either. He spent most of his money. He hurt himself with a lot of business relationships and stuff. He exhausted himself."

28

David Susskind's struggle with bipolar disorder had cost him millions of dollars and greatly diminished his standing in the television industry. Word had gotten around about his erratic behavior, but there was little or no understanding of his actual condition. He had other health issues as well. By the end of 1984, he appeared fragile to those around him. At times he had trouble recognizing former colleagues he ran into on the street or in restaurants. "We handled him very carefully," said Rebecca Halbower, who was working on Susskind's talk show at the time. "He wasn't really steady on his feet." Halbower had to check with Jean Kennedy before giving him questions for his talk show. "She'd go, 'Why don't you wait an hour.' It had to be the perfect moment or he wouldn't be focused." Still, Susskind was able to perform every week. "In my eyes, once the cameras rolled, he always seemed very sharp," Halbower said. Sometimes Susskind could seem slightly addled on the program, only to come up with a disarmingly insightful question.

In 1985, Susskind interviewed a panel of pornographic film performers that included Samantha Fox. When the discussion turned to the panelists' personal lives, Fox told Susskind she wanted her boyfriend to get out of the porno business when she did.

"I didn't want him to be doing films and having sex with other people and me not," she said.

"Why didn't you become costars as a couple and become the Lunt and Fontanne of porno films?" Sussind asked.

Even in his enervated state, Susskind was seen with attractive women by his side at events around New York. "It always amazed me," said Jean Kennedy. "David was in rather bad shape then and women still wanted to go out with him. He was really quite ill." Kennedy guided him toward one woman in particular, the fashion model Carmen Dell'Orefice.

Carmen, as she was known professionally, had met Susskind when she appeared on a 1981 talk show he did on fashion models over age forty. The panel featured Carmen and her contemporaries, Kaylan Pickford and Lillian Marcuson, who were again getting work in print ads and magazine spreads. It was an acknowledgement that the generation of consumers who grew up in America's boom times was aging. "It was about older models not being thrown into the garbage," Carmen recalled. "I was just a spearhead for people acknowledging they may live longer than they think and you'd better plan for it."

Carmen had written a book called *Staying Beautiful,* and she certainly knew about the subject. More than thirty years after she first appeared on the cover of *Vogue* as a teenager, she still looked magnificent. With her creamy skin, high cheekbones, and lustrous hair the color of winter frost, she radiated elegance. She was the daughter of an Italian concert pianist and a Hungarian dancer. Her parents had separated when she was a small child and she grew up poor in Queens, New York, during the 1930s and 1940s. She started modeling as a teenager after a bout with rheumatic fever had cut short her studies as a ballet dancer. At age fourteen, she was earning $60 a day, enough money to cover a month's rent on the apartment she shared with her mother. By her early twenties, she was the highest-paid model in the world, earning as much as $2,500 a day for work in lingerie ads. She was featured in some of the most stunning editorial work of Richard Avedon and other prominent fashion photographers.

In the mid-1960s, Carmen's classic look gave way to a new generation of younger eye-catching models. The boyish Twiggy and the towering Veruschka became pop-culture phenomena. For Carmen, modeling had been a job. As the market changed, she supplemented her income with acting work, including a role in *The Last of the Secret Agents,* a feature film with Nancy Sinatra and the comedy team of Marty Allen and Steve Rossi. She became active as a model again during the late 1970s in Europe, where her age was less of an issue.

Carmen did not care for Susskind personally at the time she was first booked on his show. "I knew David maybe thirty years before, when he was married to Phyllis and had three children and was dating Nancy Berg, a very beautiful model," she said. "I detested the man's behavior. I did not have a lot of respect for him." But she was intent on pushing her book and building on her revitalized career.

After Susskind separated from his second wife, Joyce, he got to know Carmen because Jean Kennedy booked her as a guest several more times. "I fixed her up with him," said Kennedy. "I thought she was a lovely woman." Kennedy believed Carmen was the ideal companion for Susskind at the time. She had her own storied career, her own money (although later in life she lost her savings after investing with Bernard Madoff), and was completely at ease being around a public persona such as Susskind. "She was in the business of being seen," Kennedy said. "At that point, he needed someone who was sympathetic and nice and not competitive."

Over time, Carmen felt more comfortable with Susskind as they had cocktails or dinners at Bravo Gianni, Susskind's favorite Italian restaurant on the Upper East Side, a few blocks from the WNEW studios. It was a ritual that followed each taping of his show. Before she would date him, Carmen wanted assurances from Susskind that he was not using any drugs that might worsen the effects of his bipolar disorder. "He said, 'It can never happen again because I just stopped,'" she said. "I had such admiration for that because I had been through a lot in my life with past situations. I didn't have a physical affair with him until he proved to me that he was HIV clean. I said, 'You're such a swordsman. I haven't lived this long to be so ignominious to catch something like that from you.' That's how we talked. He loved it. And he said, 'That's all? Because I can do that easily.'"

After Susskind came out of his tailspin, he no longer had the resources to be the brash, risk-taking impresario he was before. "I think he woke up from a dream almost," Andrew Susskind recalled. "He had spent all his money. There were no friends around. There was my sister Diana and myself. He was kind of wonderful, in some ways nicer then he had ever been. He didn't have a lot of productions going on. He was just him. He was fun. He was likable."

Carmen saw that side of Susskind as well, dispelling all her preconceived notions about him. "For a man I attributed to being arrogant, I found out he was the most humble, curious, delightful, engaging, wonderful human being," she said. "Nobody could follow that act. It was interesting in my development to come together with David in my life at the time that I did. He was so open and he had golden ears. He processed information so quickly and saw peripherally. He had the biggest mind I'd ever come across. I'm sure there are bigger minds in the world. But you have to understand I was a little girl from Astoria, Woodside, Sunnyside, and Bayside. No schooling and an accidental life."

By 1986, they had become a couple, appearing around Manhattan at Susskind's favorite eateries and at movie and Broadway openings. With Carmen standing at six feet and Susskind, several inches shorter even with his thick white locks, they became a celebrity sighting that was hard to miss. They enjoyed walking together along Manhattan streets and seeing which one of them passersby would notice first. "You could tell he was happy," said Susskind's daughter Samantha. "I think he really was. I think she was good for him."

Being involved in Susskind's life meant being involved in his work. Soon he was giving Carmen scripts to read, looking for an opinion. Carmen was self-conscious about it at first. She never got past the eighth grade in school and had astigmatism. "I told him I'm a really bad reader," she said. "And he said, 'You'll understand it. You don't have to be a good reader. Reading isn't just reading, it's visualizing.' He just had a way of making me feel comfortable about my intellect. Ultimately he showed me how well I do read and how well I do perceive things."

IN EARLY 1986, Susskind was reenergized enough to put together a programming deal that was worthy of his best. General Dynamics, the largest defense contractor in the United States, had seen spectacular growth after President Ronald Reagan took office in 1981. The military buildup under the Reagan administration called for enough nuclear submarines, fighter planes, and M-1 tanks to lift the company's profits 33 percent in 1984, to $382 million.

But by the spring of 1985, the public's perception of General Dynamics had been greatly tarnished. Congressional investigations had revealed the company was billing the government for dog kennel, country club, and babysitting expenses for its executives. There were suspicions of overcharges for labor costs and massive cost overruns on projects. General Dynamics found itself in the center of news stories that said the Pentagon was being charged $600 for a toilet seat and $500 for a hammer. The Defense Department stopped its contractual payments to the company until it could get its auditing procedures under control.

"They just said we're not going to send you any more money," said Chuck DeMund, a longtime executive for General Dynamics. "So we had 120,000 people waiting for a paycheck and the primary customer wasn't paying the bills. It didn't last very long. But it sure as hell got everybody's attention."

DeMund spent most of his career in the company's aerospace division in San Diego. "I worked in the motion picture and television department," he said. "Every quarter we had to make film reports on government contracts to show to congressmen who were too dumb to read any of this stuff." As the public relations crisis escalated, he was called into the company's St. Louis headquarters to help with the television end of an image-rebuilding campaign. "What we were trying to do was just to appear to be a fine upstanding good American company that made fine good wonderful products that kept the world free," he said. "We undertook a number of things to shine up the company's image and make us smell better. David had somehow gotten to the company with a proposal to do some PBS specials, and that's all anybody knew. So they asked me to go over to New York and make an appointment and find out what he was talking about."

With the assistance of his daughter Diana, David Susskind had approached General Dynamics' public relations chief Fred J. Bettinger about a series of one-man shows for PBS. They would feature actors portraying historical figures who reflect on their achievements and the challenges of their times. Susskind already had one program set up at PBS, with British actor Robert Hardy playing Winston Churchill, and a script done for another on Dwight Eisenhower. But he needed a corporate underwriter to finance the productions. It was almost a throwback to his halcyon days of the 1950s when he had to scout out advertisers to help make a network TV project happen. Susskind told Bettinger the PBS programs could earn accolades and make amends with a public that viewed General Dynamics as a poster child for government waste and the abuse of taxpayer dollars.

DeMund had approached his first meeting with Susskind with trepidation. He had worked in local television during the 1950s and still remembered Susskind's reputation as a firebrand. A lot had changed. "I went to his office, sat in a waiting room, and pretty soon this wonderful little man came out with a great head of white hair and we started to talk," he said. Susskind did not have any cachet among the newest generation of network executives in New York and Hollywood. But his name still had the patina of quality and he had not lost the ability to charm and sell. DeMund returned to his bosses in St. Louis and recommended they make the deal to underwrite Susskind's shows. "We didn't shop around," he said. "I said, 'It sounds like a wonderful idea, and he sounds like the right guy to do it.' We signed a contract for the first couple of programs. We paid about a million bucks each for those programs, which was a lot of money."

As they worked together, the two men became friends. During his visits to New York, DeMund was clearly dazzled by how Susskind was received in the city he loved. "I guess I might say everybody knew him," DeMund said. "It was astonishing. Cab drivers. Waiters. I mean, you didn't wait for a table. You didn't make a reservation. You just went, and things would just work beautifully. It was remarkable." But DeMund noted that Susskind made no pretense of being at the top of his game and spoke honestly about the difficulties he experienced in recent years. "I think the money was welcome," DeMund said. "He didn't make any bones about it. He didn't speak much of his past achievements, other than in passing. He would say, 'Yes, I worked with so-and-so' or 'We were in this place doing that,' but he didn't read off the list of his Broadway shows or go on about *Death of a Salesman*. We just talked about what we were going to do. I think he was pleased that somebody was willing to pay for the kind of quality he insisted on turning out. I don't think the guy could have done a shabby piece of work."

The shows for General Dynamics were well executed but not extravagant. Ben Edwards, the acclaimed scenic designer who had worked on many of Susskind's films and TV movies, oversaw the look of the productions with his typically refined touch. The Churchill program, a re-creation of a lecture that the prime minister gave in 1946 during a tour of the United States, was done on a single set. "David didn't throw money around," DeMund recalled. "So we taped that before a live audience in Toronto in a TV studio that was set up with a stage. Robert Hardy did it live with four cameras and one intermission. He memorized the entire thing. Not a teleprompter in the room." The second show, *Ike,* starred E. G. Marshall as Dwight Eisenhower and was also understated in its approach. Shot on location at the Wright Brothers farm in Gettysburg, it presented a retired Eisenhower being interviewed by a young student played by daytime soap actress Alice Haining.

While there were no commercials on public broadcasting programs, the rules regarding corporate underwriting messages had loosened considerably by the mid-1980s. Each of Susskind's productions opened and closed with an on-screen scroll that said: "This portrayal of one man's courage and leadership was made possible by a grant from General Dynamics" and used the company's logo. The association was as clear as any sponsored show.

While Susskind had a history of doing battle with networks and sponsors, he was overly cautious about alienating his new benefactor. "David, in his attempt not to step on anybody's toes, left out any reference to the military industrial complex in the *Ike* program—thoughts that Ike had expressed on a number of occasions," said DeMund, "because David's customer *was* the complex."

Stanley Pace, the recently installed chairman of General Dynamics, wouldn't stand for it. The former army colonel and top executive at TRW had been brought in at the urging of the Defense Department and the investment community to help restore the public's trust. He was not about to put the General Dynamics name on a program that overlooked Eisenhower's stated uneasiness about the growing political influence of the military establishment. After viewing *Ike,* he asked DeMund why the issue was not addressed.

"He said it should be in there," DeMund said.

DeMund called Susskind, who told him it had been taken out of the script.

"Well, David," DeMund said. "How much is it going to cost to put it back in?"

The filming of *Ike* had been completed for months. The final cut was done. Pace did not care. "He was very angry and upset," DeMund said. "I've probably come as close to losing my job over that as anything I ever did." Instead of returning to Gettysburg, Susskind and DeMund found a farmhouse near E. G. Marshall's home in northern Westchester and shot an additional scene, which was tacked on to the end of the show. They split the $100,000 cost of shooting it. The executives at General Dynamics were happy with what Susskind delivered and bought two more programs, *Lyndon Johnson* and *I Would Be Called John,* about Pope John XXIII.

Lyndon Johnson was a play by James Prideaux; it was based on Merle Miller's book *Lyndon* and had been presented on stage. For his PBS version, Susskind cast Laurence Luckinbill, who portrayed the rowdy but conflicted president with relentless gusto. The play became a signature piece that the actor played on stage for years afterward. (The head of the Johnson presidential library was quoted as saying Luckinbill "is L.B.J.") Making Luckinbill even more convincing was the work of makeup artist Kevin Haney, who authentically re-created Johnson's outsized ears and nose. Haney brought the same prosthetic wizardry to *Winston Churchill*. He spent two and half hours molding Hardy's face before each taped performance. His mentor, Dick Smith, an innovator in stage and film makeup who worked on many Talent Associates productions in the 1950s and 1960s, had recommended Haney to Susskind. Haney's artistry on the Susskind productions took his career to a new level as he went on to become one of the top special-effects makeup artists in movies and television. "I was relatively untested," said Haney, who won an Academy Award in 1990 for his work on *Driving Miss Daisy*. "I just got a lot of acclaim for the shows. They were very well written and well produced." Haney was well acquainted with Susskind's legacy through Smith. At the time he worked on *Winston Churchill* and *Lyndon Johnson,* he was not aware that the shows were a comeback for the producer. The Susskind he saw in 1986 was a powerful presence who elevated the performance of everyone involved in the projects. "He was very discerning," Haney said. "He knew how to get people to do their jobs. When he talked about what he wanted do and what needed to be done, there was conviction. There was a total authority." Haney believed the shows could not have been done as well, or perhaps at all, without him. Writer Eugene Kennedy, who wrote the Pope John play, remembered watching Susskind in the control room when his show was taped in Toronto. "It was like watching a symphony conductor," he recalled. "He was a graceful presence who was very pointed in the use of his baton. He made you feel that he was inside this production and really feeling along with it and seeing it from every viewpoint of his experience. That's the impression that he made on me."

IN SEPTEMBER 1986, *The David Susskind Show* aired on WNEW for the final time. The station, now owned by Rupert Murdoch's Fox Broadcasting, had moved the program out of its longtime Sunday night perch to one o'clock in the morning. The twenty-eight-year run of the program ended without fanfare. Susskind, feeling ebullient over the success of the PBS shows, quickly moved on. "There was no sense of sadness about the talk show being over," said Halbower. "He had big ideas and had money for some shows. He was trying to get funding, trying to come up with a million ideas." In the small bubble that was the Susskind Company, there was a feeling that he was back. Susskind and Carmen had traveled to London and met with Anthony Hopkins about his starring in a film project Susskind was interested in producing.

Susskind's talk show had ended, but he never stopped keeping up with the world outside of show business. Carmen recalled a trip they took to Baden-Baden in the Black Forest of Germany. They had taken two suites at the Brenner's Park Hotel. "We were together, but it was the old-fashioned thing to do," she recalled. "I traveled with one suitcase and he had three. He said, 'Is that all you're taking?' I said we're only there for ten days or whatever it was. I went to his room to see if I could help him unpack. His smallest suitcase had a couple of white shirts, a couple of navy blue ties, and another dark suit. The two other suitcases were filled with *The New York Times* and books. It was unbelievable. It was so funny. I said, 'No scripts? Only newspapers.' 'Well, I've been reading all these scripts and I have to catch up.' I said, 'Well, okay, let me know when you want to have dinner.'"

Not long after that trip, on February 20, 1987, Susskind had visited with his cardiologist. That day he had complained of being tired. According to Carmen, Susskind insisted to his doctor that he felt well enough to go home for the weekend and have an electrocardiogram at the hospital on Monday. It was possible he was going to need an angioplasty, or even bypass surgery. He had been taking medication for his heart, and in October 1986 he had been briefly hospitalized in Toronto during the making of *I Would Be Called John*.

Carmen cooked dinner for him at her Park Avenue apartment that Saturday night. They were up late talking. But Susskind said he needed to go back to his suite at the Wyndham Hotel. Andrew was to call him from California that Sunday morning at 10:30 a.m. "He's calling me on my private line and it's business," he said. "I've got to be there." Carmen escorted him out. "He got into the cab and he kind of put his butt in first and sat down hard and pulled his legs in," she recalled. "Then he pulled me in and gave me a big smooch. He said, 'I'll talk to you first thing in the morning.' 'You really are crazy,' I told him. 'Go home.'"

When Carmen hadn't heard from the always punctual Susskind by 11:00 a.m. on the morning of February 22, she knew something was wrong. She immediately contacted John Mados, the owner of the Wyndham, and asked him to have someone go to Susskind's room to check up on him. The door was opened and Susskind was found undressed on the floor, lying on his back. The tiny white nitroglycerin tablets he was taking for his heart were spilled all around him. Mados called Carmen back.

"Carmen, I'm sorry to tell you that you were right," he said. "Get right over here."

"I put on a pair of pants and a sweater with no underwear, threw on a fur coat, and ran downstairs," Carmen recalled. "Well, if that took three minutes it was a long time. When I got downstairs my doorman said, 'Oh, Miss Carmen, I am so sorry.' I said, 'Sorry about what?'" The doorman had been tuned into a police radio and heard the call come in that said David Susskind was dead. He had suffered a heart attack.

"When they saw me rush out they knew it was true," Carmen said. "That was really startling to me."

Carmen arrived at Susskind's hotel suite and the police where there shortly afterward. As she gathered Susskind's valuables for safekeeping, his sister Dorothy came through the door. "She threw herself on her brother's body and just lay there sobbing," Carmen said. "She adored him and he knew that. It was very tough on her. It was tough on all of us."

Earlier in the day, Andy Warhol had died after suffering a heart attack in his sleep that morning at the New York Hospital–Cornell Medical Center. The artist had undergone routine gallbladder surgery the day before. Carmen said right before she left the Wyndham, she learned that Warhol was in the morgue station wagon that came to take away Susskind's body. "David would have loved that," she said. The obituaries of the two men, who both had a profound understanding of the power of celebrity culture that kept them in the public eye for decades, shared the front page of *The New York Times* the following day.

Epilogue

The shows that the Susskind Company had in production at the time of David Susskind's death were eventually completed and shown by 1988. The very last program out of the company was a documentary called *JFK—A Time Remembered,* made up of filmed reminiscences of the day President Kennedy was assassinated, on November 22, 1963. It was one of many specials aired to commemorate the twenty-fifth anniversary of one of the darkest days in U.S. history. Susskind had conducted numerous interviews for the project in the years before he died. One of them, which did not make the final program, was with Johnny Carson at his house in Malibu in September 1983.

Carson had been hosting *The Tonight Show* for twenty-one years at the time. He had become a television deity who rarely gave interviews. Whatever he had to say about current events or his own life was dispensed during his late-night TV show. But Susskind was an old pal and UN Plaza neighbor for whom Carson had genuine affection. During the chat, Carson was friendly but distant. He refused to answer any question that would appear to be a political opinion, even gently halting the camera crew several times.

As Carson was cool, Susskind was emotionally molten, his eyes glistening as if he were going to cry. Carson seemed unsure what to make of him, likely unaware that Susskind was in the middle of his year of manic hell. Susskind brought up the topic of astrology, and Kennedy's astrological sign, Gemini, in particular. "David Steinberg once said he found it difficult to believe in astrology when he found out that Hitler and Sandy Duncan were born on the same day," Carson quipped, making a humorous attempt to get off the subject. "Didn't seem compatible."

Susskind barreled ahead, raising the issue of the marital infidelities of Kennedy and other presidents. "What does that say about a man?" Susskind asked. Carson carefully replied that it showed they were human. "People, I guess, tend to forgive certain things, when people are bigger than life," he said. "They kind of accept them." Susskind wondered aloud whether both he and Carson would be accorded that level of forgiveness in remembrance. "If someday long after our deaths and the deaths of our immediate loved ones it will reveal more that he admired women. . . . What would that say? Is he any less gifted? Any less of a legend, and less than a great American? . . . It means they hurt, that they're human. And God forgives him, so man and woman should forgive him, don't you think? Bible says turn the other cheek. Treat another human as you would wish to be treated."

"You would have made a great rabbi, David," Carson said.

SUSSKIND WAS THE FIERY life force that kept the Susskind Company going, and once he was gone, it was dissolved as an ongoing concern. "To me it was a sad way to end the whole chapter," said Rebecca Halbower, who Susskind had been training as a producer during the final year of his life. "It was there and it just sort of evaporated. Everyone just sort of dispersed. It was this world and then it completely disappeared. We had a little family there in a way. I saw Carmen a lot. I saw Diana. Then it was just gone."

When Susskind's estate was settled, he left $2.3 million to his children Andrew, Pamela, Diana, and Samantha, thanks in large part to the last few productions he made for General Dynamics. The amount was not insubstantial by 1987 standards, but not the kind of fortune one would expect from a man who spent much of his life as a show business impresario. Andrew Susskind never returned to his father's company after leaving in the spring of 1984, and went on to have some success on his own as an executive, director, and independent producer in television. Much of his work was in sitcoms, a genre his father generally dismissed. But while Andrew was the head of comedy development at Embassy Television he oversaw the creation of *Married . . . with Children.* The edgy and often raunchy show was designed to break every rule of the sentimental family sitcoms that proliferated in the 1980s after *The Cosby Show,* and it became the first successful series for the then fledgling Fox network. David Susskind would have fully appreciated how *Married . . . with Children* became a much bigger hit after an irate Michigan housewife tried to lead an advertiser boycott of the show. As of 2010, Andrew Susskind was teaching television at Drexel University in Philadelphia. Samantha Susskind Mannion eventually became a lawyer and was recently teaching criminal justice at Housatonic Community College in Connecticut. She shows clips of her father's last movie, *Fort Apache, The Bronx,* to students to illustrate dilemmas in police work. Her mother, Joyce Davidson Susskind, whose divorce from David Susskind was final in 1986, eventually moved back to Toronto, where she still gets recognized on the street by viewers who grew up watching her.

ON MARCH 23, 1987, a public memorial service for Susskind was held at the Metropolitan Museum of Art's Grace Rainey Rogers Auditorium. The encomiums delivered about him that day from Jack Valenti, Mike Wallace, Norman Lear, Colleen Dewhurst, and the writer Eugene Kennedy all conveyed the image of Susskind as the risk-taking iconoclast who tried to elevate television. "Always dangerous," Dewhurst said in her smoky alto. As a man, Susskind was harder to define. "I couldn't be sure how well I knew him," said Lear. Susskind shared his time, his means, his information, but really not much of himself, his cousin noted. Lear believed Susskind was best defined by his work and his choices. He spent several minutes reading a list of his production credits to the audience.

Andrew Susskind had eulogized his father as "the person I loved most in all the world." The toughness and the relentless commitment to exacting standards could not be ignored. At Susskind's induction into the Television Academy Hall of Fame in 1988, Andrew told a story about how his father had described a film they had seen as an embarrassment. Andrew was less harsh in his view. He deemed the work mediocre. The discussion came to an abrupt halt, Andrew said, when his father declared, "Mediocrity is an embarrassment."

But David Susskind could experience joy from seeing his creative vision take shape. Actor Ed Herrmann remembered how he had long kept a photograph taken on a Los Angeles soundstage during the 1976 shooting of *Eleanor and Franklin: The White House Years*. It was on a set that depicted an old Pullman train car, elevated about a foot above the floor of the stage. The photo showed Susskind on his tiptoes outside of the set and looking into the window of the re-created Pullman. "It was dark around him and there were lights inside," Herrmann said. "So all you saw was the corner of the window and the shade half down. The light was hitting his face and he looked like a kid looking at a window at Christmastime. He looked about twelve years old, I mean it was really beautiful."

Herrmann eventually sent the photo to Susskind with a note that read, "I found this and it says everything about the project, how excited we were and how wonderful you were."

"That's the way I remember David," Herrmann said. "That isn't the way he's remembered by a lot of people."

Notes

All quotations in *David Susskind: A Televised Life* are from interviews with the author for the book unless noted in the text or the source notes. The following people were interviewed in person, on the telephone, or in e-mail exchanges between May 2006 and May 2010:

Michael Abbott
Edward Albee
Burt Armus
Victor Arnold
Larry Arrick
Jane Aurthur
Irene Balsam
Martin Baum
Reza Badiyi
Alan Bell
Buzz Berger
Maureen (Hesselroth)
   Berger
Dan Berkowitz
Walter Bernstein
Gerry Bewkes
Terry Lee Bilsky
Steve Binder
Herb Bloom
Paul Bogart
Raysa Bonow
Mel Brooks
Susan Brownmiller
Ellen Burstyn
Michael Campus
Barbara Carney
Jacqueline Ceballos

Gill Champion
Bill Chastain
Lionel Chetwynd
Constance Christopher
Nicholas Christopher
Larry Cohen
Lawrence D. Cohen
Clay Cole
Ruth Conforte
Christina Conrad
Jay Cooper
Jerome Coopersmith
Madeline Coubro
Judy Crichton
Michael Dann
John Dean
Jane Deknatel
Carmen Dell'Orefice
Chuck DeMund
Dick Dorso
Jane Everhart
Barbara Feldon
Sy Fischer
Arthur Forrest
Sonny Fox
Don Francks
Michael Fuchs

Jill Spoon Gelbach
Larry Gelbart
Ed Gelsthorpe
Robert Getchell
Ron Gilbert
Anita Gillette
David Z. Goodman
Louis Gossett Jr.
Heywood Gould
Lee Grant
Dan Greenburg
Anita Grossberg
Rebecca Halbower
Pete Hamill
Kevin Haney
Rosemary Harris
Richard Heffner
Buck Henry
Stan Herman
Ed Herrmann
Alan Hirschfield
Roger Hirson
Rupert Hitzig
Robert Hooks
Barbara Howar
Nessa Hyams
Sal Ianucci

Bob Israel
Patricia Jaffe
Kenny Jackson
Lucy Jarvis
James Earl Jones
Eugene Kennedy
Jean Kennedy
Diane Kerew
Don Ray King
Emily Perl Kingsley
Ted Kotcheff
Don Kranze
Sergei Khrushchev
Verity Lambert
Edythe Landau
Eddie Lawrence
Norman Lear
Jerry Leider
Anthony Loeb
Jane Maas
Loring Mandel
Samantha Mannion
Bob Markell
Frank Marshall
Tony Marshall
Margaret Matheson
Daniel Melnick
Arthur Mercante

Jon Merdin
Marc Merson
Newton Minow
Pat Mitchell
Stan Moger
Alan Morris
Tony Musante
Pat Nardo
Elaine Noble
Paul Noble
Marc Norman
France Nuyen
David Padwa
Bruce Paisner
Fred Papert
Dorthea Petrie
Gloria Rabinowitz
Bob Rafelson
Muriel Reis
Anne Marie Riccitelli
David Rothenberg
Albert Ruben
Lynn Sackler
Molly Sackler
Marlene Sanders
Jay Sandrich
Arnold Scaasi
Daniel Schorr

Jinny Schreckinger
Barbara Schultz
Shel Secunda
George Segal
Jim Shasky
Alan Shayne
Rose Tobias Shaw
Harry Sherman
Shelley Stallworth
David Steinberg
Leonard Stern
Sandy Stewart
Larry Strichman
Viktor Sukhodrev
Andrew Susskind
Sam Szurek
Sheila Tronn
Cicely Tyson
Renée Valente
William vanden Heuvel
Ed Vane
Gore Vidal
Mike Wallace
Dale Wasserman
George C. White
Gene Wilder
Jack Willis
Elizabeth Wilson

Video research copies of *Open End* and *The David Susskind Show* were purchased from Historic Films, which licenses the programs. Audio copies and program transcripts were provided by the Wisconsin Center for Film and Theater Research in Madison, Wisconsin (cited as WCFTR), and the Hoover Institution at Stanford University. Videos of programs were also viewed at the Paley Center for Media in New York and Beverly Hills, the Museum of Broadcast Communications in Chicago, UCLA Film and Television Archive in Los Angeles, and WCFTR. A number of audio and video recordings of programs cited are from the author's private collection.

The taping and air dates for the Susskind talk shows mentioned in the text and notes are based on a list provided by Andrew Susskind and published television listings.

A number of quotes throughout the book are from David Susskind's testimony before the Federal Communications Commission on June 21, 1961. They are cited in the source notes as "David Susskind to FCC." Quotes from testimony that Susskind gave regarding his career in a deposition for the federal court cases *United States of America v. American Broadcasting Company* and *United States of America v. CBS, Inc.* on May 23 and 29, 1979, are cited as "David Susskind deposition." The transcripts, along with David Susskind's personal papers and correspondence, are located at the Wisconsin Center for Film and Theater Research.

Quotes from David Susskind's April 27, 1962, courtroom testimony at the trial of *Faulk v. AWARE* are from transcripts that appear in John Henry Faulk's book *Fear On Trial* (Simon & Schuster, 1964) and *The Age of McCarthyism: A Brief History, with Documents* by Ellen Schrecker (Bedford Books, 1994).

An audio recording of David Susskind's memorial service, held on March 23, 1987, was provided by a Susskind family friend.

All documents cited in the source notes were located in the David Susskind Papers stored at WCFTR unless otherwise noted.

PROLOGUE

On the evening of October 10: *The David Susskind Show,* October 10, 1982, Historic Films.

covering the losses out of his own pocket: A May 1982 letter soliciting contributions to PBS stations said: "David Susskind draws no salary from the program and in fact makes up annual deficits from his personal funds."

Yet he still managed to be impishly funny: *The David Susskind Show,* October 17, 1982, Historic Films.

Norman Mailer told the story: Norman Mailer, *Pieces and Pontifications* (Boston: Little, Brown, 1982), 38–43.

The reels were regularly degaussed: Undated memo listing *Open End* programs "marked for degaussing," circa 1960.

CHAPTER 1

David Susskind was dressed: Dick Dorso to Stephen Battaglio, personal communication.

"a bankrupt Dana Andrews": *The David Susskind Show,* March 30, 1968, WCFTR.

he never experienced anti-Semitism: *The David Susskind Show,* June 22, 1986, Historic Films.

When he was thirteen years old: Diane Leonetti, "The Multiple Lives of David Susskind," *New York Post,* April 26, 1959.

Mercury Players came through town: Bernice Yaffe Dworet letter to David Susskind, May 20, 1975.

"the antithesis of Father": Leonetti, "The Multiple Lives of David Susskind."

The newspapers nicknamed him "the Nylon Bandit": "Nab Nylon Bandit," *Daily Mail* (Hagerstown, MD), April 16, 1946.

having to learn Shakespeare: Ibid.

A doctor who performed cataract surgery: Lewis Gordonson to Stephen Battaglio, personal communication.

"college, fame and fortune": *The Murivan,* Brookline High School yearbook, 1938.

"I guess what I was seeking": Leonetti, "The Multiple Lives of David Susskind."

"I would hold up a card": *The David Susskind Show,* November 18, 1979, Historic Films.

"It seemed that all the wounded": Joseph H. Alexander, "Not All Flaming Spectacle for David Susskind," *Naval History,* January–February 1997.

"You can't do this kind of work": Thomas Bruce Morgan, *Self-Creations: 13 Impersonalities* (New York: Holt, Rinehart & Winston, 1965), 156.

"I hated it": Ibid., 157.

He chain-smoked cigars: Bob Israel to Stephen Battaglio, personal communication.

"Paddy came in and said": *Open End,* November 11, 1958, transcript in *Film Culture* 19 (1959): 18–45.

"Nobody knew what they were doing": Lumet to Robert Osborne on Turner Classic Movies, October 11, 2005.

The agency's New York office: Shel Secunda to Stephen Battaglio, personal communication.

"eager undertakers": Walter Bernstein to Stephen Battaglio, personal communication.

"I was known as the egghead": David Susskind, "David and the Goliaths Part 1," *Show Business Illustrated,* January 2, 1962.

"Listen," he told Lear: Norman Lear, speaking at David Susskind memorial service, March 23, 1987.

Susskind was told to go to Colgate's ad agency: Susskind, "David and the Goliaths Part 1."

"None. I have no suppressed desires": *The Murivan.*

But it became widely known: Renée Valente, Andrew Susskind, et al. recounted the circumstances of the David Susskind firing to Stephen Battaglio, personal communication.

On the morning of June 30, 1951: Medical examiner's certificate of death filed at Brookline Town Hall.

CHAPTER 2

"They counted all the television sets": *Open End,* November 11, 1958.

Within ten days, Mosel: *Ernie Barger Is 50,* viewed at Paley Center for Media.

Mosel delivered a second: *Other People's Houses,* viewed at UCLA Television Archive.

congratulating him on the fill-in work: Fred Coe telegram to David Susskind, August 30, 1953.

"almost had a heart attack": Transcript of *The David Susskind Show,* April 8, 1973, viewed at Wisconsin Historical Society.

Most of the angry calls: Sidney Poitier, *The Measure of a Man: A Spiritual Autobiography* (San Francisco: HarperSanFrancisco, 2000), 93.

Susskind secured the train yards: unpublished article by Robert Alan Aurthur.

Hoover declined the invitation: David Susskind FBI file, August 10, 1954.

Susskind said he pressured: John Henry Faulk trial testimony.

"May I close": David Susskind letter to David Levy, February 28, 1956.

In December 1954, Kim Stanley was cast: Mary Cummings letter to David Susskind, January 11, 1955.

"The protagonist": Robert L. Foreman, "Me, David Susskind and the Greatest Man in the World," *Esquire,* September 1967.

Talent Associates would be an in-house supplier: David Susskind memo to NBC, 1956.

After a few months of planning: draft of DuPont Show pitch notes, December 4, 1956.

"All of them were true": Walter Bernstein, *Inside Out: A Memoir of the Blacklist* (New York: Da Capo Press, 2000), 26.

"People would respond to his mere presence": Unpublished interview with Mary Ann Watson, November 9, 1992.

Susskind became a lover of London theater: Rose Tobias to Stephen Battaglio, personal communication.

In 1957, he enlisted: *Pinocchio,* viewed at New York Public Library for the Performing Arts.

Foreman claimed: Bob Foreman, "Inside of a Whale with David Susskind," *TV Guide,* December 8, 1962.

calling it "a world of lotus blossoms": Bob Stahl, "*Studio One* Goes West," *TV Guide,* December 28, 1957.

"Live television enlisted the kind of man": David Susskind testimony to FCC, June 21, 1961.

A few years after Andrew was born: Albert B. Ashworth Inc. Real Estate letter to David Susskind, July 27, 1956.

The apartment was described: Agnes Murphy, "At Home with . . . Mrs. David Susskind," *New York Post,* November 13, 1960.

"I tell her this is not a job": "TV's Unreconstructed Rebel: Producer David Susskind Operates with a High Resolve and a Low Boiling Point," *TV Guide,* August 16, 1958.

He maintained that he wanted to do: David Susskind to FCC.

He was unable to sell the show: Ibid.

"I was told artists are kooks": Ibid.

As the taping day approached: Reneé Valente to Stephen Battaglio, personal communication.

"I want happy shows": David Susskind to FCC.

CHAPTER 3

"I think actually it is too flippant": transcript of *The Open Mind,* WRCA-TV, October 20, 1957, provided by Richard Heffner.

the deflowering of a young Barbara Walters: Barbara Walters, *Audition: A Memoir* (New York: Alfred J. Knopf, 2008), 73.

They packaged the movies: Edythe Landau to Stephen Battaglio, personal communication.

As Susskind told it, his show opened: *The David Susskind Show,* October 10, 1982.

Susskind rolled his eyes: Ibid.

they literally walked onto the *Open End* set: clip shown on *The David Susskind Show,* October 10, 1982.

CHAPTER 4

"David did not have a hesitation": Ethel Winant interview with Sunny Parich, viewed online in the Archive of American Television.

There was also generally a limit: Molly Sackler to Stephen Battaglio, personal communication.

"It's been said you hire them": Mike Wallace interview with David Susskind, April 28, 1959, viewed at UCLA Film and Television Archive.

She was involved in the Lexington Democratic Club: Sal Ianucci to Stephen Battaglio, personal communication.

One producer who worked for Susskind: Barbara Carney to Stephen Battaglio, personal communication.

CHAPTER 5

"We are not fettered": David Susskind to Nixon, *Open End*, May 15, 1960, Hoover Institution at Stanford University.

"Since he conducts his own *Open End*": David Susskind letter to Nat Kahn, November 28, 1959.

Susskind . . . immediately wrote to the Soviet embassy: David Susskind recounted this story to Jerry Williams on WBBM radio on September 1, 1965, private collection.

"Here? Now?": Ibid.

Once Khrushchev agreed to appear: "Reminiscences of Ted Cott" (December 1960), Columbia University Oral History Research Office Collection, 186–216.

The two sides bargained: Ibid.

The office was deluged: David Susskind, "David and the Goliaths Part 3," *Show Business Illustrated,* February 1962.

"What do our files show on Susskind?": David Susskind FBI file.

"I don't think you should go through with it": Susskind, "David and the Goliaths Part 3."

"The protests and heated warnings": David Susskind, *The David Susskind Show,* November 27, 1977, Historic Films.

"This is a free country": Ibid.

"Dad, whatever you do": Ibid.

Through Sukhodrev's interpreting: Nikita Sergeyevich Khrushchev, *Khrushchev in New York: A Documentary Record of Nikita S. Khrushchev's Trip to New York, September 19th to October 13th, 1960, Including All His Speeches and Proposals to the United Nations and Major Addresses and News Conferences* (New York: Crosscurrents, 1960), 161–162.

"You are afraid of communism": Ibid., 177–181.

It was common for stations: *Open End,* October 9, 1960, viewed at Paley Center for Media.

"like an unwilling virgin": *The David Susskind Show,* October 10, 1982.

taping a sign to Susskind's door: Barbara Carney to Stephen Battaglio, personal communication.

"All of us who did interviews": David Susskind memorial service.

For years, Susskind chastised himself: *The David Susskind Show,* November 27, 1977.

CHAPTER 6

he was offered a job at MGM: Martin Baum to Stephen Battaglio, personal communication.

Negro schoolbooks: Sam Briskin and Arthur Kramer, notes to David Susskind.

Columbia would not let Susskind use location footage: Dorthea Petrie to Stephen Battaglio, personal communication.

only able to book 2,187 play dates: Charles S. Aaronson, "'Dare a Little,' Susskind's Plea to Exhibitors," *Motion Picture Herald,* January 24, 1962.

He recruited many of the real-life boxers: Arthur Mercante to Stephen Battaglio, personal communication.

Off camera, Ali charmed the cast and crew: Madeline Coubro to Stephen Battaglio, personal communication.

Even the usually prickly Gleason: Arthur Mercante and Phil Guarnieri, *Inside the Ropes* (Ithaca, NY: McBooks Press, 2006), 64.

Gleason was once so frustrated: David Susskind, *The David Susskind Show,* October 17, 1982.

Susskind sent a frantic telegram: David Susskind telegram to Hugh Hefner, November 18, 1961.

"You can only come off": Heffner letter to David Susskind, November 28, 1961.

"They barely qualify as actors": Jim Morse, "TV's Perennial 'Mad' Man," *TV-Radio Mirror,* April 1961.

"I never met Mr. Susskind": "Curtis Threatens to Slug Susskind," UPI, September 6, 1960.

The show was to be made with a television budget: David Susskind letter to Balaban.

drove the actual cost to $1.2 million: budget estimates on *The Power and the Glory,* October 10, 1961.

"I am beginning to get a thrill": Weltner letter to David Susskind, May 17, 1961.

Olivier was relaxed and playful: Michael Abbott and Renée Valente to Stephen Battaglio, personal communication.

The sets were built rapidly: James Goode, "Ordeal by Camera," *Show Business Illustrated,* September 19, 1961.

The studio lost $500,000: Balaban letter to David Susskind, December 11, 1962.

CHAPTER 7

Black Monday: Viewed at UCLA Film and Television Archive.

"If three men and their minions": David Susskind to FCC.

CBS once had an opportunity: Jerry Leider to Stephen Battaglio, personal communication.

The Witness used actual attorneys: episodes viewed at Museum of Broadcast Communications and Paley Center for Media.

parroting prepared lines: Outtakes from *Open End* taped on September 8, 1961, Historic Films. They show Truman restating answers to Susskind questions about the project.

"We're up to our necks": David Susskind to FCC.

Kennedy was a viewer: William vanden Heuvel to Stephen Battaglio, personal communication.

CHAPTER 8

"It's hard to put your finger on it": Drew Pearson, "How to Pull Wires and Influence Government," *Show Business Illustrated,* September 5, 1961.

"She'd close the door": *The David Susskind Show,* January 20, 1974, WCFTR.

both sides were looking for a way out: Harold Stern letter to James Richardson, November 27, 1961.

"Did you even submit": John Henry Faulk trial testimony.

CBS founder and chairman William Paley forced: Alan Morris to Stephen Battaglio, personal communication.

The Prestons defend: *The Defenders* episode "The Quality of Mercy," viewed at Paley Center for Media.

He signed a deal with CBS: Richard Wincor letter to David Susskind, January 23, 1963.

But Aurthur had grown tired of the chaos: Jane Aurthur to Stephen Battaglio, personal communication.

moniker of Nathan Network: "Little David Abroad," *Newsweek,* September 9, 1963.

Aubrey added an incentive: Dan Melnick to Stephen Battaglio, personal communication.

CHAPTER 9

The pilot was $24,000 over: Joel Glickman and Ron Gilbert memo to Joel Cramer, February 7, 1963.

ideal assignment for Meyers: Bob Israel personal communication to Stephen Battaglio.

The pilot episode told the story: *East Side/West Side* episode "It's War, Man," private collection.

"We certainly would not have consented": East Harlem Merchants Association letter to David Susskind, January 24, 1963.

Leslie Uggams reportedly got more fan mail: Larry Still, "TV Boom for Negro Talent," *Jet*, November 21, 1963.

issues he'd tackle on his talk show: Undated memo to Audrey Gellen regarding script ideas.

inviting him to pursue the subject: George C. Scott telegram to Arthur Miller, May 1963.

The Capital of Corruption: Pete Hamill memo to Larry Arrick, June 27, 1963.

"The real thing could never be done": Joe Liss letter to David Susskind, May 29, 1963.

"he would rather see the money go down": Irve Tunick memo to David Susskind, May 16, 1963.

"Never use that word": Kranze to Stephen Battaglio, personal communication.

"More viewers rejected the program": CBS memo, April 9, 1963.

Once two schoolboys: unpublished Scott interview by Stuart Woods.

CHAPTER 10

"the whore show": Undated memo from Jean Kennedy to David Susskind, titled "The Following Subjects Were Vetoed by Bennet Korn."

Mailer was added to a long list: Ibid.

When agents attending a Communist Party function: David Susskind FBI file, March 30, 1962.

FBI files showed that: David Susskind FBI file, June 24, 1964.

The panelists calmly debated: "Banned Sex Show" transcript.

"Under the present climate": Belafonte and Baldwin telegram to David Susskind, May 1, 1963.

They were out to celebrate: David Susskind FBI file, May 5, 1963.

"Good riddance to bad rubbish!!": Ibid.

Belafonte and King invited him: Susskind call sheet, March 1963.

On June 6, Susskind taped: *Open End*, June 6, 1963, viewed at Paley Center for Media.

CHAPTER 11

East Side/West Side premiered: *East Side/West Side* episode "The Sinner," private collection.

"She is by no means the house Negro": Undated memo to *East Side/West Side* writers.

He even wrote a detailed outline: Undated Scott memo to producers.

The network's concerns heightened: *East Side/West Side* episode "Who Do You Kill?" private collection.

"I consider it to be": Don Kranze memo to Sy Tomaschoff, September 13, 1963.

The original title was "The Gift of Laughter": Perl memo to David Susskind, Dan Melnick, George C. Scott et al., September 2, 1963.

"social guilt": Larry White memo to Perl, August 21, 1963.

rat bite–related death in Brooklyn: Emily Kaplin letter to Stowe Phillips, October 21, 1963.

never aired on the CBS affiliate in Connecticut: Richard Ahles, information director of WTIC in Hartford, said in a November 1, 1963, letter to Samuel W. Zager that the station decided not to carry the program because it was "trite and cliché ridden."

The story centered on a vagrant: *East Side/West Side* episode "One Drink at a Time," private collection.

The play by Nicholas Baehr: *Ride with Terror,* viewed at UCLA Television Archive.

Susskind and Melnick refused: John Horn, " 'Ride with Terror,' a Brutal Indictment," *New York Herald Tribune,* December 2, 1963.

the cost overruns amounted to: David Susskind letter to Giraud Chester, December 5, 1963.

"Look at me": Richard Schickel, "I've Been Just As Obnoxious As Humanly Possible," *TV Guide,* November 30, 1963.

The uneasiness of the network: *East Side/West Side* episode "No Hiding Place," viewed at UCLA Film and Television Archives.

He called a meeting: Larry Arrick to Stephen Battaglio, personal communication.

They considered building the show: Mike Campus memo to David Susskind, Dan Melnick, and Larry Arrick, December 16, 1963.

George respects the craft of acting: Singer letter to David Susskind, January 1964.

Sloane nearly came to blows: *East Side/West Side* episode "No Wings at All," viewed at UCLA Film and Television Archive.

Sloane's own son: Allan Sloane letter to Stephen Bowie, provided by Bowie.

Most of the respondents: Letters to David Susskind and Dan Melnick from Harrison Salisbury, Arthur Schlesinger Jr., Eugene McCarthy, Margaret Chase Smith, et al., dated between December 20, 1963, and January 10, 1964.

"I was not much impressed": Anslinger letter to David Susskind, December 27, 1963.

"Many stations refused": David Golden memo to cast and crew, January 27, 1964.

In the second week of March: *East Side/West Side* episode "Here Today," private collection.

East Side/West Side **was nominated:** Emmy Awards ceremony, May 25, 1964, viewed at Paley Center for Media.

CHAPTER 12

He lived in apartments at: Andrew Susskind and Shelley Stallworth to Stephen Battaglio, personal communication.

he was ordered to pay his wife: "Susskind's Wife Granted $750 a Week Alimony Here," *New York Times,* April 21, 1965.

"You make great cakes": "The Go-Go-Go Mobile," *Newsweek,* August 29, 1960.

No flights were leaving that night: David Susskind on *The Tonight Show,* February 3, 1978, viewed at Paley Center for Media.

With the new job in hand: Shelley Stallworth to Stephen Battaglio, personal communication.

led some CBC colleagues to dub her "the Snow Goddess": Don Francks to Stephen Battaglio, personal communication.

"Look, you be nice to me": William A. Coleman, "Cool Canadian," *American Weekly,* September 24, 1961.

"People always like me better": Bert Burns, "Critic of Canadians to Beautify New Show," *World Telegraph,* May 21, 1962.

"I wonder if, in a time when the hero symbol": David Susskind on *Open End,* September 10, 1961, personal collection.

"Tell me, David": Ibid.

"I noticed LBJ fixing a momentary gaze": Valenti at David Susskind memorial service.

$160,000 duplex: First National Bank letter to David Susskind, March 17, 1966.

Carson, Kennedy, and Cronkite: Andrew Susskind and Shelley Stallworth to Stephen Battaglio, personal communication.

"This past week": David Susskind on *The David Susskind Show,* February 12, 1967, WCFTR.

CHAPTER 13

Called *Mr. Broadway,* it starred: episodes viewed at private collection.

Mr. Broadway would focus on the glamorous side: Joan Walker, "The Birth of 'Mr. Broadway': The Creative Process of Madison Avenue," *New York Herald Tribune,* March 8, 1964.

Music supervisor Bob Israel hired Dave Brubeck: Bob Israel to Stephen Battaglio, personal communication.

He wanted to use writers: Kanin memos to Larry Arrick, May 4 and 7, 1964.

"Mike Bell is turning out to be a cop": Stevens letter to Dan Melnick, May 30, 1964.

The changes also created havoc: *Mr. Broadway* problems were described in a memo by Michael Campus titled "The Trials and Tribulations of *Mr. Broadway,*" November 23, 1964.

accused of racial discrimination: Frances Foster letter to Larry Arrick, November 16, 1964.

"Even I cringed": Phyllis Susskind letter to David Susskind, September 29, 1963.

Shubert told them they had forty-eight hours: Abbott to Stephen Battaglio, personal communication.

While there appeared to Susskind to be tension: *Show Business Illustrated,* January 5, 1961.

"I'm sure *Rashomon*": Andy Soroka telegram to David Susskind, December 29, 1958.

"Is that good?": "On Theatre and TV: David Susskind," *The Theatre,* March 1959.

one of the songs he wished he had written: letter to Eddie Lawrence, Library of Congress, March 2, 2000, provided by Lawrence.

"determined that we produce this show": "The Truth About 'Kelly,'" *Philadelphia Inquirer,* December 20, 1964.

Before rehearsals commenced: newsreel footage, private collection.

After Francks took the leap: Anita Gillette to Stephen Battaglio, personal communication.

"Welcome once again to Box Canyon": Don Francks to Stephen Battaglio, personal communication.

"Though the show is a bomb": Ibid.

Melnick offered to set the journalist up: Anita Gillette to Stephen Battaglio, personal communication.

CHAPTER 14

"It would be both tragic and ironic": David Susskind letter to Paul Raibourn, July 25, 1965.

"Now remember, boy, in daytime": Ed Vane to Stephen Battaglio, personal communication.

In test showings held: Peter Andrews, "The Run for the Groceries," *TV Guide,* November 19, 1966.

Susskind, who was used to wooing: Jerry Schnur memos to David Susskind and Dan Melnick, October 26 and 29, 1965.

Their early notes for the show: James Bond satire series, April 24, 27, 29, 1964.

Feldon had been an extra for a party scene: Barbara Feldon to Stephen Battaglio, personal communication.

It was a response to the news that a urine bag: "NBC Gets Smart," *Newsweek*, November 3, 1966.

Melnick came back with an offer: Dan Melnick to Stephen Battaglio, personal communication.

Sweep **tripled the size:** Andrews, "The Run for the Groceries."

"I have nothing to do with it": Ibid.

CHAPTER 15

Susskind convinced Meighan's company: Howard Meighan letter to David Susskind, September 12, 1963.

"questionable material": Meighan letter to David Susskind, June 5, 1963.

By the time the play went into production: Pilot of *Command Performance*, viewed at Paley Center for Media.

But Albee refused: Edward Albee to Stephen Battaglio, personal communication.

During the 1950s, he proposed: David Susskind to FCC.

There were weeks when Jed Clampett's clan: Steven D. Stark, *Glued to the Set* (New York: Free Press, 1997), 108.

Henry sent letters: Henry Harding, "For the Record," *TV Guide*, March 28, 1966.

Susskind claimed the unhappiness expressed: David Susskind on *The Open Mind*, March 17, 1980, viewed at Paley Center for Media.

Miller was quoted: Stanley Frank, "A Playwright Ponders a New Outline for TV," *TV Guide*, October 8, 1966.

he described the production as "condensed": Julie Salamon, "A Chance to See 'Salesman' As If for the First Time," *New York Times*, August 5, 2001.

CBS was confident enough: "Arthur Miller Hails Television's 'Death of a Salesman,'" CBS press release, April 2, 1966. Paley Center for Media.

CBS had paid Susskind $580,000: Robert Eck, "The Real Masters of Television," *Harper's*, March 1967.

The short extolled the sales profession: Kevin Kerrane, "Arthur Miller vs. Columbia Pictures: The Strange Case of Career of a Salesman," *Journal of American Culture* 27, no. 3 (2004): 280–289.

The number of viewers: Stanley Frank, "A Playwright Ponders," *TV Guide*, October 8, 1966.

"In this moment of pleasure": David Susskind at Emmy Awards, May 22, 1966, viewed at UCLA Film and Television Archive.

CHAPTER 16

"Our stories are of the first year": Undated proposal for *He & She*.

He refused to discuss producers' notes: Leonard Stern to Stephen Battaglio, personal communication.

Dick ignores the edict: *He & She* episode "A Rock by Any Other Name," private collection.

Denver gave stream-of-consciousness interviews: Kay Gardella, "Bob Denver's TV Roles: From Beatnik to Good Guy," *Daily News*, September 3, 1968.

she brought along a monkey: Leonard Stern and Harry Sherman to Stephen Battaglio, personal communication.

Susskind's shares were valued at $1.725 million: David Susskind Schedule of Securities Held, December 31, 1968.

"I have no clue": Jay Cooper to Stephen Battaglio, personal communication.

"They are playing the phonograph: *The David Susskind Show,* December 29, 1968, WCFTR.

"Most men play not to lose": "The Way I Make My Numbers Is for You Guys to Make Your Numbers," *Forbes,* February 15, 1972.

its executives testified before Congress: Ed Gelsthorpe to Stephen Battaglio, personal communication.

"As far as I know": David Susskind letter to Robert Glickman, April 3, 1970.

CHAPTER 17

Lindsay's predecessor, Robert Wagner, once granted access: William Greaves, "The Police and Susskind: His TV Series Still Is Iffy," *New York Post,* May 4, 1967.

several veterans of the force: *The David Susskind Show,* March 7, 1971.

He even rallied his show business pals: Robert Alden, "Lindsay Seeks Aid on Review Board," *New York Times,* October 3, 1966.

The pitch to the network: *N.Y.P.D.* proposal.

Leary's office had script approval: Memorandum of understanding between Howard Leary and Talent Associates, February 7, 1967.

Susskind had to state: David Susskind deposition, *Robert Blaikie v. The City of New York, Howard Leary, David Susskind and the American Broadcasting Company,* April 8, 1967.

Problems ranged from bureaucratic red tape: " 'Hawk' Folds Its Wings," *Newsweek,* December 5, 1966.

When filming on Riverside Drive: Daily production report for *N.Y.P.D.*, September 5, 1968, Robert J. Markell Papers, Northeastern University.

often paid for out of the show's wardrobe budget: Andrew Susskind to Stephen Battaglio, personal communication.

There was dialogue: *N.Y.P.D.* episode "Shakedown," private collection.

The most daring: *N.Y.P.D.* episode "Encounter on a Roof Top," private collection.

The Central Park setting: Undated memo from Lt. James J. Cleary to *N.Y.P.D.* producers, Robert J. Markell Papers, Northeastern University.

a foggy Warden could keep track: Reza Badiyi to Stephen Battaglio, personal communication.

One of Reza Badiyi's early assignments: Ibid.

He could never forget the image: Dan Melnick, who was also at the party, confirmed this scene to Stephen Battaglio, personal communication.

Just a few days before filming: Joan S. Wilson, "After 18 Hours, Just Tears; Elaine Stritch," *New York Times,* October 25,1970.

A clearly dismayed Stritch: DVD of *Company—A Soundtrack Album,* private collection.

ABC president Tom Moore: David Susskind deposition.

"One had, therefore, the comfort": Ibid.

The program was not nearly: *Laura,* viewed at Museum of Broadcast Communications.

Johnny Carson and Ingrid Bergman: David Susskind on *The David Susskind Show,* March 4, 1979, viewed at Paley Center for Media.

He took bets: David Susskind notes with share projections and wagers with Melnick et al.

CHAPTER 18

"He has probably appeared on more hours": Radio TV Reports transcript of *Firing Line with William Buckley,* May 21, 1966, copyright Stanford University.

Buckley and Susskind had a $1,000 bet: William F. Buckley letter to David Susskind, August 18, 1964.

Metromedia executives suspended him: Muriel Reis to Stephen Battaglio, personal communication.

Burke was a dandy: Jon Merdin to Stephen Battaglio, personal communication.

a woman in the audience claimed: Paul Burt letter to WNEW, August 30, 1968.

Abbie Hoffman came out: Jean Kennedy to Stephen Battaglio, personal communication.

The crowd of four thousand stood: Charles B. Willard letter to David Susskind, June 12, 1968.

Susskind wagered and won: Martin Rosenberg letter to David Susskind, November 1, 1968.

"After Nixon's victory": David Susskind letter to Richard Nixon, December 11, 1968.

Asked earlier in the year: *The David Susskind Show,* March 30, 1968, WCFTR.

Susskind lived up to his word: No recording of the show exists. Quotes are recollections of Ceballos.

"I have a private theory": Diana Lurie, "Living with Liberation," *New York Magazine,* August 31, 1970.

"Since no intelligent human": Mary McAleer letter to David Susskind, January 1, 1972.

"I've always worried about": Audio of *The David Susskind Show,* August 31, 1971, WCFTR; video of *The David Susskind Show,* October 10, 1982, Historic Films.

CHAPTER 19

"I remember meeting you": *The David Susskind Show,* April 21, 1968, viewed at Paley Center for Media.

In September 1969, they appeared: Video of *He Said, She Said,* September 4, 1969, Fremantle Media.

In the early 1970s: Ron Gilbert to Stephen Battaglio, personal communication.

CHAPTER 20

Susskind's first show: *The David Susskind Show,* February 12, 1967, WCFTR.

"Educational stations": *The David Susskind Show,* April 4, 1971, Historic Films.

"One thing I can't get over": *The David Susskind Show,* March 3, 1974, WCFTR.

"The airing of this show": Elaine Noble letter to David Susskind, February 19, 1974.

CHAPTER 21

"The minute I see a nun": Transcript of *The David Susskind Show,* March 3, 1966.

Brooks went into overdrive: *The David Susskind Show,* November 27, 1970, Historic Films.

"Mel would say": Transcript of *The David Susskind Show,* April 3, 1973.

With mock outrage: *The David Susskind Show,* November 27, 1970, Historic Films.

Always looking out for her David: Jean Kennedy, on *The David Susskind Show,* June 5, 1983, viewed at Paley Center for Media.

David Susskind honored his mother's requests: Norman Lear and Anita Grossberg to Stephen Battaglio, personal communication.

"Vile," "vulgar," "disgraceful": Viewer comments to WNEW, November 30, 1970.

"What we're doing in radio": *The David Susskind Show,* June 18, 1972, WCFTR.

As the topics and guests: Larry Strichman to Stephen Battaglio, personal communication.

In grave tones: *The David Susskind Show,* June 17, 1973, private collection.

He stayed on public TV stations: Richard Salomon letter to KCET-TV, August 25, 1982, regarding a financial contribution for *The David Susskind Show.*

CHAPTER 22

Susskind completed it at double that amount: Ron Gilbert to Stephen Battaglio, personal communication.

He passed on: Anthony Loeb to Stephen Battaglio, personal communication.

During the filming in New York: Leonard Stern to Stephen Battaglio, personal communication.

"Why you wish to delude": David Susskind memo to Martin Baum, May 26, 1970.

Howard tweaked Susskind: David Z. Goodman to Stephen Battaglio, personal communication.

The large antique bear trap: Jinny Schreckinger to Stephen Battaglio, personal communication.

There was a lot of shouting: Diana Kerew to Stephen Battaglio, personal communication.

During the summer of 1973: Talent Associates staff meeting notes, July 9, 1973.

But Calley, who had been aligned: Calley declined an interview request but made it clear in a short phone conversation with Stephen Battaglio that he disliked Susskind.

CHAPTER 23

"I've grown up": Mitch Broder, "David Susskind: Growing Up in TV," *New York Times,* February 19, 1978.

"We took a location scouting trip": David Susskind deposition.

CHAPTER 24

After suffering from years of alcohol abuse: Several colleagues of Maas described her health problems related to alcoholism.

A curved staircase: Eugenia Sheppard, "Joyce Marries American," *New York Post,* April 2, 1970.

oil portraits: seen in family photo provided by Connie Christopher.

A large Georgia O'Keeffe: Shelley Stallworth to Stephen Battaglio, personal communication.

Sukhodrev brought Samantha: Viktor Sukhodrev to Stephen Battaglio, personal communication.

KGB agents stood: Nicholas Christopher to Stephen Battaglio, personal communication.

CHAPTER 25

NSI chairman David Mahoney decided: "Why Less Is More at Norton Simon," *Business Week,* September 8, 1975.

Susskind owned his company again: Ron Gilbert to Stephen Battaglio, personal communication.

Talent Associates was sold once again: contract of sale provided by confidential source.

Early on in his tenure: David Susskind and Irving "Swifty" Lazar conversation recounted by Bruce Paisner and Andrew Susskind to Stephen Battaglio, personal communication.

CHAPTER 26

Susskind held firm: Diana Kerew to Stephen Battaglio, personal communication.

Newman wanted some support: Heywood Gould to Stephen Battaglio, personal communication.

"It is tough on Puerto Ricans": Richard F. Shepard, "Newman Rebuts Apache 'Bias' Charge; Public Session Criticizes Script," *New York Times*, April 9, 1980.

"It was a thrill for the children": Children's Circle Day Care Center letter to producers, April 28, 1980.

David Susskind did not attend: Andrew Susskind to Stephen Battaglio, personal communication.

"a six-foot-five calculator": Alex Ben Block, "Susskind Tilts at Windmills," *Los Angeles Herald Examiner,* November 12, 1982.

CHAPTER 27

Spencer Tracy cottage: Jane Deknatel to Stephen Battaglio, personal communication.

Alcohol was prevalent: Shelley Stallworth to Stephen Battaglio, personal communication.

Susskind had papers drawn up: Draft of an SEC filing dated September 29, 1983.

Susskind put $750,000 into: Andrew Susskind to Stephen Battaglio, personal communication.

Susskind indulged in other wild: Dan Berkowitz to Stephen Battaglio, personal communication.

He had gone into advanced negotiations: Ed Vane letter to David Susskind, June 16, 1983.

He attempted to use his own personal funds: Telex from the Susskind Company to David Susskind, September 16, 1983.

Susskind started hiring people he met: Anita Grossberg, Jean Kennedy, and Dan Berkowitz to Stephen Battaglio, personal communication.

Harrison was out: Salvatore Arena, "Fat Suit for Susskind," *Daily News,* November 10, 1983.

"Just tell them": Jean Kennedy to Stephen Battaglio, personal communication.

was appalled: Andrew Susskind to Stephen Battaglio, personal communication.

At some point Susskind had been prescribed: Anita Grossberg to Stephen Battaglio, personal communication.

The notes from his meetings and phone logs: David Susskind conversations, June 24, 1983; September 16, 1983; March 19, 20, 29, 1984; April 2, 28, 1984.

CHAPTER 28

David Susskind's struggle with bipolar disorder: Andrew Susskind to Stephen Battaglio, personal communication.

In 1985, Susskind interviewed: *The David Susskind Show,* November 3, 1985, viewed at Museum of Broadcast Communications.

Susskind was seen with attractive women: Paparazzi photos by Ron Galella, circa 1985.

With the assistance of his daughter: David Susskind letter to Bettinger, January 16, 1986.

Susskind and Carmen had traveled to London: Carmen Dell'Orefice to Stephen Battaglio, personal communication.

"Carmen, I'm sorry to tell you": Ibid.

EPILOGUE

The very last program: *JFK—A Time Remembered,* viewed at UCLA Film and Television Archive.

During the chat, Carson: Carson interview with David Susskind, viewed at WCFTR.

When Susskind's estate was settled: "Susskind Willed $2.3M to His Kin," *Daily News,* March 7, 1987.

She shows clips of her father's last movie: Samantha Mannion to Stephen Battaglio, personal communication.

At Susskind's induction: Tape of Fox telecast of induction ceremony, private collection.

Bibliography

BOOKS

Albee, Edward. *The Collected Plays of Edward Albee, vol. 1: 1958–1965*. Woodstock, NY: Overlook Duckworth, 2007.

Barnouw, Erik. *The Sponsor: Notes on a Modern Potentate*. New York: Oxford University Press, 1979.

——. *Tube of Plenty: The Evolution of American Television*. New York: Oxford University Press, 1990.

Bernstein, Walter. *Inside Out: A Memoir of the Blacklist*. New York: Da Capo Press, 2000.

Biskind, Peter. *Easy Riders, Raging Bulls: How the Sex-Drugs-and-Rock 'n' Roll Generation Saved Hollywood*. New York: Simon & Schuster, 1998.

Brooks, Tim, and Earle Marsh. *The Complete Directory to Prime Time Network and Cable TV Shows: 1946–Present*. New York: Ballantine Books, 2007.

Brownmiller, Susan. *In Our Time: Memoir of a Revolution*. New York: Dial Press, 1999.

Bruck, Connie. *When Hollywood Had a King: The Reign of Lew Wasserman, Who Leveraged Talent into Power and Influence*. New York: Random House, 2004.

Buhle, Paul, and Dave Wagner. *Hide in Plain Sight: The Hollywood Blacklistees in Film and Television, 1950–2002*. New York: Palgrave Macmillan, 2003.

Capote, Truman. *Breakfast at Tiffany's and Three Stories*. New York: Vintage Books, 1993.

Chayefsky, Paddy. *Television Plays*. New York: Simon & Schuster, 1955.

Cheney, Terri. *Manic: A Memoir*. New York: Morrow, 2008.

Cole, Clay. *Sh-Boom! The Explosion of Rock 'N' Roll 1953–1968*. Garden City: Morgan James Publishing, 2009.

Dann, Michael H., and Paul D. Berger. *As I Saw It: The Inside Story of the Golden Years of Television*. El Prado, NM: Levine Mesa Press, 2009.

Editors of *Broadcasting* Magazine, eds. *The First 50 Years of Broadcasting: The Running Story of the Fifth Estate*. Washington, D.C.: Broadcasting Publications, 1982.

Edwards, Anne. *A Remarkable Woman: A Biography of Katharine Hepburn*. New York: Morrow, 1985.

Faulk, John Henry. *Fear on Trial*. New York: Simon & Schuster, 1964.

Funt, Marilyn. *Are You Anybody?* New York: Dial Press, 1979.

Genet, Jean. *The Blacks: A Clown Show.* New York: Grove Press, 1966.

Goldenson, Leonard H., and Marvin J. Wolf. *Beating the Odds: The Untold Story Behind the Rise of ABC.* New York: Scribner's, 1991.

Greenburg, Dan. *How to Be a Jewish Mother: A Very Lovely Training Manual.* Los Angeles: Price, Stern, Sloan; distributed by Pocket Books New York, 1964.

Greene, Graham. *The Power and the Glory.* London: Penguin Books, 1990.

Halberstam, David. *The Best and the Brightest.* New York: Random House, 1972.

Heffner, Richard D. *A Documentary History of the United States.* New York: Signet Classic, 2002.

Howar, Barbara. *Laughing All the Way.* Greenwich, CT: Fawcett Publication, 1973.

Howard, Gerald. *The Sixties: Art, Politics, and Media of Our Most Explosive Decade.* New York: Paragon House, 1991.

Jamison, Kay Redfield. *Touched with Fire: Manic-Depressive Illness and the Artistic Temperament.* New York: Free Press, 1994.

Jonnes, Jill. *We're Still Here: The Rise, Fall, and Resurrection of the South Bronx.* Boston: Atlantic Monthly Press, 1986.

Kahn, Douglas and Diane Neumaier. *Cultures in Contention.* Seattle: Real Comet Press, 1986.

Kanin, Fay, and Michael Kanin. *Rashomon*, a drama in two acts, based on stories by Ryūnosuke Akutagawa. New York: Random House, 1959.

Kaufman, David. *Doris Day: The Untold Story of the Girl Next Door.* London: Virgin Books, 2009.

Khrushchev, Nikita Sergeevich. *Khrushchev in New York: A Documentary Record of Nikita S. Khrushchev's Trip to New York, September 19th to October 13th, 1960, Including All His Speeches and Proposals to the United Nations and Major Addresses and News Conferences.* New York: Crosscurrents, 1960.

Kisseloff, Jeff. *The Box: An Oral History of Television, 1920–1961.* New York: Penguin, 1997.

Krampner, Jon. *The Man in the Shadows: Fred Coe and the Golden Age of Television.* New Brunswick, NJ: Rutgers University Press, 1997.

Lennon, J. Michael. *Norman Mailer's Letters on* An American Dream, *1963–1969.* Shavertown, Pa.: Sligo Press, 2004.

Maas, Audrey Gellen. *Wait Till the Sun Shines, Nellie: A Novel.* New York: New American Library, 1966.

MacNeil, Robert, ed. *The Way We Were, 1963: The Year Kennedy Was Shot.* New York: Carroll & Graf, 1988.

Mahoney, David J. *Growth and Social Responsibility: The Story of Norton Simon.* New York: Newcomen Society in North America, 1973.

Marmorstein, Gary. *The Label: The Story of Columbia Records.* New York: Thunder's Mouth Press, 2007.

Maugham, W. Somerset, and Robert Calder. *The Moon and Sixpence.* New York: Penguin Books, 2005.

McCullough, David G. *Truman.* New York: Simon & Schuster, 1992.

McGilligan, Patrick, and Paul Buhle. *Tender Comrades: A Backstory of the Hollywood Blacklist.* New York: St. Martin's Press, 1997.

Mercante, Arthur, and Phil Guarnieri. *Inside the Ropes.* Ithaca, NY: McBooks Press, 2006.

Metz, Robert. *CBS: Reflections in a Bloodshot Eye.* Chicago: Playboy Press, 1975.

Miller, Gabriel, ed. *Martin Ritt: Interviews.* Jackson: University Press of Mississippi, 2002.

Miller, Merle, and Evan Rhodes. *Only You, Dick Daring! Or, How to Write One Television Script and Make $50,000,000: A True-Life Adventure*. New York: William Sloane, 1964.

Morgan, Thomas Bruce. *Self-Creations: 13 Impersonalities*. New York: Holt, Rinehart & Winston, 1965.

Murphy, Brenda. *Miller: Death of a Salesman*. Cambridge, England: Cambridge University Press, 1995.

Nizer, Louis. *The Jury Returns*. New York: Doubleday, 1966.

O'Neil, Thomas. *The Emmys: Star Wars, Showdowns, and the Supreme Test of TV's Best*. New York: Penguin Books, 1992.

Plimpton, George. *Truman Capote: In Which Various Friends, Enemies, Acquaintances, and Detractors Recall His Turbulent Career*. New York: Anchor Books, 1998.

Poitier, Sidney. *The Measure of a Man: A Spiritual Autobiography*. San Francisco, CA: HarperSanFrancisco, 2000.

Quinn, Anthony, and Daniel Paisner. *One Man Tango*. New York: HarperCollins, 1995.

Quirk, Lawrence J. *The Kennedys in Hollywood*. New York: Cooper Square Press, 2004.

Rose, Philip. *You Can't Do That on Broadway!:* A Raisin in the Sun *and Other Theatrical Improbabilities: A Memoir*. New York: Limelight Editions, 2001.

Roudané, Matthew Charles, ed. *Conversations with Arthur Miller*. Jackson: University Press of Mississippi, 1987.

Sander, Gordon F. *Serling: The Rise and Twilight of Television's Last Angry Man*. New York: Plume, 1994.

Schickel, Richard, and George C. Perry. *You Must Remember This: The Warner Bros. Story*. Philadelphia, PA: Running Press, 2008.

Schorr, Daniel. *Staying Tuned: A Life in Journalism*. New York: Pocket Books, 2001.

Simmons, Garner. *Peckinpah: A Portrait in Montage*. New York: Limelight Editions, 1998.

Smith, Martin J. and Patrick J. Kiger. *Poplorica: A Popular History of the Fads, Mavericks, Inventions, and Lore That Shaped America*. New York: HarperResource, 2004.

Smith, Sally Bedell. *In All His Glory: The Life of William S. Paley, the Legendary Tycoon and His Brilliant Circle*. New York: Simon & Schuster, 1990.

Stark, Steven D. *Glued to the Set*. New York: Free Press, 1997.

Taubman, William. *Khrushchev: The Man and His Era*. New York: Norton, 2003.

Wallace, Mike, and Gary Paul Gates. *Close Encounters*. New York: Morrow, 1984.

Walters, Barbara. *Audition: A Memoir*. New York: Alfred J. Knopf, 2008.

Wasserman, Dale. *The Impossible Musical*. New York: Applause Theatre & Cinema Books, 2003.

Watson, Mary Ann. *The Expanding Vista: American Television in the Kennedy Years*. Durham, NC: Duke University Press, 1994.

Weddle, David. *If They Move—Kill 'Em! The Life and Times of Sam Peckinpah*. New York: Grove Press, 1994.

Wilk, Max. *The Golden Age of Television*. New York: Delacorte Press, 1976.

Williams, Gordon M. *The Siege of Trencher's Farm*. New York: Morrow, 1969.

Winters, Shelley. *Shelley II: The Middle of My Century*. New York: Simon & Schuster, 1989.

JOURNAL ARTICLES

"AJC Attacks Susskind Show as Anti-Semitic." *New York Post,* October 18, 1966.

"America's Mr. TV for Britain," *Sunday Telegraph,* June 30, 1963.

"As for David Susskind. . . ." *Daily News,* February 24, 1987.

"A Special U.S. Canadian Section," *Newsweek,* June 29, 1960.

"A Talkative TV Producer." *New York Times,* June 13, 1960.

"A Sponsor Quits 'Open End' Show." *New York Times,* October 11, 1960.

"Bellicose and Still Bothered, Susskind Battles the Networks." *National Observer,* November 5, 1962.

"Blind Ambition: Television Revisits Watergate." *American Film,* May 1979.

"Boston Playhouse Offers TV Drama." *Christian Science Monitor,* December 31, 1964.

"Close-Up, *The Play of the Week,*" *TV Guide,* January 14, 1961.

"Curtis Threatens to Slug Susskind." UPI, September 6, 1960.

"David & the Goliaths." *Variety,* May 13, 1959.

"David Susskind Marries Former TV Personality." *New York Herald Tribune,* April 23, 1966.

"David Susskind, Who Sold His Talent Associates Production Company to Norton Simon Inc, in 1968, Has Bought It Back from the Consumer-Oriented Conglomerate. . . ." *Daily News,* August 5, 1975.

"Disgusting! An Editorial." *New York Daily Mirror,* October 9, 1960.

"Divorced, David Susskind. . . ." *Newsweek,* May 3, 1965.

"Do-Gooder." *Newsweek,* November 30, 1964.

"Dr. King Denounces President on Rights." *New York Times,* June 10, 1963.

"Dynamic Duo." *Manhattan, Inc.,* May 1986.

"Exalted Theater." *Newsweek,* May 23, 1966.

"Famous Feuds: David vs. the World." *Show: The Magazine of the Arts,* April 1963.

"Good Company." *Variety,* September 13, 1967.

"Here & There with Dave, Sheilah & Boom Boom." *Daily News,* August 24, 1983.

"'Hot Line'" (TV review), *New York Herald Tribune,* June 25, 1964.

"If the Suit Fits. . . ." *Daily News,* June 11, 1980.

"Joe Pyne's Fist-in-the-Mouth Show." *TV Guide,* November 6, 1965.

"Joyce Drops Brick Again: Hits Hallowe'en Fund." *Winnipeg Free Press,* November 4, 1960.

"'Justice.'" *Variety,* October 5, 1955.

"'Kelly' Court Fight Is On." *Daily News,* January 29, 1965.

"Lindsay Scornfully Snubs Drafters." *Daily News,* March 16, 1965.

"Little David Abroad." *Newsweek,* September 9, 1963.

"Marika Robert Discovers Joyce Davidson." *Maclean's,* September 10, 1960.

"Master of Controversy Weds Controversial Gal." *Daily News,* April 23, 1966.

"Movie Rights to 'Raisin in Sun.'" *Jet,* April 16, 1959.

"Mrs. Susskind Is Granted Separation; Wed 24 Yrs." *New York Post,* January 12, 1965.

"'My Life Now Is Peaceful,'" *New York Times,* October 27, 1969.

"Nothing Else Like This." *Time,* April 13, 1962.

"N. S. Khrushchev" (editorial). *Daily News,* October 7, 1960.

"Off to Court." *Daily News,* December 15, 1983.

"On 'Circle Theatre,' TV Tries the Truth." *TV Guide,* June 2, 1956.

"On Theatre and TV: David Susskind." *The Theatre,* March 1959.

"Open End Aid." *Christian Science Monitor,* February 12, 1963.

"'Open End' Commercials: For Radio Free Europe." *New York Herald Tribune,* October 10, 1960.

"Paramount Buys Half of TV Firm." *New York Times*, April 7, 1961.

"People Are Talking About . . . David Susskind." *Vogue,* September 1959.

"Police Allow Susskind to Do Series on Files." *World Journal Tribune,* February 24, 1967.

" 'Salesman' Put Off to May 8 by N.B.C." *New York Times*, March 7, 1966.

" 'Showdown in Alabama.' " *Daily News,* April 26, 1965.

"Susskind Carries His 'TV Smells' Campaign to Canadian Audience." *Variety,* February 22, 1961.

"Susskind Dancing Off in Many Directions: TV, Legit, Screen and Lectures." *Variety,* February 15, 1961.

"Susskind Divulges Theatre Pix Dream." *Variety,* July 13, 1960.

"Susskind Drops Suit." *Daily News,* January 26, 1984.

"Susskind Memorial Planned." *New York Times,* March 16, 1987.

"Susskind on Film Set, Hits at Current TV Programming." *New York Times,* October 20, 1963.

"Susskind Signs with MGM—as a Movie Producer." *Daily News,* September 26, 1980.

"Susskind: Trouble with TV. . . ." *World Telegraph,* August 8, 1964.

"Susskind's Truce with TV Industry Ends Dramatically." *National Observer,* May 6, 1963.

"Susskind's Wife Asks Separation." *New York Post,* July 6, 1964.

"Susskind's Wife Granted $750 a Week Alimony Here." *New York Times*, April 21, 1965.

"Susskind Willed 2.3M to His Kin." *Daily News.* March 7, 1987.

"Tele Follow-up Comment." *Variety,* September 9, 1953.

"Tele Follow-up Comment." *Variety,* October 5, 1955.

"Tele Follow-up Comment." *Variety,* December 17, 1958.

"Television: Review." *Time,* February 3, 1958.

"Television Review," *Variety,* September 30, 1964.

"The Clan: TV and Sympathy." *New York Post,* September 11, 1961.

"The December-December Romance Between TV's Godfather, David Susskind, and the Classic and Beautiful Model Carmen Is for Real." *Daily News,* January 14, 1987.

"The Man Who?" *Newsweek,* June 14, 1965.

" 'The Moon and Sixpence.' " *Variety,* November 4, 1959.

" 'The Power and the Glory.' " *Daily Cinema,* June 20, 1962.

"The Slow Buck." *Newsweek,* March 1, 1965.

"The Susskind Network." *Newsweek,* July 25, 1966

"The Way I Make My Numbers Is for You Guys to Make Your Numbers." *Forbes*, February 15, 1972.

"Topics: Cultivators; Talking Head." *New York Times,* February 24, 1987.

"Transsexual Seeks Divorce from Wife; Wants to Remarry." *New York Times,* October 7, 1970.

"TV: From Gadget to Greatness." *TV Guide,* January 12, 1957.

"TV Sullen over Susskind Lash." *New York Mirror,* June 22, 1961.

"TV's Handy Gal." *New York Herald Tribune,* February 28, 1960.

"TV's Unreconstructed Rebel: Producer David Susskind Operates with a High Resolve and a Low Boiling Point." *TV Guide,* August 16, 1958.

"Where All That Money's Going." *Broadcasting,* July 10, 1961.

"Why Less Is More at Norton Simon." *Business Week,* September 8, 1975.

"Wonder Boys Together." *Newsweek,* September 2, 1968.

Aaronson, Charles S. "'Dare a Little,' Susskind's Plea to Exhibitors." *Motion Picture Herald,* January 24, 1962.

Adams, Cindy. "His Secret Last Wish: To Marry Third Time." *New York Post,* February 23, 1987.

Adams, Val. "Tape Recorders for TV a Big Hit." *New York Times,* April 20, 1956.

———. "Olivier Considering TV Debut in 'Moon and Sixpence' Here." *New York Times,* July 30, 1958.

———. "Films to Be Basis of Live TV Series." *New York Times,* April 14, 1959.

———. "N.B.C.-TV Is Firm on Subway Play." *New York Times,* November 30, 1963.

———. "C.B.S. News Bars Emmy Awards for Its Staff." *New York Times,* May 13, 1964.

———. "TV Buys Salesman." *New York Times,* January 30, 1966.

———. "Willy Loman Irks Fellow Salesmen." *New York Times,* March 27, 1966.

———. "CBS Buys Watergate Book." *Daily News,* January 3, 1977.

Alden, Robert. "Lindsay Seeks Aid on Review Board." *New York Times,* October 3, 1966.

Alexander, Joseph H. "Not All Flaming Spectacle for David Susskind." *Naval History,* January–February 1997.

Amory, Cleveland. "'East Side/West Side.'" *TV Guide,* December 14, 1963.

Andrews, Peter. "The Run for the Groceries." *TV Guide,* November 19, 1966.

Archer, Eugene. "'Terror' in Transit." *New York Times,* August 30, 1964.

Arena, Salvatore. "Fat Suit for Susskind." *Daily News,* November 10, 1983.

———. "Susskind to Pay Alimony." *Daily News,* July 30, 1983.

Associated Press. "Red Labeling Told in Libel Suit." *Christian Science Monitor,* June 19, 1962.

Atkinson, Brooks. "The Theater: A Search for Truth." *New York Times,* January 28, 1959.

Aurthur, Robert Alan. "The Wit and Sass of Harry S. Truman." *Esquire,* August 1971.

Barrett, George. "Hundreds Object to Premier on TV." *New York Times,* October 10, 1960.

Battaglio, Stephen. "A Talk Show Pioneer, Before TV Talk Was Toxic." *New York Times,* April 15, 2001.

———. "Television/Radio; the Big Business of Fond Farewells." *New York Times,* July 29, 2001.

Baxandall, Rosalyn. "Re-Visioning the Women's Liberation Movement's Narrative: Early Second Wave African American Feminists." *Feminist Studies* 27 no. 1 (Spring 2001).

Broder, Mitch. "David Susskind: Growing Up in TV." *New York Times,* February 19, 1978.

Brooks, John. "Fueling the Arts, Or, Exxon as a Medici." *New York Times,* January 25, 1976.

Brown, Les. "Drama Coups Cap TA's Comeback." *Variety,* June 15, 1966.

Burns, Bert. "Critic of Canadians to Beautify New Show." *World Telegraph,* May 21, 1961.

———. "Susskind, the Critical Maverick, Finds Fall Picture Looking Brighter." *National Observer,* February 25, 1963.

Cameron, Kate. "Prize Play and Novel Now on Screen." *Daily News,* October 6, 1963.

Campbell, Barbara. "200 Start Fight on Homosexual 'Myths.'" *New York Times,* November 24, 1973.

Canby, Vincent. "Film View: Terrific, Tough-Talking 'Alice,'" *New York Times,* February 2, 1975.

Cashman, John. "Susskind Weds Press Agent; Mexican Divorce Cleared Way." *New York Post,* April 22, 1966.

Champlin, Charles. "Luckinbill Takes L.B.J. Home Again." *Los Angeles Times,* November 29, 1988.

Coleman, William A. "Cool Canadian." *American Weekly,* September 24, 1961.

Cooper, Cord. "Producer Norman Lear—His Perseverance and Innovation Helped Change the Face of TV Comedy." *Investor's Business Daily,* May 8, 2000.

Corry, John. "'JFK,' Dramatization on Channel 13." *New York Times,* June 20, 1984.

———. "'I Would Be Called John' on PBS." *New York Times,* September 17, 1987.

Crist, Judith. "Movies: 'X' Should Be for Execrable." *New York Magazine,* January 24, 1972.

Crosby, John. "Champion of Live TV from the East." *New York Herald Tribune,* January 20, 1958.

Curry, Rod. "Now Mrs. David Susskind, Joyce Abandons Own Career." *Winnipeg Free Press,* June 16, 1966.

Curtis, Charlotte. "Notables Living in U.N. Plaza 'Compound' Finally Get Acquainted." *New York Times,* May 18, 1967.

Dallos, Robert E. "Ex-Aide Explains Susskind Parting." *New York Times,* August 30, 1967.

———. "Susskind Concern Bought by Norton Simon, Inc." *New York Times,* August 20, 1968.

Daly, Maggie. "Mayor Lindsay . . . Isn't Saying If He Will Run for Mayor Again." *Chicago Tribune,* January 7, 1973.

Danzig, Fred. "Bert Parks Carries Miss America Show." *The New Mexican,* September 11, 1961.

Dean, Richard K. "Pessimistic Susskind Back—Now Exuberant." *New York Herald Tribune,* August 22, 1961.

Dehn, Paul. "Dazzling, This Father Olivier." *Daily Herald,* June 23, 1962.

Derby, R. Stafford. "Rockefeller Slams No. 2 Door; Nixon in TV Marathon." *Christian Science Monitor,* May 16, 1960.

Doan, Richard K. "David Susskind, Up to Date." *New York Herald Tribune,* November 11, 1964.

Dougherty, Philip H. "Advertising: Why TV Specials Are Special." *New York Times,* January 29, 1967.

———. "Advertising: Xerox and P.K.L. Agency Part." *New York Times,* March 6, 1968.

Easterbrook, Gregg. "Sack Weinberger, Bankrupt General Dynamics, and Other Procurement Reforms." *Washington Monthly,* January 1, 1987.

Eck, Robert. "The Real Masters of Television." *Harper's Magazine,* March 1967.

Efron, Edith. "Who Killed Neil Brock?" *TV Guide,* March 28, 1964.

Ehrlich, Henry. "The Public and Private Lee." *Look,* January 23, 1968.

Fiala, Rick. "A Gay Person Interviews a Group of David Susskinds." *Christopher Street,* March 19, 1978.

Fields, Sidney. "'PM-East' Star Keeps A.M.'s Tuned to Kids." *New York Mirror,* June 26, 1961.

Foreman, Bob. "Inside of a Whale with David Susskind." *TV Guide,* December 8, 1962.

Foreman, Robert L. "Me, David Susskind and the Greatest Man in the World." *Esquire,* September 1967.

Frank, Stanley. "A Playwright Ponders a New Outline For TV." *TV Guide,* October 8, 1966.

Fraser, C. Gerald. "Time-Life Buys Susskind TV Company." *New York Times,* July 22, 1977.

Freedman, Samuel G. "Why 'Chaplin' Is Not Opening on Broadway." *New York Times,* November 10, 1983.

Gardella, Kay. "McGavin Takes on Two Teleseries at One Time." *Daily News,* May 13, 1959.

————. "Khrushchev on 'Open End.'" *Daily News,* October 6, 1960.

————. "CBS-TV Dramatic Series Ends on Original Note." *New York Daily News,* March 22, 1961.

————. "NTA in Pay Swim." *Daily News,* March 31, 1961.

————. "Sullivan Defends Networks at the FCC TV Hearings." *Daily News,* June 24, 1961.

————. "'Open End' Panelists Play Clan for Laughs." *Daily News,* September 11, 1961.

————. "Susskind's Fall TV Plans Include Crosby in Drama." *Daily News,* August 22, 1962.

————. "Scott Applies Hard Sell to 'East Side, West Side,'" *Daily News,* April 30, 1963.

————. "Sidewalk TVing Has Its Twists." *Daily News,* June 16, 1963.

————. "Scripts Depressing—But by George, There's Scott." *Daily News,* October 8, 1963.

————. "FCC Eyeing Webs' Deals." *Daily News,* December 11, 1964.

————. "David, Now a TV Goliath, Faces the Fall with Hope." *Daily News,* July 5, 1966.

————. "Producers Prefer Landing on TV Without Any Pilots." *Daily News,* August 18, 1966.

————. "Portugal Visit of Pope on TV." *Daily News,* May 4, 1967.

————. "Lee Bailey's TV Producer Fired by David Susskind." *Daily News,* May 6, 1967.

————. "Buckley and Vidal Buttress ABC Convention Reports." *Daily News,* July 16, 1968.

————. "Good Guys Bid for Laughs." *Daily News,* August 25, 1968.

————. "Bob Denver's TV Roles: From Beatnik to Good Guy." *Daily News,* September 3, 1968.

————. "Susskind's Sex Session Still in Doubt for Ch. 5." *Daily News,* November 9, 1972.

————. "'Eleanor and Franklin'—Television Tells the Private Story." *Daily News,* December 14, 1975.

————. "Not Mad Ave, but Fun." *Daily News,* October 7, 1977.

————. "Susskind—Talk Is Chic." *Daily News,* October 7, 1982.

————. "The Susskind Legacy." *Daily News,* February 23, 1987.

Gardiner, Paul. "Sponsors Reject Top Playwrights." *New York Times,* November 18, 1963.

Gehman, Richard. "The David Who Wants to Be Goliath." *TV Guide,* November 23, 1963.

Gerard, Jeremy. "Friendly Persuasion." *New York Times,* September 13, 1987.

Goldman, Ari L. "Leslie Slote, 78, a Spokesman for Wagner and for Rockefeller." *New York Times,* August 6, 2002.

Goldstein, Marianne. "David Susskind Dead." *New York Post,* February 23, 1987.

————. "Admirers Recall His Television Legacy." *New York Post,* February 23, 1987.

Goode, James. "Ordeal by Camera." *Show Business Illustrated,* September 19, 1961.

Gould, Jack. "Reward for a Star." *New York Times,* October 16, 1958.

————. TV: Olivier and Maugham." *New York Times,* October 31, 1959.

————. "U.S. Asks Restraint in Coverage by TV of Soviet Premier." *New York Times,* September 18, 1960.

————. "Khrushchev Meets Susskind." *New York Times,* October 16, 1960.

————. "Survey of a Much-Surveyed Moderator." *New York Times,* October 30, 1960.

————. "Susskind to Vie for WNTA-TV with Landau and Citizens Group." *New York Times,* March 2, 1961.

————. "TV: Ingrid Bergman as Hedda Gabler." *New York Times,* September 21, 1963.

————. "Backstairs at 'Open End.'" *New York Times,* May 12, 1963.

Gowran, Clay. "'Death' Comes to TV and Brings New Life." *Chicago Tribune,* May 9, 1966.

Graham, Sheilah. "Hollywood Gaga over Susskind." *New York Mirror,* September 28, 1960.

Greaves, William. "The Police and Susskind: His TV Series Still Is Iffy." *New York Post,* May 4, 1967.

Greeley, Bill. "Tale of Two CBS Homo Shows." *Variety,* February 22, 1967.

Greenspun, Roger. "A Prodigiously Compound 'Lovers and Other Strangers,'" *New York Times,* August 13, 1971.

Gross, Ben. "What's On?" *Daily News,* May 20, 1959.

———. "'The Susskind Legend'—Time to Live Up to It." *Daily News,* May 22, 1959.

———. "Susskind's New Series Is Okay—but Is It Art?" *Daily News,* November 15, 1959.

———. "Susskind Has Kind Words for TV." *Daily News,* May 20, 1962.

———. "Susskind Says He'd Like to Take on Khrushy Again." *Daily News,* May 27, 1962.

———. "Brando Reveals Himself in Fascinating Session." *Daily News,* April 22, 1963.

———. "A Great Actor Never Had a Lesson." *Daily News,* September 22, 1963.

———. "Great Scott!—a Star Who Pulls No Punches." *Daily News,* September 29, 1963.

———. "Open End Bows on WPIX." *Daily News,* October 14, 1963.

———. "Why Susskind Has Changed His Mind." *Daily News,* April 25, 1965.

———. "Baldwin-Buckley Debate Old Stuff But Exciting." *Daily News,* June 14, 1965.

———. "TV's 'Death of a Salesman' an Overpowering Drama." *Daily News,* May 9, 1966.

Guidry, Frederick H. "David S, Goliath K Clash in Television Land." *Christian Science Monitor,* October 10, 1960.

Harding, Henry. "For the Record." *TV Guide,* July 8, 1961.

Harney, James. "Susskind Fans Bid Him Adieu." *Daily News,* February 24, 1987.

Harris, Harry. "'Death of a Salesman' Gains Camera Artistry in Special." *Philadelphia Inquirer,* May 9, 1966.

Hentoff, Nat. "You're Hot, You're Poor, You're Nothing. . . ." *New York Times,* November 14, 1965.

Horn, John. "No NBC 'Disclaimer' for 'Ride with Terror.'" *New York Herald Tribune,* November 30, 1963.

———. "'Ride with Terror,' a Brutal Indictment." *New York Herald Tribune,* December 2, 1963.

Humphrey, Hal. "Acting Clues for 'Laura' Watchers." *Los Angeles Times,* January 25, 1968.

Hurton, Anthony. "Lee Bailey Finds Himself a Nice Air Cushion: Money." *Daily News,* May 6, 1967.

Kenney, Harry. "New Yorkers Bid for 'Quality' TV." *Christian Science Monitor,* June 18, 1958.

Kifner, John. "Sexuality Issue Put to Rest Elaine Noble Is Ready for Office." *New York Times,* November 14, 1974.

King, Larry. "Interview with Tab Hunter" (transcript). *CNN Larry King Live,* October 10, 2005.

Kleinfeld, N. R. "Time Inc.—Bigger and Richer." *New York Times,* June 23, 1978.

Knight, Arthur. "Theatre into Film." *Saturday Review,* March 25, 1961.

Krajicek, David. "David Susskind Is Dead at 67." *Daily News,* February 23, 1987.

Kreiling, Ernie. "David Susskind—from Tiger to Pussycat." *Pomona California Progress Bulletin,* November 21, 1965.

Kubaski, Ben. "This 'Girl Friday' Has TV's Busiest Job." *Long Island Newsday,* September 24, 1959.

Lapham, Lewis H. "Has Anybody Here Seen *Kelly?*" *Saturday Evening Post,* April 24, 1965.

Larkin, Cathy. "A Chic East Sider and Her Fashion Views." *Daily News,* January 12, 1970.

Laurent, Lawrence. "WTTG Decides Against Khrushchev 'Open End.'" *Washington Post and Times Herald*, October 11, 1960.

Leonetti, Diane. "The Multiple Lives of David Susskind." *New York Post,* April 26, 1959.

Lewis, Claude. "Roles People Play When an Actor Confronted Susskind." *Philadelphia Inquirer,* February 25, 1987.

Lurie, Diane. "Living with Liberation." *New York Magazine,* August 31, 1970.

Lyons, Leonard. "The Lyons Den." *New York Post,* November 11, 1970.

Maddocks, Melvin. "All the Way Home." *Christian Science Monitor,* November 7, 1963.

Mallon, John. "4 Marriages, with a Lemon Twist." *Daily News,* January 13, 1965.

Mann, Roderick. "Susskind May Sue over Firing." *Los Angeles Times,* February 4, 1984.

Margolick, David. "Television and the Holocaust: An Odd Couple." *New York Times,* January 31, 1999.

Martino, Peter. "Captivating Carmen." *Brilliant*, March 2007.

Mayer, Martin. "How Good Is TV at Its Best?" *Harper's Magazine*, September 1960.

McCarthy, Julia. "Shelley Susskind Bride Michael Andreas." *Daily News,* June 21, 1970.

McFadden, Robert D. "David Susskind, Talk-Show Host, Dies at 66." *New York Times,* February 23, 1987.

———. "John V. Lindsay, Mayor and Maverick, Dies at 79." *New York Times,* December 21, 2000.

McGill, Douglas C. "Andy Warhol, Pop Artist, Dies." *New York Times*, February 23, 1987.

———. "Sponsor Quits 'Open End' in Hassle Over K TVer." *Daily News,* October 11, 1960.

———. "Ike, JFK Plan Political Talks." *Daily News,* October 8, 1962.

———. "Ch. 5 Fires Susskind." *Daily News,* April 30, 1963.

———. "'Open End,' Due on WPIX, Apple of Susskind's Eye." *Daily News,* July 24, 1963.

———. "Emmy Jilted Again." *Daily News,* May 18, 1964.

———. "'For the People' Ended." *Daily News,* March 26, 1965.

———. "Channel 5 Curtain Rising on a Susskind-Pyne Feud." *Daily News,* October 12, 1966.

———. "Susskind Banking on TV Remakes of Plays, Films." *Daily News,* July 31, 1967.

Messina, Matt. "'Black Sox' TVer Off." *Daily News,* September 7, 1960.

Metcalfe, Jack, and Sherwood Dickerman. "'3rd U-2' Planned, Khrush Says on TV; He's Elusive in Quiz." *Daily News*, October 10, 1960.

Mitgang, Herbert. "E. G. Marshall Stars as Eisenhower in 'Ike,'" *New York Times,* April 13, 1986.

Monahan, Anthony. "We're Having Technical Difficulties with Our Audience, Mr. Susskind, Please. . . ." *Chicago Tribune,* June 2, 1968.

Morris, Bernadine. "Wives Proud of 'Best-Dressed' Husbands." *New York Times,* January 12, 1970.

Morse, Jim. "TV's Perennial 'Mad' Man." *TV-Radio Mirror,* April 1961.

Murphy, Agnes. "At Home with . . . Mrs. David Susskind." *New York Post,* November 13, 1960.

Myers, Arthur. "David Susskind: What Turns Him On?" *Coronet,* June 1967.

O'Brian, Jack. "GoLieth Down, Dave." *New York Journal American,* May 16, 1960.

———. "Flat Reflection of 'Naked City,'" *New York Journal American,* January 24, 1963.

O'Connor, John J. "Little Rock, 1957: 'Crisis at Central High.'" *New York Times,* February 4, 1981.

Oulahan, Richard, and William Lambert. "The Tyrant's Fall That Rocked the TV World." *Life*, September 10, 1965.

Patureau, Alan. "Warn Susskind on TV Hoax." *Newsday*, November 12, 1964.

Perlow, Kenneth. "TV's Alan Burke Says: 'I Want Them to Hate My Guts!'" *National Police Gazette*, September 1967.

Prideaux, Tom. "A Boost for Rep Boom." *Life*, April 2, 1965.

Reddy, John. "Television's Fourth 'Network,'" *Christian Science Monitor* in collaboration with the *Reader's Digest*, June 13, 1960.

Robinson, Douglas. "Six Vietnam Veterans, on TV, Charge That U.S. Betrayed Them." *New York Times*, April 26, 1971.

Rosen, George. "Dick & Dave's Kid Gloves as Nixon Shares Honors with Triple Spotting," *Variety*, May 18, 1960.

Ross, Irwin. "David Susskind." *New York Post*, November 28, 1961.

Ruderman, Mel. "Docu-drama Deluge Sets Off a Storm." *New York Post*, May 14, 1979.

Ryskind, Morrie. "Nikita Never Had It So Good." *Los Angeles Times*, October 16, 1960.

Schickel, Richard. "I've Been Just As Obnoxious As Humanly Possible." *TV Guide*, November 30, 1963.

Schmeck, Harold M. "Psychiatrists Approve Change on Homosexuals." *New York Times*, April 8, 1974.

Sederberg, Arelo. "Norton Simon Inc, Agrees to Acquire Talent Associates." *Los Angeles Times*, August 20, 1968.

Shain, Percy. "TV's Susskind Says: The World Won't Let Me Be at Peace." *Boston Globe*, May 5, 1963.

———. "'Salesman' Marks Milestone." *Boston Globe*, May 9, 1966.

Shales, Tom. "The Vision of David Susskind: The TV Pioneer & His High Vision for the Screen." *Washington Post*, February 23, 1987.

Shanley, John P. "TV: Religious Discussion." *New York Times*, May 15, 1960.

———. "Networks Scared at F.C.C. Hearing." *New York Times*, June 22, 1961.

Shelton, Patricia. "Designer Roland Meledandri Means Business." *Christian Science Monitor*, September 30, 1969.

Shepard, Richard F. "Partners in Electronic Play Production." *New York Times*, August 18, 1957.

———. "Khrushchev Set as Guest Sunday on TV 'Open End.'" *New York Times*, October 6, 1960.

———. "News of TV and Radio: Perennial Best Seller Will Be Source of New A.B.C. Series—Other Items." *New York Times*, June 30, 1963.

———. "Newman Rebuts 'Apache' Bias Charge." *New York Times*, April 9, 1980.

Sheppard, Eugenia. "Joyce Marries American." *New York Post*, April 2, 1970.

Sleeper, Marvin. "Police Allow Susskind to Do Series on Files." *World Herald Tribune*, February 24, 1967.

Smith, Cecil. "KTTV Will Skip Controversial Show with Khrushchev as Guest." *Los Angeles Times*, October 14, 1960.

———. "'Hedda' Foretaste of Drama Revival?" *Los Angeles Times*, June 3, 1963.

———. "ABC Showing Its Poker Face." *Los Angeles Times*, May 27, 1963.

Stahl, Bob. "'Studio One' Goes West." *TV Guide*, December 28, 1957.

Still, Larry. "TV Boom for Negro Talent." *Jet*, November 21, 1963.

Susskind, David. "David and the Goliaths Part 1." *Show Business Illustrated,* January 2, 1962.
———. "David and the Goliaths Part 2." *Show Business Illustrated,* January 23, 1962.
———. "David and the Goliaths Part 3." *Show Business Illustrated,* February 1962.
Sweeney, Louise. "TV Drama Curtain Rises on All Three Networks." *Christian Science Monitor,* December 9, 1966.
Tallmer, Jerry. "Robert Hooks: More than Skin Deep." *New York Post,* December 9, 1967.
Taubman, Howard. "Theater: 'Kelly' Opens at Broadhurst." *New York Times,* February 8, 1965.
———. "The Theater: 'All in Good Times' Opens." *New York Times,* February 19, 1965.
Torre, Marie. "Susskind Casting Coup: Nixon for 'Open End,'" *New York Herald Tribune,* May 5, 1960.
Vincent, Sally. "Return to the First Act." *The Guardian*, July 7, 2001.
Warga, Wayne. "Newcomer to Record Industry Starts at Top." *Los Angeles Times*, November 6, 1969.
Weiler, A. H. "George C. Scott Declines an Oscar Nomination." *New York Times,* March 6, 1962.
———. "Susskind, Moooovie Producer." *New York Times,* May 26, 1968.
Wicker, Tom. "President in Plea; Ask Help of Citizens to Assure Equality of Rights to All." *New York Times*, June 11, 1963.
Williams, Bob. "The Lady Talked Herself Out of a Job . . ." *New York Post,* June 21, 1959.
———. "On the Air." *New York Post,* December 9, 1960.
Wilson, Earl. "That's Earl for Today." *Evening Standard,* December 28, 1961.
Wilson, Joan S. "After 18 Hours, Just Tears; Elaine Stritch." *New York Times,* October 25, 1970.
Zimmerman, Paul D. "Movies: Rites of Manhood." *Newsweek,* December 20, 1971.
Zolotow, Sam. "Rashomon Costs Threaten Its Run." *New York Times,* May 5, 1959.
———. "New Group Plans to Put on 'Kelly.'" *New York Times*, April 17, 1964.
———. "$650,000 'Kelly' Lasts One Night." *New York Times,* February 9, 1965.
———. "Ford Fund Aids Negro Theater." *New York Times*, May 15, 1967.

Appendix

SELECTED TELEVISION MOVIES, PLAYS, AND SPECIALS

The following is a list of selected made-for-TV movies, television plays, and specials produced by David Susskind that best represent his career. Many of these productions are currently available on DVD and more are forthcoming through E1 Entertainment.

Ages of Man (dir. Paul Bogart, 1966)
All Creatures Great and Small (dir. Claude Whatham, 1975)
All the King's Men (dir. Sidney Lumet, 1959)
Back to Back: The Dock Brief and What Should We Tell Caroline (dir. Stuart Burge, 1959)
Billy Budd (dir. Robert Mulligan, 1959)
Black Monday (dir. Ralph Nelson, 1961)
Blind Ambition (dir. George Schaefer, 1979)
Breaking Up (dir. Delbert Mann, 1978)
The Bridge of San Luis Rey (dir. Robert Mulligan, 1959)
The Browning Version (dir. John Frankenheimer, 1959)
The Bunker (dir. George Schaefer, 1981)
Caesar and Cleopatra (dir. James Cellan Jones, 1976)
The Choice (dir. Tom Donavan, 1969)
The Count of Monte Cristo (dir. Sidney Lumet, 1958)
Crisis at Central High (dir. Lamont Johnson, 1981)
Crown Matrimonial (dir. Alan Bridges, 1974)
Death of a Salesman (dir. Alex Segal, 1966)
Eleanor and Franklin (dir. Daniel Petrie, 1976)
Eleanor and Franklin: The White House Years (dir. Daniel Petrie, 1977)
Ernie Barger Is 50 (dir. Delbert Mann, 1953)
Ethan Frome (dir. Alex Segal, 1960)
Fifty Grand (dir. Sidney Lumet, 1958)
The Glass Menagerie (dir. Anthony Harvey, 1973)
Harry S. Truman: Plain Speaking (dir. Daniel Petrie, 1976)

Hedda Gabler (dir. Alex Segal, 1963)
The Heiress (dir. Marc Daniels, 1960)
The Human Comedy (dir. Robert Mulligan, 1959)
The Human Voice (dir. Ted Kotcheff, 1966)
I, Don Quixote (dir. Karl Genus, 1959)
I Would Be Called John: Pope John XXIII (dir. Charles Jarrott, 1987)
Ian McKellen: Acting Shakespeare (dir. Kurt Browning, 1982)
If You Give a Dance, You Gotta Pay the Band (dir. Fred Coe, 1971)
Lullaby (dir. Don Richardson, 1960)
Lyndon Johnson (dir. Charles Jarrott, 1987)
A Man Is Ten Feet Tall (dir. Robert Mulligan, 1955)
Mark Twain Tonight! (dir. Paul Bogart, 1967)
Medea (dir. José Quintero, 1959)
The Moon and Sixpence (dir. Robert Mulligan, 1959)
A Moon for the Misbegotten (dir. José Quintero, Gordon Rigsby, 1975)
The Norman Conquests (dir. Herbert Wise, 1978)
The Outcasts of Poker Flat (dir. Paul Stanley, 1958)
Pinocchio (dir. Paul Bogart, 1957)
The Power and the Glory (dir. Marc Daniels, 1961)
The Price (dir. George Schaefer, 1971)
Ride with Terror (dir. Ron Winston, 1963)
A Tale of Two Cities (dir. Robert Mulligan, 1957)
Three Plays by Tennessee Williams (dir. Sidney Lumet, 1958)
Transplant (dir. William A. Graham, 1979)
The Wall (dir. Robert Markowitz, 1982)

The following is a complete list of feature films, TV series, talk shows, and Broadway plays produced by David Susskind, Talent Associates, or The Susskind Company.

FEATURE FILMS

Alice Doesn't Live Here Anymore (dir. Martin Scorsese, 1974)
All the Way Home (dir. Alex Segal, 1963)
All Things Bright and Beautiful (dir. Eric Till, 1978; released in the United Kingdom in 1975 as *It Shouldn't Happen to a Vet*)
Buffalo Bill and the Indians (dir. Robert Altman, 1976)
Edge of the City (dir. Martin Ritt, 1957)
Fort Apache, The Bronx (dir. Daniel Petrie, 1981)
Lovers and Other Strangers (dir. Cy Howard, 1970)
Loving Couples (Jack Smight, 1980)
The Pursuit of Happiness (Robert Mulligan, 1971)
A Raisin in the Sun (Daniel Petrie, 1961)
Requiem for a Heavyweight (Ralph Nelson, 1962)
Straw Dogs (Sam Peckinpah, 1971)

TELEVISION SERIES

Appointment with Adventure (CBS 1955–1956)
Armstrong Circle Theatre (NBC 1954–1957, CBS 1957–1963)
Diana (NBC 1973–1974)
East Side/West Side (CBS 1963–1964)
Esso Repertory Theatre (syndicated 1965)
Faraday and Company (NBC, 1973–1974)
Festival of Performing Arts (syndicated 1961–1962)
Generation Gap (ABC 1969)
Get Smart (NBC 1965–1969, CBS 1969–1970)
The Good Guys (CBS 1968–1970)
The Governor and J.J. (CBS 1969–1970)
He & She (CBS 1967–1968)
The Hero (NBC 1966)
The Honeymoon Race (ABC 1967)
Joe and Mabel (CBS 1956)
Justice (NBC 1954–1956)
McMillan & Wife (NBC 1971–1977)
Mr. Broadway (CBS 1964)
N.Y.P.D. (ABC 1967–1969)
On Our Own (CBS 1977–1978)
People (CBS 1978)
Run, Buddy, Run (CBS 1966–1967)
The Snoop Sisters (NBC 1973–1974)
Supermarket Sweep (ABC 1965–1967)
Too Young to Go Steady (NBC 1959)
Way Out (CBS 1961)
The Witness (CBS 1960–1961)

TALK SHOWS

The David Susskind Show (WNEW-TV in New York and syndicated 1966–1986)
Good Company (ABC 1967)
Hot Line (WPIX-TV in New York and syndicated 1964–1965)
Joyce and Barbara: For Adults Only (syndicated 1971)
Maurice Woodruff Presents (syndicated 1969)
Open End (WNTA-TV in New York 1958–1961, WNEW-TV 1961–1963, WPIX-TV 1963–
    1966, syndicated 1960–1966)
Several episodes of *Open End* and *The David Susskind Show*, including "How to Be a Jewish
Son—Or My Son the Success!" are available for online viewing at www.hulu.com. Historic
Films plans to offer digital downloads of Susskind's talk shows for purchase online, possibly
as soon as 2011.

BROADWAY SHOWS

All in Good Time (opened February 18, 1965, 44 performances)
Brief Lives (opened December 18, 1967, 16 performances)
Handful of Fire (opened October 1, 1958, 5 performances)
Kelly (opened February 6, 1965, 1 performance)
Mr. Lincoln (opened February 25, 1980, 16 performances)
Rashomon (opened January 27, 1959, 159 performances)

Acknowledgments

I feel extremely privileged to have written the first biography of David Susskind. I will always be grateful to Andrew Susskind for his cooperation, candor, and trust, which allowed me to pursue the necessary paths and people to tell the story of his father's amazing life and career. My deep gratitude also goes to Susskind's daughter Samantha Mannion, his stepdaughters Shelley Stallworth and Connie Christopher, and Connie's husband, Nicholas Christopher, for sharing their thoughts and recollections.

Special thanks go to the more than 150 individuals who agreed to speak with me about working with Susskind on his TV shows, Broadway plays, and movie productions. Many of them, especially the late Michael Abbott, Dan Berkowitz, Herb Bloom, Ruth Conforte, Chuck DeMund, Jill Spoon Gelbach, Heywood Gould, Ron Gilbert, Anita Grossberg, Barbara Howar, Bob Israel, Diana Kerew, Emily Perl Kingsley, Jerry Leider, the late Daniel Melnick, Patricia Nardo, Bruce Paisner, Gloria Rabinowitz, Harry Sherman, Leonard Stern, Sam Szurek, Sheila Tronn, Renée Valente, George C. White, and Jack Willis, allowed me to repeatedly tap in to their memories about events that occurred decades ago. They generously provided introductions to their friends and former colleagues as well.

Gregory Smith, a researcher based in Oregon, Wisconsin, and Alyson Beckman ably assisted me in combing through David Susskind's papers at the Wisconsin Center for Film and Theater Research in Madison, Wisconsin. I greatly appreciate the help of the entire staff at the Center. Very special thanks goes to Robert Wasserman, the former audio specialist at WCFTR, whose tireless efforts in locating tapes of Susskind's talk show were invaluable to my research for this book. Andrea Gallo's transcription services were lightning fast and flawless. I also appreciate the assistance of the staffs at Northeastern University and the UCLA Film and Television Archive.

I am very thankful for Jane Klain, manager of research services at the Paley Center for Media in New York. She is an extraordinary resource for anyone who cares about the history of television, as is the Museum of Broadcast Communications in Chicago and its former curator, Daniel Berger.

My appreciation goes out to my many friends and associates in the media business. They provided help with contacting interview subjects, acquiring research materials and photographs, and seeking out fine dining in Madison, Wisconsin. They include Preston Beckman, Jeff Bewkes, Clay Cole, Missy Davy, Chris Ender, Ted Harbert, Richard Heffner, Kelly Kahl, Paul McGuire, Michael Mand, Virginia Mastroianni, Pat Mitchell, Joe Peryonnin, Richard Plepler, Shirley Powell, Paul Ward, and Leah Yoon. Special thanks also go to Kate Aurthur, Jon Bily, Helen Gurley Brown, Jay Cooper, Michael Davis, Samantha Graham, Louis Harris, Roy Harris, Dan Heffner, Jakob Holder, Graham, Carmen La Via, Elizabeth Maas, Ron Mandelbaum, Gregg Mitchell, Pamela Morrison, Joseph Morsman, Marilyn Pessin, Colette Phillips, Mark Quigley, Faigi Rosenthal, Molly Sackler, Michael Schneider, David Schwartz, Gretchen Sherman, Pamela Steigmayer, Laura Stern and the staff at Exprimo, a Moscow-based translation service. Longtime friends David Bushman, Tamara Haddad, Richard Huff, Susan Kim, Laurence Klavan, Scott Klavan, and Sara Nelson eagerly helped when I called.

My colleagues at *TV Guide Magazine*—Nancy Schwartz, Rose Fiorentino, and Eileen Spangler O'Malley—provided tremendous assistance and guidance regarding the use of photographs, as did Liz Pressman and David Boyle at the *New York Post*.

Mary Ann Watson, professor of electronic media and film studies at Eastern Michigan University, was gracious enough to allow me to use a 1992 interview she conducted with TV director Paul Bogart. Her 1992 piece about Susskind in *Television Quarterly* was an insightful guide to Susskind's TV producing career. TV historian Stephen Bowie provided a memo by writer Allan Sloane on *East Side/West Side* that I had heard about but never imagined I would actually locate. His 1997 article on *East Side/West Side* for *Television Chronicles* was also an excellent resource.

Thank you to my agent PJ Mark, now at Janklow & Nesbit, who saw the potential in this book, and to Elizabeth Beier, my editor at St. Martin's Press, who helped me realize it. Also thanks to Michelle Richter of St. Martin's Press for her assistance.

My brother-in-law Matt Rufrano deserves credit for having first suggested that I write this book after reading my piece about David Susskind for the *New York Times Arts and Leisure* section in 2001. The encouragement of my mother, Dolores Rizzo-Tesch; my father, Michael Tesch; Amelia Battaglio, Roger Sorcio, Raphael Sorcio, Luke Sorcio, and Billie Taylor was also greatly appreciated.

Finally, this book would have been impossible for me to pursue or complete without the aid and unwavering support of my wife, Candice Agree. She willingly gave me her time and valuable help in every stage of this project, from photocopying documents to expertly proofreading the final manuscript. She never once complained about the mess in our living room over the last three years. *David Susskind: A Televised Life* is dedicated to her.

Index